SUCCESSFULLY IMPLEMENTING TURNAROUND STRATEGIES IN STATE-OWNED COMPANIES:

SAA, Kenya Airways and Ethiopian Airlines as Case Studies

Kaizer Mabhilidi Nyatsumba

VERITY PUBLISHERS

Pretoria

SUCCESSFULLY IMPLEMENTING TURNAROUND STRATEGIES IN STATE-OWNED COMPANIES:

SAA, Kenya Airways and Ethiopian Airlines as Case Studies

Published in the Republic of South Africa

Successfully Implementing Turnaround Strategies in State-Owned Companies:

SAA, Kenya Airways and Ethiopian Airlines as Case Studies

Copyright © 2021
Kaizer Mabhilidi Nyatsumba
First Published under the imprint of Verity Publishers
© 2021

This edition is published in paperback and digital
©2021
Published in the Republic of South Africa
Copyright ©2021
Verity Publishers
Pretoria 0001
www.veritypublishers.co.za

ISBN 978-1-990985-11-9

Cover Design by Verity Graphix

CONTENTS

Chapter Twelve

Chapter Thirteen

Chapter Fourteen

Chapter Fifteen

Chapter Sixteen

References

List of Acronyms & Symbols

ACSA	– Airports Company South Africa
AfCFTA	– African Continental Free Trade Area
AGM	– Annual General Meeting
ANC	– African National Congress
ASAP	– Association of Star Alliance Pilots
ASI	– Adam Smith Institute or Adam Smith International
BASA	– Bilateral Air Services Agreement
BoD	– Board of Directors
BRICS	– Brazil, Russia, India, China and South Africa
BRP	– Business Rescue Practitioner
CASK	– Cost per available seat-kilometre
COP	– Capital Optimisation Process
COSATU	– Congress of South African Trade Unions
DG	– Director-General
EAL	– Ethiopian Airlines
DPE	– Department of Public Enterprises
GCIS	– Government Communication Information Service
IATA	– International Air Transport Association
ICAO	– International Civil Aviation Organisation
IFC	– International Finance Corporation
JKIA	– Jomo Kenyatta International Airport
KALPA	– Kenya Airline Pilots Association
KATA	– Kenya Association of Travel Agents
KQ	– Kenya Airways
KSh	– Kenyan Shilling
LCC	– Low-cost carrier
MNJV	– Metal Neutral Joint Venture
MRO	– Maintenance, repair and overhaul

NED	– Non-Executive Director
NIPP	– National Industrial Participation Programme
NUMSA	– National Union of Metalworkers of South Africa
OHI	– Organisational Health Index
ORTIA	– Oliver Reginald Tambo International Airport
PIIP	– Privately Initiated Investment Proposal
R	– South African Rand
RASK	– Revenue per available seat-kilometre
SAA	– South African Airways
SAAPA	– South African Airways Pilots Association
SAATM	– Single African Air Transport Market
SAP	– Structural Adjustment Programme
SACAA	– South African Civil Aviation Authority
SACCA	– South African Cabin Crew Association
SACP	– South African Communist Party
SAPA	– South African Press Association
SATAWU	– South African Transport and Allied Workers Union
SAX	– South African Express
SCP	– Strategic Commercial Partner
SEP	– Strategic Equity Partner
SMF	– Significant Materiality Framework
SOC	– State-owned Company
SOE	– State-owned enterprise
TMT	– Top Management Team
UAE	– United Arab Emirates
US$	– United States Dollar
$	– United States Dollar

Definitions

Cost-per-available-seat kilometre – "the total operating cost for a flight, route or network divided by the corresponding seat-kms produced by that flight, route or network" (Doganis, 2019)

Revenue-per-available-seat kilometre – "the total revenue for a flight, route or network divided by the available seats offered" (Doganis, 2019)

Ancillary revenues – "any revenues which are additional to those generated from the sale of the different fare categories or branded fares" (Doganis, 2019)

Passenger load factor or seat factor – "an expression of the number of passengers carried as a percentage of the seats available for sale" (Doganis, 2019)

Yield – "the average revenue collected per passenger-kilometre or tonne-km of freight carried" (Doganis, 2019)

Legacy airlines – "old, established traditional airlines usually operating a hub-and-spoke network" (Doganis, 2019)

Network airlines – "airlines operating hub-based networks as opposed to low-cost airlines that operate a matrix network" (Doganis, 2019).

INTRODUCTION

Ethiopian Airlines (EAL), South African Airways (SAA) and Kenya Airways (KQ) have consistently ranked among the top 10 African airlines in terms of both the number of passengers flown and reputation. They are by far the most established and best known airlines in Sub-Saharan Africa, with EgyptAir, Royal Air Maroc, Air Tunisia and Air Mauritius completing that list on various independent organisations' ratings when the entire continent is considered.

According to Wikipedia, which ranks EgyptAir and Royal Air Maroc ahead of SAA in terms of the number of passengers carried, African airlines account for only 6% of the world's traffic, with the vast majority of it carried by foreign airlines. This is despite the fact that Africa is the second largest continent by size and population.

This percentage is bound to grow, should the Single African Air Transport Market (SAATM) adopted by the African Union in January 2018, following the adoption of the Yamoussoukro Decision in July 2000, be implemented.

A World Bank study found that, while Africa is home to 12% of the world's population, the continent accounts for less than one per cent of the world's air service market (Schlumberger, 2010). That was because many African countries restricted air services markets to protect the share held by their respective national carriers, going back to the early 1960s when countries which had obtained their independence established their national airlines "in part to assert their status as nations".

Airlines, therefore, are a major part of African countries' economies, as will become clear in the chapter dealing with the contribution of air travel and tourism to countries' Gross Domestic Products (GDP). However, at least two of the continent's most prominent airlines, SAA and KQ, have experienced serious financial and strategic challenges in the last 10 and five years respectively. As a result, they have had to implement various turnaround strategies.

SAA has been implementing different turnaround strategies over the past decade. Without exception, none of those strategies has ever been implemented successfully. Instead, the airline – which last recorded a profit in 2011 – has had a series of Chief Executive Officers, with most of them having been in the role in an acting capacity.

SAA is not the only State-owned company (SOC) to have found itself in trouble in South Africa in recent years. A number of them have found themselves in similar trouble. To be found on that list, which has been growing progressively longer, have been the following: South African Broadcasting Corporation (SABC), Passenger Rail Agency of South Africa (PRASA), Eskom, Denel and South African Post Office, among others.

All of them have had to implement – or are in the process of implementing – turnaround strategies of some kind. At the time of writing, none could claim to have done so successfully.

On the other hand, KQ – which was privatised in 1996 and listed on the Nairobi Stock Exchange – performed so well in the years following its privatisation that it even challenged SAA, which was then the most successful African airline. Things changed, however, following that airline's adoption of an ambitious growth strategy, called Project Mawingu. Since 2015, the airline has been working to turn its fortunes around, so far without much success.

What are the factors which facilitate or impede a possible successful implementation of a turnaround strategy in African business, but especially in a SOC? That was the question to which I attempted to respond, in the form of comprehensive research for a PhD study, over the past three years as I sought to develop a framework for successful implementation of turnaround strategies. It is my humble opinion that the answers to that question and the framework that I have developed should help South Africa and other African countries significantly as they struggle to arrest and reverse the fortunes of their SOCs.

This book is based on that PhD thesis, which focused on the aviation sector and honed in on SAA and KQ as case studies. Since aviation was the area of focus, Africa's most successful airline, Ethiopian Airlines (EAL), also formed part of the study.

It is my contention that, although the study focused on the three airlines, the findings of this research are equally relevant to businesses – especially State-owned businesses – in any other sector of the economy.

Although all three airlines are an important part of this book, SAA features most prominently than KQ and EAL. That is because, unlike Kenya, which was under colonial rule before attaining its independence, and Ethiopia, which is one of two African countries never to have been colonised, South Africa has had a long history of both colonialism and white minority rule under a policy known as apartheid. As the last African country to rid itself of white rule and as the one to have the biggest white population, South Africa has had far more dynamics which have impacted on its national carrier following efforts to reverse the legacy of apartheid, among other things.

In order to avoid boring the average reader, two chapters which are part of that thesis are excluded from this book. Those are the chapters dealing with the methodology followed to carry out this research and the one dealing with comprehensive literature review on turnaround strategies. Those chapters are likely to be of interest to academically-inclined readers with an interest in the field of strategy or, to be precise, turnaround strategy. In that case, they will be able to access them in the thesis at the University of Johannesburg.

In addition, much work has gone into converting the thesis into a readable book of wider interest, but all important claims made in this book remain duly referenced.

At the time of putting this book together, SAA was still in the process of undergoing business rescue, which was preceded by intense conflict between Business Rescue Practitioners Les Matuson and Siviwe Dongwana on the one hand, and the Government, as represented by Public Enterprises Minister Pravin Gordhan, on the other hand. A new SAA was said to be likely to rise, like a phoenix, from the ashes of the old SAA. Kenya Airways, which was once so successful that it was dubbed the "Pride of Africa," was in the process of being nationalised.

Both developments occurred even before the advent of the Corona Virus Disease 2019 (COVID-19), which has had a devastating impact on the global aviation sector.

Ethiopian Airways, on the other hand, was a great African success which had long overtaken SAA as the best African airline and had begun to benchmark itself against world-class carriers like Singapore Airways, Emirates and British Airways, among others.

Adding an important African perspective

Schoenberg, Collier and Bowman (2013) reviewed literature that included 22 empirical studies which had investigated business turnaround strategies completed during recessionary periods from the mid-1970s to the early 1990s, and which was based on turnaround and recovery strategies used by almost 1 300 companies. They found that there was a great deal of convergence in the conclusions of those studies.

Schoenberg *et al.* (2013) found that the literature identified six predominant turnaround strategies as being effective, with four of them related to the main objectives of the strategy and the other two related to change processes necessary for implementation.

In their conclusion, Schoenberg *et al.* (2013) remarked that they were unaware of any research on turnaround strategies that was conducted outside of Europe and the Americas. They believed that this presented an opportunity for future studies to identify turnaround strategies that are effective in different cultural contexts and to establish the reasons for the success or otherwise of individual strategies in those circumstances.

Trahms *et al.* (2013:1297) say a lot more remains unknown or understudied when it comes to organisational decline and turnaround compared to what is known, and express the view that a study that includes an assessment of the impact that strategic leadership, stakeholder management and resource orchestration plays in the turnaround process would be helpful.

O'Kane and Cunningham (2014:966) describe corporate turnaround as an area of academic study where "theory is nascent or immature," and contend that a study which includes an assessment of the management of key activities and tensions by turnaround leaders in companies with different ownership structures (family run, publicly owned or State owned) would be beneficial.

The research done on the implementation of turnaround strategies at SAA and KQ presents an important African perspective and, through the developed framework, contributes to the body of knowledge on turnaround strategies.

How the book is ordered

In order to ensure that the reader has better appreciation of the challenges which have confronted SAA and Kenya Airways and their respective responses to them, the book opens with a chapter on turnaround strategies, followed by another on the aviation industry. It is my view that understanding of both a highly-summarised version of the concept of turnaround strategies and the aviation industry is critical for the reader to benefit from the detailed discussion which follows and the recommended framework for successful implementation of turnaround strategies.

It is my hope that policy makers in South Africa and elsewhere on the continent, who are charged with the important responsibility of overseeing SOCs, will find benefit from this research.

Appreciation

Finally, my thanks go to all the 49 men and women – in South Africa, Kenya, Ethiopia, Sudan and Britain – who were so generous with their time and insights during this research. This is a product of their collective wisdom.

Collectively, these men and women were the primary source of the data used in this book. Other sources were media reports, annual reports and other publications. All but one of the interviews took place in 2019. To avoid repeatedly indicating the year 2019 when the interviews are quoted either directly or indirectly, the year is indicated at first mention and sometimes dropped in subsequent mentions, unless the citation is to something said or written in another year.

I am particularly grateful to Ethiopian Senior Minister and academic Dr Arkebe Oqubay, who offered me invaluable advice and guidance on converting what was a highly academic manuscript based on my thesis into a readable book.

Kaizer M. Nyatsumba
January 2021

Foreword

Dominikus Heil, PhD, Managing Director, Reputation Institute of South Africa; Global Partner, Reputation Institute; and Associate and Tutor, Praxis Centre, University of Cranfied School of Management, UK.

The flag carriers of nations are a cornerstone of their respective economies. Kaizer Nyatsumba's analysis of the turnaround efforts at South African Airways and Kenya Airways gives a timeous, well-researched and honest insight into the inner workings of a successful as well as a failed turnaround effort in this sector. South African Airways is likely to remain a key issue in the political discourse for years to come.

The insights that are presented here are relevant well beyond just flag carriers, but provide a thorough insight into the day-to-day inner workings of State-owned companies. Whether you are a supporter of ideas of the developmental state or not, the fact remains that State-owned companies will continue to play a critical role in the functioning of the nation's economy. That they deliver on their mandate will be paramount to the nation's success; it is, therefore, vital that the broad public gets a deep insight into how they have been working and how decision making has been taking place within and around them in our recent troubled past.

This book is a critical read for anybody who wants to participate in the national discourse on the future of South African Airways in particular and State-owned enterprises in general. Whether you are a decision-maker or influencer in the sphere of government, a political and economic commentator, an academic in an associated field or just a responsible citizen who wants to understand the dynamics and know what is going on in South Africa's State-owned companies, you would want to read this book with great diligence.

Kaizer Nyatsumba has been an insightful observer and commentator as well as an active participant in the economy for a number of decades now. It is his skill as a journalist, his understanding of being a decision maker from experience and his skill as an academic that make this book an outstanding contribution. Through his own reputation, he was able to gather information from the critical role-players that the public typically does not have easy access to, and much less elicit such open and honest responses from.

Since in South Africa's recent troubled past State-owned companies have been in the headlines for State capture, corruption, cronyism, cadre deployment and poor decision-making, this book gives the depth of insight the South African public has been yearning for.

Note on Style

In this book, a capital "G" is used when reference is made to a specific Government, and a small-letter "g" for the institution of "government" in general or when reference is made to the apartheid government, which was lacking in legitimacy.

Chapter One

A BRIEF OVERVIEW OF CORPORATE DECLINE AND TURNAROUND STRATEGY

The study of turnaround strategies dates back to 1976, when Schendel and Patton (1976) published a paper on "corporate stagnation and turnaround." Schendel, Patton and Riggs (1976) published another article, "Corporate turnaround strategies: A study of profit decline and recovery" in the same year in the *Journal of General Management*.

There is a reason why that was the case. Between 1948 and 1973, the US economy grew at an average rate of 3,7% per annum and both unemployment and inflation were relatively low. American companies supplied not only their domestic market with their products and services, but also Europe, Asia and South America. The US was a net exporter, with a trade surplus of $157 billion (Whitney, 1987).

Whitney (1987) argues that turnarounds were not only unheard of in that environment, but they were also unnecessary. However, that changed in the early 1970s. In 1973, when the Arab-Israeli war broke out, Arab members of the Organisation of Petroleum Exporting Countries imposed an oil embargo against the USA following the US government's decision to support Israel and to supply military weapons to the Israelis. The embargo was extended to other countries which also supported Israel, such as the Netherlands, Portugal and South Africa (USA Department of State, 2020:online).

As a result, oil prices soared in the US (and the other embargoed countries), inflation increased until it reached 20% in 1981 and fell to 8% in 1986, and the country's growth rate fell to an average of 2,3% per annum until 1985. The US's trade surplus was halved to $79 billion as foreign-based products started flooding the US market. Additionally, the rate of technological changes accelerated to the extent that foreign substitutes posed a real threat to long-established American products (Whitney, 1987).

It was then, when corporate declines and stagnation began to be experienced in the USA, that turnaround management as a discipline was born in that country (Whitney, 1987).

Four years later, Hofer (1980) distinguished between operational and strategic turnarounds, and Bibeault (1982) built on that knowledge by identifying three critical stages during a turnaround: the emergency stage, the stabilization stage and the return-to-growth or redevelopment stage. Arogyaswamy, Barker and Yasai-Ardekani (1995), Robbins and Pearce (1992) and Pearce and Robbins (1993; 2008) subsequently came to be recognised for their prominent contribution to the body of knowledge on turnaround strategies, and Trahms, Ndofor and Sirmon (2013) built on their contribution.

Therefore, compared to other academic disciplines, turnaround strategy is relatively new. It came into existence following growing failure of some companies and the need for interventions to be made to turn them around, especially financially.

Given the growing complexity of the business environment today, there is a higher probability of businesses struggling or failing at some stage. In the course of their lifetimes, most companies find themselves confronted by a situation that requires them to embark on urgent interventions to turn the business around. It is that management intervention that will determine if such companies are able to return to their original health or wither away to oblivion (Bibeault, 1999; Hofer, 1980; Trahms, Ndofor & Sirmon, 2013; Reeves, Haanaes & Sinha, 2015).

Bibeault (1999) calls the business state that requires that decisive management intervention a turnaround situation. He describes it as "an abnormal period in any company's history" which requires unique management approaches that are vastly different from those used during a normal period. During such a period, proven management principles routinely used during moments of stability are no longer valid (Bibeault, 1999:1-2; Trahms *et al.*, 2013:1278).

Turnaround situations arise when criteria normally used to measure a company's performance, such as financial measures, are "sufficiently depressed" to require turnaround efforts. When a company's absolute decline in performance occurs relative to that of its peers in the industry, explicit turnaround actions are warranted (Pearce & Robbins, 1993:625-30). Then, a company can only be considered to have been turned around when its performance before and after the decline has changed at a greater rate than the industry average.

For Chowdhury (2002:250-1), a turnaround occurs when a company goes through "an existence-threatening performance decline," adopts a combination of strategies, systems, skills and capabilities to contain the decline and ultimately emerges with "sustainable performance recovery." He argues that a turnaround is a process and not a single event, but a series of events which, when combined, reveal an improvement in performance over a particular time span.

Reeves *et al.* (2015) say the fast pace of environmental and technological change increases the chances of a company's strategy being ill-matched to the changing environment. They say their analysis shows that, because of the frenetic pace of change, businesses now move more quickly through the different stages in their product and overall life cycles "from question mark to star to cash cow to dog." As a result, more and more companies' overall life cycles are reduced.

Their study found that in 75 percent of industries, the average time a firm spends at any state of its life cycle has now halved.

Reeves *et al.* (2015) call the turnaround process a renewal, transformation or streamlining, and Pearce and Robbins (2008:122) say that in recent years it is also increasingly referred to as "restructuring."

Bibeault (1999:81) defines a corporate turnaround as "a substantial and sustained positive change in the performance of a business." The need for a turnaround arises as a consequence of years of declining profitability which may result in significant losses that over time may threaten a company's continued financial viability or, in its mildest form, have serious negative consequences for market competitiveness, customer confidence and employee morale.

Hofer (1980) says that turnaround strategies are occasioned by the seriousness of a company's situation, a sense of crisis or urgency in which the company finds itself, which threatens its existence.

Walshe, Harvey, Hyde and Pandit (2010:202) distinguish between chronic and acute causes of organisational failure. They say the former tend to exist over an extended period and contribute to a gradual reduction in performance, while the latter are often the triggers which "force or precipitate a crisis" that makes management finally acknowledge the possibility of impending failure.

Panicker and Manimala (2015) describe a corporate turnaround as being "a doubly entrepreneurial act" that has to lead an enterprise "from negative to breakeven and from breakeven to growth," with the strategies used to accomplish this goal being "similar to those adopted by entrepreneurs."

Hopkins (2008) says poorly-performing companies need a turnaround strategy to get back on track, with such a strategy explicitly intended to halt the decline and restore the company to good health. He says that successful turnaround strategies directly address the causes of the firm's problem, and this makes an accurate diagnosis of a problem very important.

Hopkins (2008) stresses the importance of asking the right questions to make the diagnosis, followed with another series of questions about the appropriate course of action to arrest the decline and reverse the situation. He says an accurate diagnosis of a problem may be the most important step in devising a turnaround strategy with a higher chance of success.

Ravaghi, Mannion and Sajadi (2017) concur, arguing that understanding the causes of decline and the factors that can lead to success is crucial if effective strategies are to be designed to counter underperformance.

Pearce and Robbins (2008:129) say not only can turnaround situations be managed to improve the chances of a company's survival, but they can also set a company in a new direction and, in the process, form the basis of "unprecedented future performance."

According to Pretorius (2008), a business is considered to have been turned around when it has recovered from "a decline that threatened its existence" – through various interventions, including a strategic reorientation – to resume normal operations and achieve performance acceptable to its stakeholders. Using munificence theory, Pretorius (2008) indicates that a company needs to meet the minimum threshold of financial capital if it is to avoid failure. He stresses the importance of organisational resources being matched with environmental munificence (an enabling environment) in order for a turnaround strategy to succeed.

He warns that if nothing is done about companies that are in distress or if wrong strategies that drain resources are pursued, then a crisis situation develops that might see a company on its death bed. Relating his turnaround matrix to Michael Porter's (1998) generic strategies, Pretorius (2008) says that

- a company that is performing well should devote its energies to pursuing growth,
- a company that is underperforming should focus on improving efficiencies as a turnaround strategy,
- a company in distress has to pursue "a forced repositioning strategy" (forced by the circumstances), and
- a company in a crisis has to embark on "a last-resort strategy such as going into receivership or debt rescue and asking for debt forgiveness."

Pretorius (2008) says that, in essence, repositioning a company in distress fundamentally boils down to making a choice from one of Porter's three generic strategies.

Bibeault (1999) and Reevel *et al.* (2015) share the view that successfully implementing a turnaround strategy is not easy. Bibeault (1999) says trying to effect meaningful improvements in a company in trouble is a much more onerous test for management than running a stable company. He points out that managing a turnaround situation is fraught with challenges like customer and creditor pressure, employee resistance, "the risks of change" and people's impatience, which "all become acute."

Bibeault (1999:3-7)) says turnaround situations are different and success is heavily dependent on "the visible hand of management." He says success or failure in a turnaround situation depends heavily on how management responds to "a predictable series of organizational and people crises."

Bibeault (1999:23-38) says that while businesses decline for both uncontrollable external reasons and controllable internal reasons, in most cases business problems are internally generated. He says that if a company's management is poor, it makes two types of mistakes: errors of omission and errors of commission, with one example of the former being a company's failure to respond timeously and properly to changes in its external environment.

Reeves *et al.* (2015:151-2) concur, saying that putting together a renewal strategy must be characterised by "a swift reaction to an early indication of a harsh environment:"

> *Recognizing and responding quickly to signals that your firm is in a harsh environment is the most critical step to improving the odds of survival: as in medical situations requiring CPR, the timelines of the first response in a potentially life-threatening situation often dictate the outcome.*

Bibeault (1999:81-2) says typically the decline and renewal scenario takes a familiar pattern which sees absent or poor management leadership resulting in a firm's decline in various performance measures, including return on investment. This decline is followed by a company's failure to invest in order to preserve cash and, eventually, outright losses and possibly even "ultimate oblivion." The replacement of "sleepy or complacent management" with "new and eager management" reverses that trend, with the result that employee morale and customer confidence improve and, once again, the company becomes profitable.

Bibeault (1999:82) says change – of leadership, product lines or divisions – is the distinguishing feature of turnaround situations. He says that in order for a turnaround effort to stand a chance of success, it is vital that the necessity for change is accepted.

"When this acceptance ceases in any company, hardening of the arteries starts to set in," he cautions.

Most of the research into organisational failure and turnaround has been conducted in the private sector, with little of it taking place in the public sector (Boyne, 2004:97; Walshe *et al.*, 2010:204). Therefore, the bulk of the knowledge that has been accumulated on turnaround strategies in the past five decades has been based on the private sector (Boyne, 2004; Paton & Mordaunt, 2004; Ravaghi *et al.*, 2017). Studies which have been conducted by Boyne (2004), Paton & Mordaunt (2004), Ravaghi *et al.* (2017) and Walshe *et al.* (2010) into turnaround strategies in the public sector have focused on the provision of public services like education, health, transport, social services, criminal justice and local government.

Chapter Two

THE AIRLINE INDUSTRY AND ITS DYNAMICS

The Birth of Aviation

The story of aviation is generally thought to date back to American inventors and pioneers the Wright brothers, Wilbur and Orville, who made history in 1903 when they flew the first airplane flight (Ryabinkin, 2004; History.com, 2009). Following a number of unsuccessful attempts, on 17 December 1903 the brothers finally managed to fly "the first free, controlled flight of a power-driven air plane." Wilbur Wright accomplished this feat when he piloted their plane at Kitty Hawk, North Carolina for 59 seconds, at 852 feet (History.com, 2009).

When their accomplishment did not meet with immediate acclaim in the United States of America (USA), elder brother Wilbur left for Europe in 1908, in search of more recognition and greater commercial success. He settled in France, where he was received more warmly. His younger brother Orville joined him in Europe some months later, where they became "huge celebrities" who were often featured in the media and were feted "by royals and Heads of State." Their popularity enabled them to sell their planes on the continent, before their eventual return to the United Sates in 1909 (History.com, 2009).

However, in 1900 – three years before the Wright brothers' achievement – German military officer Count Ferdinand Graf von Zeppelin flew his first airship, the *Lufftschiff Zeppelin 1* (called the *LZ1* in short). The airship made three flights before Zeppelin ran out of money and had to dismantle it (Meyer, 2004). Von Zeppelin, who believed that an airship supported by a rigid framework could be strengthened sufficiently to render it useful, is described by Meyer (2004:12) as "perhaps the most important person in the history of lighter-than-air flight."

Von Zeppelin established the Deutsche Luftschiffahrts-AG (DELAG) company in 1909 to purchase airships and transport passengers between German cities (Meyer, 2004). The DELAG, which became the first-ever commercial airline, offered flights before the outbreak of the First World War (Petrescu & Petrescu, 2011). By the time the First World

War broke out in July 1914, the DELAG had covered about 160 000km without any problem, carrying more than 34 000 passengers (Meyer, 2004:14).

Given the outstanding success of Von Zeppelin's design, the word "zeppelin" came to be used to refer to rigid airships in general. Following the outbreak of the First World War, the German army used zeppelins extensively as bombers and scouts (Petrescu & Petrescu, 2011).

Aviation spreads to different parts of the world

Following the progress made by Count von Zeppelin in Germany and the Wright brothers in the United States of America and Europe, aviation soon spread to different parts of the world.

In 1919, an aviation conference held in Paris, France led to the signing of an agreement known as the Paris Convention, which accepted that governments have "sovereign rights in the air space above their territory" (Doganis, 2019:22). With a country's air space being "one of its valuable natural resources," governments started intervening directly in air transport, and that led to the end of what Doganis (2019:22) calls "the free-trade laissez-faire approach towards air transport of the early years of aviation" and its replacement with bilateral agreements between countries which had airlines, as well as those countries through whose air space the airlines wanted to fly.

By 1919 various governments had begun to form their own national airlines (Barrett, 2006). In 1919 the Dutch government established the Koninklijke Luchvaart Maatschappij (KLM), which means Royal Aviation Company in English; the German government set up Lufthansa in April 1926; the French government established Air France in 1933 and the Irish government set up Aer Lingus in 1936. These airlines were all owned by the governments of those countries and benefitted from the fact that competition was officially restricted (Barrett, 2006:160).

Elsewhere in the world, the first air service in India began in 1912. Twenty years later, Indian entrepreneur RJD Tata established Tata Airlines, the first Indian airline, which was subsequently renamed Air India. Its inaugural international flight on 8 June 1948 was from Mumbai to London, United Kingdom. In 1953 the Indian government passed the Air Corporations Act, through which nine privately-owned airlines were nationalised to form the Indian Airlines Corporation, which catered for the domestic market, and Air India International, which catered for international travel (Chattopadhyay, 2015).

In South Africa, aviation began in 1929 with an airmail service provided by Union Airways, which was founded by Major Allister Miller (Ssamula, 2014:228). Over time, Union Airways operated more like a commercial airline (Pirie, 2006:9). Between 1939 and 1945 when the Second World War was being fought, all aircraft used for civil aviation purposes in South Africa were taken over by the military, leaving the country fully dependent on foreign airlines for the supply of air transport services (Gavin, 2013:9).

Having had its origin in Europe and the USA, aviation soon spread to different parts of the world, with various governments setting up national airlines which prominently displayed their countries' flags. As more countries launched their own airlines, it became imperative for some form of international coordination to be introduced. That led to the convening of a major international aviation conference in Chicago, USA in 1944.

The landmark Chicago Aviation Conference

Given the rapid development of aviation across the world, an important international conference on aviation was held in Chicago, USA in 1944 to discuss the introduction of rules to govern the industry (Barrett, 2006; Belobaba, Odoni & Barnhart, 2009; Chattopadhyay, 2015; Doganis, 2019). In particular, the conference sought to reach a multi-national agreement on three areas of international transport: the exchange of air traffic, the control of fares and freight tariffs, and the control of flight frequencies and traffic (Belobaba, *et al.*, 2009:20; Doganis, 2019:22).

Fifty-four countries attended the conference (Belobaba *et al.*, 2009; Chattopadhyay, 2015; Doganis, 2019). At the Chicago Aviation Conference, the Convention on International Civil Aviation (known simply as the Chicago Convention), which listed the rules governing international aviation, was signed. The Convention also stablished the International Civil Aviation Organization (ICAO), which was charged with the responsibility of "fostering the planning and development of international air transport" (Chattopadhyay, 2015:146).

The International Air Transport Association (IATA) was formed in 1945, a year after the Chicago Convention, and was charged with the responsibility of coordinating international airfares. It was only after 1978, when the US government raised concern about the anti-competitive nature of the practice, that IATA stopped setting international airfares (Belobaba *et al.*, 2009:42).

The ICAO, which came into existence in 1947 and subsequently enjoyed the status of a specialised United Nations agency, has its headquarters in Montreal, Canada. All bilateral and multilateral air services agreements concluded between and among countries, in terms of the Freedoms of the Air concept which originated at the Chicago Aviation Conference, must be registered with the ICAO. About 4000 such agreements were lodged with the organisation in 2008 (Belobaba *et al.*, 2009:41).

At the Chicago Aviation Conference, the USA Government proposed the concept of "open skies," a more relaxed dispensation that would facilitate easy international travel between and among countries. However, the US lost the fight, following fears by European countries – led by the United Kingdom – that such a dispensation would lead to the US dominating international aviation after the Second World War (Barrett, 2006; Belobaba *et al.*, 2009). As Barrett (2006:159) puts it, international aviation ended up being organised "on a bilateral 'Noah's Ark' basis," with international flights between countries having to take place only through prior agreements between the governments and airlines concerned.

In terms of the Chicago Convention, international flights could not take place over or into the territory of another country without the express permission of that country. In the years that followed, the ICAO adopted "a series of traffic rights" – variously called "Freedoms of the Skies," "Freedoms of the Air" or "Degrees of Freedom" – which continue to bind the aviation industry to this day. These freedoms formed the basis of the degree of latitude a country has to operate an aircraft registered in its territory over another country's air space (Belobala *et al.*, 2009:21; Zalagenaite, 2017), based on an agreement between the States or governments concerned.

There were five Freedoms of the Skies agreed upon at the Chicago Convention and recognised by the ICAO. These were the First Freedom Rights, the Second Freedom Rights, the Third Freedom Rights, the Fourth Freedom Rights and the Fifth Freedom Rights (Belobaba *et al.*, 2009; Chattopadhyay, 2015; Doganis, 2019; Zalagenaite, 2017; ICAO, 2020:online). The First and Second Freedoms are considered the most basic rights and are generally granted "automatically in all but exceptional cases" (Zalagenaite, 2017).

The First Freedom grants an airline from a specified country permission to fly over the territory of another country, carrying passengers, but without landing; while the Second Freedom permits an airline from a specified country to land in the territory of the country granting permission for non-traffic reasons such as maintenance or refuelling. The Third and Fourth Freedoms are granted bilaterally between two countries. The Third Freedom grants a government the right to designate an airline from that country to carry passengers from that country to the State which granted the right, and the Fourth Freedom grants that airline the right to carry passengers on the return flight from the State concerned back to the country of its origin (Belobaba *et al.*, 2009; Chattopadhyay, 2015; Zalagenaite, 2017; Doganis, 2019); ICAO, 2020:online).

The Fifth Freedom, the last one to be recognised by the ICAO, allows an airline from a specified country to carry passengers between two countries and also to stop over in a third country for passengers' embarkation or disembarkation before landing at its final destination. The ICAO regards the other four freedoms which subsequently came into existence between and among countries as "so-called freedoms" (Belobaba *et al.*, 2009; Chattopadhyay, 2015; Zalagenaite, 2017; Doganis, 2019); ICAO, 2020:online).

Chattopadhyay (2015:147) draws special attention to two rights, the Seventh Freedom and the Eighth Freedom. The former is a right that a government grants to another government for an airline registered in that foreign country which has applied for the air services agreement to carry passengers between the country which has granted permission and a third country, without the flight in question having to originate from or conclude in the country whose government was granted freedom for the route/s. It requires the express permission of the third country in question. The Eighth Freedom – which "is almost never granted" (Chattopadhyay, 2015:147) – would allow a foreign airline to operate domestic flights in other countries, a practice which is known as consecutive cabotage (ICAO, 2020:online).

An "Open Skies" agreement completely removes any government restrictions on the kind of air service that foreign airlines can offer between two countries (Belobaba *et al.*, 2009; Chattopadhyay, 2015; Zalagenaite, 2017; Doganis, 2019); ICAO, 2020:online).

In order to be able to carry passengers or cargo between two countries, an airline has to be "designated" (which means that it has to be specifically indicated by name) by the state entering into a bilateral air services agreement (BASA) with another state as the airline which will carry passengers or cargo between the two states concerned (Belobaba *et al.*, 2009; Chattopadhyay, 2015). In terms of traditional or restricted agreements, each country may designate only one of its airlines to operate between itself and another country, with the host government reserving the right to control capacity and price for the home market. However, such restrictions on capacity and pricing are usually eliminated in progressive or liberal BASAs, which may make allowance for a government to designate more than one airline for routes which have high-demand volumes (Belobaba *et al.*, 2009; Chattopadhyay, 2015).

Once concluded, BASAs remain valid indefinitely, until they are renegotiated (Doganis, 2019:24).

All airlines have been associated with a nationality since the 1944 Chicago Convention. To this day, most governments have laws which limit foreigners' ownership and effective control of airlines in their respective countries if these airlines are to operate in the domestic market and to qualify for designation in BASAs. Examples of such limitations are given in table 2.1 below, which shows that the USA has some of the most stringent requirements. In that country, US citizens have to own a minimum of 75% of an American airline and at least two-thirds of the Directors (including the Chairman) on US carriers' Boards of Directors have to be American citizens (Belobaba *et al.*, 2009:27).

In South Africa, foreign ownership of South African airlines is limited to 25% (Joffe, 2020), but it is capped at 20% for the national carrier, South Africa Airways, with possible South African private ownership capped at 49% (Kingston, 2019) .

According to Belobaba *et al.*, (2009:27), the nationality rule for airlines probably resulted from governments' need to be able to use airlines in their countries for national emergencies, which may include wars, in addition to a desire to protect jobs, as well as countries' "lingering fondness for the notion of 'flag carriers'." It is that nationality rule, which is found in all traditional BASAs, which has made it impossible for the international airline industry to be fully normalised (Doganis, 2019:23).

It follows, therefore, that the Chicago Aviation Conference of 1944 – which gave birth to the Chicago Convention, the ICAO and IATA – formed the basis of international aviation. Among the most important offshoots of the Chicago Convention was the concept of the Freedoms of the Skies or Freedoms of the Air, on the basis of which governments have concluded bilateral and/or multilateral air services agreements.

Table 2.1: Restrictions regarding foreign ownership of airlines in selected countries

Country	Limits of foreign ownership
Australia	49% for airlines engaged in international operations (25% on any single shareholder); 100% for solely domestic airlines
Canada	25%
China	35%
Chile	100%, as long as airline's principal place of business is in Chile
European Union	49%, applies to non-EU citizens
India	49%, but foreign airlines cannot hold shares in Indian airlines
Japan	33,33%
Korea	49%
Malaysia	45%
New Zealand	49% for airlines engaged in international operations; 100% for solely domestic airlines
Singapore	27,51%
Taiwan	33,33%
Thailand	30%
USA	25%; one-third of the Board of Directors; Chairman/woman must be US national

Source: Chang & Williams (2001)

Having outlined the solid foundation that was laid by the Chicago Convention for the international aviation industry, we now turn to what is probably the most important part of that industry for the purposes of this study: commercial airlines.

The nature of the commercial airline industry

Not only is the airline industry among the most regulated economic sectors in the world, but it is also very capital intensive and hyper-sensitive to external factors like natural disasters, health emergencies and socio-political developments, all of which have the potential to affect its financial health. In addition to being intensely competitive, the sector is also labour intensive and faces numerous structural challenges which include the fluctuating cost of Aviation Turbine Fuel (also called jet fuel), airport charges, rigid labour laws and a higher cost of capital, among others (Belobaba *et al.*, 2009; Chattopadhyay, 2015; Doganis, 2019).

Among the challenges facing airlines is the fact that their products, namely seats on a commercial flight or space on a cargo flight from one city or country to another, are homogenous and cannot be stored in the form of an inventory (Chattopadhyay, 2015:147; Doganis, 2019). The industry is vulnerable to high levels of seasonality and cyclicality and labour has considerable bargaining power because "airlines use capital-intensive equipment that is useless unless flown" (Chattopadhyay, 2015). This bargaining power has enabled unions to negotiate "generous pay packages and exceptionally good working conditions for employees," with the result that workers' contracts are very complex and generous to labour (Chattopadhyay, 2015).

In addition to the homogeneity of airlines' products, which cannot be stored in the form of inventory, Doganis (2019:4) says another one of airlines' main characteristics is the fact that demand for their services is a derived demand. This means that individuals and companies book seats on a commercial flight or space on a cargo flight not because they desire the experience of being airborne *per se*, but because they are going on holiday, visiting friends or attending meetings in another city or country, or they want a parcel or cargo moved from one place to another.

While global aviation markets operate like oligopolies, suppliers to the airline industry are "very monopolistic in nature:" not only are airports natural monopolies, but there are also only two major aircraft manufacturers in the world, Boeing and Airbus (Chattopadhyay, 2015:148). This reality leaves airlines with weak bargaining power, hence it is a challenge for them to remain consistently profitable. As a result, the industry's profitability is weak or negative even during periods of high economic growth and times when demand for air travel is growing fast (Chattopadhyay, 2015).

WNS Holdings Ltd (2017) concurs, pointing out that until recently the commercial aviation industry was not regarded as a good sector in which to invest.

Belobaba *et al.* (2009:3) point out that passenger growth in the airline industry averaged about five per cent a year in the 30-year period between 1988 and 2008, although it was impacted upon by differences in economic growth in different parts of the world. They point out that growth in air travel is heavily dependent on the economy's performance, and has often taken place at twice the annual growth in gross domestic product (GDP).

With the exception of 1991 and 2001, following the Gulf War and the terrorist attacks in the USA on 11 September 2001 respectively, passenger traffic has grown every year. Generally, non-American airlines have experienced higher levels of global passenger growth when compared to their American counterparts. This led to the proportion of international passenger traffic carried by American airlines declining from over 40% in 1987 to less than 32% in 2007 (Belobaba *et al.*, 2009:4).

Mott MacDonald (2017) agrees that economic growth is the main driver of air traffic demand, and shares the view that air travel, as shown in available seat-kilometres (ASK), has grown "significantly more rapidly than GDP," as illustrated in figure 2.1 below.

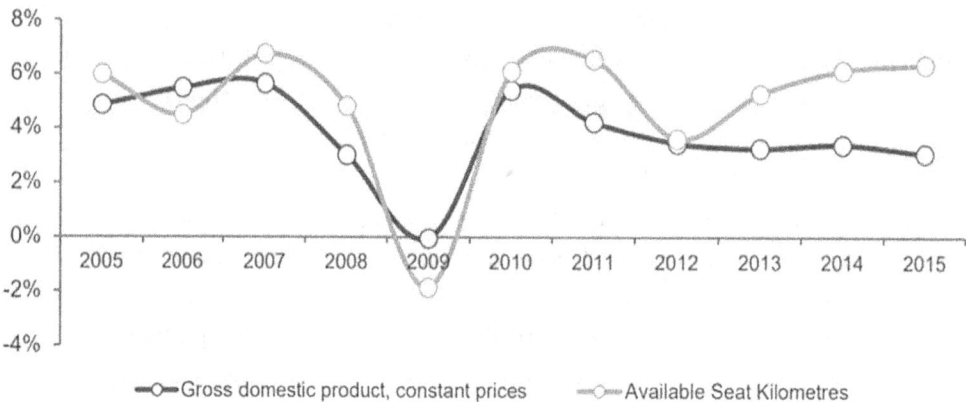

Source: IMF and SRS Analyser, 2016

Figure 2.1: Relationship between GDP growth and air travel between 2005 and 2015
Source: IMF and SRS Analyser, 2016

Figure 2.1 above shows that world air travel, as shown in ASK, grew faster than global GDP, except in the years 2006 and 2009. While the reasons for the 2006 decline in air travel when compared to GDP are unknown, the decline in 2009 was attributable to the global financial crisis which occurred that year (Mott MacDonald, 2017).

However, North America continued to be the busiest region in terms of air traffic, followed by Europe and Asia-Pacific. Growth in the Asia-Pacific region has been much higher than that experienced in North America and Europe, so much so that by 2007 Asia-Pacific had the same level of passenger traffic as Europe – and the region was expected to emerge in later years as the second largest in terms of air traffic (Belobaba *et al.*, 2009:4).

Doganis (2019:1) pointed out that in most years the airline industry is only marginally profitable, and only experienced growth which "more than covered the cost of capital" between 2015 and 2018, an era he calls "a period of golden profits." Otherwise, the pattern was one where, between 1970 and 2000, "five or six years of profits were followed by three to five years of losses," with the years of losses rendering the industry one where long-run profitability was only marginal.

However, Doganis (2019:2) noted that something unprecedented happened between 2010 and 2018 when airlines came close to experiencing "almost a decade of continuous profits," largely because of a huge drop in the price of aviation fuel in mid-2014. During this period, but especially between 2014 and 2018, airlines "recorded super-profits."

In 2015, in particular, the airline industry achieved record levels of profitability, with operating margins reaching what was until then an unprecedented 8,8% at a time when average air fares fell by 5%. Aviation jet fuel prices were also 44% lower, on average, than they were in 2014 (Mott MacDonald, 2017). American carriers were the most profitable, followed by European, Middle Eastern and Asian carriers. Three major US legacy carriers (American Airlines, Delta Airlines and United Airways) excelled in all global rankings, namely revenue, operating profit, revenue per passenger-kilometre and number of passengers. This performance followed consolidation by those airlines in their home market (Mott MacDonald, 2017).

Internationally, operating profit reported by airlines increased steadily between 2010 and 2015, and in 2015 18 global carriers reported operating profits of more than $1 billion. Despite a lower economic growth level of 1,6% GDP in the region, European carriers recorded $7,4 billion in operating profits in 2015, up from $1 billion the year before. Lufthansa, low-cost carrier Ryanair and the International Airlines Group (IAG, which owns British Airways and Aer Lingus, among others) were the most profitable (Mott MacDonald, 2017).

Collectively, low-cost carriers (LCCs) recorded a 3% growth in passenger volumes in 2015, which equalled a 20% share of global passenger volumes. Air traffic grew the fastest at mega-hub airports in the Gulf region, but African airlines experienced a pedestrian 0,6% growth in passenger volumes as a result of security instability in the north and poor economic performance by countries dependent on commodities. Chinese airlines like Air

China, China Eastern Airlines and China Southern Airlines also recorded growth in passenger volumes, as did the Middle Eastern carrier Emirates, which moved to the global top 10 of the most profitable airlines (Mott MacDonald, 2017).

With international air traffic passenger demand growing by 7,4% in 2015 (compared to GDP growth of 3,1%), at a time when available capacity supply grew by 6,7% year on year, airlines experienced "record load factors exceeding 80% on average." European airlines carried 311 million passengers, which was a 4% growth on 2014 figures, and averaged a load factor of 81% (Mott MacDonald, 2017).

Belobaba *et al.* (2009:7) point out that load factors (described as the proportion of available seats filled with revenue-paying passengers) have increased steadily since the mid-1990s for the international airline industry. The growth in the load factor increased considerably and approached "almost 80%" in the USA (which was 10% higher than in 2000) and 77% in other parts of the world. Until then, those were unprecedented levels, which boded well for future airline profitability.

However, in the Middle East, when air traffic passenger demand reached double-digit levels in 2015, more seat capacity was added (Mott MacDonald, 2017).

Globally, there were more than seven billion departing and arriving air passengers in 2015, which was a growth of 6,4% on the previous year, which had itself registered a 5,5% growth on 2013. High growth levels were recorded in North America and Asia-Pacific but, with 9,6% growth, the Middle East – with the Gulf area's mega-hub airports – emerged as the world's fastest-growing region. Global airports also recorded increased profitability in 2014 following faster growth in operating revenues (at 7,3%), compared to operating costs. As an industry, global airports achieved a return on invested capital (ROIC) of 6,3%, although those situated in emerging economies registered a higher ROIC of 9,9% when compared with airports in advanced economies, whose ROIC growth was 5,6% (Mott MacDonald, 2017).

In 2016, the number of international air passengers grew by 6,3% to a new record of 3,7 billion. That impressive performance was a continuation of the recovery in the industry after the 2008/9 global financial crisis, and followed a 3,1% growth in the world economy and a reduction in air fares following a 43% drop in the price of jet fuel (Mott MacDonald, 2017).

However, not all airlines were profitable even during that period. Others made losses or registered negligible profits, and in 2017 three European airlines – Air Berlin, Monarch and Alitalia – went into bankruptcy (Doganis, 2019:2).

Fuel is the single largest cost for airlines, accounting for up to 40% of their operational costs (Bekele, 2019). That, argues Doganis (2019), means that airlines must always watch costs carefully and seek to contain them.

Doganis (2019:76) and Belobaba *et al.* (2009:10) point out that US airlines were the first to tackle the challenge of high labour costs in the early 1980s, but especially after 2001 following the grounding of airlines in that country in the aftermath of the terrorist attacks at the World Trade Center in New York and at the Pentagon in Washington DC. These airlines were able to use the threat of imminent collapse and Chapter 11 bankruptcy rules, which are similar to South Africa's business rescue proceedings, to cut staff numbers by up to one-third, while simultaneously reducing salaries by 25% to 30%. American airlines were again able to do the same thing following the global recession of 2008/2009, hence US airlines have relatively lower wage levels (Doganis, 2019) when compared to their counterparts in other parts of the world.

Between 2001 and 2005, four of the six legacy US airlines – namely US Airways, United, Delta and Northwest – declared Chapter 11 bankruptcy, which enabled them to downsize and restructure considerably. The other two airlines, American and Continental, were able to do the same after they also threatened to file for Chapter 11 bankruptcy. Collectively, these airlines retrenched more than 100 000 employees and reduced salaries by around seven per cent (Belobaba *et al.*, 2009:10).

According to the ICAO (2020), the aviation sector directly employs 10,2 million people around the world and supports a total of 65,5 million jobs internationally. On their own, airlines, air navigation service providers and airports employ an estimated 3,5 million globally, while the civil aerospace sector (which includes aircraft manufacturers) employs 1,2 million. Another 5,6 million people are employed in other positions related to airports, with an additional 55,3 million people working in indirect, induced and tourism-related jobs (ICAO, 2020).

In 2019, airlines carried an estimated 4,3 billion passengers per annum, contributed 3,6% to the world's GDP and had a multiplier effect of $2,7 trillion in the world economy (ICAO, 2020), as illustrated in figure 2.2 below.

Economic Context for Civil Aviation

Aviation provides the only rapid worldwide transportation network, which makes it essential for global business. It generates economic growth, creates jobs, and facilitates international trade and tourism.

PER YEAR		
4.3 BILLION PASSENGERS	**48,500** ROUTES WORLDWIDE	**38** MILLION SCHEDULED COMMERCIAL FLIGHTS

PER DAY		
100,000 FLIGHTS	**12** MILLION PASSENGERS TRANSPORTED	**240,000** HOURS FLOWN

ECONOMIC BENEFITS		
65.5 MILLION JOBS SUPPORTED	**3.6** PER CENT OF GDP SUPPORTED	USD **2.7** TRILLION ECONOMIC IMPACT

Source: Aviation Benefits Report, 2019

Figure 2.2: Global economic impacts of civil aviation
Source: ICAO Aviation Benefits Report, 2019

Figure 2.2 above shows that in 2019 the airline industry, among other things, sustained 65,5 million jobs, contributed 3,6% to the world GDP, operated 100 000 flights and flew a total of 4,3 billion passengers (ICAO, 2020).

Although airlines have been known to have very tight profit margins, it is evident that trends in the last decade have shown growing profitability. However, given the homogeneity of airlines' products and growing competition, it is those carriers whose managements have been good at cost containment and productivity improvements that have been able to take full advantage of the growing demand for air travel services.

The industry, which was until then heavily regulated, was to experience major changes from 1978 onwards, following the enactment of legislation in the USA which encouraged greater competition. That change, whose effects continue to be felt in the sector across the world, is outlined in the section below.

Dregulation of the airline industry and the birth of low-cost carriers

The biggest change to affect the airline industry over the past five decades came in 1978 when American President Jimmy Carter signed the Airline Deregulation Act into law on 24 October (Doganis, 2019:30; Lawton, Rajwani & O'Kane, 2011). That legislation followed Carter's pledge, during his election campaign, to support consumers (Doganis, 2019).

The Airline Deregulation Act of 1978 marked a major turning point for the industry, first in the USA itself and subsequently around the world, and resulted – as was intended by the authorities – in more intense competition for airlines which were already in existence and which subsequently came to be known as "legacy airlines" (Lawton *et al.*, 2011).

Until then, most airlines were owned by the governments of their respective countries and enjoyed the benefits of being entrenched monopolies in their respective routes. Generally, they offered higher service levels to their passengers and had higher fixed costs when compared to the new, low-fare airlines (LFAs) or low-cost carriers (LCCs) that subsequently sprang up (Belobaba *et al.*, 2009; Lawton *et al.*, 2011).

According to Button (2003:5), airline deregulation – or liberalisation of the airline markets – was based on observations in smaller markets that American customers enjoyed better service and lower fares where there was no economic control. From the assertion by Button (2003), it follows that the lawmakers' intention was to ensure that similar benefits were extended to the rest of the country.

Button (2003) argues that another motivation for the deregulation of the sector was the belief that competition would be far more effective in ensuring that airlines were much more responsive to societies' needs than government regulations would be.

Deregulation refers to the process of removing barriers to entry to an industry, or the gradual weakening of centralised authority in an industry in order to expose it to market forces by facilitating greater competition within that industry (Njoya, 2013; Pirie, 2006; Wensveen, 2011). Abate (2013) says that, in the case of the airline industry, deregulation refers to the removal of regulations related to entry and exit control and the protection of some routes from competition, while simultaneously tightening controls over safety.

Markman (1999) calls the resulting change in the operations of airlines "an international revolution … in the liberalisation of transport markets." Until then, the airline industry in the USA was highly regulated and had been caught in "a virtually static regulatory framework for 50 years." The aftermath of the Airline Deregulation Act of 1978 was "a surge in the establishment of new airlines and in mergers leading to price wars and increased flight frequencies," which benefitted US passengers (Markman, 1999).

Belobaba *et al.* (2009:5) point out that while passenger numbers have grown phenomenally over the years, average air fares declined so sharply in the USA following deregulation that in 2008 they stood at less than half the level where they were in 1978 as a result of new entrants – mostly LCCs – into the market. That forced airline managements to prioritise cost management and productivity improvements in order to survive.

Other countries around the world – such as Australia and Japan – soon followed suit with similar pieces of legislation to deregulate their own airline industries. Australia eventually went as far as relaxing airline ownership rules to make it possible for foreigners to own up to 100% of that country's airlines (Doganis, 2019).

In Europe, the Republic of Ireland was the first country to deregulate its aviation industry in 1986. National flag carrier Aer Lingus, which was established in 1936 at a time when the Irish government was strongly protective of its industries, found itself facing competition from LCC Ryanair. That happened after Aer Lingus, which had been very successful in its efforts to lobby the Irish government to reserve the market for it, was deemed to have "achieved regulatory capture of its parent government department" (Barrett, 2006:160).

Ireland's aviation deregulation took place 11 years before the European Union (EU) did the same thing in 1997, and Ireland was also the first country within the EU where a new entrant, Ryanair, grew so popular that it ended up being four times bigger than the long-established national airline, Aer Lingus, in terms of passengers carried (Barrett, 2006:161). So successful was airline deregulation in Ireland that it created a favourable impression of deregulation in other sectors of the economy (OECD, 2001).

Similar legislation was passed within the EU in 1997, leading to complete deregulation of the aviation industry within that region. The result was a situation where legacy airlines within the union found themselves struggling to adjust to a new competitive landscape (Lawton *et al.*, 2011).

In South Africa, a White Paper on Privatisation and Deregulation published by the National Party government in 1987 advocated for the deregulation of the aviation industry, "based on the American experience" (Goldstein, 2001:230). Four years later (1991), the industry was deregulated, with South African Airways open to direct competition for the very first time in its history (Shaw, 2011:35).

In Africa, airline deregulation was first approved by continental Ministers in October 1998 when the Yamoussoukro Declaration on a new African Policy was signed in Ivory Coast. When no progress was registered, African Transport Ministers came up with "The Decision Relating to Liberalization of Access to Air Transport Markets in Africa," known as the Yamoussoukro Decision, which was endorsed by Heads of States of the African Organisation of African Unity on 12 July 2000 and came into effect on 12 August 2002 (Munene, 2012).

Although it was ratified by many countries, the Yamoussoukro Decision was mainly observed in breach. In January 2018, the African Union established the Single African Transport Market (SATS), with 23 countries signing the agreement. The aim of the SATS aim was "to implement provisions of the Yamoussoukrou [Decision] and create an African open skies area similar to that in Europe" (Doganis, 2019:39).

In India, in 1986 the government gave privately-owned airlines permission to offer air taxi services (Chattopadhyay, 2015). Four years later, the government embarked on deregulation and allowed "air-taxi operators to operate flights from any airport." In 1994, the government repealed the Air Corporations Act of 1953, which had granted a monopoly to Indian Airways and Air India, and replaced it with the Air Corporations (Transfer of Undertaking and Repeal) Act, which granted private airlines the right to offer air transport services (Chattopadhyay, 2015).

However, important limitations still remained: foreign airlines could not own any equity in any Indian airline and foreigners could not own more than a 49% stake in an Indian airline, but Indian citizens who lived elsewhere in the world ("non-resident Indians") could have full ownership of an airline registered in the country (Chattopadhyay, 2015).

Losses sustained by Air India since its merger with State-owned domestic operator Indian Airlines in 2007 forced Prime Minister Narendra Modi to announce in March 2018 a sale of a 76% stake in the flagship national carrier, along with two-thirds of the loss-making carrier's $7,8 billion debt in a move described by Bloomberg News (2018) as India's "most high-profile asset sale in decades." Air India had survived on government bailouts for a number of years. In January 2018, Prime Minister Modi amended the law restricting ownership by a foreign airline to a maximum of 49% of an Indian airline to include Air India, which was previously not covered by those regulations (Bloomberg, 2018).

In China, the airline industry, like many others, has been "heavily regulated" for many years, with all aspects – "market entry, route entry, frequency, fare levels and aircraft purchasing" – being controlled very tightly by the Civil Aviation Administration of China (Chen, 2017; Zhang & Chen, 2003). Although partial deregulation of the sector occurred in 2004 when five privately-owned airlines – United Eagle Airlines, Okay Airways, Lucky Air, Spring Airlines and China Express Airlines – were established, severe regulatory constraints remained in place, with privately-owned airlines hardly ever granted the right "to serve the most profitable routes" (Chen, 2017; Fu, Lei, Wang & Yan, 2015).

However, since then more privately-owned airlines have entered the market. Chen (2017:114) quotes information from the OAG Database as indicating that by the end of 2015 at least 32 airlines were operating in China, although the three State-owned airlines (Air China, China Southern Airlines and China Eastern Airlines) continued to dominate.

Deregulation changed the commercial aviation industry (Barrett, 2006; Chen, 2017; Hazledine, 2011; Mhlanga & Steyn, 2016). It left massive damage in its wake, with the industry today looking very different from the way it looked before deregulation. Established airlines that were well known at the time – like Pan American (PanAm) and

Trans-World Airlines (TWA) in America and SwissAir in Europe – went out of existence. Air France merged with Dutch airline KLM, Aer Lingus re-invented itself as a semi-low-fare carrier (Barrett, 2006; Lawton *et al.*, 2011) and Alitalia was privatised, with United Arab Emirates airline Etihad buying a 51% stake in it (*Corriere della Sera*, 2014), but finally filed for bankruptcy on 2 May 2017 (Bloomberg, 2017).

By the end of 2017, Lufthansa and British Airways had acquired or merged with other European airlines. The Lufthansa Group owned Lufthansa, SWISS, Austrian Airlines and LCCs Brussels and Eurowings, while BA was part of the International Airlines Group (IAG), which also owns Iberia, Aer Lingus and low-cost Spanish carrier Vueling (Doganis, 2019:159). IAG also launched Level Airlines, a low-cost carrier intended to compete with WOW, a low-cost airline owned by Norwegian Airlines (Zhang, 2017).

Kumar (2006:110) points out that BA first set up LCC Go to counter competition from EasyJet and Ryanair, but subsequently sold that carrier to EasyJet in 2002 to concentrate on long-haul flights because LCCs do not offer competition on long-haul international routes. The British flag carrier also reduced its capacity on flights to several European destinations, "effectively conceding victory to low-cost carriers."

In South America, Chile's LAN Airlines merged with Brazil's TAM to form LATAM, which had subsidiaries in Colombia, Ecuador, Paraguay, Argentina and Peru. That transformed LATAM into "a global player" (Doganis, 2019:160).

Button (2003:6) points out that deregulation transformed many airline markets around the world "from regulated monopolies to more free market-based structures." He says that, between 1980 and 2003, the proportion of the capacity of the largest 25 global airlines owned by governments had fallen from 38% to 10%.

Lawton *et al.* (2011) point out that the challenges that followed airline deregulation – such as the privatisation of State-owned airlines and the entry of new competitors in the form of LFAs or LCCs, among others – necessitated a strategic rethink on the part of the "former flag carriers." They say it has been mostly start-up LFAs, rather than legacy carriers, which have accounted for the most recent airline industry success stories around the world: "The nimble, ultra-lean business models of LFAs often make the legacy carriers cumbersome, anachronistic and financially unappealing" (Lawton *et al.*, 2011).

Barrett (2006:166) says the case study of Aer Lingus, which responded to competition from LCC Ryanair by reducing its fixed costs and lowering its fares, shows that the old legacy carriers tend to be more expensive and are, therefore, deserted by passengers the moment there is a choice in the form of a LCC. Goldman Sachs (2004) says that most governments no longer consider ownership of airlines as "an important element of public policy," but now use other means "to achieve their objectives as airline stakeholders."

Barrett (2006:166) observes that the era of protectionism in the aviation industry in Europe has revealed that sheltered airlines which were not exposed to competition employed many more people in support services, and this impacted negatively on their average earnings. Low-cost airlines, on the other hand, employed fewer people in similar roles, paid performance-related salaries and were more productive.

The entry of LCCs into airline markets had the effect of significantly lowering travel costs, thereby forcing "a fundamental restructuring" of many existing legacy or full-service airlines (FSAs) (Chen, 2017: 113; Njegovan, 2006; Papatheodorou & Lei, 2006). Chen (2017) refers to the existence in the US of a phenomenon known as "Southwest effects," which refers to the fact that a market entered by Southwest Airlines in that country routinely saw "a dramatic increase in passenger volumes," which was always accompanied by a decrease in average fares.

Dresner, Lin and Windle (1996:311) point out that, before the passage of the Deregulation Act of 1978, Southwest Airlines operated only within the state of Texas in the USA, but started offering point-to-point services to other parts of that country following deregulation. The airline flew only a single type of aircraft – the Boeing 737 – on all its routes, avoided congested airports and had quick turnaround times in order to ensure that its aircraft spent as much time in the air as possible. So successful was Southwest Airlines that, when all other American carriers were experiencing huge losses in the early 1990s, Southwest was the only profitable carrier (Dresner *et al.*, 1996).

Following a study that they conducted, Windle and Dresner (1995) concluded that the entry of Southwest Airlines into a route in the US had the effect of decreasing fares by up to 48% on average and resulted in a 200% increase in passenger volumes. This is the phenomenon that came to be known as "the Southwest effects" (Chen, 2017; Zhang, 2017).

According to Kumar (2006:108), until the year 2000, Southwest Airlines had the lowest costs (excluding fuel) among all airlines in the USA, namely 6,2 cents per available seat-mile when compared to legacy carriers like Delta, Northwest Airlines and United Airlines, whose costs were 8c per available seat-mile. However, JetBlue – which was launched in 2000 – had even lower costs than Southwest Airlines, at 4,7 cents per available seat-mile and offered tough competition to the latter (Kumar, 2006:108).

According to Chen (2017), in Europe "Southwest effects" were replicated by LCCs like Ryanair and EasyJet.

In order to survive, legacy airlines have had to respond to the threats posed by LCCs. Responses have ranged from Aer Lingus's reduction of its fixed costs and air fares (Barrett, 2006; Hazledine, 2011), establishing their own LCCs as "fighting brands" on routes where they are challenged by LCCs, or – as Air Canada and Air New Zealand did – using their higher costs and improved service levels to their advantage (Hazledine, 2011).

Kumar (2006:110) also makes the point that in the 1990s a number of legacy carriers responded to competition from LCCs by setting up their own "no-frills second carriers" as fighting brands: Continental Airways launched Continental Light, Delta Airways set up Delta Express, KLM established Buzz, US Airways created MetroJet and United Airways established Shuttle. However, the efforts to counter competition from LCCs did not succeed, and these legacy airlines shut down or sold their low-cost fighting brands because trade unions were vehemently opposed to them paying their subsidiaries' employees salaries that were comparable to those paid by Southwest Airlines and JetBlue (Kumar, 2006:110).

Delta's LCC, Song Airways, was launched in 2003 and ceased to exist in 2006, while United Airways Ted Airlines, which was launched in 2004, went bankrupt during the global financial crisis in 2009 (Zhang, 2017). Following the failure of their no-frills fighting brands, US legacy carriers resorted to competing with LCCs through the introduction of "a basic economy, discount-fare class" in their economy cabin, which saw passengers on a basic-economy fare restricted to one carry-on bag that would fit underneath the seat (Zhang, 2017).

Hazledine (2011:130) contends that FSAs' fixed costs "can actually deliver market value, that this value can be enhanced by shrewd and innovative pricing and marketing practices, and that such practices cannot easily be replicated by LCCs and so can deliver a source of competitive advantage to the legacy carriers which may compensate for the LCCs' lower variable costs."

Hazledine (2011:130) points out that LCCs' share of the domestic market in the USA, in terms of passenger numbers, increased from 4% in 1990 to 20% in 1999 and ultimately to 33% in 2008, while the six largest legacy carriers' collective market share was 63,3% in 1997 and 63,1% in 2005. He says that since, on average, legacy carriers fly longer routes, their revenue passenger miles also tend to be "substantially larger," thus leading to their larger share of revenue because their fares tend to be higher than those of LCCs.

In Europe, more than 40% of air passengers flew on LCCs in 2016. These included Ryanair, EasyJet, Norwegian and KLM's Transavia (Zhang, 2017).

Low-cost carriers (LCCs) like AirAsia "massively disrupt[ed]" the airline industry in Southeast Asia, where commercial air travel was previously dominated by established legacy carriers like Singapore Airways, Thai Airways and Malaysia Airlines. In 2016, LCC AirAsia had a 49% market share in Malaysia and a 22% market share in Thailand (Zhang, 2017).

According to Zhang (2017), LCCs accounted for 28% of all air passenger traffic around the world in 2016, which represented a 10% increase since 2014. Zhang (2017) pointed out that, while LCCs had transformed the way people fly in the developed world, these low-cost airlines had actually made air travel possible for many people in the developing world.

Hazledine (2011:133) concludes that there is little evidence which supports the proposition that competition from LCCs, based on its overall impact on fare structures, has made legacy carrier pricing practices – but particularly price discrimination – obsolete. He says his study on Air Canada's response to competition from its LCC rival Westjet showed that there are passengers who are prepared to pay – or to get their companies to pay – "for various perks and frills" supplied by the legacy carrier, which the LCC does not or cannot provide.

Kumar (2006:112) shares that view, arguing that while some consumers may be price sensitive, there will always be others who are "partial to value" and are willing to pay for it.

Hazledine (2011:135) argues that his study into the responses by Air New Zealand and Air Canada to competition from LCCs in their respective markets showed that "even well-run LCCs are not *a force majeure,* sweeping aside all resistance." Instead, argues Hazledine (2011), legacy carriers can successfully exploit LCCs' low-cost business model, which can also be a source of weakness for them.

Doganis (2019: 239) posits that some government-owned airlines tend to have other priorities, such as job creation, facilitating tourism and ensuring that a country has adequate connections to its trading partners, with profit seen as "a desirable longer-term objective rather than a short-term priority." He says that was the thinking which informed the establishment of Qatar Airways in 1993 and Abu Dhabi's Etihad Airways in 2003.

It is clear, therefore, that President Jimmy Carter's Airline Deregulation Act of 1978 has had a big ripple effect in the airline industry around the world, where competition – especially from cheaper, no-thrills LCCs – became much stiffer. As more air travel became affordable, the number of air passengers grew phenomenally over the years, but air fares became cheaper.

Africa was not untouched by developments in aviation elsewhere in the world, as will be clear in the next two sections, which trace the evolution of aviation first in South Africa and then in Kenya, the countries where the two airlines which are the primary case studies for this study are domiciled.

Aviation in South Africa

Major Allister Miller, who came to be described as "the father of civil aviation in South Africa," founded Union Airways in 1929 as an airmail operation, after having won a government contract to fly airmail between Cape Town and major centres in the country (SAA Museum Society, 2020:online). Union Airways was registered on 24 July 1929 and started operating on 26 August 1929. Later on, it started operating passenger flights (Pirie, 2006:9); it carried its first passenger from Cape Town to East London on 3 September 1929 and, subsequently, sick persons on mercy flights (SAA Museum Society, 2020:online).

Following a crash in which Union Airways' Junkers W34 aircraft was lost in bad weather near Eshowe in 1933, which was a serious financial blow to Major Miller, the government of the day took over the airline's assets and liabilities on 1 February 1934, renamed the airline South African Airways (SAA) and made it part of South African Railways and Harbours (SAR&H), which was later renamed Transnet (SAA Museum Society, 2020:online). During the Second World War between 1939 and 1945, SAA aircraft were transferred to the army, thus leaving the country fully reliant on foreign airlines for the provision of domestic air transport services (Gavin, 2013:9).

In 1946 a new private airline, Comair, was established (Goldstein, 2001:230). The airline offered a charter flight from Rand Airport in Germiston to Stamford Hill Aerodrome in Durban. In 1948 Comair introduced its scheduled service between Johannesburg and Durban via Kroonstad, Odendaalsrus, Bloemfontein, Bethlehem and Ladysmith, using a new Cessna model 195 aircraft (The Comair Story, 2020:online).

Three years later, the government passed the International Air Services Act Number 51 of 1949, which sought to protect SAA from competition. The new law stipulated that airlines wishing to compete against SAA in the main domestic routes had to prove the existence of a need that could not be met by SAA (Brits, 2010:27; Mhlanga & Steyn, 2016). As a result, SAA operated as a sole monopoly on the main routes and controlled both airports and landing slots (Gavin, 2013:9), with Comair left with the feeder routes (Goldstein, 2001:230).

Thanks to the International Air Services Act (also called the Air Services Act), SAA continued to be sheltered from competition for more than 40 years (Pirie, 1990:238). This protection meant that SAA – which maintained some services that did not make economic sense and enjoyed automatic rights to the major routes and the dominance that flowed therefrom – "was not a true business concern" (Vlok, 1992:20).

As the fight against apartheid intensified at home and abroad, with a growing number of countries ostracising both South Africa and the national carrier following the passing by the US Congress of the Comprehensive Anti-Apartheid Act in 1986, SAA found itself denied landing rights in countries like the USA and Australia and Australian airline Qantas stopped flying to South Africa, landing in Harare, Zimbabwe instead (CAJ News, 2015:11; Ndhlovu & Ricover, 2009:17; Ryan, 1992:9). SAA also found itself banned from flying over Africa and had to fly around the west coast of the continent and refuel at Ilha do Sol in Cape Verde (Pirie, 1990:238; Pirie, 2006:9).

In an effort to improve its performance, SAA embarked on a number of initiatives, among them the introduction of a cheaper, "see South Africa" fare, business class and a Frequent Flyer Programme (subsequently called Voyager). These initiatives paid off at first, with passenger numbers and revenue increasing by 14% and 16,5% respectively in 1984 and 1985. However, when the economy worsened in 1995, the airline's performance also declined (Mhlanga & Steyn, 2016).

The deregulation of the aviation market in 1991 did not immediately lead to the full levelling of the playing field. SAA continued to exercise the exclusive right to control airports, allocate landing slots to its competitors (Pirie, 1992:345) and operate luggage conveyor belts at all local airports (Bennett, 2005:419). This forced SAA's competitors like Flitestar to enter into agreements with it for ground handling services (Kemp, 2001).

To compound matters, there was no transparency when it came to SAA's financial performance since the airline's financial results were published as part of those of the Transnet group to which it belonged (Bennett, 2005; Goldstein, 2001).

From its inception, Comair continued to operate along a few, secondary routes, adding new routes only when these were deemed likely to be profitable. The privately-owned airline served low-cost routes and grew from carrying around 100 000 passengers in 1992 to carrying over one million passengers by 1997 (Ssamula, 2008:9).

When private airlines like Comair and Flitestar – which had entered the market following the industry's deregulation – complained about SAA's privileged market position, the new democratic Government resolved that operation of the services which gave the national carrier an unfair advantage should be placed under the control of a neutral organisation. That was accomplished through the passage of the Airports Company Act of 1993, which established the Airports Company of South Africa, whose responsibilities were "the acquisition, establishment, development, provision, maintenance, management, control and/or operation of an airport, or part of an airport, or a facility or service of an airport crucial to the functioning of such an airport" (Frederico, 2013:721; Pirie, 2006:9; Steyn & Mhlanga, 2016; Ssamula, 2014:226).

Now able to operate more routes, including those previously the preserve of SAA, in 1996 Comair entered into a franchise agreement with BA, in terms of which the local airline could use BA livery on its aircraft, change its interior and staff uniforms to those of BA and be part of BA's Frequent Flyer Programme, known as the BA Executive Club

(Cochrane, 2001; Heinz & O'Connell, 2013). The agreement enabled Comair, while it remained an independent South African company, to upgrade its aircraft and services to include a business class offering at a more competitive price than that offered by SAA (Cochrane, 2001; Heinz & O'Connell, 2013).

More importantly, the franchise agreement gave BA direct access to the South African market through Comair, while the latter gained direct access to international routes (Ndhlovu & Ricover, 2009:17). In response, in 1997 SAA concluded a franchise agreement of its own with SA Express and SA Airlink (Chalmers, 2001), and in the same year Nationwide Airlines – which had come into existence after the deregulation of 1991 – also entered into a strategic partnership with Belgium's SABENA World Airlines (Chingosho, 2005:17).

The new, post-deregulation entrants into the market included low-cost carrier (LCC) Kulula.com, which was established by the BA/Comair partnership in August 2001 (Bennett & George, 2004:117). Five years later, SAA countered with the launch of its own LCC, Mango Airlines. The national carrier also purchased a 49% share in Air Tanzania in 2003 when the latter was partially privatised (Chalmers, 2003:9).

The biggest beneficiaries of deregulation were passengers, who had a wider choice of service providers and higher frequencies of service throughout the day (Mhlanga, 2017). Kulula's success on the Johannesburg to Lusaka, Zambia route led to a reduction of 33% to 38% in ticket fares and a 38% increase in the number of passengers (Mhlanga, 2017).

In September 2018, Comair announced a profit of R325,6 million for the 2017/18 financial year, described as "the highest after-tax profit" in its history, up from R296,97 million in 2017, with its revenue having increased to R6,5 billion, up from R6,064 billion the previous year. This meant that the airline had recorded 72 successive years of profits (Blom, 2018). It recorded a seven per cent growth in revenue, a four per ent increase in passenger volumes and a three per cent increase in the average fare per passenger (Blom, 2018).

At the same time, SAA reported a financial loss of R5,7 billion for the same year, which was R3 billion worse than initially expected. However, the national carrier's route rationalisation had begun to show results (Gernetzky, 2018).

Of the 17 airlines that entered the industry between 1991 and 2016, nine went out of business and only eight were still in existence by the middle of 2016, with SAA and Comair (Kulula.com) the only airlines to have operated "for a lengthy period" (Steyn & Mhlanga, 2016). SAA itself had suffered a series of financial losses "requiring several Government bailouts and guarantees" (Ismael, 2015:6).

Between 2006 and 2016, SAA accrued losses of over R18 billion (Businesstech, 2016). Between 2011 and 2016 it received Government bailouts, in the form of guarantees, worth an estimated R14,4 billion as part of its turnaround strategy (Businesstech, 2016). It had moved from controlling "more than 95%" of the domestic airline market before deregulation in 1990 to controlling an estimated 38% of the market in 2016 (Centre for Asia-Pacific Aviation, 2016).

In 2017, 2018 and 2019, SAA lost R5,6 billion, R5,5 billion and R5,1 billion respectively and was placed in business rescue on 5 December 2019 (Paton, 2020). In May 2020, Comair was placed in business rescue, following a loss of R564 million in the first half of 2020 and the global lockdown as a result of the CoronaVirus Disease 2019 (COVID-19) pandemic which saw borders closed and many airlines around the world grounded (Smith, 2020).

Therefore, it is evident from this section of the chapter that deregulation has had the same effect in South Africa as it has had in the USA since 1978 and in other parts of the world once it was embarked upon. SAA, like other legacy carriers, suddenly found itself vulnerable to competition from LCCs and other competitors and was unable to hold onto to the kind of market share that it enjoyed in the days when it had a monopoly in the domestic market.

In the next section, the early days of aviation in Kenya, including the formation of that country's national flag carrier, Kenya Airways, are outlined.

Aviation in Kenya

Kenya Airways was founded on 22 January 1977 following the liquidation, on 31 January 1977, of the East African Airways Corporation, which was jointly owned by the governments of Kenya, Uganda and Tanzania (Debrah & Toroitich, 2005). Collectively, the three countries constituted the East African Community which was formed in 1967 as an economic union after those countries had each won their independence from their former colonial power, the United Kingdom. A government-owned airline and Kenyan flag carrier, Kenya Airways (hereafter referred to as KQ, its International Air Transport Association code name) was established with a fleet of seven aircraft, little technical expertise, few competent employees and without an effective management (Debrah & Toroitich, 2005).

At its formation, KQ was poorly capitalised and its management team highly inexperienced. In its early years, KQ's financial and related performance deteriorated, thus impacting negatively on the airline's financial health and its reputation (Debrah & Toroitich, 2005).

Like SAA, KQ had a range of other managerial problems. Over an 18-year period, from its inception in 1977 until 1995, the airline had 10 different CEOs appointed by its sole Shareholder, the Kenyan Government. The situation was aggravated by the fact that the Board was made up of "political appointees with no specific experience either in managing a business, in general, or an airline in particular," and this left the airline without any "clear strategic direction" (Deborah & Toroitich, 2005).

Although KQ had the largest market share of the East and Central African regional routes and some international routes, it lost customers because of its poor flight services and late departures and arrivals. By 1991 it was unable to pay its debts, which had run into millions of US dollars, and the Kenyan Government had to step in and bail it out continuously by paying its foreign loans, which the Government had guaranteed (Debrah & Toroitich, 2005).

In the end, corrective action was taken through the appointment of a Probe Committee, which recommended commercialisation of the airline, stressing that KQ could not succeed commercially unless it was privatised. The Kenyan Government accepted the recommendations, dismissed the CEO and the entire Board and replaced them with a new Board headed by Phillip Ndegwa as Executive Chairman and David Narmu as Chief General Manager, with the latter two considered "the best and ablest people in the country to run the company" (Debrah & Toroitich, 2005).

The new Board – which soon concluded that KQ would be profitable only if it were run as a commercial entity, "free from political interference" – appointed a consulting company and subsequently accepted its recommended turnaround strategy. With the concurrence and support of the government, a 26,73% stake in KQ was sold to Royal Dutch Airlines (KLM) as a strategic partner, the airline was listed on the Nairobi Stock Exchange and employees became co-owners through an Employee Share Ownership Plan (Debrah & Toroitich, 2005).

KQ's privatisation in 1996 was a major turning point for the airline. From then onwards, KQ has operated as fully-fledged private business, in which the Kenyan Government happened to be one of the two largest Shareholders.

In the next section, prospects for the commercial airline industry are discussed.

Changes in and prospects for the commercial airline industry

Global business process management services company WNS (Holdings) Limited (2017) identified six top trends shaping the airline industry. These were rising passenger demand and rebounding cargo volumes, a boost from the addition of higher capacity, thereby improving airline operating metrics, high load factors driving revenue, intensifying competition from Low-Cost Carriers (LCCs) and Ultra Low-Cost Carriers (ULLCs), as well as ancillary revenue opportunities.

WNS (2017) noted that while the commercial aviation industry was not considered a good investment until recent years, with US businessman Warren Buffet having described it as "a death trap" for investors in 2013, the industry's performance changed for the better from 2015. WNS said the industry's growth had remained steady, notwithstanding poor global macro-economic conditions and a rising tide of anti-globalisation sentiment.

In its 2017 Annual Review, IATA (2017) noted that in 2016 the airline industry's return on capital exceeded its cost of capital, and that this marked a trend which had emerged "only for the second time on record." WNS (2017) stated that in 2016 the average airline reported a positive return on invested capital (ROIC) for the third consecutive year "and only the third time in history," and that the ROIC was expected to be around 8,8% in 2017 as a result of "persistent growth in air travel" since the global economic recession of 2008-09 and airlines' single-minded focus on cost reduction and efficiency improvements, especially by keeping aircraft airborne as much as possible, rather than on the ground.

According to WNS (2017), passenger numbers were expected to grow by an estimated 7,19% in 2017 to an unprecedented 4,1 billion, which significantly outpaced the 20-year trend of a 5% growth rate, and cargo demand was expected to rebound. That scenario would have resulted in airlines posting a 5,3% growth in revenue on an aggregate basis, from $705 billion to $743 billion in 2017.

According to WNS (2017), "almost 100 airlines" have declared bankruptcy since the advent of the 1978 Airline Deregulation Act in the USA. An ongoing focus on costs will see legacy airlines or full-service carriers (FSCs) in Europe and developing nations facing major challenges of the same kind as LCCs and ULLCs reduce their market share. Legacy airlines would have to continue to find ways to generate ancillary revenues through services such as priority boarding, on-board entertainment, bag fees and in-flight entertainment, among others.

However, notwithstanding challenges and exogenous factors like global pandemics, overall the airline sector was considered to be healthy, with the number of passengers having grown by 6,6% in 2017 (Business Insider, 2018). In 2017 alone, the world's 20 busiest airports saw an estimated 1,5 billion passengers pass through their terminals (Business Insider, 2018).

IATA expected the industry to grow for a fourth consecutive year in 2018, with passenger volumes increasing by more than 6% (Blom, 2018).

Diaz (2019) stated that over one billion more people were flying in the last decade, with another one billion people set to join the ranks of airline passengers in the next decade. He said demand for intra-Africa travel was also growing, although at a lower rate than elsewhere in the world.

Diaz (2019) points out that between 58 million and 60 million tourists visit Africa per year. He says African governments have to work hard to increase the number of tourists to the continent to 70 million per annum, targeting especially Americans and Russians.

According to Tafiranyeka (2014), Rupp (2015) and Eze (2016), governments in southern African have been quick to bail out national airlines financially because they consider them to be their countries' status symbols. Mananavire (2016) points out that southern African governments retain veto power over the airlines' commercial decisions, "including route network, fleet acquisition and, most significantly, payroll cuts," and McCann (2015) makes the point that, owing to political pressure, SAA has had to introduce routes that are not commercially viable, but which are deemed to be of strategic importance "in growing economic relationships and dependencies between the BRICS [Brazil, Russia, India, China and South Africa] countries."

However, Barrett (2006) makes the important point that in a study conducted in 2004 for the government of Ireland, Goldman Sachs found that of 18 European countries examined, only five – Malta, Czech Republic, Hungary, Greece and Portugal – still retained 100% state ownership of the national airlines at that time. In their concluding remarks, Goldman Sachs (2004) stated that "most governments" no longer considered public ownership of airlines to be "an important element of public policy and use other means to achieve their objectives as airline stakeholders."

Button (2003:6) concluded that many airline markets had been transformed from regulated monopolies to "more free market-based structures," with the proportion of the world's largest 25 airlines – which accounted for about 62% of total capacity – that were owned by governments having decreased from 38% to 10%.

It follows, therefore, that in order to remain profitable, most network airlines have been privatised or part-privatised and have adopted business practices which have helped them to reduce costs and improve productivity levels. Legacy carriers have had to find alternative ways of making money, through the introduction of various kinds of ancillary services, in order to make themselves attractive to the growing number of air passengers.

Aviation and the Coronavirus Disease 2019

Before the outbreak of the Coronavirus Disease 2019 (COVID-19), which started in Wuhan, China in November 2019 and subsequently spread to other parts of the world, including South Africa, Doganis (2019:327) cautioned that airlines were vulnerable to "both sudden and unexpected external shocks and internal disruptions" as a result of either changes in technology or decisions made by company managements. He said that it was likely that the decade of global profits in the industry, which started in 2010, would be "disrupted in the not-too-distant future."

Following the outbreak of the COVID-19 pandemic, many countries closed their borders and limited domestic travel to control the spread of the virus. As a result, the international airline industry was badly affected (Mazareanu, 2020).

According to Serra and Leong (2020), it is the very first time in history that almost 90% of the world's population finds itself in countries with travel restrictions, with airlines, travel companies and tourism being among the most affected industries. The COVID-19 pandemic placed about 25 million jobs in aviation at risk, along with an additional 100 000 jobs in travel and tourism (Serra & Leong, 2020).

That picture is illustrated in graph 2.1 below, which shows the precipitous drop in passenger numbers in 2020.

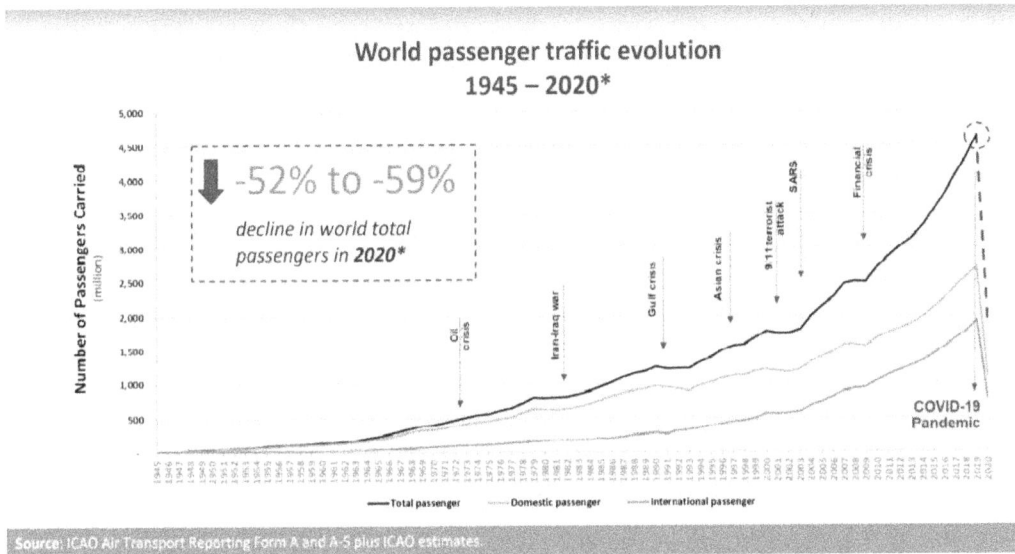

Graph 2.1: Drop in air traffic passengers in 2020 as a result of COVID-19
Source: ICAO, 2020

The graph shows a steady growth in overall airline passenger numbers from 1945 until 2020, with some small declines indicated in years when some global crises were experienced. International passenger numbers fell from around 4,6 billion when the Coronavirus pandemic spread beyond the borders of China to various countries in the second quarter of 2020 to just below 2 billion, which was a drop of between 52% and 59%.

During the week of 4 March 2020, the number of scheduled flights globally had decreased by 69,9% when compared to the same period in 2019, with the year-on-year decline in passenger flights in some countries reaching 90% (and 98% in Italy) (Mazareanu, 2020). According to Mazareanu (2020), airline capacity was down by around

88% in Europe on March 22, when compared to the same period in 2019, and in China air travel was expected to decline by an estimated 87 million passengers in the first half of 2020.

In a statement issued on 14 April 2020, the International Air Transport Association (IATA, 2020) estimated that COVID-19 would lead to a drop in airline passenger revenues of US\$314 billion in 2020, which would be a 55% decline on 2019 revenues. That was an upward revision of an initial estimate – issued two weeks earlier (on 24 March 2020) – of a US\$252 billion loss in revenues, equivalent to 44% of revenues generated in 2019.

IATA (2020) said its revised figure reflected "a significant deepening of the crisis since then," the existence of "severe domestic restrictions" in various countries lasting for three months, international travel restrictions lasting longer than three months and a severe worldwide impact of the virus, including in Africa and South America, which were less affected by COVID-19 at the time. The Association (2020) further expected domestic and international passenger demand to almost halve (48% down) in 2020, when compared to 2019.

IATA (2020) said this was due to the fact that there was a looming global recession, with a contraction of 6% expected in the international Gross Domestic Product in the second quarter of the year, as well as to travel restrictions which had been imposed by a growing number of countries.

IATA Director-General and Chief Executive Officer Alexandre de Juniac said COVID-19 resulted in more than half of passenger revenues – amounting to \$314 billion – disappearing overnight. He said there was a possibility that airlines could spend as much as \$61 billion from their cash reserves in the second quarter of the year alone, which could place up to 25 million aviation-dependent jobs at risk. De Juniac called on governments to do everything possible to assist airlines with "new or expanded financial relief measures" and other "stabilization packages," without which many airlines would not survive to lead the industry's economic recovery (IATA, 2020).

De Juniac argued that urgent government assistance for the sector was crucial because airlines were at the centre of a value chain which supported about 65,5 million jobs internationally and directly employed 2,7 million people, each of whom supported "24 more jobs in the economy" (IATA, 2020).

The UN World Tourism Organisation (UNWTO, 2020) indicated in August 2020 that COVID-19 led to a fall of between 47% and 60% in international tourist arrivals in different regions of the world between January and May 2020 when compared to the previous year, with Asia Pacific being the worst affected, followed by Europe, as reflected in figure 2.3 below.

Coronavirus Cuts International Tourism in Half

Change in international tourist arrivals
from January through May 2020 vs. 2019

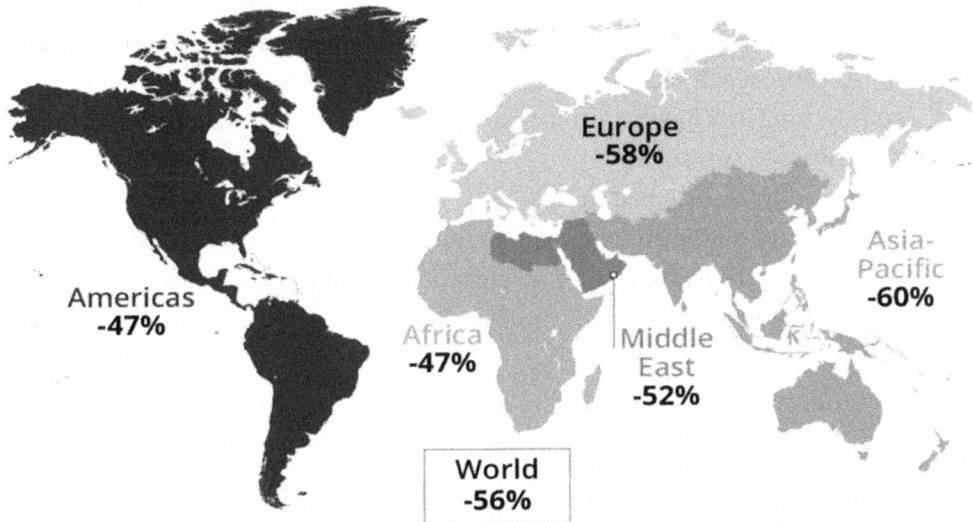

Europe
-58%

Asia-
Pacific
-60%

Americas
-47%

Africa
-47%

Middle
East
-52%

World
-56%

Source: UNWTO

Figure 2.3: Changes in international tourist arrivals between January and May 2020
Source: *Business Maverick*; UN World Tourism Organisation

Figure 2.3 above shows that the 56% drop in international tourist arrivals affected different world regions differently. Asia-Pacific, which Belobaba et al. (2009:4) indicated had experienced higher levels of growth in air passengers than North America and Europe, was the worst affected by COVID-19, with the drop in international tourist arrivals reaching 60%. Next came Europe (58%) and the Middle East (52%), with the Americas and Africa each recording a 47% drop in international tourist arrivals.

IATA (2020) called on governments to support airlines through direct financial assistance: loans, loan guarantees and "support for the corporate bond market by governments or central banks," and rebates on payroll taxes or the extension of payment terms for the rest of the year, in addition to other measures like a temporary exemption from ticket taxes and other levies.

In June 2020, IATA (2020) estimated that airlines in Europe would lose an estimated $21,5 billion, with passenger demand falling by more than half, placing between six million and seven million jobs supported by aviation at risk.

A study conducted by the International Civil Aviation Organisation (2020) estimated that COVID-19 would have cost the aviation sector a loss of between 2,5 billion and 2,8 billion passengers and between $343 billion and $383 billion in gross passenger operating revenue in 2020, and between 290 million and 562 million passengers and between $44 billion and $80 billion in gross passenger operating revenues in the first quarter of 2021. The ICAO (2020) said the actual quantum of the losses would depend, among other things, on how long and how severe the pandemic was and the measures put in place by different countries to contain it.

This information is presented in figures 2.4 and 2.5 below. The yellow triangle on the left shows the most optimistic scenario indicating a V-shaped recovery, and the red triangle on the right shows the worst-case scenario indicating a U-shaped recovery.

Global Estimates of Impacts in brief

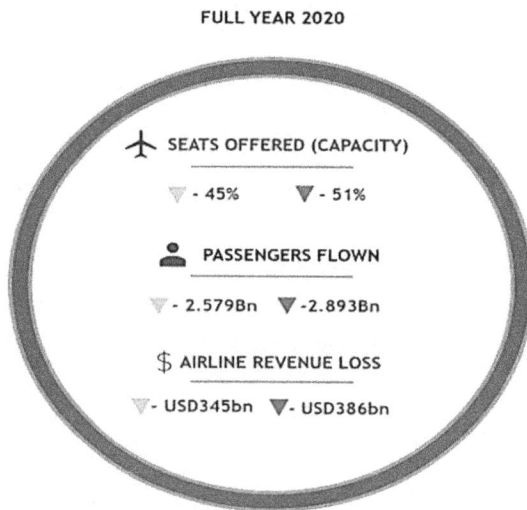

FULL YEAR 2020

✈ SEATS OFFERED (CAPACITY)

▽ - 45%   ▼ - 51%

👤 PASSENGERS FLOWN

▽ - 2.579Bn   ▼ -2.893Bn

$ AIRLINE REVENUE LOSS

▽- USD345bn   ▼- USD386bn

Figure 2.4: Estimates of the economic impact of COVID-19 on airlines in 2020
Source: ICAO, 2020

Figure 2.4 shows that the COVID-19 pandemic is estimated to have cost airlines between $345 billion and $386 billion in lost revenues as a result of decline ranging from 45% to 51% in the number of seats sold. In passenger numbers, that equates to a decline of between about 2,6 billion and about 2,9 billion (rounded off).

Figure 2.5 below indicates the ICAO's (2020) estimate of the likely cost of the COVID-19 pandemic to the airline industry in the first quarter of 2021.

Q1 2021

✈ SEATS OFFERED (CAPACITY)

▽ - 20%   ▼ - 40%

👤 PASSENGERS FLOWN

▽ - 312M   ▼ -590M

$ AIRLINE REVENUE LOSS

▽ - USD46bn   ▼ - USD83bn

Figure 2.5: Estimates of economic impact of COVID-19 on airlines in Q1 2021
SOURCE: ICAO, 2020

Figure 2.5 above indicates that, according to the ICAO (2020), it is estimated that COVID-19 will cost airlines between $46 billion and $83 billion in lost revenues in the first quarter of 2021 as a result of a decline ranging from 20% to 40% in the number of seats sold. That would equate to a decline of between 312 million and 590 million in passenger numbers.

It is clear, therefore, that COVID-19 has left massive devastation in its wake in the global economy, with aviation and related sectors being among the worst affected. International passenger numbers have been decimated and grounded airlines found themselves unable to generate revenues over a minimum of four months, depending on the countries where they found themselves.

The future of aviation

Although the Coronavirus Disease 2019 has presented aviation with its worst crisis to date, the sector will survive and emerge stronger in the long term, better prepared to deal with future challenges. That is the view held by the overwhelming majority (89%) of aviation professionals who took part in an interactive poll organised by Inmarsat Aviation and APEX in June 2020 (Leigh, 2020). Sixty per cent (60%) of the respondents estimated that it will take between 18 months and three years for the sector to return to pre-COVID-19 levels, while 26% believed that aviation will have recovered by the beginning of 2021.

While 69% of the aviation professionals believed that the post-COVID-19 aviation sector would look quite different from the way it did before the pandemic, they were also optimistic that it would be both stronger and healthier than it was before (Leigh, 2020). The changes are likely to include the adoption of new technological innovations like the World Economic Forum's Known Traveller Digital Identity, which would see travellers sharing personal information like their identities and health data electronically ahead of any trip, thus enabling airline and immigration officials to conduct risk assessments before passengers even present themselves at airports. Standardised digital travel credentials, which promote the use of biometrics, will be among the new innovations (Serra & Leong, 2020).

Airbus Chief Executive Officer Guillaume Faury, who called COVID-19 "the gravest crisis the aerospace industry has ever known," shared the view that, upon recovery, aviation will "look very unfamiliar" compared to what it was like before the onset of the pandemic (Nunes, 2020).

Before the Coronavirus broke out, the worst crisis to have affected aviation was the grounding of airlines in the USA following the 11 September (9/11) 2001 terrorist attacks on the World Trade Center in New York City and the Pentagon in Washington, DC. However, the industry recovered remarkably well almost immediately, following increased security levels at airports. A year later, 1,63 billion passengers flew internationally, marginally less than the 1,66 billion who had flown in 2001, according to the World Bank (Skapinker (2020).

Skapinker (2020) reported on the views of Donald Carty, Rod Eddington and Barbara Cassani, who were the CEOs of American Airlines, British Airways and the low-fare airline Go at the time of the 9/11 attacks on the US. Carty's American Airlines (AA) was affected directly in those attacks: one of its planes, which had taken off from Boston, was the first to crash into the World Trade Center, followed by a United Airlines plane; another AA aircraft crashed into the Pentagon.

Having survived that dark period in aviation's history, Carty, Eddington and Cassani were confident that over time aviation would survive the current crisis occasioned by COVID-19, provided that a vaccine was found. Carty believes that people's demand for travel is insatiable and that travel will normalise within a year if a vaccine is found. However, the three former airline CEOs felt that business travel may not return to the pre-COVID-19 era because working from home has shown that meetings can be held almost as effectively remotely via technologies such as Zoom and Microsoft Teams, among others (Skapinker, 2020).

Following the 9/11 terrorist attacks on the USA, the airline industry posted cumulative net losses of over $40 billion between 2001 and 2005, and only returned to profitability in 2006 when a net profit of over $3 billion was registered (Belobaba *et al*, 2009:6). In the aftermath of those attacks, US carriers laid off up to 20% of their employees in total in anticipation of a decline in passenger numbers. It was not until mid-2004 before passenger numbers returned to the level where they had been before the 9/11 attacks (Belobaba *et al.*, 2009:7).

Although the industry has experienced various market shocks in the past, it has proved to be resilient. Between 1986 and 2016, aviation had to contend with challenges such as "recessions, oil-price shocks, near pandemics, wars and security threats," and yet it continued to grow at an average of 5% per annum (Mott MacDonald, 2017). Those challenges included the oil shock in 1980, the Gulf War in 1991, the 1997 Asian financial crisis, the September 11 2001 terrorist attacks on the USA, the severe acute respiratory syndrome (SARS) epidemic of November 2002 (which lasted until 2004, affected 5 300 people in China and claimed 349 lives), and the global financial crisis (GFC) of 2009.

That airline industry's resilience is depicted in graph 2.2 below.

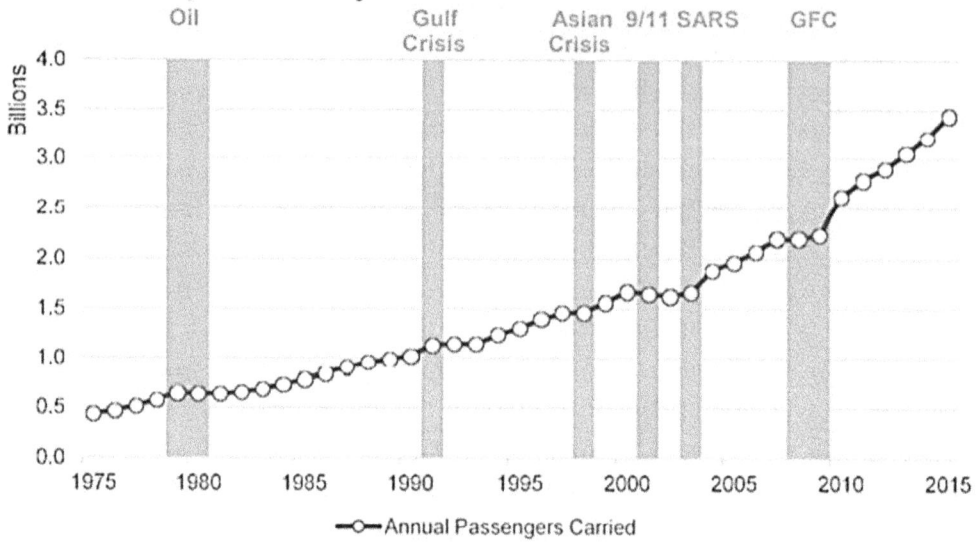

Graph 2.2: Airline resilience shown in terms of the number of passengers carried
Source: Mott MacDonald, 2017; Airbus; ICAO

Graph 2.2 above shows the airline industry's resilience in the face of various global challenges. It is clear from the graph that, despite initial declines occasioned by various crises (oil price shocks, the Gulf War, the Asian financial shock, the terrorist attack on the USA in September 2001, the SARS epidemic in Asia and the 2009-10 global recession), international air traffic passenger numbers rebounded shortly thereafter and continued to grow.

Among the reasons for this resilience has been steadfast growth in tourism during the same period. Not only does the UNWTO expect tourism to grow at an annual rate of 3,3% between 2010 and 2030, reaching a number of 1,8 billion tourists, but the organisation also reported that international tourism grew by 52 million in 2015, which was a 4,6% growth on the previous year, reaching almost 1,2 billion tourists (Mott MacDonald, 2017). According to Mott MacDonald (2017:30), 2015 marked the sixth consecutive year of above-average growth in tourism following the 2009 global financial crisis (GFC).

Of the 1,19 billion international tourists, just over 50% travelled to their respective destinations by air. France, the USA, Spain and China were the most popular tourist destinations and countries from which tourists originated, with China being the biggest source of tourists: the number of Chinese tourists increased by 10% in 2015 to reach 128 million, and their spending increased by 26% during the same year to reach $292 billion (Mott MacDonald, 2017).

In an annual report compiled for the European Commission's Directorate General for Mobility and Transport, Mott MacDonald (2017) revealed that the Americas and the Asia-Pacific region recorded a 6% growth in international tourist arrivals, with Europe – described as "the most visited region" – having recorded a 5% growth in international tourist arrivals.

In forecasts developed before the onset of COVID-19, both aircraft manufacturers Boeing and Airbus expected airline passenger numbers to grow by between 4,5% (Airbus) and 4,8% (Boeing) respectively between 2016 and 2035. The fastest growth rates (6%) are expected in developing regions like Asia-Pacific, the Middle East, Africa and South America, with mature markets like Europe (3,7%) and North America growing at rates between 2,9% (Airbus) and 3,1% per annum (Boeing) (Mott McDonald, 2017).

These forecast growth rates are shown in figure 2.6 below.

Air Traffic Growth Projections by Region for 2016-2035

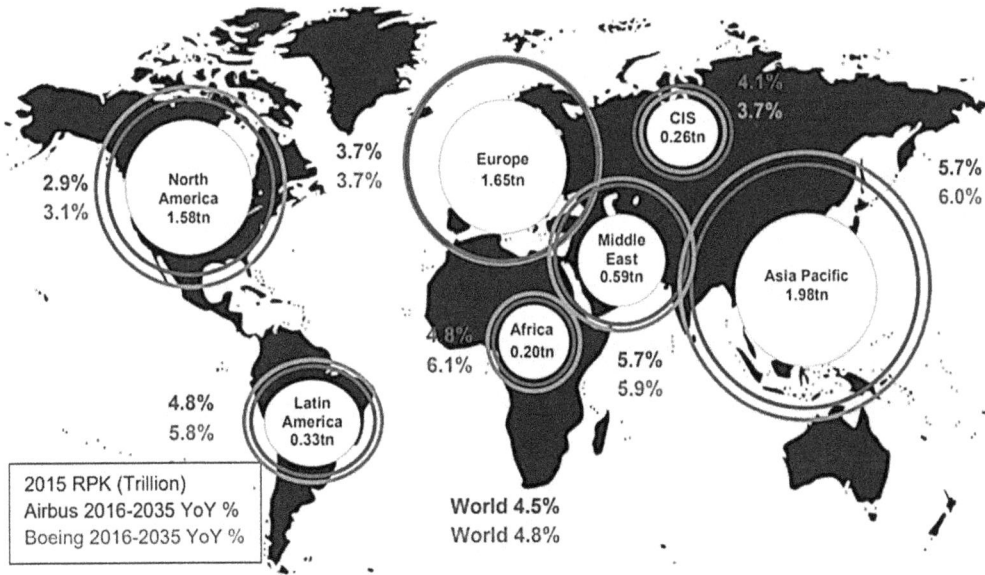

Source: Airbus/Boeing, 2016

Figure 2.6: Global air traffic growth projections by region
Source: Airbus/Boeing 2017

Figure 2.6 shows that, pre-COVID-19, Airbus and Boeing expected international airline passenger numbers to grow by 4,5% and 4,8% respectively (Mott MacDonald, 2017), with much of the growth to come from Asia-Pacific (5.7% and 6% respectively), Africa (4,8% and 6,1% respectively) and the Middle East (5,7% and 5,9% respectively).

The factors which impact on a region's growth in air travel can be grouped into three categories. These are economic performance, ease of travel and local market factors. Local market factors include the degree to which consolidation has taken place or can occur in a region and the extent of congestion at a region's airports. Airport congestion, argues Boeing in its 2016 Current Market Outlook, has the potential to limit passenger growth (Mott MacDonald, 2017).

Airbus and Boeing also expect growth in demand for air travel to result in the delivery of between 33 070 and 37 340 new wide-body, commercial aircraft respectively during the same period (2016-2035). Airbus anticipates greater demand for narrow-body aircraft, with wide-body aircraft demand constituting only a third of the total expected demand (Mott MacDonald, 2017).

Research into the impact of COVID-19 on aviation, conducted by Fast Future and Future Travel Experience, came up with four scenarios for the industry over the next two years. Completed by 269 aviation professionals from 47 countries and drawing from more than 900 participants in a subsequent webinar, the research focused on economic recovery and the degree of collaboration within the industry, and the result was a matrix featuring four possible scenarios (Taylor, 2020).

The four scenarios are (Taylor, 2020):

- "Survival and the Safest," which is premised on a deep global recession and a fragmented industry response;

- "Love in a Cold Climate," which is premised on a global recession during which there is a coordinated industry response;

- "Hope and Glory," which would see a strong global economic recovery, but a fragmented industry response; and

- "Sealed and Secure," which envisages global economic recovery and a strong, coordinated industry response.

The "Survival and the Safest" scenario would see passengers reluctant to travel as a result of "confusing protocols differing by country, airline and airport," while the "Love in a Cold Climate" scenario would see demand for air travel coming mostly from business travellers and the wealthy, who would feel sufficiently comfortable to fly. In the "Hope and Glory" scenario, travel demand would rely on passengers taking responsibility for their own testing, vaccination and certification with regard to COVID-19. The most ideal scenario, "Sealed and Secure," would see growing demand for travel as passengers would be required to show, through a certificate, that they have previously contracted COVID-19 and survived it or that they have been vaccinated against it (Taylor, 2020).

The four scenarios are shown in figure 2.7 below.

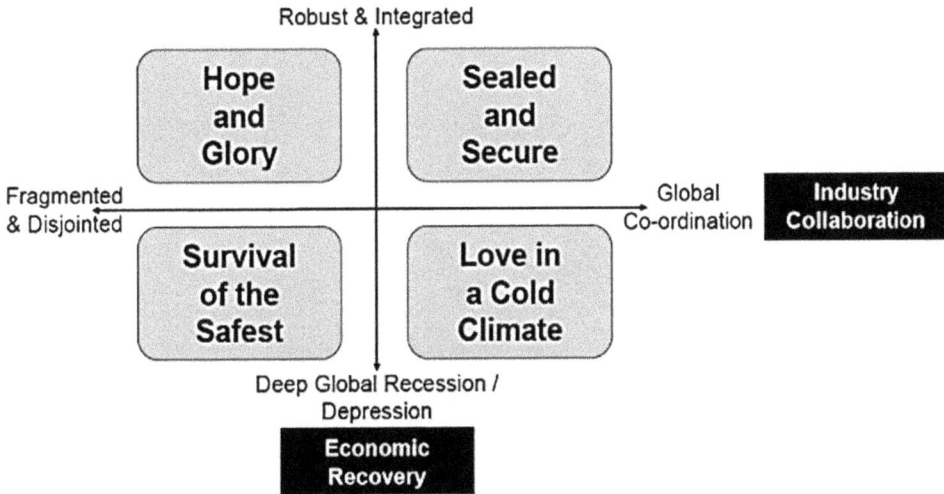

Figure 2.7: Post-COVID-19 recovery scenarios for aviation
Source: Fast Future and Future Travel Experience, 2020

According to the research participants, the likeliest scenario is "Survival of the Safest" (32%), followed by "Love in a Cold Climate" (30%) and "Hope and Glory" (20%), with "Sealed and Secure" being the least likely scenario (18%). The majority of the participants (39,7%) believed that safety kits – which would include sanitiser bottles, wipes and masks – would have to be provided to all passengers in order to encourage people to fly again, and airlines would have to be flexible enough to allow for travel cancellations without imposing penalties on passengers (Taylor, 2020).

It follows, then, that while the aviation industry is among the worst affected by the COVID-19 pandemic, with some airlines' survival threatened, it will continue to survive into the future, albeit with some changes. A lot will depend on either a vaccination or a cure being found for the pandemic. Although the COVID-19 crisis is by far the most serious to have affected the sector to date, the airline industry has previously confronted – and survived – numerous other challenges.

Chapter Three

BACKGROUND TO THE THREE AIRLINES' TURNAROUND STRATEGIES

The three airlines had very different origins: while SAA rose from the ashes of Union Airways and Kenya Airways (KQ) from the ruins of the regional East African Airways Corporation (EAAC), which was owned by three East African governments, Ethiopian Airlines (EAL) started life in its own incarnation. EAL came into existence following the Ethiopian Government's conclusion of a management agreement with American airline Trans-continental and Western Airlines (TWA, later renamed Trans-World Airlines) in September 1946.

SAA was born 1934, 14 years before the National Party came into power in what became a minority-ruled white republic. It existed from the era of British colonialism through the apartheid government and into the black-led democratic dispensation which began on 10 May 1994 when Nelson Mandela was sworn in as the country's first president to have been elected by a racially inclusive Parliament.

Twelve years after SAA's birth, EAL came into existence, following the conclusion of an agreement between the Ethiopian Government, led by Emperor Haile Selassie, and TWA. With Ethiopia being one of only two African countries never to have been colonised (the other one being Liberia), that meant that EAL was born into a very different milieu from SAA.

Both KQ and its predecessor, the EAAC, were born into a post-colonial era when Kenya, Uganda and Tanzania, which collectively co-owned the East African Airways EAAC, were independent from Britain. KQ was incorporated on 22 January 1977 in a country which was entering the 14th year of its independence.

In cataloguing the early years of these airlines, we will start with SAA, followed by KQ, given the nature and circumstances of their respective births, and then EAL will be last.

The SAA Story

When the government of the Union of South Africa took over the assets and liabilities of a struggling Union Airways on 1 February 1934, it renamed the airline South African Airways (SAA) and made it part of South African Railways and Harbours (SAR&H), which was itself established in 1910 (SAA Museum Society, n.d.). SAR&H, which incorporated the country's rail, ports and air travel services, was renamed South African Transport Services (SATS) with effect from 1 April 1981.

In both its incarnations as SAR&H and as SATS, the entity was part of the government's Department of Transport. On 1 April 1990, the government established the group as a business enterprise, Transnet Limited, with the government as its sole Shareholder (Transnet Freight Rail, n.d.).

In 1996, two years into South Africa's democracy, Sakumzi Macozoma – who, at the time, was a Member of Parliament for the majority party, the African National Congress (ANC) – was appointed the first black Managing Director of Transnet Ltd, succeeding Anton Moolman (Macozoma, 2019). The new company inherited the pension liabilities of all those who were in the employ of SATS and, before it, SAR&H.

As Macozoma (2019) put it, these pension liabilities – which the State did not provide for financially when the company was formed – "meant that the balance sheet of Transnet was constrained from the beginning." The different Transnet divisions did not have their own balance sheets.

According to Macozoma (2019), Spoornet, Portnet, Petronet, Metro Rail and SAA were the main divisions, but Metro Rail was subsequently transferred back to the Department of Transport. Each one of these divisions had its own Board of Directors, its own Chief Executive Officer (CEO) and its own Management Team. While most of the members of the Boards of the business units were either members of the main Transnet Board of Directors (BoD) or its Executives, some were also independent individuals who were not on the holding company's employ.

As Group MD, Macozoma sat on all the Boards of the Transnet divisions "as and when it became necessary." Divisional CEOs reported to Transnet Group Executive Directors who, in turn, reported to him. At the time, SAA CEO Mike Myburgh reported to Transnet Executive Director Zukile Nomvete.

Macozoma (2019) said that, ideally, SATS's pension liability (and, before that, SAR&H's) should have been absorbed by the Government. He said the Government's failure to do so created a major "pension burden" for Transnet and its divisions, which did not themselves have their own balance sheets. He said the majority of the people in the company's leadership, during Moolman's tenure, were of an advanced age and would soon be going on pension. As a result, "their orientation was to fund the pension fund by any means necessary, and so people talked about Pension-net rather than Transnet."

"This is one of the mentalities that I had to deal with to say look, you can't have this thing feeding the pension funds. You are always in the negative [as a group], yet the company is profitable, because you have this provision. It's demoralising on management and it's doing all kinds of things to their psyche," he said.

Macozoma (2019) said it soon became evident that, although the different divisions constituted the Transnet Group, in essence some of them had little in common. There was, he said, "no relationship between an airline and a port operations company," and matters became complicated in the Transnet central bargaining council where labour negotiated on behalf of all employees across the divisions. Among the workforce, he said, were stevedores on the one extreme and pilots on the other extreme.

"We then started saying even if these companies don't have their own balance sheets, let's write pro-forma ones. Let's start doing pro-form balance sheets," he said.

Macozoma (2019 and his Management Team then decided to corporatise SAA, and that exercise took "about two years or so." He said corporatising the airline meant that, even though it continued to be a Transnet subsidiary, nevertheless it would have its own stand-alone balance sheet. The long-term intention was to take the airline out of the Transnet stable.

Macozoma (2019) said the process of creating a balance sheet for SAA "began with the pension fund; how much of the pension liability was SAA going to take"? To determine the percentage of the Transnet pension liability that would be allocated to SAA, the Transnet leadership interrogated historical information and the number of employees. Among the professionals involved in this process were lawyers, accountants "and all kinds of people to try and say this we apportion to this entity and this we apportion to that entity," Macozoma (2019) said.

He said that within the group, Spoornet had the highest number of employees when compared to the other divisions. He said while, logically, Spoornet should then have been assigned a higher portion of the pension liability, doing so would have led to a situation where that division "would have been totally unviable."

SAA was the first division to be corporatised. During that process, one of the main challenges that the Transnet leadership encountered was "the funding structure of the aircraft of SAA." Macozoma said that since some of the aircraft were purchased during the time when there were still punitive economic sanctions imposed against apartheid South Africa, the funding structure was "opaque and difficult:" "Every aircraft or group of aircraft was funded by a different group, with different conditions."

Macozoma said some of the aircraft were funded through the Japanese Samurai bonds. This required that he and relevant members of his team had to travel "all around the world" to talk to the different groups of investors who owned the aircraft to inform them about their decision to create a separate balance sheet for SAA, with the debt guaranteed by Transnet until the airline's corporatization, at which point SAA as a separate juristic entity would inherit the debt, with the State as the guarantor.

"And so we had to go intricately into each and every agreement to make sure that all bases were covered and we did not trigger events of default. Some of these lenders refused to novate their loans to this new entity because it has no track record and it has no balance sheet. The pro-forma balance sheet that we had on the table, with the pension issue, actually made SAA unviable," Macozoma explained.

He said that, as a business, SAA was profitable: "There was absolutely nothing wrong with SAA. Operationally, SAA was profitable at the time, but the balance sheet was the challenge," he said.

However, aviation economist and chartered accountant Joachim Vermooten (2019) said Transnet had already lost R13 billion on SAA by that time.

Macozoma and his team then informed the government that SAA's corporatisation would not succeed – unless Pretoria took over some of the airline's debts. They explained that, in drawing up an SAA balance sheet, they would apportion some of the airline's debt to SAA and then ask the Government to take over some of it. Although then Finance Minister Trevor Manuel initially baulked at the idea, eventually the Government agreed to the proposal because the plan at the time was to acquire a strategic equity partner (SEP) for SAA. Otherwise, with that huge debt, SAA would not have been attractive to a possible SEP.

"The idea was that the SEP was going to bring in new technology, capital when required (at least 20%), but also integrate SAA into the network, whatever network that it had," Macozoma explained.

In 1999, once the airline's new balance sheet was finalised, bids for a stake in SAA were invited and Swissair, which Macozoma described as "a very good strategic partner," took a 20% equity in the African carrier, with an option to buy an additional 10% (Bell, 2002). The airline was then moved out of the Transnet stable, but remained a subsidiary and no longer a division.

SAA Non-Executive Director Martin Kingston (2019), who was with Deutsche Bank at the time, revealed that he was appointed transaction adviser to SAA during that transaction. He said Lufthansa Airways and Singapore Airways had been the Government's preferred strategic commercial partners (SCP) for SAA. However, upon completion of their due diligence, the two carriers decided to withdraw from consideration. Kingston said the two airlines concluded that they could not "make the numbers work," that there were "too many uncertainties and too many questions," and they were concerned about the South African regulatory environment, "the competence of the team, the strategy [and] the political interference."

That left Swissair to conclude the deal at the cost of US$200 million (which was R1,382-billion at the time) for a 20% stake in SAA, Kingston said.

Macozoma said at the time the SAA Board and the CEO had "full operational autonomy" and did not have to call his office or the Department of Transport, which has responsibility for transport policy, when they needed to make decisions. However, when it came to decisions on aircraft procurement, which created a liability for the State, it became imperative to rope the Government in.

Macozoma said in that case the SAA Board would constitute a committee which would include the Departments of Transport and Finance (Treasury) "not to decide on which aircraft to buy," but to establish if the business rationale made sense. If the decision was found to be sensible, then it was Management's prerogative to make the procurement decisions.

Macozoma left SAA in January 2001 after a fall-out with then Public Enterprises Minister, Jeff Radebe (FlightGlobal.com, 2001). He told me that, once he had left the Transnet Group, the Government began to get involved in the choice of aircraft to be purchased and the manufacturer from whom to buy it. He said that followed Radebe's appointment as Minister. He said that, had he still been Transnet Group MD, he "would not have agreed" to that situation.

He said that SAA's operational autonomy extended to decisions on which routes the airline was to fly or exit. Such decisions, he said, would be made by the Top Management Team (TMT), which would then sell them to the Board's Strategy Committee, with the airline's Board making the final decision, without any involvement by the Transnet Group BoD.

Macozoma said it was only once he had left the Transnet Group, when Mafika Mkhwanazi was MD and Radebe was the Minister of Public Enterprises, that important decisions required ministerial approval. He said his departure from Transnet was hastened by his "major disagreement with Radebe on the basis that I wasn't going to do what he was telling me to do." This fallout with the Minister happened at a time when his five-year contract was coming to an end, so he decided to leave earlier.

Macozoma said that while at first the change in operational autonomy was "a governance issue," it later became necessitated by the deterioration in the airline's financial performance, which led to SAA becoming reliant on Government bailouts.

Macozoma (2019) said he believed that SAA was sufficiently capitalised at the time, otherwise Swissair would not have paid US$200 million for a 20% stake in the airline.

However, he agreed that SAA's challenges were attributable to a number of "legacy issues," among them the facts that some of the aircraft were "too old and were burning fuel at a time when fuel prices were high," that there were different types of aircraft with different configurations "like 11 different cabins and cockpits." That situation, he said, meant that a different crew was needed per aircraft configuration. Therefore, among the airline's priorities was the acquisition of new, standard aircraft.

However, Malusi Gigaba (2019), who became Minister of Public Enterprises on 1 November 2010, argued that SAA was not appropriately capitalised when it was taken out of SAA. He said that non-capitalisation had "a massive bearing on its capital structure" because the airline had huge overheads, lots of routes, an ageing fleet, a huge head office with different layers of decision making, and "a massive lack of domestic skills."

Gigaba (2019) said he believed SAA was not properly capitalised because of the naïve belief that the airline would continue to be dominant in the domestic market and grow significantly in the regional market and, in the process, be able to "fund itself, its own growth, its own fleet replacement and its own modernisation out of its revenues." He said the Shareholder did not do "proper scenario planning to anticipate, for example, the impact of the 1998 Asian contagion and the more devastating 2008 global recession," which impacted negatively on bookings and, therefore, revenue generation.

Former SAA CEO Sizakele Mzimela (2019) also strongly held the view that the airline was "never capitalised properly:"

> *Even today, by the way, that's really going to be the biggest challenge in that every single time SAA requires some level of support, they are given an additional guarantee. A guarantee is not capital. So, what are you doing? You are just increasing the liabilities of the entity and weakening it, actually. There's a huge public outcry, "they've got another guarantee," but it means nothing.*
>
> *Basically, it's as good as somebody saying "I'm putting you more in debt." All you do with a guarantee is that it actually helps you to be able to release your financials, or you use the guarantee to go and raise a facility with the banks. It comes at a price. All you have done is that you have increased the liability.*

Mzimela made the point that SAA's high gearing ratio meant that the airline had to pay a premium whenever it purchased goods and services, compared to airlines with lower gearing ratios which enjoyed better discounts. "When SAA enters into negotiations with the same suppliers, because of its weak balance sheet, no discounts were forthcoming. So, at every point, you're already starting off from a highly disadvantaged position," she said.

Department of Public Enterprises (DPE) Acting Deputy Director-General for Transport Enterprises, Avril Halstead, said her own personal view, based on her experience at the Treasury where she was Chief Director dealing with SOEs, was that while SAA may not have been "as well capitalised as it should have been, but it was actually capitalised."

Writing in SAA's Integrated Annual Report in 2017, Chairman JB Magwaza (2017:38) argued that the airline had "long struggled with adequate capitalisation and a lack of capital injection from the Shareholder." He said that lack of capitalisation had weakened the airline's balance sheet and impacted negatively on the implementation of the Long-Term Turnaround Strategy.

Former SAA Executive Vice-President and, subsequently, Board Member Bonang Mohale (2019) argued that most South African SOCs have not been adequately capitalised. He said he did not believe that, during the 25 years of South Africa's democracy, the Government had "thought about their [SOCs'] capital structure properly to solve it." He said he would "absolutely agree" that SAA was not properly capitalised. He said had an exercise been done to establish if a stand-alone SAA would be financially sustainable, the national carrier would not have "become an un-rehabilitated alcoholic that every year goes back to the Shareholder, National Treasury, and says give us more."

SAA Operations Research Head Josua Du Plessis (2019), who has been in the airline's employ for more than three decades, shared the view that SAA was not properly capitalised, saying airlines like Qantas, Etihad and Emirates have "a very strong capital base to start building on, to grow on and to develop." However, Du Plessis said the one thing that must never be discounted was "the incredible impact when the rand took a massive dive" in 2002 and SAA lost R8 billion in a period of two years because of hedging during Andre Viljoen's tenure.

"They had some money hedged, the currency dropped and we lost R8 billion. That wiped our capital base. Since then, we were never properly recapitalised from that point," Du Plessis said.

He said SAA would never be able to pay its debt back if it was not recapitalised, adding that it was urgent that the recapitalisation issue be resolved speedily.

Another legacy issue, Macozoma said, was the way in which pilots were contracted, which was not sufficiently flexible for an airline with ambitions of being a global player.

Vermooten (2019) – who, having been an SAA competitor since 1979 through Trek Airways (which traded as Luxavia and operated Luxair-registered aircraft) where he was Executive Director, joined the DPE in October 2006 as Aviation Specialist – said Swissair and its holding company, the SAirGroup, enjoyed contracts with SAA that went beyond its 20% shareholding. According to him, all aircraft requirements had to be leased from

Flightlease, Swissair's leasing company, and all the computer system requirements had to go through Swissair group companies.

The sale of equity in SAA was consistent with the Government's view at the time that State-owned companies (SOCs) that were not essential for the Government's functioning had to be sold off. Vermooten said before 1994 the DPE was the Bureau for Privatisation under National Treasury, with all State-owned enterprises (SOEs) that fell within it meant to be sold off.

Gigaba said the National Party government had decided to shut down SOEs and had established an office for privatisation. He said when the ANC took office in 1994, it established the DPE, but wanted to continue with privatisation of SOEs until it was prevented from doing so by its labour ally, the Congress of South African Trade Unions (COSATU). However, the new Government did not "develop an alternative vision" for SOEs.

Gigaba said from 1994 the ANC-led Government had a belief – which informed the Growth, Employment and Redistribution policy adopted during the first administration – that SOEs had to be privatised. That, he said, explained the sale of a 20% stake in SAA to Swissair.

Matsietsi Mokholo (2019), who joined the DPE on 1 March 2007 as Chief Director: Legal, Governance and Risk and was appointed Deputy Director-General in 2012, concurred that the Department was established as an office for privatisation. She listed Iscor, Telkom, the Cape Town Waterfront and Vironeck among the entities that were privatised at the time or in which a significant stake was sold off. She said SAA, Eskom and Transnet were on the list of SOEs to be privatised.

Mohale said the reversal of the privatisation policy during the Jacob Zuma presidency was motivated by selfish – as opposed to national – interests.

When Swissair went into liquidation in 2001, Kingston advised the Government to buy its 20% stake back. The Government bought that stake back "for less than 15% of the price we sold it for 18 months before," he said. He said since then, there had been "a litany of changes" in Board Members and the TMT, "with no stability and no consistency in alignment."

Mohale revealed that the 20% stake in SAA was sold to Swissair for R1,5 billion, but bought back for R434 million. He said although part of the agreement was that 1 314 SAA technicians would be sent to Switzerland to study over a three-year period, "only two ever left because we were not focusing on it."

Vuyisile Kona (2019) worked in the Transnet Group Finance Department at the time when SAA was incorporated as a stand-alone company. Keen to acquire operational experience, he was seconded to SAA in 1998, at his own request, and worked in the airline's Corporate Finance Department under Chief Financial Officer Andre Viljoen. For a year, he worked for both Transnet and SAA, and later transferred to the airline permanently.

In 1996, Transnet commissioned SBC Warburg Investment Bank to assess SAA's financial position. Having concluded that "SAA was in a financial crisis and that the existing management team did not have the capability to improve the situation," the bank recommended the appointment of a turnaround specialist. Shortly after SBC Warburg Investment Bank's assessment, the situation at SAA worsened (GCIS, 2001).

When, in 1998, Transnet proposed an SAA turnaround strategy that would see an international turnaround specialist appointed to run the airline, the Government supported it (GCIS, 2001).

In June 1998, when SAA was heading for a loss of R500 million (News24, 2001) Macozoma appointed American Coleman Andrews CEO of SAA. He was previously CEO of charter company World Airlines Inc. That appointment proved to be controversial for a number of reasons, among them the amount of money that Andrews was paid. However, Andrew Shaw (2019), former DPE Deputy Director-General and later Director-General, said that Andrews "created a more global sense of how to position the airline," given that South Africa had just emerged from apartheid.

"We had a terminally ill airline, and we needed someone who could take determined action very quickly. We couldn't afford to subject [business decisions] to the kind of dithering that you had previously," Macozoma later told the *Washington Post* in an interview (Jeter, 2001).

However, Vermooten (2019) argues that Andrews was a wrong appointment from the beginning. He points out that running a charter company is different from running a scheduled commercial airline. He says that running the former is easy because such a company solicits for contracts and only flies when enough contracts for the specific flights have been secured, while a scheduled airline flies according to a fixed time-table, whether the aircraft is full or empty, much like the reliability of a train service.

According to Vermooten, Andrews contracted the services of Baines Consulting, a company where his wife was a partner, and it had "in excess of 200 senior consultants at SAA at any point in time." However, he acknowledges that Andrews and team trained SAA employees "very well."

Andrews and Swissair sold off SAA's A320 aircraft and leased back smaller, "very, very old B737s via Flightlease." The B737-200 and B737-300 aircraft were narrow-body, short-haul aeroplanes, and this skewed the capital costs for the number of available passenger seats.

"And then they found out, while they were in the process, that due to the high cost of the new 737 aircraft, the project was actually not viable. To reduce the capital costs of the

B737s, SAA bought very, very old aircraft, 25 to 28 years old, from South America to reduce the unit costs," Vermooten said.

He said that the sale and lease-back of SAA's A320 aircraft resulted in abnormal profits, from which Andrews would have been entitled to a profit share. According to reports at the time, SAA recorded a profit of R350 million in the 1999/2000 financial year (News24, 2001).

Andrews's contract was terminated in February 2001, a month after Macozoma's resignation as Transnet Group MD, owing to "significant tension" between the former and top officials at Transnet and at the DPE. His contract still had 14 months left to run before its expiry. He was paid a severance package of R232 million for two-and-half years' service, including for shares that were allocated to him (News24, 2001).

In December that year, Macozoma told the *Washington Post* that he had known all along that Andrews was not the right person for SAA in the long term. Instead, he was the right person to turn the airline around, "but the fact that he was a white, conservative American did not make him a good fit for more than a few years, simply from a cultural standpoint" (Jeter, 2001).

Following Andrews's departure, Viljoen was appointed CEO. He, in turn, appointed Kona as Head of Strategy. In 2003, Kona (2019) was appointed Executive Vice President, with a responsibility for SAA and all subsidiaries within the airline group. These included maintenance, repair and overhaul (MRO) company South African Technical (SAAT).

In 2004, Khaya Ngqula (2019) succeeded Viljoen as SAA CEO. He and Minister Erwin shared a background in rugby and had been close from their student days (Ngqula, 2019; Vermooten, 2019).

Professor Jakes Gerwell, who had been Director-General in the Presidency when Nelson Mandela was Head of State, was the Chairman of the Board.

Ngqula, who had previously run the successful Industrial Development Corporation, said he found the airline bankrupt and reliant on State funding, with the State having "a big say in how it is run." Shaw concurred, saying that although SAA was still dominant domestically and regionally, at the time the airline was "bleeding." He said Ngqula encountered a challenge where SAA's revenue was not meeting the airline's cost base, with the cost base inherited from the Andrews era being high.

According to Vermooten, Ngqula, owing to his background in sports administration, had the "very rare" ability of selecting and building a good team. Among his appointments were Vera Kriel as Head of Corporate Strategy and Business Planning, Chris Smythe as Chief Financial Officer and Bhabhalazi Ngqulunga as Head of Human Resources, as well as Captain Colin Jordan (General Manager: Flight Operations), Captain Johnny Woods (Chief Pilot and Head of Flight Operations) and Jan Blake as General Manager: Commercial. Smythe had come from Kenya Airways, where he had held a similar position; Ngqulunga had worked with Ngqula at Norwich Insurance, where Ngqula (2019) had been CEO, and Kriel joined SAA from consulting firm Deloitte (Kriel, 2019).

It was in October 2006 that Vermooten joined the DPE, which was – and still is – SAA's Shareholder Ministry. At the time, the plan was for the Department to be a private-equity company, according to Vermooten, who was appointed in the role of Aviation Specialist to assist in restructuring the national carrier as a service to his country. His primary responsibility, he said, was to implement the Government's purchase of SAA from Transnet and to assist in Shareholder oversight over State-owned airlines.

When he joined the DPE, Adam Smith International (ASI) – which is a consulting arm of Adam Smith Institute in Britain – was working with the DPE to structure it in a modern way to be able to run SOEs professionally (Vermooten, 2019). He said the work done by ASI, whose services were paid for by the British Government, was "really world class." The organisation had done a good job of training DPE employees "to understand what their roles should be and actually to get work done." Vermooten argued that most of the systems and structures still being used within the Department "dated back to the ASI project."

Vermooten said the negotiations with Transnet over the sale of SAA to the State were tough. Transnet provided guarantee letters for SAA, without any time limitations. He said creditors and suppliers "saw it [the transaction] as an opportunity to get a National Treasury guarantee, which was higher-rated security than Transnet guarantees."

While the sale of SAA to the State was concluded in 2006, the enabling legislation that was required to effect the transaction could not be passed until 2007 (Vermooten, 2019). That was because some members of the National Assembly's Portfolio Committee on Public Enterprises had expressed concern that clause 4(1) of the enabling legislation, the South African Airways Act, empowered the Minister "to convert South African Airways (Pty) Ltd into a public company having a share capital in accordance with the Companies Act." That clause, the MPs argued, indicated a hidden intention to privatise the airline in years to come.

Vermooten said that, in the end, it took the insertion of a preamble to the South African Airways Act which stated expressly the State's intention to promote air links with South Africa's "main business, trading and tourism markets within the African continent and internationally" and the Government's intention "to retain it [SAA] as a national carrier," given the fact that the State has "a developmental orientation," to get the law approved by the Portfolio Committee. The preamble described SAA as "a national carrier and strategic asset that would enable the State to preserve its ability to contribute to key domestic, intra-regional and international air linkages" (South African Airways Act, 2007).

Specifically, the South African Airways Act No.5 of 2007 had three purposes: "the transfer of SAA shares and SAA interests from Transnet to the State, the conversion of South African Airways (Pty) Ltd into a public company with share capital, [and] the listing of SAA as a major public entity in Schedule 2 to the PFMA [Public Finance Management Act]" (South African Airways Act, 2007).

The preamble to that enabling legislation also had the effect of laying down SAA's mandate.

Vermooten (2019) said his initial analysis of SAA revealed that the airline had "too many types of aircraft, with no compatibility among aircraft in the fleet," hence staff required different licences and spares holdings, among other things. He said Erwin informed the SAA Board that the Government would back the airline and make funding available, but SAA would be required to come up with a restructuring plan.

South African Airways last made a profit in 2011 (Whitehouse, 2019). Although the airline often did not publish its results because of concern about its going-concern status (Kingston, 2019), various estimates indicate that SAA's losses over a 13-year period totalled R28 billion (Planting, 2020), with cumulative losses of R26,1 billion having been made between 2015 and 2020 (Maeko, 2020). Vermooten's calculations put the losses suffered by the airline between 2007 and 2019 at R26,9 million, as shown in figure 3.1 below.

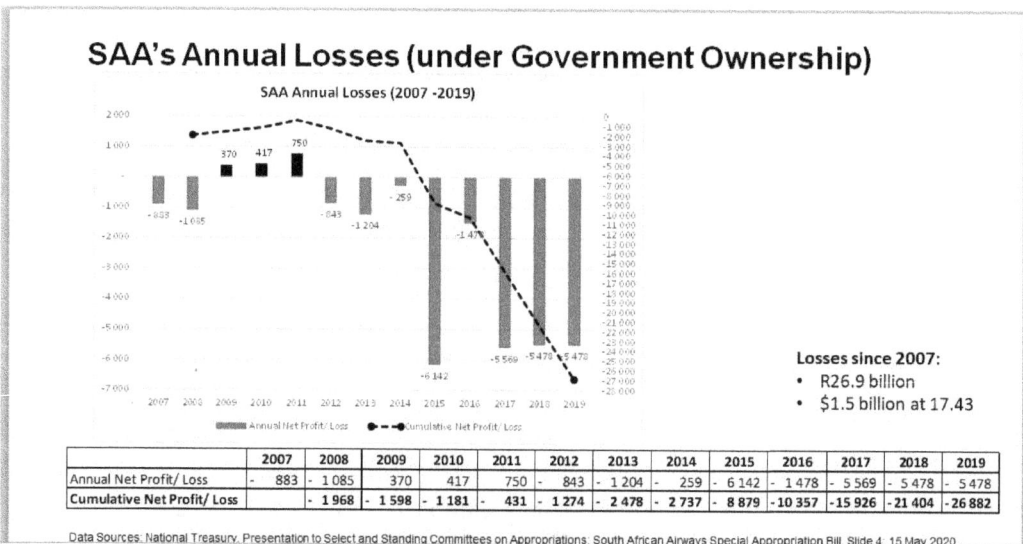

SAA's Annual Losses (under Government Ownership)

SAA Annual Losses (2007 -2019)

	2007	2008	2009	2010	2011	2012	2013	2014	2015	2016	2017	2018	2019
Annual Net Profit/ Loss	- 883	- 1 085	370	417	750	- 843	- 1 204	- 259	- 6 142	- 1 478	- 5 569	- 5 478	- 5 478
Cumulative Net Profit/ Loss		- 1 968	- 1 598	- 1 181	- 431	- 1 274	- 2 478	- 2 737	- 8 879	-10 357	-15 926	- 21 404	-26 882

Losses since 2007:
- R26.9 billion
- $1.5 billion at 17.43

Data Sources: National Treasury. Presentation to Select and Standing Committees on Appropriations: South African Airways Special Appropriation Bill. Slide 4: 15 May 2020.

Figure 3.1: Cumulative SAA losses between 2007 and 2019

Source: Joachim Vermooten (2020)

Quoting from correspondence sent in March 2020 by business rescue practitioners Les Matuson and Viwe Dongwana to all unions active at SAA, Maeko (2020) reported that SAA's biggest loss of R5,6 billion was registered in March 2017 for the 2016-17 financial year when Dudu Myeni was Chairperson of the Board, compared to a R1,5 billion loss made the previous year. In 2017-18, SAA registered a R5,5 billion loss, followed by a loss of R5,1 billion in 2018-19 (Paton, 2020).

Figure 3.2 below shows that as annual revenues plateaued around R30 billion from 2013 onwards and started declining in 2015, costs worsened, with the exception of the 2015/16 financial year. The increase in costs started when the airline embarked on a growth strategy in 2011, and its losses got progressively worse.

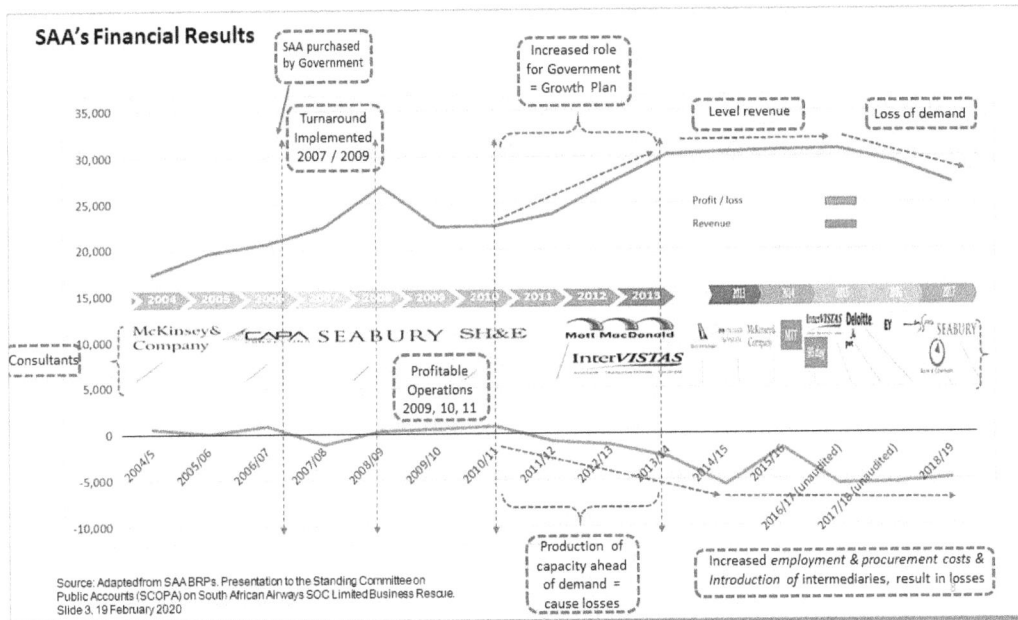

Figure 3.2: Depiction of SAA's costs and financial performance
Source: Joachim Vermooten (2020)

SAA was heavily insolvent in the 2016/17 financial year, with its liabilities exceeding its assets by R17 billion (Solidarity Research Institute, 2018; Vermooten, 2019), and Vermooten's (2019) calculations indicated that the airline was already insolvent by R12,3 billion on 31 March 2016.

In 2018, Vermooten (2018) told the National Assembly's Standing Committee on Appropriations that, from the time it became a stand-along company in March 2007 until March 2018, altogether SAA had received financial support from the Government to the value of R31,3 billion, and financial support worth R45,9 billion from the Government and Transnet between April 1999 and 31 March 2007. These amounts included both cash transfers and guarantees.

In a revised presentation in May 2020, Vermooten (2020) indicated that Government's financial support to the airline between 31 March 2007 and March 2020 stood at R53,3 billion, with R32,2 billion of it being in cash and R19,1 being in guarantees, while total financial support for SAA by the Government and Transnet during the Transnet era (April 1999 to March 2007) amounted to R14,6 billion. Altogether, total financial support to SAA by Transnet and the Government between April 1999 and October 2019 added to R67,9 billion.

Table 3.1 below gives Vermooten's calculation of the financial assistance given to SAA by the Government and Transnet between April 1999 and March 2007 when the airline was still owned by Transnet:

Table 3.1: Financial assistance given to SAA during Transnet's ownership of the airline between April 1999 and March 2007:

AMOUNTS GRANTED TO SAA, WHEN SAA WAS UNDER DIRECT TRANSNET CONTROL (1999 to 2006)

Government assistence to SAA under Transnet ownership		Guarantee	Cash Transfer
April 1999	Total Unallocatble Debt taken over at SAA Privatisation		1 333

Under Transnet ownership		Guarantee	Cash Transfer	Total Cash & Guarantees
April 1999	- Total Unallocatble Debt at Privatisation		4 057	4 057
	- Less: Unallocatble Debt allocated to SAA		-1 000	-1 000
	- Less: Unallocatble Debt allocated to Government		-1 333	-1 333
	Unallocatble Debt allocated to Transnet		1 724	1 724
April 1999	Original Net Assets Transferred		3 127	3 127
2005/03/31	Conversion of Transnet Loan		6 089	6 089
2007/03/31	Conversion of Transnet compulsory convertible loan to shares less share buy back		2 361	2 361
			13 301	13 301

Total financial assistance to SAA by Transnet & Government under Transnet Control		14 634

Source: Joachim Vermooten

Table 3.2 and figure 3.3 below give Vermooten's calculation of the total financial support given to SAA by the Government and Transnet between April 1999 and March 2020:

Table 3.2: Total financial support given to SAA between April 1999 and March 2020

SUMMARY OF FINANCIAL ASSITENCE TO SAA ACCORDING TO DIFFERENT SOURCES

R' Millions	Information provided to SCOPA		Calculations based on National Treasury 2018 and 2019 Annual Reports and Previous Transnet and SAA Reports		
	DPE Submission to SCOPA	DPE Submission to SCOPA with Correction of Addition Error	Previously provided to SAA under Transnet Ownership	Provided to SAA under Government Ownership (based on National Treasury 2018 and 2019 Annual Reports)	Total financial Assitence to SAA
Cash Injection	31 243	38 243	14 634	34 204	48 838
Guarantees	19 114	19 114		19 114	19 114
Total	50 357	57 357	14 634	53 318	67 952

Source: Joachim Vermooten

Financing of SAA's Losses

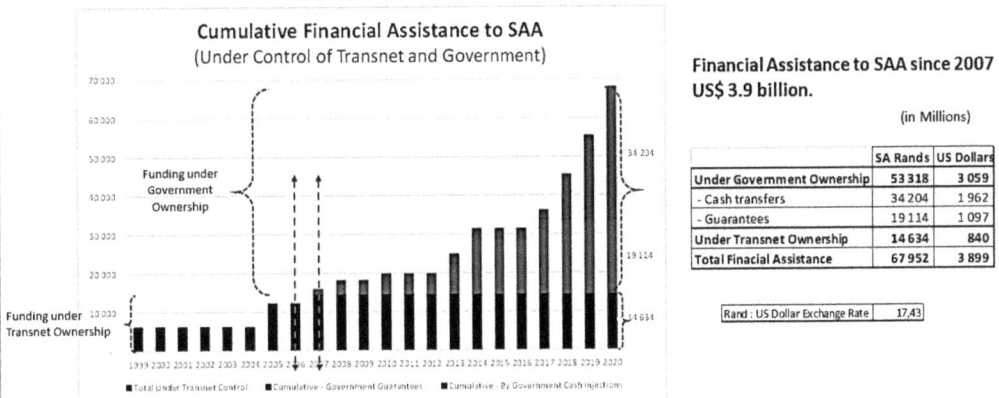

Figure 3.3: Total financial support given to SAA between April 1999 and March 2020
Source: Vermooten (2020)

According to the National Treasury, of the R291 billion which was to have been spent on bailing out SOEs between 2008 and March 2022, R244,7 billion was to have gone to electricity utility Eskom, with SAA in second position with "a total bailout package ... of R38,4 billion" during that period (Paton, 2020).

Since becoming a stand-alone company in 2007, SAA registered profits only in three out 14 years (including 2020).

The Kenya Airways Story

By the time the EAAC collapsed and Kenya Airways was formed in January 1977, the International Air Transport Association (IATA) had already assigned the code "KA" to Korean Air, the national carrier of South Korea. As a result, the East African carrier got assigned the code "KQ" because "KA" was already taken (Kosgei, 2018).

Following the passing away of Phillip Ndegwa, who was Chairman of the airline's BoD, former Cabinet Minister Isaac Omolo Okero was appointed KQ Chairman in February 1996 (Kenya Cabinet, 2018). That was a month after the Dutch Royal Airlines, KLM, had bought a 26% stake in KQ and five months before the airline was listed on the Nairobi Stock Exchange.

The success of KQ's privatisation led to KQ's Scheduling Manager at the time, who was unnamed, telling Debrah & Toroitich (2005) that, following KQ's profitability, the East African airline's "extended ambitions" were "to replace South African Airways in this coveted position [of being] Africa's leading carrier." KQ went on to register profits over the next six years, leading Debrah and Toroitich (2005) to conclude that the airline's turnaround strategy was "a resounding success" for the airline and all its stakeholders: customers, employees, shareholders, the Government and the Kenyan economy (p. 221).

Concluding their paper, which was headlined "The Making of an African Success Story: The Privatisation of Kenya Airways," Debrah and Toroitich (2005) wrote:

> *It remains to be seen how Kenya Airways will perform in the future, given its illustrious performance in the recent past. One factor that will be crucial for assessing its future performance is the political environment in Kenya and the countries in which the airline operates. The political crises and conflicts in Central Africa pose serious threats to the airline's growth.*
>
> *More important, the continued success of the airline will depend on the government's ability to curb the soaring numbers of crime and criminal activities in the country and tackle terrorist activities such as the 2003 hotel bombing in Mombasa. Failure to do so will have devastating consequences on the Kenyan tourist industry and, consequently, on the growth of Kenya Airways.*

Following the privatisation, KLM had two seats on the KQ BoD, and the Kenyan Government also had two seats (Kinyanjui, 2019).

During my interview with him in September 2019, Kenyan researcher and writer Morris Kiruga (2019) made the important point that the privatisation of KQ was not just an economic decision. Instead, external politico-economic pressure played an important role. Kiruga (2019) said around the time of KQ's privatisation, the heavily-indebted Kenyan government was under immense pressure from donors to embark on structural adjustment programmes (SAP) which culminated in the privatisation not only of KQ, but also of Mumias Sugar Company and Uchumi Supermarkets (Munaita, 2015), among others.

Taboi (2019) confirmed that KQ's privatisation was part of "the externally-driven processes that happened in 1996-97 where the government divested over a period of time, with the assistance of the IFC."

The Ethiopian Airways Story

EAL had a humble beginning on 8 April 1946 when it started operating with five surplus war aircraft, following the Ethiopian Government's conclusion of a management agreement with TWA in September 1945. That original agreement gave TWA "full authority to establish and manage" EAL, and the American carrier assumed all responsibilities, including for the selection and procurement of all aircraft needed to start the aviation industry in Ethiopia (Oqubay & Tesfachew, 2019:3-4).

In return for a management fee and minority equity (which option the American airline never exercised), TWA recruited all employees from abroad – mostly the USA – for EAL and facilitated credit for the airline from American banks. Employees recruited by TWA included the Chief Executive Officer (CEO), the Management Team, pilots, technicians, cabin crew and catering staff (Oqubay & Tesfachew, 2019:5).

Although there was initially a tacit understanding that TWA would prepare Ethiopians for eventual take-over of posts occupied by the expatriates, it was not until the signing of a second agreement between the Ethiopian Government and TWA in 1953 that a clause stating explicitly that "the ultimate aim is that EAL shall eventually be operated by Ethiopian personnel" was included (Oqubay & Tesfachew, 2019:5). In 1959, a third agreement was signed, which reinforced the need for the development of Ethiopian expertise, and in 1966 an agreement transferring management of the airline from TWA to EAL was concluded, and led to the appointment of Ethiopian Semret Medhane as Deputy CEO. Medhane was appointed the first-ever Ethiopian CEO of EAL in November 1971 in celebration of the national carrier's silver jubilee (Oqubay & Tesfachew, 2019:5).

The fifth agreement between the Ethiopian Government and TWA, signed in 1970, changed the American carrier's role from managing EAL to being an adviser. Five years later, the partnership between the two parties ended "when TWA found the venture less attractive," but the latter continued to provide services to EAL on request (Oqubay & Tesfachew, 2019:5)

The agreements between the two parties are shown in table 3.3 below.

Table 3.3: Agreements between EAL, as represented by the Ethiopian Government, and TWA:

Agreement	Year	Key content
First	1945	Established EAL, undertook full operation and the procurement of aircraft
Second	1953	Stated clearly the ultimate objective of Ethiopianization
Third	1959	Reinforced the urgency of the Ethiopianization agenda
Fourth	1966	Transferred management from TWA to EAL and appointed an Ethiopian deputy CEO
Fifth	1970	Shifted TWA's role from management to advisory until 1974

Source: AfDB HDI 2019, 2(1)

Oqubay and Tesfachew (2019:5) say there were "constant differences of opinion" between TWA and the Ethiopian Government about the pace of "Ethiopianisation," with the Ethiopian authorities feeling that it was too slow and TWA officials feeling that it was too fast. They say that given widespread racism at the time, Ethiopian trainees "had to show exceptional skill and competence" before they could be given an opportunity to replace American pilots.

In order to accelerate the pace of skills development among Ethiopians, an aviation school under the Ethiopian Civil Authority was built with assistance from TWA and pilots and technicians from the Ethiopian Air Force – who were trained in Ethiopia and the United States – were recruited. Oqubay and Tesfachew (2019:5-6) say "even the candidates for CEO and other positions came from the air force."

In 1956 the Ethiopian Aviation Academy was founded and the Pilot School was established in 1964, with the training of Ethiopians and people from other African countries beginning in 1970. EAL opened an MRO facility in 1957, which conducted its first overhaul of jet engines in 1964. Again, trainees came from both Ethiopia as well as other African and Middle Eastern countries (Oqubay & Tesfachew, 2019:6).

According to Oqubay and Tesfachew (2019:6), from the very beginning EAL was a stand-alone company with a Board of Directors (BoD), and not a government department. TWA and the Ethiopian Government each had two seats on the Board, and the Minister of Transport was Board Chairman (Oqubay & Tesfachew, 2019:6).

"From the early days, TWA instilled in EAL a culture of corporate independence, a need for intensity of learning and the importance of a strategic approach to marketing. Consequently, EAL's marketing of both domestic and international destinations was aggressive from the start … EAL thus vigorously developed its operations and market capability, with TWA as the main driver and as an effective mentor," Oqubay and Tesfachew (2019:6) wrote.

However, the airline was to run into serious challenges between 1975 and 1991 following political upheavals in the country. In February 1974, Emperor Haile Selassie was overthrown by the Derg, described as "a totalitarian military regime," which seized power in 1975. Oqubay and Tesfachew (2019:7) say the Derg's socialist economic outlook posed a serious challenge to EAL, with whose running they interfered and, "solely on political grounds," replaced Semret Medhane with a military general as CEO (Oqubay & Tesfachew, 2019:7).

The Derg government's interference at EAL extended to labour relations and, in the process, affected the airline's performance, "staff discipline and conformity with industry practice, which later led to major financial losses." An airline which had been profitable since inception suddenly found itself facing bankruptcy up until the early 1980s (Oqubay & Tesfachew, 2019:7).

However, EAL did not surrender. Instead, the airline fought back valiantly against the interference by the Derg government, calling on the experience gained during the long partnership with TWA to demonstrate "corporate independence, self-reliance, ability to operate in an unconventional setting and capacity to manage and survive setbacks." EAL Management pressured Derg officials to appoint a CEO who understood the aviation industry, and they eventually succeeded (Oqubay & Tesfachew, 2019:7).

In 1980 "aviation veteran" Captain Mohammed was appointed CEO, and he accepted the appointment "on condition that State intervention in internal matters would stop and that the airline would operate under international business practices rather than socialist doctrine." The Derg authorities accepted Mohammed's conditions, and he went to work to turn the airline around from the state where it was almost bankrupt (Oqubay & Tesfachew, 2019:7).

In a second act of defiance, EAL Management threatened to resign *en masse* if the Derg persisted with its demand that EAL – which had used Boeing aircraft from inception – should purchase Russian aircraft and no longer buy from the American manufacturer. Again, the Derg authorities compromised by reversing their decision, and EAL was able to introduce Boeing 767s, which enabled it to fly non-stop long-distance flights of up to

13 hours across the Atlantic Ocean. The airline also replaced its Boeing 720 aircraft with the new Boeing 737s and expanded its technical services and training facilities.

Oqubay and Tesfachew (2019:7) said that throughout the 1980s, EAL – "driven by its motto, 'Bringing Africa Together'" – "vigorously expanded its route to all African regions."

Another important act of independence was shown by the EAL leadership in 1991. When the Ethiopian People's Revolutionary Democratic Front (EPRDF) marched on Addis Ababa, "practically placing it under siege" in an effort to oust the Derg government from office, the EAL Management took a decision "to protect and save the assets of the company from damage and destruction," in the event that the conflict spilled over into the city. The EAL Top Management Team (TMT) "unilaterally decided to move EAL's aircraft to Nairobi, negotiating with the Kenya Aviation Authority to operate and service EAL's customers from Nairobi until the political tension in Ethiopia abated" (Oqubay & Tesfachew, 2019:7).

"This remarkable corporate independence, commitment and responsibility," wrote Oqubay and Tesfachew (2019:7), "was only possible because of the corporate culture developed in EAL and the training and commitment of its Management."

Even with the Derg government ousted in 1991, EAL's problems were not over. Oqubay and Tesfachew (2019:8) say, according to EAL insiders, the carrier "remained in crisis mode as a result of Government interference and the ambiguities of the political and economic environment." To support their argument, Oqubay and Tesfachew (2019) point to the fact that between 1991 and 2000, the Board "appointed three successive CEOs from within and outside the airline, creating uncertainty and disrupting EAL's long-standing coherent and stable corporate management structure and culture," and fired 37 senior staff members who constituted the airline's TMT following a disagreement over EAL's strategy and future.

In addition, the EPRDF government implemented "a series of ill-advised reforms and policy experiments" which impacted negatively on EAL and undermined staff morale, thus leading "many Executive Officers and technical personnel to resign." As a result, Oqubay and Tesfachew (2019:8) say the 1990s were, for EAL, "a period of transition, confusion and policy experimentation," and that the Government's "delay in resolving the situation caused unwarranted setbacks in EAL's recovery, growth and expansion."

"This episode shows that a firm's learning and catch-up can be hampered or accelerated by the type of governance and leadership provided. Internal and external crises can waste capabilities created over decades. But crisis in the political and economic environment can also present opportunities for learning by problem-solving and policy experimentation," argue Oqubay and Tesfachew (2019:8).

Chapter Four

SAA'S MANDATE AND STRUCTURAL CHALLENGES

Unlike its Ethiopian and Kenyan counterparts, SAA has had to juggle two tough mandates and to operate under severely restrictive conditions imposed by the Public Finance Management Act (PFMA) which governs Government Departments and all State-owned companies (SOC) in South Africa. In addition to being expected to be successful commercially, the airline has also had to deliver on an ill-defined "developmental mandate."

KQ and EAL, on the other hand, had one clear mandate, to be profitable and self-sustaining, and enjoyed the benefits of agility when it came to decision making.

Although, during their era, Khaya Ngqula and his team interpreted SAA's mandate to be that the airline had to "to operate profitably" (SAA Business Restructuring Plan, 2007), they also acknowledged that they were simultaneously expected to operate within the strictures of the PFMA and, more importantly, to discharge a developmental mandate, as articulated in the preamble to the South African Airways Act of 1997. Specifically, the preamble said SAA – which had "a developmental orientation" – was to be "a national carrier and strategic asset that would enable the State to preserve its ability to contribute to key domestic, intra-regional and international air linkages."

That meant that, as far as the Government was concerned, the carrier was meant to be an instrument that would be used to link South Africa's big cities and to connect the country to its business partners and tourist markets regionally and internationally.

Bonang Mohale (2019) said even during Coleman Andrews's tenure, SAA had "a confused dual mandate." He said that, on the one hand, the carrier's mandate was meant to be developmental because it had to fly to areas where other commercial airlines would not find it profitable to fly, and on the other hand it was meant to be commercially successful to "fund our own expansion, our own operations and buy our own fuel and our own aircraft."

Mohale said it was common knowledge that successful state-owned airlines enjoyed "strong backing" from their governments. He said Emirates was similarly funded by the United Arab Emirates government to "bring them here to the biggest shopping mall in the world, Dubai." However, SAA's mandate "continues to be confused."

Asked how SAA was supposed to combine the commercial and developmental mandates and how the developmental part of that mandate was meant to be funded, former Public Enterprises Minister Barbara Hogan (2019) was stumped. She replied:

> *The question to ask is what, frankly, is a developmental mandate for an airline, a commercial airline? It's a question I often ask myself. You know, an airline is there to move freight and passengers, and that's central to an economy. Okay, so we can talk about far-flung areas where there's not much traffic, but to insist that an airline flies to countries where there is going to be very little passenger traffic and an enormous cost, in the name of development, is to place a huge burden on what is effectively a commercial company.*

Hogan said she felt that, of all the SOCs for which the DPE was the Shareholder Ministry, SAA was the one that should have been allowed to operate commercially.

"I never understood the notion of a developmental mandate for SAA. What does that mean? I don't know what it means. I think there was a great deal of confusion in Government about what was a developmental agenda. Very often it was limited to the notion of transformation – and that was all. I still think there are very few Ministers who could tell you what the developmental agenda is for SAA," she said.

Hogan said while the SAA value chain was one area where "real transformation" could be advanced, situating intermediaries in SAA's supply chain, thus leading to an inflation of prices for the goods or services procured, was "a gross abuse of the notion of development."

She added that what compounded matters was the fact that the developmental agenda can – and does – change depending on who the Minister is, and "from one government [administration] to the next."

Dr Andrew Shaw (2019), who was at DPE during Hogan's time and left the Department in 2011, said he did not think that the Government ever got the balance right for SAA "when I was there, or before or after" when it comes to the airline's mandate. He said the Government wanted the carrier to be commercially viable and have a developmental mandate, without the developmental mandate having been clarified.

"So, it's worse than just having those two [mandates]; it's actually worse," he said.

Shaw said, as far as he could remember, the developmental mandate only came up when there was a problem. For instance, when SAA wanted to pull out of a route, they would then be told: "Ahh, but your developmental mandate says you must be in there."

"No one has been clear what the development mandate is and what it isn't. Is it these five routes or these five cities, or these? What is this developmental mandate? Is it to appoint different people or get supplies from different sources? What is it?

"So, SAA is very challenged by that mandate. It's a great excuse at times, but it's also an excuse not to do anything. In a competitive environment, I think that it's almost impossible to have a developmental mandate which comes with costs and be commercially viable," Shaw said.

He said SAA, unlike new market entrants like low-cost carrier FlySafair, had "a whole lot of history which gives them excessive debt, a very aggressive affirmative action programme and suppliers which come at higher costs because of how they drive procurement," among other things. In this situation, the national carrier was "disabled before you put it into the market," without the Government funding that developmental mandate.

Shaw's reference to how SAA drives its procurement refers to the practice by the airline to buy certain products, such as aviation turbine fuel, from third parties which were not among the oil majors, but who would procure the fuel from the oil majors, add a considerable mark-up and on-sell it to the airline, thus making a generous profit for themselves. The rationale for the practice of using black intermediaries was that they were "black business people" who needed to be empowered, hence that advanced the national carrier's transformation agenda.

Dr Joachim Vermooten (2019) said reference to SAA's dual mandate was first made in 2013 after SAA had suffered a huge loss in 2012. He believed that the Ministry at the time used the reference, in the preamble to the South African Airways Act, to "a developmental orientation" to justify the losses when, in fact, "there is no clause in the SAA Act that requires SAA to achieve a particular developmental mandate."

Vermooten described the developmental mandate as "an excuse for people to raid SAA." He said there were people who were situated in the SAA supply chain and earned high margins "from a company in an industry with low margins of about 3,5% in good times."

Former DPE Deputy Director-General: Legal Matsietsi Mokholo (2019) said the Department tried to define SAA's commercial and developmental mandates. She said the DPE set different types of targets for the airline. These were financial, developmental, "socio-economic and governance" targets. The socio-economic targets required the SAA leadership to "make sure that you contribute to job creation, you support emerging enterprises, you do skills development and you assist with regional integration."

Mokholo said once the targets were set, there were times when SAA would complain that the targets related to the developmental mandate would leave very little room for it to be profitable:

> *We said if you are not making a profit, at least break even; but more and more it became problematic to say if we are not able to break even, we then need to reduce the developmental mandate. We said if you reduce the developmental mandate, you are operating akin to a private company. We said we are not a Shareholder that is interested in a dividend per se; we would rather take a dividend in a different form.*

However, Mokholo conceded that this approach caused problems not only for SAA, "but even for us as Government because juggling those two mandates was very, very problematic." She said the Government did not have "a yard stick" to assess performance on the developmental mandate.

Mokholo said in 2019 SAA's mandate was now "beginning to be clearer to say remain profitable; the fiscus can no longer continue to bail you out." She said the national carrier was now required to cut loss-making routes and its overheads in order to be commercially viable. She said Vuyani Jarana, who was the airline's CEO when the interview with her took place, was "doing exactly that."

She said the DPE had "made good strides to convince the Cabinet" that SAA should jettison the developmental mandate.

Martin Kingston (2019, who was still on the SAA Board when he was interviewed, said development and subsidy went "hand in glove." He said somebody had to pay for a developmental mandate – "and it is not going to be the consumer, which means it's got to be the taxpayer or the Shareholder." He said if the taxpayer and the Shareholder were not prepared to fund such a mandate or did not have the resources to do so, "we've got a problem; that I would characterise as unfinished business:"

> *If you look at the SAA strategy, we have spent most of our time removing the words "developmental mandate" because we don't think that can be the responsibility of the Board. That can be the aspiration of the Shareholder; then the Shareholder has to facilitate our ability to acknowledge and incorporate that particular objective of the Shareholder.*

Hogan said that, "within hours of being appointed Minister of Public Enterprises," she had to deal with a request from SAA for a Government guarantee. She said she got the impression that the airline was in the habit of relying on Government guarantees. She said while the extent to which shareholders recapitalised a business was "an essential and critical question," during her tenure as Minister the issue of SAA's recapitalisation never arose "because the reliance on Government guarantees just became the norm."

Former Public Enterprises and former Finance Minister Malusi Gigaba (2019) said SAA, as a State-owned carrier, had different goals from those of its private counterparts. It had developmental goals which conflicted with achieving the bottom line. He said the Government, as a political Shareholder, was influenced by different factors like electoral cycles, political alliances, the state of the economy and the objectives of the governing party.

Gigaba said when he succeeded Hogan, he discovered – and was advised – that the airline's problems were structural in nature. The challenge, he said, lay in the Shareholder's unclear approach to the airline. He said he believed that the Shareholder needed to clarify its position on SAA "and be very clear because that would inform how, then, SAA structures itself, how it is supported, how it operates and what the goals are that we set for it."

He said the problem was larger than just SAA, but affected all State-owned enterprises (SOEs). He argued that the post-1994 Government was "very unclear" about its objectives for SOEs, including the national carrier. His instruction to Transnet during his time as Minister, for instance, was that the logistics company had to "be bold, stimulate demand, show confidence in the economy." However, SAA could not do the same because it was not capitalised when it was taken out of Transnet.

Gigaba argued that things would have been different if clear instructions had been given to SAA:

> *If the Shareholder had said to SAA, these are the objectives we set you and this is how we are going to support you to achieve them, then come up with a strategy, what would be the example? For example, you say to them: "Okay, firstly we want you to be commercially viable. We want you to take over routes that are going to bring in money. Secondly, we want you to dominate the African air space. Thirdly, we want you to take us to every capital in BRICS. Fourthly, we want you to keep employment at this level and, within that range, we want you to bear in mind that these are the transformation objectives that we want you to achieve in terms of pilots, your captains and your senior officers, in terms of your cabin attendants, your management and all of that."*
>
> *When you have said that, you then say to the airline: "To keep you afloat, we need to take several decisions. One, we need to keep your overheads manageable. Two, we need to keep your fuel levy affordable. Three, we need to subsidise you on routes which are not profitable, but which we need for*

strategic purposes as a country because we must fly to New Delhi or Mumbai, we must fly to Sao Paolo, we must go to Moscow – and then the African routes."

Gigaba said all SOEs had a dual mandate: to be commercially sustainable and to deliver on defined developmental goals. He said their commercial success was meant to fund the developmental objectives.

Former Finance Minister Nhlanhla Nene (2019) said if interested Departments like Tourism as well as Trade and Industry, for instance, were able to quantify the monetary value of the service rendered by SAA as part of its developmental mandate, then an argument could be made that, as part of its annual budgeting process, the Treasury would have to provide for the airline to discharge that mandate. He said doing so would require convincing taxpayers that annual budgetary allocation to SAA had "the best social and economic return." However, not much progress was made in that regard because "everybody actually thought just give them the money and they will run."

Former Finance Director-General Lungisa Fuzile (2019) said both SAA and the DPE often justified the airline's losses on the basis that it had a greater impact on the economy, through flying tourists and business people to the country, than could be told from its financial performance. He said the National Treasury then asked for a clear distinction to be made of SAA's commercial role, which would be self-funding, from its developmental mandate, which the Government could choose to subsidise transparently.

"When taken to its logical conclusion, what we wanted, through that intervention, was that if there is a proposal that SAA should fly to Sudan and say we are not doing this because we think there is a commercial reason for it, but there is a developmental reason, they put a price on it and let the Government say: 'SAA, fly there; we know you may not be able to price the tickets and get enough bums on sits to be able to recover your costs. This is what flying there costs, all inclusive, but you are only going to cover 50%, therefore the rest of the costs will come from the Government,'" Fuzile said.

He added that the airline could even "demand a return of y%" on every non-commercially viable route because it was carrying out business for the Government. That would have enabled the Government to decide if it was happy for the airline to continue to service those routes as part of its developmental mandate. Fuzile said while the Government accepted the framework, neither SAA nor any other SOE ever applied it to its logical conclusion.

Avril Halstead (2019), who was previously Chief Director responsible for SOE oversight at the National Treasury, said the Department of Finance believed that quantifying the cost of SOEs' developmental mandates so that they could be funded directly from the National Budget would improve transparency and public accountability and result in trade-offs about how public resources were used. However, she said when it came to SAA, nobody was willing to spell out what its developmental mandate was.

"So, SAA would say everything that they did that was loss making was their developmental mandate, and the Government would say 'no, it wasn't' or 'yes, it was,'" Halstead (2019) said.

Former SAA CEO Monwabisi Kalawe (2019) said the Government had to decide if it wanted SAA to be a commercial success or to drive a developmental mandate. If the Government wanted the airline to play the latter role, then it would have to provide funding to make that happen. However, if the airline was to be commercially viable, then the Government would have to ask itself if it was the right group to own the airline, or if SAA would be better off owned by a third party with experience in operating airlines.

Mokholo said SAA had a serious challenge with the developmental mandate because it operated in a competitive space, unlike electricity utility Eskom and logistics company Transnet, for example. She said while it was easy to define the commercial mandate, it was not as easy to set developmental targets for the airline. Financially, SAA was expected to generate a profit or break even, but developmentally it was supposed to "make sure that you contribute to job creation, you support emerging enterprises, you do skills development, you assist with regional integration."

Mokholo said the DPE informed the SAA leadership, when it complained about the extent of the developmental mandate, that a reduction of that mandate would mean that the airline was operating like a private company: "We said we are not a Shareholder that is interested in a dividend per se; we would rather take a dividend in a different form."

She added: "So now it was problematic not only for the entities, but even for us as Government, because juggling those mandates was very, very problematic. We did not have a yard stick; we did not have a test of saying this is the developmental mandate and for it to be achieved, this must be done."

Former SAA Acting CEO Musa Zwane (2019) said the Government was not clear if SAA was "a tool for development" or "a tool for making money for the Shareholder." As a result, SAA itself was confused about its mandate. The airline found itself having a Shareholder who expected it to "exist sustainably, but you had to be developmental at the same time."

He said unlike SAA, EAL had "clarity of Shareholder expectations." Not only was the Ethiopian Government's expectation of that airline clear, but it was also backed up by "a financial muscle that can sustain it."

Josua Du Plessis (2019) supported calls for SAA's mandate to be "very clearly defined." He said if the airline was meant to discharge a developmental mandate, then it had to be subsidised; and if it was meant to be commercially viable, then it needed to be supported.

If the national carrier's mandate was a mixture of those two, then "the best route is developmental growth through profitability of the airline creating the growth."

Du Plessis said if the Government wanted to use SAA for a developmental agenda, then it would be important that a "whole-of-State" approach is adopted to aviation. That would ensure that the SAA Group worked closely with the Government's other aviation assets, including the Airports Company South Africa (ACSA), and that international traffic was routed through Johannesburg as an African hub. It would also mean that "you do not put unabridged birth certificates in and cost us half a billion rands in revenue."

He was referring to a controversial policy that was introduced by the Government, through the Department of Home Affairs, requiring people travelling with minor children to and from South Africa to carry on them and produce on demand the children's unabridged birth certificates which gave the details of both parents and indicated that the travelling parent had the permission of the other parent to travel with the child or children. That policy has since been abandoned.

"You need a very clear strategy that says we want to grow SAA; we want to support it. We want to route traffic through Johannesburg. We want to make Johannesburg a hub of choice," Du Plessis said.

He said while the Airports Company South Africa (ACSA) made R2 billion in revenue a year, SAA was making a loss. He said this was a zero-sum game for the Government, "except that ACSA's high rates are chasing passengers to rather connect through other countries." Du Plessis said connections through Ireland were booming because the airport in Dublin charged "a tenth of [our] airport's taxes."

Du Plessis blamed national-versus-regional agendas for the undermining of Johannesburg as Sub-Saharan Africa's main hub:

> The other thing is that you have got a national agenda versus the regional agendas. The national agenda is to make Johannesburg the biggest hub in the southern hemisphere. Is it logical for the provinces to go and subsidise people through discounted tariffs to fly to Cape Town and Durban and go against the national agenda of creating a main hub for Africa at Oliver R. Tambo International Airport?

Du Plessis was referring to the fact that the Western Cape and KwaZulu-Natal provincial governments had successfully lured a number international airlines to land and depart from Cape Town International Airport and the King Shaka International Airport in Durban respectively, in the process undermining Johannesburg as the regional hub.

In its Integrated Annual Report for the 2016-17 financial year (the last one to be issued by the airline at the time of writing), SAA re-affirmed its mission as being "to deliver commercially sustainable, world-class air passenger and aviation services in South Africa, the African continent and our tourism and trading partners." The airline stressed its dual mandate, which it said was to offer aviation services in support of the State's desire "to promote air links with the Republic's main business, trading and tourism markets within the African continent and internationally." The airline was to carry out this dual mandate "in a manner that is financially sustainable" (SAA Annual Report, 2017:5).

In the Annual Report (2017), SAA said it had five specific strategic objectives. These were, in that order, to:

- "Support South Africa's National Developmental Agenda;"
- "Achieve and maintain commercial sustainability;"
- "Provide excellent customer service;"
- "Achieve consistent, efficient and effective operations;" and
- "Foster performance excellence."

As earlier indicated at the beginning of this chapter, as a SOC, SAA is subject to the PFMA, which entails, among other things, "extra-bureaucratic requirements" (Halstead, 2019) like lengthy procurement processes (Fredericks, 2019; Halstead; 2019). Halstead explained: "Every time they want to open or close a route, they have to get approval from the Government, and so on and so on. They want to purchase a new aircraft, they have to get approval from the Government; they want to lease a new aircraft, they have to get approval from the Government."

Halstead said these approvals were in terms of "the contentious" Section 54 of the PFMA, which assigned to the Shareholder "authority for making relatively operational decisions." She said the majority of SAA Board Members came from the private sector, where they were accustomed to the Companies Act 71 of 2008, and did not "like the fact that there are certain approvals that they have to seek from the Minister because that's not in line with their experience in private-sector companies."

However, SAA Interim Chief Financial Officer Deon Fredericks (2019) revealed that the SAA leadership team could not even arrange an off-the-record briefing with the media without first getting approval from – or informing – the Shareholder.

Mokholo said, as Chief Director: Legal, Governance and Risk at the DPE, she handled all Section 54 transactions that were referred to the Shareholder Minister. She was also involved in the development of the Significance Materiality Framework (SMF), in terms of Section 54 of the PFMA, which indicated the threshold for transactions that required Shareholder approval.

She said that, in terms of the PFMA, the Board must submit to the Minister requests for approvals of transactions that fall within the SMF for consideration within 30 days. She acknowledged that often the Shareholder did not respond within the 30-day period:

The 30-day requirement is a big problem. Legislation is a big problem for SOEs because the Shareholder, in most cases, does not respond within 30 days. When you are in a competitive space like SAA, by the time you want to enter or change a route, you come for Shareholder approval and, three months later, Emirates is already in there. Meanwhile, we are still going to consult.

The PFMA says nothing happens without the Treasury. If the Treasury and the DPE are not aligned, they are fighting, who suffers? The airline. We have not mastered this in terms of the powers which should reside with the Shareholder and the powers that the Shareholder should delegate to the Board in terms of the Shareholder Compact, and the powers that the Board delegates to the Executives.

SAA Chairman JB Magwaza and Board Members Ahmed Bassa and Akhter Moosa were very frustrated that the SAA Board could not make senior appointments at subsidiaries like Mango Airlines and SAA Technical without the prior approval of Public Enterprises Minister Pravin Gordhan. On at least one occasion, Gordhan took months to respond to their recommended candidate for the position of Chief Financial Officer and the successful candidate ended up taking a job at a rival South African airline, while on another occasion the Minister vetoed the SAA Board's choice of a CEO for Mango Airlines.

Neither KQ nor EAL had similar problems. Instead, their respective Top Management Teams and the Boards of Directors made all the kinds of decisions which SAA had to refer to the Shareholder Minister and wait for weeks – and sometimes months – on end for a response. Not only were their Shareholders not involved in decision making, but their respective Boards also delegated sufficient authority to the airlines' CEOs.

Chapter Five

SAA'S AND KENYA AIRWAYS'S EARLY TURNAROUND STRATEGIES

South African Airways (SAA) and Kenya Airways (KQ) had opportunities to implement some turnaround strategies before the advent of their main turnaround strategies which were the subject of this research: the Long-Term Turnaround Strategy (LTTS) in the case of SAA and Operation Pride (which was accompanied by a Cost Optimisation Plan known internally as Project Safari). Predictably, given the respective pictures of the two airlines which will have begun to emerge by now, SAA had more attempts at implementing such strategies than KQ did.

While SAA had the Three-Spokes Strategy, the Business Restructuring Plan (SAA BRP) and the Growth Strategy, KQ had the Kenya Airways Turnaround Plan (KATAP) and Project Mawingu. The interesting thing to note is that the SAA BRP and the Growth Strategy took place around the same time as KQ's KATAP and Project Mawingu respectively. Even more interesting is the fact that SAA's Growth Strategy and KQ's Project Mawingu (itself a growth strategy) took place over five years after Ethiopian Airlines (EAL) had embarked on its own growth strategy, called Vision 2010.

The big difference between SAA and KQ is that, with the exception of the SAA BRP, during which considerable progress was made, its turnaround strategies were not implemented (Zwane, 2019).

In the 1990s and the early 2000s, SAA was widely acknowledged to be the best African airline and won African Airline of the Year Awards year after year. During this period, other African carriers like KQ, EAL, EgyptAir and Royal Air Maroc aspired to SAA's standards and reputation.

In 1998, Coleman Andrews introduced a three-phase plan to return SAA to profitability and to get the airline to be "one of the top five airlines in the world." Although details of that turnaround plan are sketchy, its first phase was to "stop the bleeding," followed by "strengthen[ing] the mind and body" in the second phase, with "develop[ing] the heart and the soul" being the final phase (Stockport, Cowie & Dockrat; 2000).

Bonang Mohale (2019), who was Executive Vice-President for Strategic Alliances, Global Sales and Revenue Management in Andrews's team, said they developed a turnaround plan called the Three-Spokes Strategy at the time, that would take SAA into the rest of Africa. He said then Public Enterprises Minister Alec Erwin had approved the strategy, which was awaiting implementation "as to how we can merge the three business units of SAA: SA Express, Mango and SAA Technical into SAA Group so that we run all of them out of the same back-office support."

Mohale said that meant that support services like booking, ticketing, human resources and legal would service all three business units, resulting in cost savings. He said the integration was "quite advanced" and they were at a point where they were deciding who was going to be Joint CEO for the Group and who would be in the SAA Group Executive Committee – "and it [the plan] sat with Minister Alec Erwin."

Vuyisile Kona (2019) said as SAA came under growing pressure domestically from competition, especially from LCCs, the national carrier wanted to create "a lot of domestic sectors" for itself by partnering with African governments to form SAA-operated airlines in those countries. One such airline was Air Tanzania, to which SAA's old, "tired" planes were moved. He said although the East African airline was losing money, SAA made money from the deal by charging a management fee.

Kona (2019) said efforts to conclude a similar partnership with Nigerian Airlines, which was a virtual airline, fell apart when an agreement could not be reached on the Nigerian government being assured of a stake in SAA in the event that the South African carrier was ever privatised.

"Our expansion in West Africa fell flat. We were supposed to have put up a footprint in West Africa to grow the business because we knew that as the domestic sector gets depressed, it's only regional routes that would support it because the fares regionally are dollar based. It's difficult to depress that, because guys have dollars and they can afford it. Here you don't have dollars and the rand will keep on depreciating. We wanted to make sure that we bring in third-party additional revenues. That's what the plan was for SAA going forward," Kona (2019) said.

Dr Andrew Shaw (2019) said Andrews had, "despite many of the negativities, brought many of the correct disciplines" to SAA and created "a more global sense of how to position the airline." Shaw (2019) said that "no one had ever done that before."

Du Plessis (2019), who had been with the airline "for so many years," said Andrews moved the airline from being "a State Department with budgets" to making progress in his efforts "in terms of changing us far more into a commercial airline." He said while

Andrews "did a lot of work" to turn SAA into a commercial airline, he had also concluded some deals which had implications for the carrier's future.

"The view was that we were in big trouble, so let's rather sell the fleet and lease it back. Let's go and take aircraft with increasing balloon payments and we'll sort it out later when we have more money – that later was the problem," Du Plessis said.

Next came *Bambanani* – Let's Join Hands Together, a restructuring plan initiated by then Chief Financial Officer Tryphosa Ramano early in Khaya Ngqula's tenure as CEO. It focused on cost savings and financial efficiencies, but was "not good enough" (Ngqula, 2019). It was followed by the SAA Business Restructuring Plan, which was driven by Vera Kriel as Head of Corporate Strategy and Business Planning (Kriel, 2019; Ngqula, 2019).

That is why Zwane (2019) said the airline has had many strategies: "You must remember that SAA has had numerous strategies. It means that you turn around from a strategy that was not implemented and turn around from another that was not implemented," he said.

SAA's first main turnaround strategy was drafted with the assistance of Seabury, a consulting firm specialising in aviation (Kriel, 2019; Shaw, 2019; Vermooten, 2019). Kriel joined SAA as Head of Corporate Strategy and Business Planning in May 2006 and Vermooten joined the DPE as Aviation Specialist in October of the same year. Shaw joined the DPE in the same year as Deputy Director-General with responsibility for the transport portfolio, which included SAA, SA Express and Transnet.

That was the time when efforts to get the South African Airways Act endorsed by the Portfolio Committee on Public Enterprises were on the go, but did not succeed in the same year. However, that year [2006] SAA joined the Star Alliance (Ngqula, 2019).

Kriel joined SAA from Deloitte, for which she had worked for two years in New York, USA because the airline was no longer part of Transnet and was going to develop its own major strategy for the very first time, when in the past it had relied on Transnet resources. Ngqula was the CEO at the time.

Kriel said an analysis of SAA, which was conducted as part of the strategy process, quickly revealed that the airline was "in big trouble from a sustainability point of view." She said the airline was running out of cash and was in danger of not being a going concern. She said Ngqula's team had inherited a lot of contracts that Transnet had concluded, which were "not very good for SAA." Since they could not get out of those contracts, they sought to renegotiate some of their terms with the aircraft lessors.

She said one of the legacies of Transnet's ownership of the airline was residual contracts with balloon payments required at the end of their term. She said the lease agreements had the effect of making SAA's financials appear fine, but the balloon payments hit the airline badly at a time when there were more fuel-efficient aircraft being released to the market.

"So, we had the double whammy that we had balloon payment and we had aircraft that was not fuel efficient when compared to some of our competitors. It was fine for them [the Transnet leaders] because their financials looked fine, but it was kicking the can down the line for the next generation," Kriel said.

Following that analysis, the SAA leadership presented the DPE with three options: shut the airline down, get an equity partner or embark on a major restructuring. A decision was taken that it was possible to save SAA, provided that a turnaround plan was implemented. According to Vermooten (2019), Minister Erwin informed the SAA Board that the Government would provide funding, provided that the airline came up with a restructuring plan.

Vermooten said the protocol was that the Minister spoke to the Chairperson of the Board, the Director-General interacted with the CEO and other officials in the Department each had people that they liaised with at SAA. As Aviation Specialist, he worked closely with Kriel and was part of the process of selling the plan, once it was approved, to the other Government departments.

However, Vermooten said when the SAA Board took a major decision that had "a materiality that required the permission of the Minister," Chairman Jakes Gerwel would write to Minister Erwin, who would pass that correspondence on to him for analysis and a recommendation. Only then would the Minister reply to the SAA Board.

"That was a long process," Vermooten said.

Following a tender process, the airline appointed international aviation specialists Seabury to help it in the development of a restructuring plan which was approved by the Board of Directors early in 2007.

To formulate the restructuring plan, the airline took its mandate from a letter sent by Erwin to Gerwel on 28 February 2007. Based on Erwin's letter, the airline concluded:

> *The interpretation of SAA's mandate is, in fact, to be an African Airline with Global Reach. It is, therefore, the DPE['s] expectation that SAA concentrate[s] its operations in Africa, a more limited number of profitable routes into each of the major continents linking to key cities and airports and focus only on the golden triangle in South Africa's domestic market. It is, therefore, SAA's interpretation that the mandate is to operate profitably* (SAA Business Restructuring Plan, 2007).

"The golden triangle," Kriel explained in a subsequent e-mail to me in response to a question, referred to the lucrative routes between Johannesburg, Cape Town and Durban. That meant that the airline would stop flying to and from Port Elizabeth and

East London, with the routes to be taken over by SAA's LCC, Mango Airlines. There was considerable opposition to the plan from Members of Parliament from those areas because Mango did not have business class (Kriel, 2019).

Based on its understanding of its mandate, the SAA team adopted "An African airline with global reach" as its vision, with its mission being "to deliver sustainable profits and to grow our market share through world-class service to our customers internally and externally" (SAA Business Restructuring Plan, 2007).

The SAA team observed that while the fundamental economics of the airline business had improved globally, SAA had lagged behind. Although the airline's revenue had increased, nevertheless "in almost all areas of [its] business" SAA spent much more than it generated revenue. The analysis revealed that the carrier suffered from low productivity levels among employees and that high ownership and aircraft lease costs exacerbated the high cost base (*op. cit.*).

That situation impacted negatively on SAA's domestic and international routes, where competition had grown considerably, thus resulting in most of the airline's international routes being unprofitable. As a result, "a fundamental restructuring" was required to capitalise on the airline's strengths domestically, in regional African routes and in connecting traffic and routes in the southern hemisphere (*op.cit.*).

To ensure SAA's survival into the future, Kriel's team – assisted by the consultants – concluded that the airline's entire business had to be overhauled. That would include its strategy, its processes, its employees and its systems. The restructuring, which would take place under the theme "simplify, right-size, re-skill and incentivise," entailed more than just financial recapitalisation or changes in the organisational structure. The intention was to return the airline to profitability – "without artificial accounting" – by 2009 at the latest (SAA Business Restructuring Plan, 2007).

To achieve its goals, the plan committed SAA to achieving a R2,7 billion saving (which equated to a 7,5% profit margin before tax) over an 18-month period. It benchmarked the airline against "world-class peers" like British Airways (BA), Cathay Pacific, American Airlines and Qantas Airways, among others, to which it wanted its performance metrics to be comparable. It identified the grounding of the Boeing 747-400 aircraft, the reduction of management headcount and better management of the relationship between SA Express (SAX, fully owned by the State) and the private SA Airlink in which SAA had equity through the State as being crucial for the attainment of its R2,7 billion saving.

The airline owned one B747-400 aircraft and leased five others, with a fleet of 21 wide-body A340 aircraft. The additional complication was that the B747-400 aircraft also had two engine variants, thus adding "complexity and cost to their operation," and was more expensive to operate compared to the A340. Given the B747-400 aircraft's operational inefficiency, SAA proceeded to retire them as part of its cost-saving efforts, "notwithstanding the absence of replacement A340 aircraft." Simultaneously, it increased the utilisation of the A340 aircraft already in its possession as part of its fleet (*op.cit.*). Elimination of the B747-400 was expected to be completed within a year.

At the time, the airline's baseline forecast projected a net loss of approximately R1 billion in the next three financial years (2007/8, 2008/9 and 2009/10). It said its "transformation forecast" incorporated both the R2,7 billion improvement in operating performance and R2,5 billion for "one-time expenses associated with implementing the initiatives" (*op.cit.*).

In terms of the SAA Business Restructuring Plan (2007), SAA would seek to dominate "key Southern African routes by offering regular direct services from Johannesburg, thereby positioning Johannesburg as the network hub for international traffic to/from Southern Africa." The airline would further seek to serve profitably those international destinations that it was better placed to serve from its Johannesburg hub, that were relatively large enough to warrant daily flight services and that were considered to be "friendly gateways."

According to the Plan (2007), SAA's location in Southern Africa provided it with a competitive advantage in serving "the growing South-South traffic flow between South America, Africa and Asia." Johannesburg, as a hub, was ideally positioned to offer passenger traffic connections between the three continents. It was believed that providing direct services would increase the airline's share of premium international traffic, while direct daily services would ensure that SAA captured business traffic.

The Plan (2007) committed SAA to rationalising its international route network, where "more than half" of its international routes were not profitable. To that end, the airline would exit two unnamed European routes that year, shifting capacity to Munich, Germany as a new hub. Capacity would also be shifted to profitable routes like Sao Paolo, Brazil and Australia in the southern hemisphere.

However, Middle Eastern carriers like Emirates, Qatar, Etihad and Gulf Air were identified as posing "the main threat" to SAA's international strategy. In Africa, Egypt Air, Kenya Airways (KQ), Ethiopian Airlines (EAL) and Virgin Nigeria were SAA's largest competitors. The Plan (2007) also made the observation that, while some of SAA's competitors were among the most profitable airlines, SAA's cost base on international routes was "at least 30% too high."

However, SAA's Africa routes were the most profitable, when all costs were taken into consideration. Domestically, Johannesburg-Cape Town was the only profitable route, while internationally Sao Paolo, Frankfurt, Perth and Hong Kong contributed positively to profitability. However, the contribution of the Hong Kong route was doubtful "when all accruals are taken into consideration" (SAA Business Restructuring Plan, 2007).

As part of the Plan (2007), SAA was to forge strategic alliances with Air Senegal and Egypt Air in Africa, and with Saudi Arabian Airlines, El Al and Emirates in the Middle East in order to grow its network reach in North, West, East and Central Africa. Further afield, the airline would leverage its membership of the Star Alliance group by flying into Star Alliance carriers' hubs in order to contribute to its passenger volumes on trunk routes. It was also to engage in discussions with EAL with a view to enhancing their cooperation and increasing the revenue-earning potential of their code-share agreement.

According to the Plan (2007), SAA would no longer seek to meet the aviation needs of the entire market. Instead, it would position itself as "value-led as opposed to price driven," which meant that it would seek to offer value to customers who were not price sensitive, and not compete on price. Instead, its LCC, Mango, would focus on servicing the price-sensitive segment of the market.

In addition, SAA would no longer serve hot food in economy class on all flights lasting under two hours, while meals in business class on those flights would be rationalised "to an appropriate level for the length of flight and time of day."

Shaw (2019) described the four pillars of the turnaround strategy as having been the need to downsize the SAA network, to increase the revenue generated, to reduce the number of employees and "to get out of non-essential services." He said those pillars have formed the core of every subsequent SAA turnaround strategy.

Kriel (2019) concurred, saying the Plan (2007) involved "a full restructuring" which included cost cutting, revenue generation and a critical review of the network.

Except for some modest profit reported in March 2005, SAA had experienced "significant losses over the past few years." Its performance had lagged, notwithstanding the fact that the economics of the international airline business had improved. While its revenue had increased, SAA was dogged by the challenge of cost outpacing revenue gains (SAA Business Restructuring Plan, 2007).

A benchmarking exercise conducted by Seabury and the SAA team revealed that the airline was over-staffed in most departments, "with a significant overlap of functions and duplications of efforts, resulting in inefficiencies and excessive costs." The SAA Business Restructuring Plan (2007) contended that a new organisational design with a more streamlined reporting structure for Senior Management would result in a saving of R110 million.

The benchmarking exercise, against four airlines of similar size, also revealed that SAA was more expensive in Europe (11%), Asia (21%) as well as domestically and in its regional African routes (7,8%), and that many of its third-party contracts for goods and services were above market rates and at times included "non-market terms and conditions." The airline also paid Global Distribution System an average of US$5,60 per passenger segment, as opposed to a global average of US$2 to US$2,50 per passenger segment.

The SAA Business Restructuring Plan (2007) indicated that a Section 189(A) notice, in terms of the country's Labour Relations Act when retrenchments were contemplated, was issued earlier that year. The SAA team said the planned headcount reduction, which affected primarily managers based at head office, was expected "to be very deep and culturally difficult" for the airline. Alternatives to retrenchment would include "redeployment, [an] early retirement option, voluntary retrenchment [voluntary severance packages], [a] salary freeze/reduction [and] flexible work practices."

Kriel said that it helped that the staff reduction started at the top, where there was a 30% cut. She said that showed rank-and-file SAA employees that the TMT "would not touch the bargaining units if we have not touched the management first."

Kriel said Ngqulunga met with labour "if not every week, then twice a week to tell them what's going on." Unions were invited to SAA's organisation design workshops in order to ensure that they were on board. That ensured that labour was consulted and felt involved in the process. As a result, "a portion of labour restructuring" took place, without any industrial action.

Consequently, "for the first time ever in SAA's history," the SAA leadership was able to conclude a no-increase deal with the pilots.

Seabury formed a Cash Conservation Office (CCO), which scrutinised "every single invoice and every single payment" that was made by the airline (Kriel, 2019; Ngqula, 2019; Shaw, 2019). The airline could not spend money on anything at all without first having to justify it to the three-man CCO. Even Ngqula, as CEO, had to go through the CCO. He said the CCO approved even the hiring of new staff members.

"If I had a request, it had to go through Seabury," Ngqula (2019) said.

Shaw (2019) said while it was necessary, the CCO was not popular and led to "a lot of tension." However, the CCO – which was made up of people who had previously worked in the airline business and, therefore, understood the sector – brought "the right discipline to the airline," Shaw said.

Kriel (2019) said the CCO amounted to "a significant closing of the taps." She said while it was frustrating because the power to buy things was taken away, nevertheless it presented "a mind-set change in that everyone started to become quite cost conscious" and led to transparency when it came to what money was spent on.

The SAA Restructuring Business Plan (2007) noted that network airlines focused much more closely on simplification of processes, network and fleet in order to improve operating margins and sought to integrate into their network models best practices from LCCs. It also stated that consolidation and rationalisation would continue through airline mergers and global alliances.

The SAA-Seabury team identified a number of challenges and risks that would threaten achievement of the targets spelt out in the SAA Business Restructuring Plan (2007).

In addition to growing competition from South African and foreign LCCs, "a high legacy cost base" which included "'ever-green' pilot agreements," high staffing ratios and tough labour unions, the SAA-Seabury team said "an unwieldy governance structure" which included a minimum of three Government departments – which sometimes had competing expectations – posed a threat to a successful implementation of the turnaround plan. Specifically, these were the DPE, which was the Shareholder Department; the National Treasury, which was a source of funding; and the Department of Transport, which was responsible for aviation transport policy (*op.cit.*).

In an analysis of where the airline found itself in terms of its regulatory environment, the SAA-Seabury team said the carrier used to operate "in a fairly interventionist environment" which, while designed to protect the airline, also handicapped it at times. However, on the commercial continuum, SAA found itself "focuse[d] largely – but not entirely – on profitability." This tension is reflected in figure 5.1 below.

The SAA restructuring team concluded that this situation reflected competing Government expectations: "While [the] DPE and National Treasury have given SAA a formal mandate to pursue profits, other informal pressures serve to blunt that focus somewhat" (*op.cit.*).

The restructuring team said SAA often found itself facing various demands from different Government departments, and the airline found itself "discouraged" from reducing staff numbers because of the country's high employment rate. That left SAA in a situation where it had a higher employee-per-passenger and a higher employee-per-available-seat-kilometre ratio than its competitors:

> *Despite – or, perhaps, because of – this ambiguous mandate, SAA often seems to please no one. Its harshest critics are the agencies whose constituencies use air transport – DEAT [the Department of Environmental Affairs and Tourism], DTI [the Department of Trade and Industry], Agriculture, and*

Foreign Affairs. These agencies fault SAA for offering too little capacity on too few routes.

Some of them would like SAA to focus more on volume and less on profits so as to drive economic growth directly. At the same time, other agencies fault SAA for the burden its periodic financial losses impose on Treasury. All these Government departments have different expectations of SAA, which at times are in conflict. SAA as an SOE is expected to fulfil national objectives such as tourism, job creation, being a profitable airline and not depend on State funding, and also facilitate trade between SA and other states (SAA Business Restructuring Plan, 2007).

SAA Restructuring Plan

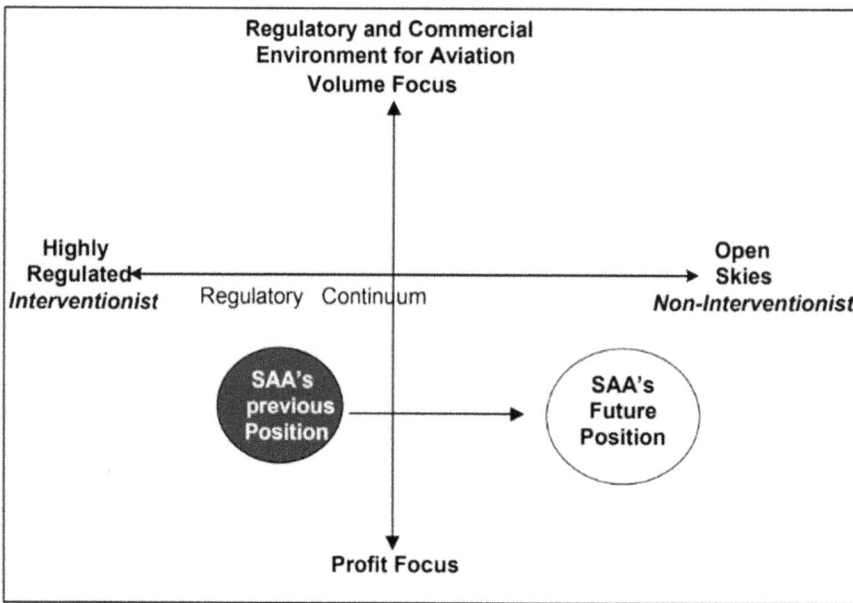

Figure 5.1: SAA Restructuring Plan

Source: SAA Restructuring Business Plan, 2007

Figure 5.2 below captures the competing Government expectations of SAA.

However, Ngqula's leadership team said that, going forward, it understood SAA's "formal mandate" to be profit maximisation. That was based on the DPE's policy framework of August 2000, which was subsequently clarified by Erwin in the letter to Gerwel in February 2007, as well as "ongoing guidance from the Department of Finance, which does not want the carrier to be a burden on the Treasury." Therefore, the SAA-Seabury leadership team concluded that SAA's mandate was "to operate profitably."

Among the top 10 risks identified by the SAA leadership team in its restructuring plan, which could impact negatively on its ability to achieve its turnaround goals, were South Africa's labour laws, "lack of Shareholder understanding and participation," delays in obtaining approvals in terms of the PFMA which could slow down the implementation of identified restructuring plans, an increase in fraudulent activities, as well as failure to achieve its R2,7 billion savings target. With regards to the risk posed by "lack of Shareholder understanding and participation," the SAA team identified a need for "a restructuring protocol" to be agreed upon between the airline, the DPE and National Treasury (SAA Business Restructuring Plan, 2007).

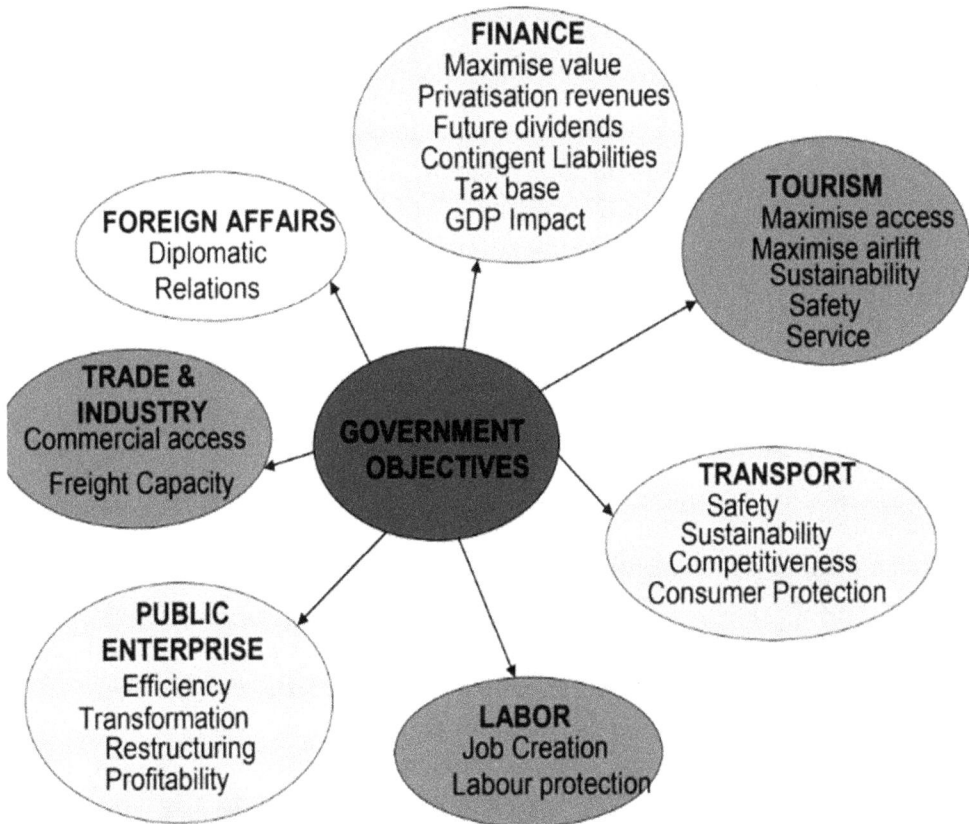

Figure 5.2: Competing Government expectations of SAA

Source: SAA Business Restructuring Plan, 2007

To improve the chances of the restructuring plan's success, Kriel (2019) said the SAA TMT held monthly meetings with the DPE and the National Treasury in order to ensure alignment. The Government Departments were represented at the levels of the Deputy Directors-General. The monthly meetings took place at the DPE, which was represented by Shaw as DDG and Vermooten as Aviation Specialist, who, with their colleagues from the DPE and the National Treasury, "were also committed to making it work."

"They even came on a regular basis to SAA to have meetings with us. When they picked up stuff, they let us know. It was a real team effort. It wasn't like an us-and-them. We knew that we wanted to do this. They needed us and we needed them; we wanted to make it work," Kriel (2019) said.

Vermooten (2019) said a joint DPE and National Treasury team monitored the implementation of the turnaround plan. He said Kriel appointed Ernst & Young to run the numbers and ran process teams to make presentations. The joint DPE-National Treasury team interrogated both the restructuring plan and the monthly and quarterly reports submitted by the airline. That formed the bulk of Vermooten's responsibilities.

The restructuring plan formed an important part of the Performance Contracts of the SAA TMT, who were "made accountable." In order to ensure leadership stability, people who were critical for the restructuring's success during that two-year period were identified and approval was obtained for retention bonuses for them. Kriel said there was a retention bonus and a performance bonus linked to the restructuring, which was payable only after the successful implementation of the turnaround.

Kriel said the Government funded the restructuring through a bank guarantee that enabled SAA to borrow money from the banks to cover once-off costs like the renegotiation of the airline's inherited onerous lease agreements and the voluntary severance packages that were offered to staff to reduce employee (especially Management) numbers.

Ngqula said SAA broke even at the end of his second year as CEO.

According to Kriel, the restructuring plan featured prominently at all meetings of the SAA Executive Committee (Exco) and enjoyed the full support of both the BoD and the Shareholder Ministry. "The Board was very committed," she said. "We had fantastic support from the Board. You can't do this without the Board's support. The Board was so committed that it established a Special Restructuring Sub-Committee for that period."

Kriel said once the Board had approved the detailed restructuring plan, it was presented to the Shareholder, who signed off on it. Once Erwin had approved it, Management was then fully responsible for operational decisions. Important day-to-day decisions were made by the SAA TMT, but route closures required the Shareholder's approval, in terms of the airline's Shareholder Compact.

Kriel cited an example when SAA wanted to exit some unprofitable routes. The carrier's primary Shareholder Ministry of Public Enterprises facilitated a meeting for the SAA leadership attended by Deputy Ministers from Finance, Tourism, Transport, Trade and Industry. She said when the SAA leadership explained its rationale for wanting to exit one of the routes, the Ministry of Tourism objected, arguing that the decision would have an adverse impact on tourism.

Kriel explained: "We said it's fine, but this route is losing us (I'm just using a number now) R60 million a year. If you cover that R60 million in our budget, we will keep that route open. They said no, and then we could close it. Those were quite interesting negotiations and discussions to say 'people, we have all these conflicting messages that we are getting from Government; which one do we actually have to execute and live by?'"

Shaw said the SAA leadership team faced Government push-back whenever it wanted to exit a route. As a result, the airline found itself "with exactly the same position they have now, where they have the wrong aircraft on the wrong route." These routes performed badly when it came to earning revenue, with yield management equally poor.

However, Ngqula was complimentary about his leadership team. He said he had "a very good Executive Team" made up of specialists and "a good Board, which did not compete with us as Management." He said he got mandates from the Board and he and his team "ran the show."

He said he also had ready access to Minister Erwin whenever he needed to discuss something with him.

Kriel explained that, although SAA was supposed to be financially sustainable, in reality it continued to have a dual mandate: to be profitable and to deliver on "a developmental mandate." She said while compromises were made from time to time, the SAA leadership accepted that the airline could not indefinitely be "a drain on the fiscus because if the airline goes under, you can't do anything about the developmental mandate."

She added that, given the airline's dire financial situation, the SAA leadership argued that "a perfect balance" between the commercial and developmental mandates could not be reached because the carrier could not compete with essential services like social grants, education and health for funding by the fiscus. As a result, the developmental mandate was of secondary importance in the order of priorities.

"There can't be a perfect balance – ever," Kriel said.

She said the restructuring plan paid off. She said within 18 months to two years, SAA was operationally profitable and the airline was turned around. She said while overall the airline recorded a net loss because of the hedging loss incurred during the tenures of Viljoen and Andrews as CEOs, operationally it made a profit.

Kriel said that, before "that hedging debacle," SAA had a positive balance sheet of R6 billion. She said the 2003/4 hedging loss wiped SAA's balance sheet out, sending the airline into the red. The Government then recapitalised SAA "back to R0, and not to the original R6 billion."

That, said Kriel, marked the beginning of SAA's liquidity challenges: "After that, SAA was never properly capitalised. The Government did not bring it back to the R6 billion that gave you breathing room for growth; they just brought it to R0. So, from then onwards, SAA has hobbled. That's just the truth of the matter."

Barbara Hogan (2019), who became Minister of Public Enterprises in 2009 when Jacob Zuma became President, said "that hedging disaster just ate into its [SAA's] entire capital base."

In June 2008, Kriel (2008) informed the Parliamentary Portfolio Committee on Public Enterprises that by the end of March 2008 SAA had achieved a saving of R209,3 million through operational improvements of its fleet and a sub-lease to Angolan carrier TAAG. It had put in place a new organisation design which had a streamlined reporting structure for Senior Management, and 235 Managers had exited the company, resulting in a R40 million saving. She said the SAA TMT believed that the saving was sustainable and that the airline would reach its target of R110 million by the end of March 2009.

Ngqulunga (2008) informed the Portfolio Committee that labour had agreed to a wage freeze that year "as part of its commitment to supporting the restructuring process." He said the South African Airways Pilots Association (SAAPA) had also agreed to both a three-year suspension of its Maintenance of Parity Agreement and to a wage freeze that year in support of the restructuring process.

Ngqulunga (2008) – who described the relationship between Management and the unions as being "constructive and productive" – informed the Committee that 1 992 people had left SAA's employ in the 2007/08 financial year, with the majority of them leaving "within a six-month period." Of this number, 963 (including 118 Managers) had taken voluntary severance packages and 869 (including 105 Managers) had resigned.

Kriel (2019) said when she left SAA in 2010, they had managed to make an audited, sustainable cost saving of R3,2 billion and SAA had "about R4 billion cash in the bank." That, she said, meant that if the next SAA TMT and the next BoD had "just managed that and not increased staff," those savings were sustainable. She said Ngqula's team had also put in place a plan which, based on the operational improvements, would have enabled SAA to acquire a new fleet in 2017 "if it had just kept on that path."

Vermooten (2019) said implementation of the turnaround plan was a success, with the airline being operationally profitable in 2009, 2010 and 2011. He said when the restructuring cost was isolated from the ongoing cost, SAA was already operationally profitable in 2008. He said while there were some things that still needed to be done, nevertheless SAA's finances were stabilised within 18 months "and it remained so until I left."

Ngqula (2019) said when he was dismissed from SAA in 2009 following "unfounded allegations" against him, SAA had R3,4 billion cash in the bank. He said his dismissal was intended to make room for people aligned to President Jacob Zuma – who had succeeded Thabo Mbeki a year earlier – to have easy access to lucrative contracts on the carrier. Following his departure, the leadership team that he had put in place was dismantled.

"That's what happened. It was painful. People like Vera were hounded out of there. Everybody was hounded out of there. Everybody. They got rid of the whole team. They started with me. They took out the whole Executive, even the next layer of leadership, and hounded the whole Board. That's when Dudu Myeni came in [first as a Board Member and subsequently as Chairperson]," Ngqula said.

Kriel (2019) agreed with Ngqula. She said the whole Management Team and the Board were affected by the change at the Presidency because the latter had a plan to bring in their own people. "That's what happened. It's what happens every time there is a change in leadership," she said.

During the years when SAA was implementing the Three-Spokes Strategy and *Bambanani*, KQ was a profitable enterprise. However, the airline's profits were gradually declining each year.

Titus Naikuni was appointed CEO of KQ in February 2003 (*Business Times*, 2019), replacing Briton Brian Prestbury (Brinson, 2002), thus becoming the first Kenyan to run the airline after its privatisation. According to Limo Taboi (2019), that marked a period of the airline being led by Kenyan Managers, with KQ "really on the up and up" and winning "many Company of the Year awards in 2004 and 2005."

Kevin Kinyanjui (2019) joined the airline at the beginning of 2004 as Chief Information Director and Thomas Omondi Achola (2019) joined it in February 2005.

Kinyanjui (2019), who left the airline's employ at the end of 2017, said KQ underwent "very rapid growth as an airline" during his "first seven or eight years" with the carrier. He credited Naikuni for the airline's "rapid growth" during those years, saying he had "managed very successfully to bring courage to the company, to dare to dream and to spread its [KQ's] wings." He said while other African airlines were content with their respective sizes at the time, Naikuni seized on opportunities presented by global economic liberalisation and growing intra-African trade and trade between Africa and Asia to reposition KQ.

Kinyanjui said the fact that Middle Eastern and Asian airlines started targeting African destinations aggressively from "around 2010/11" vindicated the prescience of the KQ TMT.

Kinyanjui said the Kenyan Government was happy with and "very confident in" the partnership that it had with KLM, an airline which had "survived for 100 years," hence it did not seek to involve itself in the running of KQ. Instead, the Government "literally left the running of the airline to the Board and the Management."

Although KQ continued to be profitable in the years after its listing on the Nairobi Stock Exchange, the quantum of its profits grew progressively smaller between 2000 and 2003. Kinyanjui said it became clear that if Naikuni and his TMT did not change course, the airline would find itself "in a loss-making territory" within a year or two. As a result, Naikuni introduced the Kenya Airways Turnaround Plan (KATAP), which focused on cost containment and revenue generation.

Kinyanjui said both companies and human beings were prone to become complacent over time and "wastage comes into play" after a sustained period of success. That complacency, he said, had resulted in the annual halving of KQ's profits in the years 2000, 2001, 2002 and 2003, which necessitated the adoption of KATAP as a strategy. He said KATAP "was really about the entire team" and involved a critical examination of all aspects of the airline which involved costs, ranging from "each core area of the operations," through to "those who were working in cargo and ground handling."

He said KQ employees were encouraged to come up with suggestions to increase revenue generation and contain costs. He said profit generated as a result of suggestions from employees led to a company-wide bonus, and not only for the individuals or group from whom the suggestion had originated. The idea, he said, was to ensure that the benefit was shared across KQ, and that was done over three successive years – "and I know it was a very, very good motivator across the airline," Kinyanjui said.

He said those staff members who were part of the KATAP secretariat received recognition certificates, were mentioned in the airline's internal newsletter and a party was thrown for them. The idea, he said, was to celebrate the team, and not an individual.

"They were celebrated. If people came from outside the organisation, coming for references and success stories, they [secretariat members] are the ones who told the stories," he said.

Kinyanjui (2019) explained:

> So, in a way it was quite good, but especially the company-wide bonus scheme really had the biggest impact. It got sustained for about three or four years because it was premised on a certain minimum clear growth on growth, and there were certain years when we didn't attain that.
>
> People did not begrudge the airline because the rules were very simple. They were global; one percentage was applied literally to everybody. I think especially when you are struggling to be able to get good team work, it's a very

important component. When you celebrate, let everybody celebrate; when you have hard times, all of you share the hard times together. Otherwise, you make it individualistic.

And this has been seen in many organisations where, you know, the top team is disengaged because they will get a certain bonus, no matter what. They don't have any empathy with the staff on what they are going through. So, I think it's much better when it is just shared across the board.

Kinyanjui said that in order to succeed, KATAP required "somebody who could be pragmatic, but also have good leadership qualities to be able to rally all the people in the airline." Naikuni, he said, was such a person, who enjoyed the full confidence of the TMT, the BoD – which included the KLM CEO at the time – and the Shareholders. Kinyanjui said Naikuni held a series of town-hall meetings with KQ employees, explained the profit trend to them and exhorted them to come up with proposals to improve efficiencies, reduce costs and increase revenue.

He said Naikuni was very effective in rallying the troops:

He is an extremely good communicator. I mean, for those who know him in the business community, he is not technical. Despite the fact that he is a mechanical engineer by profession, he talks or defines the problem, breaks it down into very simple messages that everybody – even on the shop floor – can be able to understand. I think that was a very critical component of that turnaround.

So, very simply, when he ran town halls across the business, when he explained "look, this is how our profits are going down, year on year" and extrapolated that in one or two years we will be making a loss, it was an extremely simple graph which people saw over and over again until it was ingrained in people's minds that the airline is going to be in serious trouble.

Kinyanjui said it was crucial for a leader to be able to marshal all the troops in one direction during a turnaround. He said Naikuni was able to accomplish that goal during KATAP, without the pilots pulling in a different direction. He said pilots were "at the core and the heart of the operation," hence their support for a turnaround was vital. Naikuni, Kinyanjui said, had "good skill and qualities to be able to connect with people" and to persuade them of the course of action which needed to be taken.

"I think those qualities of his stood the test of time. In my mind, I am very convinced that having strong leadership skills and courage, and ability to communicate and rally people around behind a common cause is very, very important for a major turnaround of a large organisation," Kinyanjui said.

He said to deliver on KATAP in 2004 and 2005, KQ engaged the services of McKinsey, with the consulting company playing the role of an adviser. He said "a very small secretariat" was established to run KATAP, with all other KQ employees participating in the programme in addition to their normal jobs. That, he said, had the effect of "the KQ family being trained and coached [by McKinsey] on how to look at things, how to have a view on them, how to analyse them and be able to come up with another programme to be able to bring in success."

One suggestion that Kinyanjui recalled was about the monetisation of excess luggage, an issue that was "not being policed or pursued" by the airline at the time. KQ, he said, did not even have a cost centre for excess luggage at the time, with it being "put with the rest of passenger revenue." Flowing from that suggestion, targets were set and performance was monitored against those targets.

Kinyanjui said the KQ team that analysed the various suggestions from employees was coached by McKinsey, with the ownership of those ideas "never taken away by McKinsey." He said that suggestions came directly from employees who participated in the "very many town halls and focus groups [which] were created in every area," and the KATAP secretariat served as the first stage gate "to be able to see if something was worth the while to be pursued or not." The approach adopted by the secretariat, he said, was one which sought to increase the potential of every suggestion made, "rather than shooting the idea down altogether."

"So, in effect, the majority of the ideas came from employees and got captured within the programme, especially if there were resources available to be able to do the implementation and to do the tracking," he said.

Kinyanjui (2019) said the various focus groups met weekly to review progress, and on a monthly basis they met with the Executive Committee "to see how they were doing." He said it was "very important" that both the generation of ideas and the measurement thereof took place at shop-floor level, with subsequent "reporting done at that level:"

> *I remember a very distinct part of it always used to be the question to the people doing the presentations: Do you have enough resources to be able to achieve success? What do you need? Now whatever resources were required for that were easily made the priority because, remember, the town hall was being run by the Chief Executive; it's attended by all the Management Directors. If, for example, they said there is something that they needed on the technology side, I am actually called out to be able to confirm whether or not we can make the resources available. So, it enjoyed a very, very, very high priority.*

Kinyanjui said until then, KQ held annual strategic planning sessions. He said as Divisional Directors waited to see if KQ would hold its strategic planning session in 2004, Naikuni informed them that KATAP "is the strategic plan; this is supposed to grow the airline by a tremendous pace, and that's what we really exist for, so let's not distract ourselves by also having other plans." He said Naikuni informed them that, when it came to the issue of the budget, "the initiatives you are working on are either delivering revenue or managing costs, so they should impact on your P&L at the end of the day."

Kinyanjui added: "KATAP was the strategic plan of the airline, and that's what we did. It gave focus, and nobody was being distracted by having other competing priorities to deal with. It was a very clear mandate."

Kinyanjui said KATAP was focused entirely on revenue generation and cost containment, and did not include the airline's recapitalisation by the Shareholders. Instead, KQ relied on its operating capital to deliver on KATAP. That, he said, was the only constraint within which Naikuni's team had to work at the time.

According to Kinyanjui, one of KATAP's benefits was getting KQ employees to be super-conscious of the costs involved in everything they did. That included the sourcing and control of in-flight consumables like blankets and headphones, which "used to just walk off the aircraft and nobody – not even the cabin crew – could really be bothered about it." He said the fact that measurement was introduced to everything led to a sense of heightened responsibility by KQ employees.

He said:

The good thing about measurement is that you start to get a sense. Before that, many people in their work perhaps did not know what the costs of some of those components were, but once they were aware and then could see that by just doing some simple things around control and usage they could be able to actually seriously impact on the airline's bottom line, they wholeheartedly owned it and ran with it. In fact, some became like the airline's protectors.

I remember many instances where people went, for example, into a market place and found some of the stalls there selling some of the cutlery that was used on the aircraft and they would actually seize it and say: "Look, I am from Kenya Airways; these things are not sold in the open market. What are they doing here?"

They would put pressure on those people working there to tell them or lead them to where they got the cutlery. Actually, at the end of the day some few arrests of people who were actually pilfering from the airline took place. They took ownership of it completely.

Kinyanjui said KATAP resulted in "around 30-40% of the costs being slashed in one year alone," with many opportunities for revenue generation identified. He said the pilots chipped in with "pilot techniques" which saved fuel consumption upon take-off and landing in order to reduce costs and, in the process, impacted positively on the bottom line.

Former Strategy Director Thomas Omondi Achola (2019) said when he joined KQ in 2005, KATAP was at its tail end. However, there were some projects which were still ongoing. He said the town-hall meetings took place on Friday afternoons and he remembered attending "a few sessions chaired by the CEO." He also said that he knew that "there were things that were implemented" which had come out of the recommendations by employees.

Although she was not with KQ at the time, former Communications Manager Wanjiku Mugo (2019) said 800 people were retrenched as part of KATAP, and the airline's structure of how it employed people changed. Instead of employing people permanently, KQ moved to employing people on contract. She said "that was not very good for staff and they were not happy about it, but that was what the business needed at the time."

Back at SAA, following Ngqula's dismissal, CFO Smythe was appointed Acting CEO "and did well" (Vermooten, 2019). Shaw (2019) said SAA then went "into this period where everyone was acting." Smythe remained in the role until Sizakele Mzimela was appointed CEO in 2010.

Kriel said she and others stayed on "a little longer," but then realised that they had to leave when Ngqula's successors "started to unravel our plans and all the stuff." She said while Ngqula's TMT had reduced the size of Management and fixed salaries, the new leadership paid itself "10% to 30% more and started to appoint people left, right and centre."

"So, where we had brought the number of employees down to between 8 500 and 9 000, it ballooned again back to 11 000. Not only did they appoint these people, but they appointed them at far higher salaries than we got," Kriel said.

Shaw (2019) said when Ngqula left, among the first things to be done was the scrapping of the Seabury-manned CCO "not because it wasn't helping, but because there wasn't enough discipline in that business."

According to Vermooten (2019), Ngqula's exit from SAA was engineered by jealousy within the DPE because, at the time, a DG earned about a third of what a CEO in a SOC earned. He said the main charges against Ngqula were that he had approved SAA sponsorship of South American golfer Angel Cabrera and some partnership with the Professional Golfers' Association of America. He said he doubted that the SAA Board did not know about the Cabrera sponsorship because he had seen "many photographs" of Minister Erwin and SAA Board Members with Cabrera.

Vermooten said it made sense for a small airline like SAA, which had international ambitions, to seek to promote its profile in its targeted international markets:

> *Now if you want to operate on an international basis, you need international exposure. So, where the civil service in South Africa only operates locally, if you operate an international airline you need international exposure. You can have many long debates about what is necessary and what is not, and they deemed it necessary to enter into those partnerships – and they did create a lot of exposure for SAA. I saw it on TV the whole time, you know.*
>
> *You must remember that when it comes to network airlines, SAA is very small. So, a small network airline is normally about 200 to 250 aircraft strong; SAA was 47, so it was very small. If you want to lift yourself in the public eye, you have to do something.*

Upon her appointment as CEO in 2010, Mzimela jettisoned the SAA Business Restructuring Plan, focusing, instead, on growing the airline's network (Shaw, 2019). Shaw said then SAA Board Chairperson Cheryl Carolus, who had been South Africa's Ambassador to the United Kingdom, had "come from this very global perspective that said SAA must play a more dominant, more substantial role." At the time, the carrier had "benefited dramatically" from South Africa's hosting of the 2010 FIFA World Cup, and that had led Mzimela and Carolus's Board to believe that a turnaround strategy focused on network expansion was ideal (Shaw, 2019).

At the time, EAL had grown phenomenally, thanks to a successful implementation of its own growth strategy, Vision 2010. More on that strategy and the actions taken to implement it is contained in the chapter dealing with how success looks like in aviation in Africa.

I was not able to establish if EAL's positive experience at the time had influenced Mzimela's thinking in any way.

Shaw, who was Director-General at the DPE at the time, said the approach of Mzimela's Growth Strategy was to expand the network and to buy new wide-bodied and narrow-bodied aircraft. He said Mzimela drove an expansion plan into Africa, which was something with which he agreed, and was "very focused on the service dimension."

Mzimela (2019) said hers was a growth strategy: "Our strategy was a strategy of growth... Our argument was that you have to grow yourself out of trouble; you can't shrink yourself out of trouble."

Shaw said his view then was that previous SAA strategies by McKinsey and Seabury "had shown that that [expansion] was an unlikely strategy to work with." He said that, until then, "everybody had said the network should be more constrained."

Following Mzimela's resignation when most members of the Carolus-led Board stepped down shortly after Gigaba's appointment as Minister of Public Enterprises, the new Minister ordered the reconstituted Board to come up with a long-term strategy to get SAA to be "competitive and well run" (Gigaba, 2013). That became the origin of the Long-Term Turnaround Strategy.

According to Ethiopian aviation journalist Kaleyesus Bekele (2019), in 2010 SAA was stronger and more dominant in the marketplace than both Ethiopian Airlines (EAL) and KQ. Bekele, who said he regarded all African carriers as "equally home-grown airlines" despite his Ethiopian nationality, said he had since come to notice that KQ had "an unhealthy competition with their rivals, EAL."

Bekele (2019) said when EAL came up with Vision 2025 in 2010, which included aggressive route expansion and fleet acquisition, a year later KQ launched an ambitious, 10-year growth strategy called Project Mawingu. In KiSwahili, "mawingu" means "clouds," which aptly captured KQ's ambition to conquer the African clouds (Amollo, 2015; Munaita, 2015; Thiong'o; 2012). Through Project Mawingu, KQ aimed "to connect Africa through Nairobi to North America (USA and Canada), South America and Australia" and to launch seven new routes into China, six in the Indian sub-continent and three across North and Southeast Asia (Amollo, 2015).

According to Amollo (2015), KQ wanted to take advantage of its growing presence in Europe and the Middle East "to strive to become Africa's largest and one of a few airlines to serve every inhabited continent in the world."

Project Mawingu involved increasing the size of the KQ fleet from 42 to 115 aircraft by 2021 and increasing the airline's destinations from 58 to 117 "in 77 countries in six continents" (Amollo, 2015; Thiong'o, 2015). With Jomo Kenyatta International Airport (JKIA) in Nairobi as a major African hub for flights from the East, KQ and its partners (KLM was since acquired by Air France) would "pick up fares to the rest of Africa and Europe" (Munaita, 2015).

The envisaged growth resulting from Project Mawingu is illustrated in figure 5.3 below.

According to Munaita (2015), while regionally targeted at EAL, Project Mawingu's impact was "also likely to occupy the strategists for Gulf carriers and their operating bases in the United Arab Emirates."

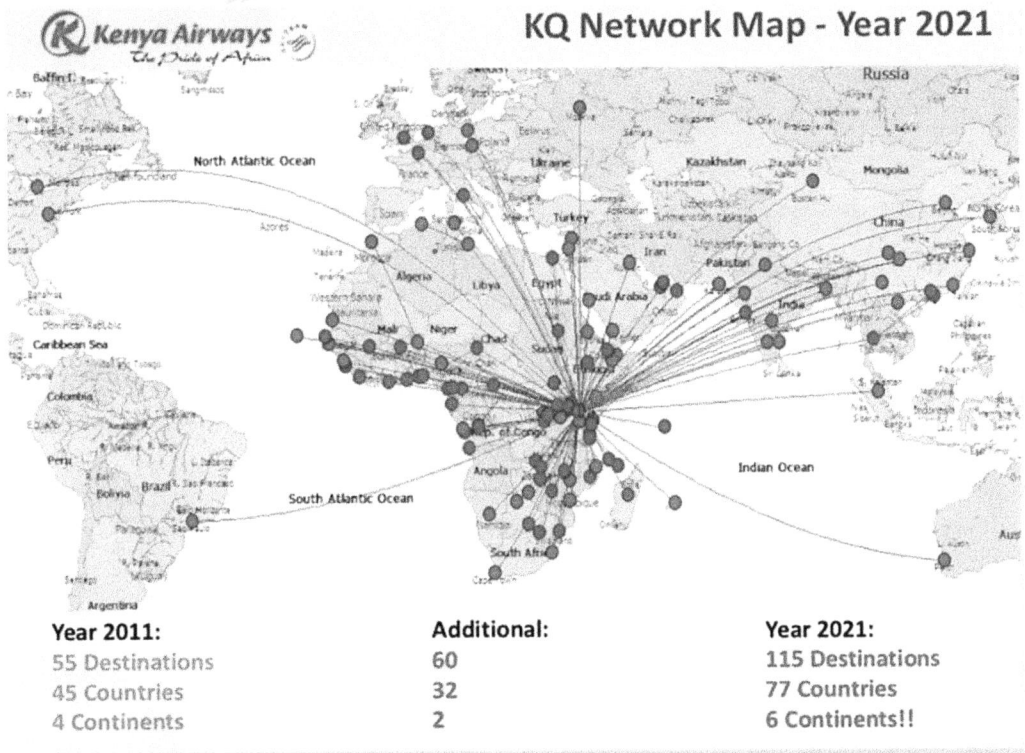

Kenya Airways *The Pride of Africa*

KQ Network Map - Year 2021

Year 2011:	Additional:	Year 2021:
55 Destinations	60	115 Destinations
45 Countries	32	77 Countries
4 Continents	2	6 Continents!!

Figure 5.3: Envisaged KQ network growth by 2021
Source: Thiong'o (2012)

To acquire the new fleet and grow its routes, KQ needed an estimated US\$3,7 billion in financing cover during the first five years, with much of it provided through "cash flows and traditional sources of finance such as debt and capital markets" (Amollo, 2015). KQ planned to issue 1 477 million shares at a price of KSh134 per share and raised KSh20,7 billion (US\$250,1 million), which formed part of the airline's initial pre-delivery payments for aircraft acquisition in the 2014 and 2015 financial years. The airline described the rights issue as "the largest of its kind in East Africa" at the time (Amollo, 2015).

KQ also took out a hedge against the fuel price (Mungai & Bula, 2018).

The first phase of KQ's fleet renewal programme, which involved acquisition of 10 Boeing Dreamliner aircraft and the exit of the Boeing 767 fleet, was completed successfully in 2015 (Amollo, 2015).

At the time, KLM owned 26% of KQ, the Kenyan Government owned 23%, foreign institutions owned 13,2%, Kenyans owned 22,14% and Kenyan institutions owned 15,12%, as shown in table 5.1 below:

Table 5.1: Breakdown of KQ Shareholders

Kenya Airways
The Pride of Africa

Shareholder Analysis as at 31 Dec 2011

Domicile	Shares	%	Holders
KLM	120,020,026	26.00	1
Foreign Institutions	60,123,604	13.02	49
Foreign Individuals	3,283,304	0.72	484
Government of Kenya	106,171,561	23.00	1
Local Institutions	69,807,876	15.12	3,415
Local Individuals	102,209,112	22.14	69,299
Total	461,615,483	100.00%	73,249

GOK and KLM have provided irrevocable commitment to fully subscribe

Source: Thiong'o (2012)

The KQ team identified seven key risks for delivery on Project Mawingu, among them airport infrastructure, shortage of pilots and other skilled personnel, as well as delayed aircraft delivery. It had mitigating plans for the other six, with the exception of equipment availability (Thiong'o, 2012). Not as much attention was paid to possible exogenous factors and competitor behaviour.

Identified risks and mitigating steps against them are listed in table 5.2 below.

According to Bekele (2019), Project Mawingu was KQ's way of blindly copying EAL's Vision 2025, given the stiff competition that existed – and continues to exist – between the two East African carriers. He said while EAL conducted feasibility studies before opening new routes, KQ would immediately open similar routes "without doing a feasibility study." He said things got so bad that the EAL leadership asked him not to report on its plans "when they were starting to open new routes in certain countries ... because you are going to promote it and then Kenya Airways, before we start the flight, will have started."

He said he was told the same story by some KQ employees: "So, without doing a proper market study, they (KQ) were opening new routes just because their rival started first. I have myself witnessed this. Immediately after Ethiopian Airlines had launched a flight, Kenya Airways also launched a flight. Okay, two or three routes would be by coincidence, but when it happens now and then, you say oh, these people are right," said Kaleyesus.

However, Achola (2019) accused EAL of having copied KQ's Project Mawingu.

He said the decisions on Project Mawingu were taken in consultation with KQ employees. He said Alex Mbugua, who was the airline's Chief Financial Officer at the time, was the Chairman of Project Mawingu, with a team working under him. Project Mawingu, he said, had three scenarios: a pessimistic view, an optimistic view and one in between. He said CEO Titus Naikuni asked KQ Senior Executives which scenario was most preferable:

I remember that when the plan was done, there was an optimistic view, a pessimistic view and a middle one. There were three plans. I still remember vividly Titus, who was the CEO at that time, standing up there and asking: "Which one of these three options should we go for?" It was a vote from the Senior Executives that we should go for the aggressive option, which was to grow to 150 destinations. Just like any team, we had a set of ambitious leaders who were confident that we were going to deliver on the strategy.

Table 5.2: Risks identified for Project Mawingu

Kenya Airways
The Pride of Africa

Risks

Risk Area	Issue	Response/Mitigation
1. JKIA Infrastructure	Timely delivery of new terminal and facilities	• Get commitment from the Government/KAA to fast tract Greenfield Project
2. Captains	Insufficient numbers	• Obtain approval from Government & Union to recruit expatriates
3. Fleet Acquisition & Re-delivery	Capacity/ Capability	• Set up a fleet delivery dept with director
4. Availability of equipment	Boeing delay experience Lease market volatility	• ???
5. Skilled Manpower	Availability of skilled local labour	• Pride centre • Expatriates
6. Fuel Cost	High volatility of fuel costs which are largest direct costs	• Hedging • YR
7. Funding	Large capital required	• Good credit history / Capital market access (KLM and Kenya Govt Support)

10

Source: Thiong'o (2012)

Mugo (2019), Achola (2019) and former KQ CEO Mbuvi Ngunze (2019) are confident that Project Mawingu would have succeeded, were it not for a series of exogenous factors over which the airline had no control. Although she was not with KQ at the time, Mugo (2019) said the Operation Mawingu plan that she saw upon joining the airline in 2015 was "actually a good project." However, "Murphy's Law happened: anything and everything that could go wrong, went wrong."

Mugo (2019) said a series of terrorist attacks in Kenya between 2010 and 2015 scared off foreign tourists, who were among KQ's main passengers. The airline, she said, "had basically survived on tourism, and when tourism numbers dropped, that drastically affected KQ." Next was the Ebola epidemic in West Africa, a destination that was "going to be a money maker for KQ," and that led to the Kenyan carrier suspending its flights to West Africa "for almost eight months." Then there was also the fuel hedge decision which affected the airline adversely when the fuel price went down, with KQ losing in the region of KSh5 billion at some stage.

Mugo said internal issues like "a bit of mismanagement" were also a factor "because there were no checks and balances" at the time. She cited an example of staff members flying to Amsterdam, Netherlands for meetings with KLM when they could have discussed matters with their KLM counterparts via a video facility.

While acknowledging the impact of the various exogenous factors, Achola attributed the challenges spawned by Project Mawingu to "pure strategic failure." He said KQ experienced "shocks along the way" following its decision to embark on its growth strategy, and the airline was unable to withstand them.

He reeled these off:

> *If you look at it, there were certain events. The airport (JKIA) burnt in August during peak, the peak of peaks. When the airport burns during peak, many of the people who were booked think, actually, there is no airport. There was an Ebola attack in West Africa, where we ended up stopping to operate to Freetown and Monrovia. The airline lost $50 million. There was the Westgate attack. There was the Mpeketoni attack. So, there was a series of events.*
>
> *Alongside that series of events, we had various aircraft entry events, because remember we had a strategy to grow. You are getting in aircraft, you are anticipating a certain level of revenue, but because of the shocks in the market, the revenues plummet. So, if you look at the first year, for example, that's when the airport burnt and, subsequently, there was the Westgate terrorist attack. Same year. That had a huge impact on the bottom line.*
>
> *So, I would say for me it's just strategic failure, either on account of Management's strategic ability or lack thereof.*

The Westgate Mall terrorist attack took place in October 2013 (Howden, 2013), the fire at JKIA took place in August 2013 and the outbreak of the Ebola Virus Disease in West Africa started in February 2014 (Centers for Disease Control and Prevention, n.d.). The Mpeketoni attack, in which at least 48 died, took place in June 2014 (BBC, 2014).

Former KQ Marketing Director Chris Diaz (2019) said the KQ team, which put tanks on the runway and converted local fights into a cargo warehouse, showed great resilience and was able "to turn flights around within one day" after the JKIA fire. He said the terrorist attacks and the Ebola outbreak in West Africa led to the US, French and British Governments publicly warning their citizens against travelling to Kenya. "That grossly affected the number of tourists coming into the country," he said.

Achola's (2019) recollection was that Project Mawingu's goal was to take KQ to 150 destinations by 2030 and to increase the number of aircraft from "about 40" to 105 by 2030. Project Mawingu, he said, was "a well-planned strategy." He said KQ "made money all the way from 2004 to 2010" and that the Boeing 787 Dreamliner aircraft to be acquired as part of the strategy were ordered in 2004, hence "these were well thought-out – and not knee-jerk – acquisitions."

Achola said the rights issue that was meant to raise US$22 billion for the aircraft acquisition raised only $14 billion, leaving a shortfall of $8 billion. He said it was hoped that the shortfall would be financed from operations, but KQ was "not even making an operating profit" at the time, thanks to the aforementioned shocks in the market. That, Achola said, forced KQ to "go to the banks to borrow money to finance both [aircraft] pre-delivery payments and the operations."

Kinyanjui said Operation Mawingu led to KQ flying into "very serious headwinds," with costs overrunning revenues. He said financing aircraft "is a very expensive venture and an aspiration for a certain level of growth to try and counter especially the Middle East carriers flew into very strong headwinds."

Half-way into Project Mawingu, KQ reported a loss of KSh25,7 billion for the 2015 financial year, which included unrealised losses on fuel derivatives of KSh5,8 billion. Gross profit declined from KSh18,2 billion to KSh8,2 billion, with an operating loss of KSh16,3 billion (Amollo, 2015).

Diaz was recruited to KQ in 2012, when the position of Marketing Director was created in preparation for the delivery of the aircraft as part of Project Mawingu. He said at the time the airline was already making "huge losses" and there was no money available for marketing purposes. It was "a tough time," he said, with KQ "borrowing even to pay salaries."

Diaz (2019) said at the time KQ was taking delivery of 10 new, 96-seater Embraer aircraft and removing the Boeing 737 classics. Using a hub-and-spoke strategy, KQ sought to fly passengers and cargo "from all over the world, using global alliances, into Nairobi and feeding the rest of Africa from Nairobi." A trained pilot himself, Diaz said Kenya has "a very good geographical location, by far better even than Addis Ababa in terms of altitude."

He said the Embraer aircraft expanded KQ's reach across the continent, with some of the routes "making very good profit." The challenge, however, was the aircraft's limited luggage storage capacity, and that led to frustration on the part of passengers whose bags would be left behind in Nairobi, to be brought on the next flight on the same day because the airline had frequent flights. He said baggage tampering emerged as a growing challenge.

Diaz said with the Embraer and Boeing 777 aircraft, KQ had "a great product" with state-of-the-art Wifi and Instrument Flight Procedures. He said the airline could fly the new aircraft longer and at less cost, and was able to carry "19 to 20 times of the belly cargo" of the Boeing 777s.

"That meant we certainly became a major player in connecting Africa to the world and the world into Africa in terms of cargo. At that time, what KQ did was to hold two cargo freighters within Africa. So, dedicated cargo freighters had certainly come into the strategy so that we could chase freighters, bags and special cargo within the African destinations. That meant more revenue," Diaz said.

He said KQ increased revenue by KSh6 billion to KSh98 billion per annum from "sweating the assets much better" and "for the first time beat South African Airways by being the Best Business Class African airline." KQ was also named "the Best African Airline" for the first time in its history, beating both SAA and EAL in the process.

However, Diaz said as KQ's revenue grew, its costs "continued escalating." He said fuel price hedging cost the airline between KSh4 billion and KSh6 billion: "We found that the branding team was discussing every week forex (foreign exchange) losses. In one year, we made billions of forex losses in Kenyan Shillings, so the Commercial team was questioning the Finance team why KQ is saddled with forex losses. Those were the key challenges," he said.

Diaz said unlike SAA, which "had very old aircraft," KQ had "very good aircraft" and won "a lot of awards" at the London World Travel Market, where the World Travel Awards are "the Hollywood awards for airlines."

"The good thing is we had a great product and revenues went up, but unfortunately costs went up and we could not bring down our pricing on tickets a lot because our costs were very high. That's one of the problems and the challenges and the failures of [Project] Mawingu, that the costs were really high. We had to bring in consultants like McKinsey to help the airline to reduce costs. Costs were just messing the airline's driving strategy," Diaz said.

He said some of the new aircraft were fully owned by KQ, while some were on a 12-year loan to the airline from GE Capital and other financiers. He said the loans "were running in" the moment the aircraft left the USA, when the aircraft still had to "sit on the ground for one month for final setting and final training before they started commercial flights." He said the monthly aircraft servicing costs were very high.

"The only way you can make money is to put the aircraft in the air. The more you are flying, the more you are making money. While you are in the air, the cabin factor that brings most airlines even is between 80-85% because fuel cost is over 42% of any airline's cost on average. So, you need an 80% cabin factor on most routes because it's a game of yield and cabin factor," said Diaz.

He said if KQ flew with a cabin factor of 70% and above, it made money, but if it flew with a cabin factor below 68%, that was "a loss-making flight." However, KQ's high ticket prices reduced the chances of filling an aircraft.

Diaz said KQ had four months of high season, which were the northern-hemisphere summer tourist season of June-August and a mini-peak at Christmas, while the remaining months were low season. He said the airline came up with various promotions like "KQ Holidays" to ensure that it broke even during the low holiday season.

Diaz said Project Mawingu enabled KQ, with its "good product" and "really passionate, polite, respectful and warm people," to increase the number of its passengers from 3,6 million to 4,6 million per annum and revenue grew from KSh98 billion to KSh106 billion (up to KSh110 billion in year four) with the same aircraft. However, costs remained doggedly high, in the process seriously negating the benefits of the growth plan:

> So, we were successful in terms of top-line revenue growth, in terms of winning global awards; product experience was very much enhanced and the brand was very strong. We were doing very well in the global alliance of Sky Team, working with 23 airlines. We had audits with the Sky Team, and in all audits we were scoring very well, on par with the other airlines. We pulled our benchmarking to another level in the implementation.
>
> The only challenges we had are that we had very high fuel hedging, which was hedged the wrong way; we had forex losses and we had a lot of demands for higher wages from the pilots. One thing is that the airline was trying to reduce costs, and at the same time 80% of the salary bill is for pilots. Pilots were asking for salary increments. There were a lot of union issues. The organisation has a very strong union, so you find that the relationship between Management and the pilots was sometimes a little bit frosty.

Kenyan business journalist Edwin Okoth (2019) said by the time KQ took delivery of its first batch of the Boeing Dreamliner aircraft, EAL had already taken delivery of its own and was "already exciting the market with its new aircraft." Limo Taboi (2019) said delivery of the Boeing 787 Dreamliner aircraft to KQ was delayed, thus forcing the Kenyan flag carrier to enter into some lease agreements, which meant that they had to retain planes they had planned to retire, in the process "incurring financial expenses for the new planes they didn't have." He said KQ eventually received the new aircraft in 2014.

According to Munaita (2015), KQ received its Boeing 787 Dreamliner aircraft some two years after EAL had received its order. He said KQ's personnel costs more than doubled from $70 million in 2007 to $157 million in 2011 as a result of pressure from labour.

Kenyan researcher and writer Morris Kiruga (2019) said the growth registered by KQ between 2000 and 2010 was "on steroids." He said during the late 2000s, Kenyans "were the untouchables and Kenya Airways was everywhere." Neither the country nor the airline realised at the time "that success is very hard to keep up with, especially in a business with such high costs and very little room to manoeuvre, beyond opening new routes."

Project Mawingu, according to Taboi (2019), was "very ambitious." He said a rival airline executive once told him that KQ's growth strategy "never envisaged competition."

Subsequent to the adoption of Project Mawingu, KQ recorded huge losses four years in a row (KSh7,8 billion in 2012/13, KSh3,38 billion in 2013/14 and KSh27,7 billion in 2014/15), with its worst performance (a KSh26,2 billion net loss) registered in 2015/16, and its share price dropped by a massive 87% over a five-year period. Once-off items (such as foreign exchange losses worsened by capital restrictions imposed in Nigeria, Angola and South Sudan) accounted for KSh17 billion of the losses in 2015/16 (Mungai & Bula, 2018).

In the same year (2015/16), fellow East African airline EAL recorded a net profit of $148 million (Aglionby, 2016).

KQ recorded a net loss of KSh11,9 billion ($107,2 million) for the half year ending in September 2015 (which was worse than the KSh10,5 billion reported during the same period in 2014), and a KSh26,2 billion net loss for the year ending in March 2016, compared to a net loss of KSh25,7 the previous year (Mungai & Bula, 2018).

The losses between 2012 and 2016 are attributed to "a poorly-timed expansion strategy" by the airline, and left KQ needing KSh100 billion "to pull off a complete turnaround" (Kuo, 2016).

Okoth (2016) reported that KQ's 2015/16 loss was "the worst performance in the country's corporate history" and made the airline "one of the highest loss-making companies in East Africa." The loss, he said, sparked fears that KQ, which was "once one of the most profitable airlines in the world for its size," could be heading for a collapse.

Taboi (2019) said: "It was very painful for me as a Shareholder and as an aviation fan when I would take off from Jomo Kenyatta International Airport, because I would see the new 777s parked there, sitting in the sun. They were not going anywhere."

Following this turn of events, Naikuni went on retirement at the end of November 2014, "a few months before the airline declared its worst financial performance in March 2015."

In a statement carried on its website, Kenya's National Treasury (2015) said while "poor management and investment," "un-strategic decisions" and "the buying and leasing of planes" had left KQ "highly indebted," the national flag carrier had to be saved:

> *The slogan of Kenya Airways (KQ) is "The Pride of Africa." Therefore, KQ is an important entity for this country. In the past, KQ has been an envy of the continent. It carries our national flag and identity globally. With that in mind, the national carrier must be saved from the KSh25,7 billion loss which signals imminent collapse of the airline.*
>
> *… In order to save the "Pride of Africa," the challenges which contributed to the huge loss must be known. Currently, some challenges have been pointed out. The slump in tourism did affect many sectors of the economy and Kenya Airways was not immune. It is also true that the Ebola outbreak in West Africa affected the KQ business.*

The Kenyan National Treasury (2015) said it "might be appropriate" for the airline to make a capital call on Shareholders "partly because the capital structure, holding other factors constant, is less optimal and more significantly immediate." It said the Kenyan Government – which owned 29,8% of KQ at the time – and KLM (which owned 26,7% equity at the time) would "need to consider major capital injections to rescue the airline." Kiruga (2019) said Project Mawingu did not have to be done at once because "it was too expensive and would saddle you with debt for years." The added challenge, he said, was that the airline was paying for the aircraft, but they did not belong to it because they were registered in the names of other companies.

Chapter Six

SAA'S LONG-TERM TURNAROUND STRATEGY AND KENYA AIRWAYS'S OPERATION PRIDE AND PROJECT SAFARI

The two airlines' main strategies which were the primary subjects of this research were SAA's Long-Term Turnaround Strategy (LTTS) and Kenya Airways's (KQ's) Operation Pride and Project Safari. SAA's LTTS dates back to 2013, while KQ's Operation Pride – which was the main turnaround strategy, with the Cost Optimisation Plan (known internally as Project Safari) being its offshoot – started in 2015. The airlines were still busy with the LTTS and Operation Pride by the end of 2019.

Typically, between the two airlines, these turnaround strategies had different origins: SAA's LTTS was then Public Enterprises Minister Malusi Gigaba's brain child, with the Board directed to embrace it and implement it, while KQ's Operation Pride came from the East African flag carrier's Chief Executive Officer (CEO) and the Board of Directors (BoD).

In October 2009, a few months after assuming office as Minister of Public Enterprises, Barbara Hogan announced the appointment of a new Board of Directors, replacing the Board led by Professor Jakes Gerwel, whose term had expired. In that announcement, Hogan thanked Gerwel and the outgoing Board "for a good set of results in the 2009/10 year and for their commitment in [sic] ensuring that the airline is turned around to become a profitable enterprise" (Department of Public Enterprises, 2009).

The new Board appointed by Hogan included Johannesburg Stock Exchange Chief Executive Officer Russell Loubser, Shell SA Country Chairman and Vice-President Bonang Mohale, Advocate Lindi Nkosi-Thomas and Dudu Myeni, who was described as "CEO of Skills Dynamics." Former South African Ambassador to the UK, Cheryl Carolus, was appointed Board Chairperson (DPE, 2009). Also appointed at the same time were Cyril Jantjies and Margie Whitehouse, described as human resources and marketing professionals respectively.

Established by Myeni in 1999, Skills Dynamics was a consulting firm "which was involved in social development projects in Richards Bay for government." Myeni was also the founding Director and Executive Chairperson of the Jacob Zuma Foundation (Pather, 2016).

Hogan (2019) described the SAA Board that she appointed as "a very strong Board." She said President Zuma was "very angry" with her for having appointed those individuals onto the Board. Since it was the first SAA BoD appointed during the first few months of his presidency, Zuma was not at that stage "watching me to that extent," Hogan said.

She said when Gigaba, who succeeded her as Minister of Public Enterprises in November 2010, did not inform Carolus and her fellow Directors if they would be re-appointed, they resigned because "any decision they took that post-dated their termination date would have been illegal."

However, Carolus informed the media that her resignation – together with that of six others – was a result of a breakdown in the relationship with Gigaba as Shareholder Minister. She said she was under the impression that SAA and the DPE had agreed on a strategy, and was frustrated "that this notion continues to exist that there is no strategic vision on the table at SAA" (iol.co.za, 2012).

First to resign a few days earlier was Loubser, who had cited "lack of support from the Department of Public Enterprises." Resigning at the same time with Carolus were Mohale, David Lewis, Jabulani Ndlovu, Louis Rabbets, Whitehouse and Teddy Daka. The resignations followed Gigaba's decision to cancel SAA's Annual General Meeting and to request Parliament for a two-month postponement of the tabling of the airline's Annual Report (iol.co.za, 2012).

Carolus later told national talk-radio station SAFM that the relationship with the new Minister had broken down irretrievably: "The Board has just become untenable. Our reputation and professional integrity had just been dragged through the mud, without any clarification or support, and I believe this had reached a point where the relationship has been broken irretrievably" (SAPA, 2012).

On the same day, Gigaba announced new Board members to replace those who had resigned. His spokesperson, Mayihlome Tshwete, said the Minister had learned through the media about the resignations, and accused Carolus and the six others of "creating a distraction" and a sideshow that had become a talking point, when "the talking point should be about how we can return the company to public health" (SAPA, 2012).

Tshwete said although Gigaba was planning to announce the new Board Members at the SAA AGM two weeks later, he was forced by circumstances to announce the new appointments on the same day. He said their names had been approved by the Cabinet at its meeting on 19 September 2019, and revealed that the resigned Directors would not have been re-appointed upon expiry of their term in October (SAPA, 2012).

The new Board Members were Vuyisile Kona (who was appointed Executive Chairman), Andile Mabizela, Andile Khumalo, Bongisizwe Mpondo, Dr Rajesh Naithani, Carol Roskruge, Raisibe Lepule and Nonhlanhla Kubeka. Kona had previously occupied a senior executive role at SAA (Kona, 2019).

A few days later, Mzimela resigned as CEO and informed SAA employees through a letter that her decision was "not a random move." She confessed that there had "not always been a uniform understanding and appreciation of this [SAA's] mandate from stakeholders, which bred a myriad of challenges – as if the operating environment was not daunting enough without this unnecessary discourse and misinformation" (Smith, 2012).

The resignation of Mzimela and two other Senior Executives (Commercial General Manager Theunis Potgieter and Legal and Risk Head Sandra Coetzee) led to Richard Baloyi, Acting Minister of Performance Monitoring and Evaluation at the time, issuing a public statement indicating that the Cabinet had noted developments at the national carrier "with concern" (South African Government News Agency, 2012).

According to the South African Government News Agency (2012), SAA had generated a net profit of R581 million in the 2009/10 financial year, a profit of R782 million in the 2010/2011 financial year "and contributed R11,7 billion to the Gross Domestic Product as tourists flocked to the country." However, the airline was expected to report a loss of R1,25 billion for the 2011/12 financial year (SAPA, 2012).

Kona was appointed Acting CEO in December 2012, but was placed on "precautionary suspension" on 11 February 2013 (Smith, 2013). Nico Bezuidenhout, CEO of SAA subsidiary Mango, was appointed Acting CEO (CAPA, 2013). When Kona assumed the position of Acting CEO in December 2012, Myeni became Acting Chairperson of the Board (Skiti, 2013).

Kona (2019) said that, after obtaining Gigaba's approval to engage the services of a company that would assist SAA to develop a business plan, a tender process was initiated and Lufthansa Consulting was appointed. He said a business plan was "extremely critical" because airlines had to take a long-term view.

"You cannot make a mistake. The difference with other business plans is that here [at SAA], if I make a mistake, it's a 10-year or 20-year mistake. In other businesses, if I make a mistake, I can fix it next year," Kona (2019) said.

However, the Lufthansa Consulting tender marked the beginning of the end of his short stint at Acting CEO. Kona (2019) said an adviser to Minister Gigaba (whom he named to me) told him to go to the residence of the Gupta family in Saxonwold, Johannesburg for an unstated purpose. Once there, he was allegedly offered money

(R100 000 at first and, when he turned it down, R500 000) as a gesture of a welcome to "the family."

"Then it clicks to me what's going on. Now, I come from the old school, Kaizer. My father was a school principal and he used to beat us very hard. My father always used to say there is no free lunch; nobody is going to give you money that you have not worked for. If somebody gives you money and you take it, you will work for that person," Kona (2019) told me.

He said although he had not been paid for three months ("remember, as Chairman or as CEO, your salary needs to be approved by the Minister; the Board recommends and the Minister approves") and the Guptas seemed to have known that, he turned the offer down, telling them that they were insulting him. An excerpt from the interview with him follows below:

> **Kona**: *I say: "No, I get my instructions from the Minister, so if the Minister gives me instructions, I'll do what the Minister tells me to do. You don't need to pay me; I'm a civil servant. If the Minister has given me an instruction, I'll do it. I'm a civil servant. I don't need to be paid for doing my job. The Minister must pay me well. We'll fight about my salary. Why should you pay?"*
>
> *I make my money on my own private ventures here [in his Pretoria office where the interview is taking place], Kaizer.*
>
> *I see now the mood changes when I turn the money down. Then they ask: "By the way, that consulting thing, how far is it?" I said no, that consulting thing is done; it's awarded to Lufthansa. They said: "Noooo! How could that thing not be awarded to …? Have you signed a contract?"*
>
> *I said: "Yes, we have notified Lufthansa."*
>
> *Oh, oh, that was the end of my meeting, Kaizer.*
>
> **Researcher**: *To whom did they want it offered?*
>
> **Kona**: *McKinsey.*
>
> **Researcher**: *R40 million?*
>
> **Kona**: *Yes. Now you can imagine jumping from R7 million to R40 million. How do you justify that? How do I tell my guys, no, you should have given it to …? Even if I were corrupt, how do I instruct my guys to say guys, let's give it to McKinsey? This thing [SAA] is bankrupt at the moment. How do I say I am prepared to pay a premium of R40 million?*
>
> *Moreover, now I must be a puppet? I'm nobody's puppet. I'd rather not do the job, Kaizer; then you would rather fire me, but don't make me a puppet. I think that's*

where the miscalculation for them was, that I am greedy, I love money, blah, blah, blah. I am a rural guy. My parents are poor, so I am used to poverty.
Then immediately they phoned Tseliso Matona.

Researcher: *In your presence, right there?*

Kona: *Yes, yes.*

Researcher: *And he is the DG at the time?*

Kona: *He is the DG. "Tseliso, where are you?" they ask. "I am on my way to you, Chief. I am on my way to you," he says.*
"Do you know that Vuyisile has given this thing to Lufthansa?" they ask.
So, the whole meeting ends there. Kaizer, you do not know. That's when my shit started. The whole nonsense; now I am being investigated. The Board is instructed: "Investigate this contract." I can't do my work now. DPE is sent to come ask what process was followed. I give them the process. The guys made [deposed] affidavits, but they can't find anything. How do you fault a man who has not done anything? So, I've not done anything; they started to harass me. Then you realize that, no, akusebenzeki lapha [it is not possible to continue to work here].
… They went through my e-mails. They followed me. They had these bogus spies investigating me, calling me an American spy, and what have you. I had all that nonsense done on me.

Kona (2019) said that, when nothing incriminating was found on him, he was offered a position as CEO of another SOC, but he turned it down and walked away.

He told the same story to the *Sunday Times* in 2013 (Skiti, 2013) and to the Commission of Enquiry into State Capture (Mahlati, 2020) chaired by Deputy Chief Justice Raymond Zondo.

At the October 2012 SAA AGM where Kona was Board Chairperson, Gigaba (2013) gave the new Board very specific instructions to come up with a long-term strategy to turn the airline around. He informed the Board that it was appointed "primarily to turn the airline around to a position of financial independence and operational efficiency." He said for that goal to be accomplished, it was imperative for "a long-term vision and strategy" to be developed to get SAA to become competitive and well run, "with clear plans and targets for the future, including on such issues as fleet procurement." He said the process of stabilising the airline would see his Department, the SAA Board and the Management Team collaborating to review the carrier's business model, structure and strategy.

Gigaba (2013) said the envisaged Long-Term Turnaround Strategy had to be drafted in collaboration "with all stakeholders."

In September that year, Gigaba (2013) informed the Portfolio Committee on Public Enterprises that a task team comprising SAA, SA Express (SAX) and the DPE was established, "under the leadership of a special SAA Board Sub-Committee," to draft the strategy. He said work done or commissioned by previous SAA Boards, the Management Team and third-party consultants was considered and revalidated. That included an SAA business overview that was commissioned by the DPE to Mott MacDonald and Spectrum Capital.

That strategy, he said, had to "highlight the conditions required for an improved and profitable operating model, with efficiencies of scale ... as well as the strategic importance of the proposed route network to achieve Government's objectives." Gigaba (2013) ordered that the strategy should include:

- "an aircraft optimisation model for the current fleet programme and replacement fleet programme, which is in line with the route network and long-term strategy;"

- "an assessment of the State's aviation assets, including SAA and SAX in relation to Airlink, and the most appropriate structure to advance the State's objectives in the airline industry;"

- "the development of a cost-management and revenue-enhancing framework on the proposed route network plan and operations;" and

- "the incorporation of the Department of Public Enterprises' African Aviation Strategy as part of the long-term strategy."

Gigaba (2013) informed the Portfolio Committee on Public Enterprises that he had told the Board that its mandate was to provide "a stable platform for future growth and sustainability, with a focus on reversing recent trends and challenges." He had told the Board, at that SAA AGM on 15 October 2012, that the airline's constant requests for Government financial support had placed both the carrier and his Department in a negative light, hence it was imperative that SAA was self-sufficient and focused on growth.

Four months earlier, when he visited the SAA office to announce the appointment of new CEO Monwabisi Kalawe with effect from June that year, Gigaba (2013) informed SAA employees that he had asked the new Board to focus on cost reduction and revenue maximisation, and tasked it with delivering a turnaround strategy that would see the airline being competitive and operationally efficient, "with clear plans and targets for the short, medium and long term." He said an Executive Task Team had subsequently met weekly during the intervening four months to draft the strategy.

Gigaba (2013) said the product of that task team's work, simply called the Long-Term Turnaround Strategy (LTTS), was submitted to him on 2 April 2013. He described it as "a 20-year plan that will see the airline evolving in many respects," and welcomed the fact that the LTTS was "the first strategy in the history of SAA that has been crafted by SAA staff for SAA." Therefore, Gigaba (2013) said, the LTTS belonged "to all the employees of the airline and its success is dependent on their commitment to its implementation."

Gigaba (2013) informed the SAA employees that the LTTS sought to focus the airline on "maintaining a commercially-sustainable business model" which would make it possible for the airline to compete globally by ensuring a "network with an African footprint and a global reach," strategic alliances that would enable SAA to reach destinations beyond those to which it flew at the time, have fleet that is "appropriate and efficient" to meet its customers' expectation, and a diverse workforce that is "highly skilled, motivated and engaged."

In his address to the Portfolio Committee on Public Enterprises in September that year, Gigaba (2013) said the resulting turnaround strategy had "sought and gained insights into best-practice learnings from leading and successful airlines around the world," with its projected financial outcomes having been modelled with assistance from consulting company PriceWaterhouseCooper (PWC) personnel. He said it placed an emphasis on "managing SAA's high-cost structure and on improving yield."

The Minister (2013) said through the LTTS, which was "a holistic document" incorporating short-term and long-term targets, SAA would "sweat its assets," build the required capabilities, "optimise operational efficiencies of strategic routes, and prioritise both fleet renewal and strategic fleet acquisitions" as well as cost-saving measures in order to ensure a healthy balance sheet. In the short term, the network strategy formed "a critical component" of the LTTS.

Gigaba (2013) said the plan also prioritised strategic initiatives "to minimize the loss-making, long-haul international route network, including exiting certain routes that will most likely reduce the airline's operational losses."

As was the case with the SAA Business Restructuring Plan, the LTTS would see SAA focusing "on the most profitable areas of the network, domestic South Africa and regional Africa."

"There is no luxury to fail in the implementation of this strategy. SAA will improve operations and strengthen its balance sheet to the point that the airline is able adequately to leverage off its balance sheet without the stringent conditions imposed by lenders due to a weak financial position. Our collective focus right now is to ensure that the strategy is fully implemented. We have developed an action plan that clarifies roles and duties for the different components of the LTTS," Gigaba (2013) informed the Portfolio Committee.

He said his Ministry would focus "both on hardware as well as heart-ware" to ensure a successful implementation of the LTTS. He said the LTTS's "steadfast implementation is crucial" and would be aligned to SAA's four corporate plans spanning over a 12-year period, "with clear milestones." For its part, the DPE would "strengthen its monitoring and oversight role" to ensure that the strategy was implemented successfully (*loc.cit*).

From then onwards, the LTTS would be an important part of the DPE's Shareholder Compact with SAA and the Department's Director-General would meet quarterly with the SAA CEO "to review progress regarding the implementation of the strategy." Gigaba (2013) said although it was "a living document," nevertheless the LTTS would "form the bedrock against which SAA's success will be judged for future generations" and that it would be "a litmus test for the role of the developmental state in the economy."

Gigaba (2013) said while SAA and its subsidiaries operated in "highly competitive global markets which are rapidly liberalising and consolidating," the LTTS was still premised on SAA having a dual mandate "to fulfil both the commercial as well as [the] developmental mandates of this Government."

He said in order to assist the national carrier to transition "into a commercially sustainable model," the LTTS had identified the following six opportunities:

- Adoption of "a new, collective Group Vision and Mission" which would guide SAA in its work to deliver on "its Shareholder's Mandate as South Africa's national strategic asset which supports the country's National Development Plan;"

- An Integrated Airline Group, SAA Group Holdings, would be formed, incorporating SAA, Mango and SAX "to improve the overall efficiency of operations and the capital allocated to the airlines;"

- A new network, alliance and fleet strategy would be implemented for SAA "as a full-service, world-class premium carrier," Mango as "Africa's leading, world-class low-cost carrier" and SAX as the continent's "world-class regional feeder airline;"

- A "Whole-of-State Aviation Framework" would be developed to consolidate the policy approach to aviation in the country;

- New staff training ("human capital development") interventions would be rolled out immediately; and

- There would be immediate and ongoing efforts to implement "new business infrastructure interventions."

Gigaba (2013) committed that his Department would "ensure that SAA achieves the critical milestones of the LTTS," with the airline moving "from a diagnostic paradigm to a 'learning-by-doing' paradigm." He revealed that he had interceded with the Finance Minister, on behalf on SAA, in an effort to secure "the prerequisite funding to ensure the airline's going-concern [status]," and that he had had "several engagements" with both SAA Chairperson Dudu Myeni and CEO Monwabisi Kalawe to raise his concerns and emphasize his expectations "and the need for an active approach from the Board."

Gigaba (2013) said his Department would arrange a series of meetings with other Government Departments in an effort to resolve "some of the major policy concerns facing SAA currently." He also revealed that his Department had initiated research on the drafting of a Fly South Africa Policy/Act, as proposed by the LTTS, in an effort to compel everybody employed in the public sector "to fly airlines owned by the State where Government is funding the travel."

The Minister (2013) informed the Portfolio Committee that SAA had requested assistance "in finalising its decisions on key routes" like Mumbai, India and Beijing, China, which were not financially sustainable. He said while SAA's decisions may be based on commercial viability, those decisions "may also have far-reaching diplomatic implications, especially given the strategic objectives of the BRICS countries." He said that he had cautioned the SAA leadership to be "mindful of short-term responses to current challenges which may have long-term implications."

As a solution, Gigaba (2013) said a proposal had been made that the Government should identify "all strategic routes, irrespective of whether they are profitable or not," and strategies should be developed to deal with strategic but non-profitable routes. He said that, learning from other countries how to respond to "the dynamic market forces," the Government would explore alternative priority initiatives to support "these strategic interventions."

Minister Gigaba (2013) said while the DPE and the National Treasury were reviewing SAA's capital requirements, in the short term the national carrier had to prioritize cost containment and improve its debt-to-equity ratio. The airline had to improve its operations and strengthen its balance sheet "to a point where [it] is able adequately to leverage off its balance sheet without the stringent conditions imposed by lenders due to a week financial position."

He said with the LTTS having received "boisterous support from the Cabinet," what remained was for SAA to implement it rigorously to ensure a return to profitability, with "the agility of the business model [being] critical in ensuring that the airline is able to react positively to changes in its environment." He said the Cabinet had shown confidence both in the DPE, working with other Departments, and in SAA to turn things around.

Gigaba (2013) informed members of the Portfolio Committee that "the airline's governance structures are stable, its management is stable and its operations are solid." He expressed confidence that the LTTS provided a lucid "road map into the future," notwithstanding SAA's financial challenges, which were receiving urgent attention from the Government.

Gigaba (2013) concluded his presentation with a flourish: "We are confident that a turnaround is within our reach: it is palatable, it is plausible. It can be done ... Failure is not an option."

Kalawe (2019) said the LTTS was a synthesis of the previous turnaround strategies for SAA ("I think there were nine or 10 of them," he said) and the Cabinet had signed off on it. Vuyani Jarana (2019), who became SAA CEO in November 2017, said there had been "five or six" turnaround strategies for the airline, which had been written "many years ago." Kalawe (2019) said while he had inherited the strategy, he was given an opportunity to review it and was "impressed with what I saw."

He confirmed that the LTTS had four main pillars: withdrawal from loss-making routes, getting an equity injection from the Government, reducing headcount and procuring wide-body aircraft. As the person charged with implementing the strategy, he could not register success on any one of the pillars.

Kalawe (2019) said on the Johannesburg-Beijing route, SAA lost "approximately R300 million a year." He said a decision was taken to exit "in support of the strategy:"

> I didn't know this, but to withdraw from a destination, we were required to consult with [the Departments of] Tourism as well as Foreign Affairs. I personally met with both Ministers. I started with [Tourism Minister] Marthinus van Schalkwyk, and his response was that the growth strategy for South African Tourism hinges on there being a connection between South Africa and China, and if you guys withdraw, you would be killing the tourism strategy. We're friends, but, sorry, I'm not going to support you.
>
> Then I went to Maite Nkoana-Mashabane, the Minister of Foreign Affairs [International Relations and Co-operation], and she said: "I'll support you on condition that Tourism supports you." I said, look, I'm not getting any support from Tourism, and she said "tough luck."
>
> That was a key pillar because we wanted to reduce losses very, very quickly. In crafting the strategy, the guys didn't consider that those parties would have to be canvassed separately in order for us to implement. We assumed that because the Cabinet had signed off on it, the Ministers would be supportive.

Kalawe said at the time SAA needed a R6 billion cash injection from the Government to strengthen the balance sheet. He said that when he asked the Board, in his third month in office, when SAA would receive the R6 billion, the Board did not know. He was advised to talk to Lungisa Fuzile, who was the Director-General of the National Treasury at the time. Kalawe said Fuzile informed him that the Government did not have money and that the best it could do was to give him guarantees. However, he said Fuzile had warned that the National Treasury could not give SAA a guarantee if it continued to fly loss-making routes.

When he reported back to the SAA Board on his meeting with Fuzile, the Board asked Kalawe what the alternatives were. One alternative, he said, would be for SAA to get an equity partner. With the Board's approval, he then embarked on a process to persuade the Government to agree to bringing an equity partner on board, but "the result was negative because of the experience that they had during Coleman Andrews's time when Swissair had taken a 20% stake in SAA."

By then, Gigaba was the Minister of Home Affairs and Lynne Brown was the Minister of Public Enterprises. Kalawe (2019) said Brown advised him to talk to Enoch Gogongwana, Head of the Economic Transformation Committee of the governing African National Congress (ANC). That committee is responsible for coordinating economic policy in the ANC, and the theory is that its positions inform the Government's economic policy.

Kalawe (2019) had a few meetings with Godongwana (which the latter subsequently confirmed to me). He said he "eventually convinced him [Godongwana], and he went back and convinced the ANC." He said SAA was then allowed to consider an equity partner, and that when SAA Chairperson Dudu Myeni suspended him in October 2014, Brown "had just signed off on us getting an outside equity partner."

Kalawe (2019) said when it came to the third pillar of the LTTS, the SAA staff complement at the time was 11 000 and the calculation was that the airline would approach break-even point if employee numbers were to be reduced to 9000. He said he approached Gigaba for approval to proceed with retrenchments:

> *I said to him: "Chief, I need your approval to retrench about 2000 people. It's part of the strategy; you signed off on the strategy."*

> *He said: "Yeah, yeah, yeah; but you can't do it now. You must do it after the elections. I can't be heading elections and giving you approval to retrench people."*

Kalawe said to implement the fourth pillar of the strategy, a tender process was initiated before he joined SAA. The motivation for the tender, he said, was the high price of jet fuel at the time, which was over $100 per barrel, hence the need for new, more efficient aircraft. He said according to calculations done by the SAA team at the time, SAA would break even if the fuel price fell below $100 per barrel, hence "the desperation to acquire the planes."

Kalawe said Gigaba cancelled the tender because "there were two camps in the Cabinet at the time: some guys were supportive of Airbus and some were supportive of Boeing."

"All the key pillars that were supposed to drive the strategy did not get support from the key stakeholders. If an environment had been created for us to implement those pillars, SAA would be better today," Kalawe said.

He was suspended in October 2014, "at the behest of Board Chairperson Dudu Myeni," and Mango CEO Nico Bezuidenhout was appointed Acting CEO. He explained in an affidavit filed with the Labour Court in 2015 that the reason for the breakdown in his relationship with Myeni involved the acquisition of 23 new, wide-body aircraft. In April 2015, SAA reached an out-of-court settlement with him (Hogg, 2015).

In December 2014, SAA was transferred from the DPE to a new Shareholder, the Ministry of Finance (Ministry of Finance, 2014). Nhlanhla Nene was Minister of Finance at the time (KaNkosi, 2018).

After Bezuidenhout, Human Resources General Manager Thuli Mpshe was appointed Acting CEO in July 2015, after the former returned to his position as Mango CEO. Mpshe was in that position for just under four months, and was succeeded in November 2015 as SAA Acting CEO by Musa Zwane, who was CEO of SAA Technical. Zwane became the seventh SAA CEO, whether full time or acting, in four years (Hill & Bowker, 2015).

Zwane continued in that position until the appointment of Vuyani Jarana as CEO, with effect from 1 November 2017. Like Kalawe before him, Jarana (2019) said he had reviewed the LTTS and previous SAA turnaround strategies, and soon came to the conclusion that much of what was supposed to have been implemented was not done.

"Now, a plan is a multi-year plan; it assumes that you start doing things today," he said.

He said failure to get things done immediately, in accordance with the approved strategy, impacted negatively on the timing outlined in the LTTS and the anticipated revenue gains. Jarana said he soon realized that there was no way in which he could deliver on the turnaround strategy "based on what Seabury had written," hence he had to revise the strategy. That process entailed a look at the commercial side of the business, remodelling it based on market trends, and a review of the fuel price movement.

He said the national carrier was in an unhedged position at the time and did not have the money to hedge against the fuel price. He said five months after assuming office, he had remodelled the strategy to cover a five-year period and started implementing it, balancing and dividing domestic routes between SAA and sister company Mango.

He said although Mango was an SAA subsidiary, the two airlines "did not work together as a group," hence they had to be pulled together. Before that, the two airlines had different cultures and "worked as if they belonged to different ownership structures." By mid-April 2019, that was still work in progress.

Jarana (2019) said another one of his priorities was fixing SAA Technical, the national carrier's maintenance, repair and overhaul (MRO) subsidiary, in order to make sure that it would have quick turnaround times. That, too, remained work in progress, with Jarana and his team being "still far from getting that kind of success."

In a presentation to the National Assembly Standing Committee on Appropriations in April 2018, when Jarana was in office for six months, SAA reported that "while numerous attempts" had been made to restructure the airline, these had met with "limited success" for a number of reasons. These included lack of "a coherent, integrated strategy," too much focus on cost reduction without simultaneously addressing constraints in the airline's operating model, reduced customer focus and "limited commercial and business skills to drive revenue growth." Other reasons were cited as management instability and "breakdown of culture," as well as "slow decision making often due to increased Management restrictions" (SAA, 2018).

The SAA team also made the point that increased competition had led to the carrier's loss of market share and reduced yields, which was graphically presented in figure 6.1 below.

The SAA team informed the Standing Committee on Appropriations that the FY2017/18 budget and the LTTS were based on five key assumptions. These were the sale of five, SAA-owned A340-300 aircraft (which was not accomplished), a R900 million capital budget, purchase of two A340-600 aircraft (one was bought), R13 billion recapitalisation over three years and the airline continuing to be a going concern. The last two assumptions were met following a R10 billion cash injection from the National Treasury in the course of that year, which was used to service the carrier's immediate debt obligations and to meet its working needs.

Increased competition has resulted in a loss of market share and reduced yields

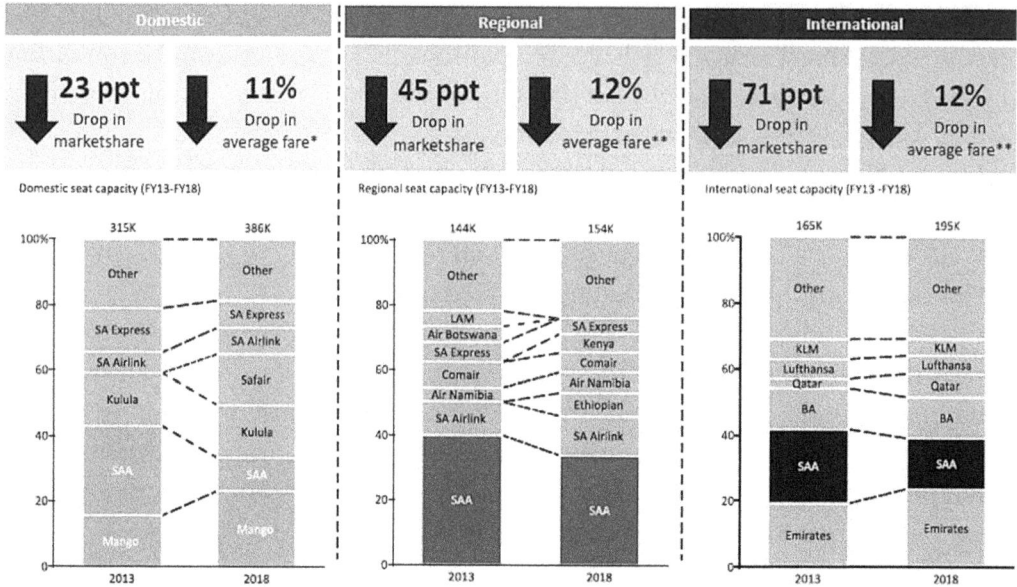

Figure 6.1: SAA market loss and reduced yields
Source: SAA Group Presentation to Standing Committee on Appropriations (2018)

Now called the "SAA Change Agenda," the turnaround strategy had 10 key strategic priorities, namely:

- Transforming SAA into a commercially capable organisation whilst defending its safety track record ("Flying for Profits");

- Establishing an efficient production and operating platform for SAA;

- Winning the battle for premium and business travellers in the domestic market;

- Winning the battle for the price-sensitive segment of the market in South Africa through Mango;

- Becoming a focused niche player in the international market, leveraging alliances and partnerships;

- Growing scale in the regional market through organic growth, commercial partnerships and the Single African Air Transport Market (SAATM);

- Leading in customer experience management;

- Developing aviation skills for the group and achieving workforce diversity in all occupational categories;

- Shaping the aviation policy in South Africa and the continent to defend SAA's market and enable growth in the market; and

- Strengthening the balance sheet and addressing liquidity challenges.

The SAA Change Agenda is illustrated in figure 6.2 below:

The SAA Change Agenda is driven by ten key strategic priorities

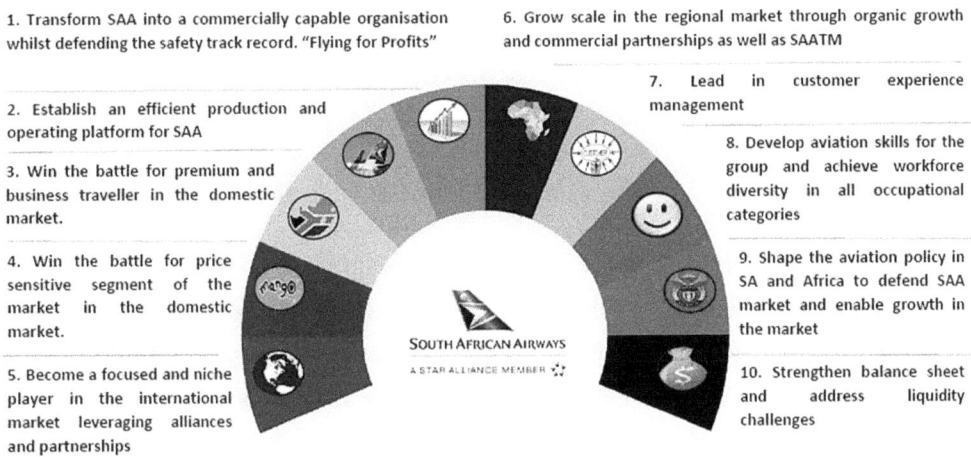

1. Transform SAA into a commercially capable organisation whilst defending the safety track record. "Flying for Profits"

2. Establish an efficient production and operating platform for SAA

3. Win the battle for premium and business traveller in the domestic market.

4. Win the battle for price sensitive segment of the market in the domestic market.

5. Become a focused and niche player in the international market leveraging alliances and partnerships

6. Grow scale in the regional market through organic growth and commercial partnerships as well as SAATM

7. Lead in customer experience management

8. Develop aviation skills for the group and achieve workforce diversity in all occupational categories

9. Shape the aviation policy in SA and Africa to defend SAA market and enable growth in the market

10. Strengthen balance sheet and address liquidity challenges

Figure 6.2: SAA Change Agenda
Source: SAA Group Presentation to Standing Committee on Appropriations (2018)

There were four phases of the SAA Change Agenda, as shown in figure 6.3 below. These were Arrest, Change, Stabilize, and Grow. The first phase focused on quick wins, over a six-month period, like cost reduction and service improvement, while the second phase focused on revenue and customer service optimisation, over a three- to 18-month period. The stabilisation phase, to last between one-and-a-half years and two-and-a-half years, would focus on internal efficiency improvements and restructuring as well as on external alliances and strategic partnerships. Finally, the grow phase, between years two and three, would focus on network and revenue growth, with SAA being recognised as the "Promoter of the African Experience" (SAA, 2018).

However, Jarana and his team indicated that for successful implementation of the SAA Change Agenda, four conditions had to be met:

- SAA needed to remain a going concern;
- there had to be "close collaboration between the Shareholder and the Board;"
- there had to be "good governance and Board responsiveness;" and
- SAA had to have the required "executive capacity and skill" (SAA, 2018).

While no clarity was given in the presentation about what "Board responsiveness" meant, Jarana (2019) said in the interview with me a year later that Board members needed to be prepared to challenge the Shareholder when the situation required it.

Alongside the four conditions were four "key dependencies." These were "successful manpower productivity right-sizing," which referred to staff retrenchments; "organisational culture and [an] agreement with labour; "speed and agility of contract revisions and renegotiations;" as well as the provision of funding to effect the turnaround and the restructuring of the airline's debt beyond 2019 (SAA, 2018).

In terms of the Change Agenda, which was a revised version of the LTTS, Jarana and the SAA Board committed to a reduction of losses over the next three years to get the airline to break even in 2021, as illustrated in figure 6.4 below.

Jarana and his team informed the Portfolio Committee on Appropriations that the National Treasury, as the Shareholder, and the SAA Board had formed a joint task force, called the Oversight Forum, to facilitate discussion on a joint search for solutions to the airline's funding challenges and to create an enabling environment for a successful implementation of the turnaround strategy. They said the Oversight Forum, which was chaired by Deputy Finance Minister Mondli Gungubele, followed appreciation by both the SAA Board and the National Treasury that "an urgent solution must be found to address the funding challenges facing South African Airways."

Among its duties, the Oversight Forum would:

- "Determine the optimal capital structure for SAA;"
- "Determine mechanisms to implement the optimal capital structure and funding model for SAA;"
- "Define a work programme to plan and monitor the realisation of the objectives of the Oversight Forum;" and
- "Design appropriate mechanisms to oversee and monitor the implementation of the turnaround strategy beyond the term of the Oversight Forum."

Plan leverages a structured approach consisting of 4 phases; initial phase focuses on addressing immediate remedial actions

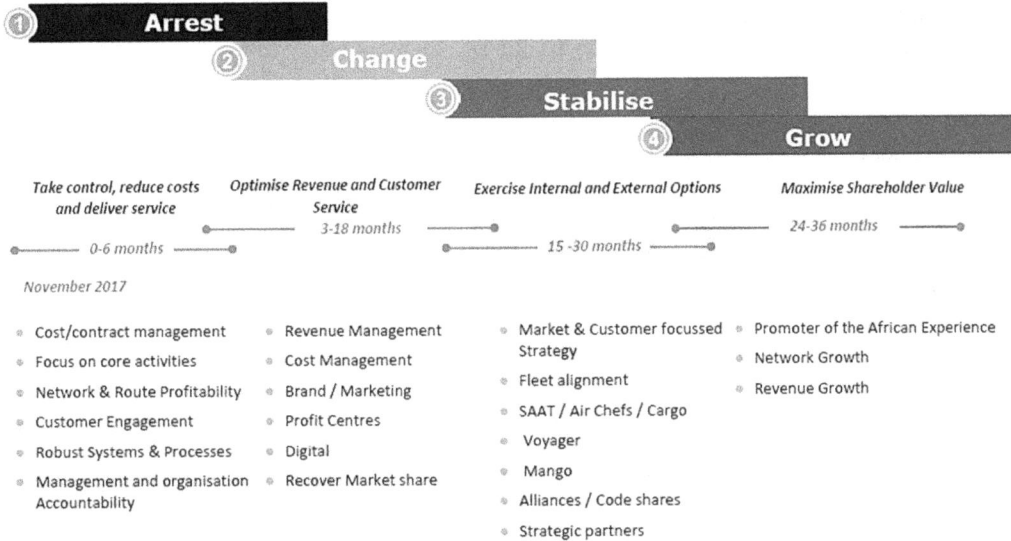

① **Arrest**

② **Change**

③ **Stabilise**

④ **Grow**

Take control, reduce costs and deliver service	Optimise Revenue and Customer Service	Exercise Internal and External Options	Maximise Shareholder Value
0-6 months	3-18 months	15-30 months	24-36 months

November 2017

- Cost/contract management
- Focus on core activities
- Network & Route Profitability
- Customer Engagement
- Robust Systems & Processes
- Management and organisation Accountability

- Revenue Management
- Cost Management
- Brand / Marketing
- Profit Centres
- Digital
- Recover Market share

- Market & Customer focussed Strategy
- Fleet alignment
- SAAT / Air Chefs / Cargo
- Voyager
- Mango
- Alliances / Code shares
- Strategic partners

- Promoter of the African Experience
- Network Growth
- Revenue Growth

Figure 6.3: Four Phases of SAA Change Agenda
Source: SAA Group Presentation to Standing Committee on Appropriations (2018)

Jarana (2019) said the Oversight Forum, which worked well while SAA had the National Treasury as its Shareholder, made decision making quicker "at the highest level." However, when SAA was returned to the DPE in August 2018, the Oversight Forum did not work as well because "the Minister is over-stretched with many things." That left the SAA Board and Management with "the vagaries of submissions." They had to ask for appointments with Minister Pravin Gordhan, and "it will take you a month because there is no time; everyone is busy."

Jarana (2019) said the idea of an Oversight Forum was his in order to ensure quick decision making: "It was purely my idea to fast-track decisions to say this is an ailing company; it's in ICU [intensive care unit]. You can't treat it as an out-patient, as if it's a patient in an out-patient system. You see, in ICU the doctor doesn't leave the ward. Therefore, we needed that mechanism so that we are together with the Shareholder consistently to make decisions."

Figure 6.4: Path to SAA's break even in 2021

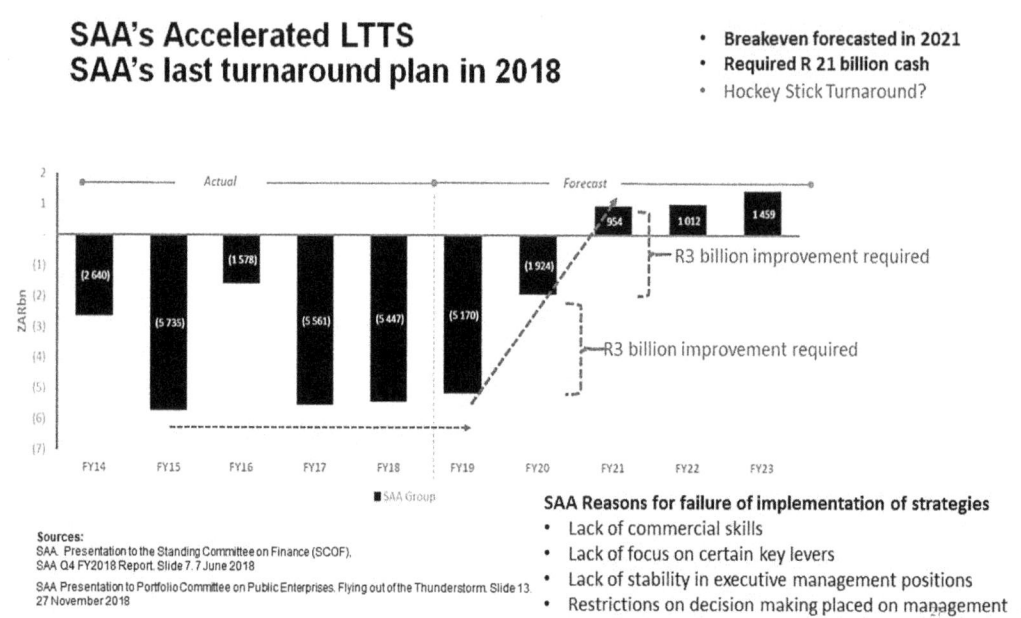

Source: Joachim Vermooten (2020)

However, following the collapse of the Oversight Forum after the airline's return to the DPE, Jarana (2019) proposed that two senior Deputy Directors-General – one from the National Treasury and the other from the DPE – be appointed onto the SAA Board to improve the pace of decision making by the Shareholder:

> *I don't want the extras in the movie; I want people who make decisions so that when they discuss SAA at the National Treasury and at the DPE, they don't second-guess us. These people sit on the Board; they have all the packs, all the information. Therefore, as a transitional mechanism to close the gap – because there is an information gap and a gap around the urgency – when we bring them in as Directors, they are equally liable like us for fiduciary responsibility. Today they can call it as they see it as DGs or DDGs and not sign anything. They are not exposed.*
>
> *So, I'm calling for equal exposure, so you bring skin in the game. Once you bring people in as Directors, somehow there's skin in the game.*

Jarana (2019) said if his proposal was not accepted, SAA would not be agile and he and his team would not succeed in implementing the turnaround strategy.

Meanwhile, after years of profitability, KQ was experiencing serious financial challenges following the unsuccessful implementation of Project Mawingu.

When former KQ Chief Operations Officer Mbuvi Ngunze was appointed CEO with effect from 1 December 2014, the carrier was already in deep trouble financially. Ngunze immediately launched a turnaround strategy called Operation Pride, through which KQ hoped to "derive at least $200 million in value from increasing revenue and cutting costs," and engaged the services of both McKinsey and Co. and Seabury Group as consultants (Bekele, 2016).

As part of Operation Pride, KQ reduced its fleet by almost a third, leased its Boeing 777 and 787 jetliners, agreed to loan its under-utilised pilots to Ethiopian Airways, sold its take-off and landing slot at Heathrow International Airport in London and planned to retrench 15% of its workforce (600 employees) in order to return to profitability. Ngunze and his team embarked on this plan with the full support of KQ's main Shareholders, the Kenyan Government and Air France-KLM (Bekele, 2016).

However, the Kenya Airline Pilots Association (KALPA) insisted that "any turnaround strategy amounts to an exercise in futility if implemented by the same management team [that] carries responsibility for the 'poor' decision-making that dragged down the airline" (Bekele, 2016).

Kinyanjui (2019) said KQ suddenly found itself "with a lot of capacity," with its competitors already having established themselves "and already having made names for themselves" in markets which it had targeted. That made the situation "very, very difficult," especially since in the past KQ "used to think of a market, decide this is the number of aircraft that we have, deploy them and they make money."

"It's no longer like that. Even an airline right now trying to come into the market, as much as it becomes a bit obvious that your local market is your low-hanging fruit, I think in terms of global travel, your destination markets are not as easy to define as they were before," Kinyanjui (2019) said.

In October 2015, Thomas Omondi Achola (2019) was appointed Strategy Director, in addition to being Acting Commercial Director. In 2016, when a substantive Commercial Director was appointed, Achola assumed the additional position of Chief Transformation Director, in addition to his role as Strategy Director, and remained in both positions until he left KQ in February 2018. He was, therefore, the Executive responsible for Operation Pride, working alongside Ngunze.

Achola (2019) said Operation Pride's end goal was to return KQ to profitability, to maintain the airline's licence to operate and to "operate the business for cash." He said the airline's losses unnerved aviation regulators and had the potential to compromise KQ's licence to operate. A licence to operate, he said, was about "safety, ability to pay critical suppliers and making sure that you don't violate any covenants."

Achola (2019) said the main elements of Operation Pride were waste elimination, revenue generation and asset disposal, which the KQ team called "'one time', which is just things that you can cut off which are not core business, or which you don't need as assets." The latter were sold to generate cash.

He said KQ entered into new ventures and partnerships, came up with new revenue ideas and set up a Cash Committee which vetted all expenses. "As the Cash Committee," he said, "basically, we said there were certain things which must be justified, before you even commit the company. We also, by necessity, said that we shall not pay suppliers just because they are due. We prioritised suppliers which we paid."

That Cash Committee operated exactly like the Cash Conservation Committee which was introduced by Seabury at SAA during Khaya Ngqula's era.

Achola (2019) said eight areas fell within the scope of the Cash Committee (CC), with travel, recruitment, IT expenditure, new product acquisition and capital expenditure being among them. He said only those suppliers which were "very, very critical to the continued operation of the airline from a perspective of safety and being a going concern" were paid. He said the CC, which made sure "that there was no spend when we never needed it," met twice a week and was made up of two people from the Transformation Office.

Achola (2019) said the budget was suspended and "a completely zero-based budget[ing]" system was adopted.

Other initiatives that were taken included a sale of unused KQ land, a sale of Boeing 777-200 aircraft which was "spare capacity" and a lease of aircraft to Oman Air and Turkish Airways. He said KQ lost "a lot of people," especially pilots and engineers, who left out of fear that "the airline was going under." He said "more than 300" pilots and engineers were lost, which was "a huge number for the size of the airline."

"That allowed us to eliminate about US$8 million a month from the P&L. In total, we achieved almost $800 million in terms of savings just by grounding aircraft and leasing some out. In some cases, we actually sold some aircraft to be able to generate cash," Achola (2019) said.

He explained how the CC worked:

> The Cash Committee was made up of only two people from the Transformation Office. They are the ones who chaired the Cash Committee. It was not people from Finance. So, the Cash Committee was an ad-hoc committee. You sent all your requirements in advance. They looked at them and you came to defend your requirements.
>
> It was either accepted or rejected, depending on the priorities of the business, because remember we were running the business for cash, and cash

was a very, very big issue. So, we needed to conserve cash, and the way to conserve cash is just to withdraw the ability of people to spend it.

Former Communications Manager, Wanjui Mugo (2019) said that each department was asked to contribute to the success of Operation Pride. She said different work streams were created to look at different aspects of the business, such as the KQ network, fleet management, revenue generation and human resource rationalisation, among others.

She said KQ had just taken delivery of the last batch of Boeing 787 Dreamliner aircraft, but it did not need all nine of them. Two of them were leased, together with two of the newer Boeing 777 aircraft, with plans to sell the two older Boeing 777 aircraft. She said the sale of the Heathrow International Airport slot led to KQ having one aircraft flying to London, UK in the morning and then flying back in the evening, "instead of having two aircraft criss-crossing each other."

Mugo (2019) said KQ had "a lot of land" and sold "a lot of it," and other efforts involved renegotiating contracts. She said laying off "about 600" staff members was one of the last things that were done as part of Operation Pride.

Mugo (2019) said competition from EAL and Emirates was "very tough," hence KQ worked closely with tour operators in order to bring them closer and incentivise them to support the airline. A programme for staff members, called Buddy Ticket, was introduced, which incentivised KQ employees to get their friends to fly the airline at a discount.

Both Achola (2019) and Mugo (2019) said Operation Pride was a success. Achola (2019) said a year after KQ's biggest loss in the 2015/16 financial year, the airline recorded an operating profit the following year and again in December 2017, when KQ changed its financial year from April to March to a calendar year (January to December). However, the airline still made losses before tax "predominantly because of financing costs."

Mugo (2019) said during that period, KQ cut its gross losses by 35% and grew operational profit "by over 100%." The challenge, she said, was that the carrier still had aircraft that it could not pay for and owed both local banks and the US Export-Import Bank, which were part of the consortium that had helped KQ to acquire the new aircraft.

Achola (2019) said as in the case of the Kenya Airways Turnaround Plan (KATAP) a decade earlier, KQ again involved its employees in the formulation of ideas to generate revenue and contain costs. He said all employees were told very clearly that KQ's focus was on "profitability, licence to operate and we are doing the business for cash." He said employees were told that "the airline is dying," and that they had a role to play to prevent that from happening.

Achola stressed the importance of clarity during such a process:

> *Clarity has to be there. The numbers have to be very clear. You have to tell people. In this case, we were trying to generate cash of KSh890 billion, so people are focused. That strategic clarity is important, but also, from a direction point of view, role clarity is important. Every person in the business needs to understand: "So, we are doing this. This is where we are going. This is where the team leader says we are going. What is my role?"*

He said KQ approached Operation Pride "from the bottom up," through "ideas sessions," in order to get employees involved and to take ownership. As a result, he said, "all the ideas that were turning around the airline came from the troops," and not from McKinsey. He said employees whose ideas were adopted and implemented received "a financial incentive."

Achola said staff members who came up "with an idea that just turns on a light bulb" received a coffee voucher; but if their ideas went through the stage gates and were implemented, they got a reward of "about $500" about two months after those ideas had generated revenue. He said individuals who achieved their milestones quicker were called Pride Stars and received a call "directly from the CEO and the CEO invited them either for dinner, lunch or a conversation with them and their spouse or partner."

Achola said that, as part of Operation Pride, KQ had to "stop side-shows and non-core activities," like its sponsorship of the Kenyan national rugby team, and focused on markets that were cash cows.

Kaleyesus Bekele (2019) said Ngunze "sat on a very hot seat" and "found himself paying a price for some bad decisions made some years back." He said that, as part of Operation Pride, Nguze downsized the fleet, rationalised some routes, released some aircraft and even sold the KQ slot at Heathrow International Airport.

Operation Pride architect Ngunze (2019) said the strategy was focused on three things:

- Improving the top line, reducing costs and increasing the level of profit through an operational turnaround;

- a strategic focus on Africa, particularly "southern trans-continental routes," through building partnerships; and

- financial restructuring.

Ngunze (2019) said the most important thing concerning the operational turnaround was renegotiation of lease agreements, supply contracts, financing arrangements and staff costs around the crew, all of which impacted on the cash flow. He said the retention of McKinsey as an operational restructuring adviser "really facilitated a lot of the conversation."

"We used McKinsey, and that was very intentional. It was intentional in the sense that what we were looking at is helping to bring credibility to the process and to drive the execution. Typically when you have a strategic process, a lot of times you fail not because you don't have a good plan, but because you fail to executive at the tempo or in a pace that you can, if you understand what I mean," Ngunze said.

He said KQ had "a good execution strategy," was "relentless" in its follow up and effective in managing its stakeholders.

Ngunze – who joined KQ in 2011 and was not there when KATAP was implemented – said he and his team had decided on the "bottom-up" ideation approach because "ideas for staff restructuring, cost optimisation and revenue rest among staff." He said of the 700 initiatives that were put through a funnel, the airline ended up focusing "on around 440 of them, and all of these were led by a team of people in different parts of the organisation."

He said that was done in order to ensure that they "involved as many people as possible and also celebrated their wins as part of that process."

Ngunze (2019) said by the time he stepped down as CEO in May 2017, they had achieved 75% of KQ's operational turnaround targets. Negotiations with aircraft lessors were concluded successfully, aircraft that KQ wanted to sell had been sold and those that it wanted to sub-lease had been sub-leased. Collectively, these efforts "took out $280 million worth of cost in terms of aircraft cost."

Mugo (2019), who worked closely with both Achola and Ngunze and reported first to Diaz and subsequently to Ngunze as CEO, said while Operation Pride's focus was internal, the externally-focused part of the strategy was the Capital Optimisation Plan (COP), which was known within KQ as Project Safari. Project Safari's primary aim, she said, was to "try and save the airline, without necessarily nationalising it."

While Operation Pride kicked off in 2015, Project Safari (or the COP) began towards the end of 2016. She said while it was initially hoped that Project Safari would take six months to complete, in the end it was concluded in November 2017.

Mugo (2019) said that, in essence, the COP was about the renegotiation of KQ's debt to foreign aircraft financiers and restructuring of KQ's debt of KSh20 billion to Kenyan banks. With the internal restructuring done, it then became possible for KQ to approach the banks.

She said the Kenyan Government was approached with a request for it to give KQ guarantees for the money owed to foreign banks, with that money turned into equity to increase the Government's shareholding. Mugo (2019) said although the Kenyan Government had never given any guarantees to the airline before, it "came on board very quickly and was happy to do it," and both the Ministers of Transport and of Finance supported the proposal, with the latter Minister subsequently chairing the COP Committee.

Former KQ Information Technology Director Kevin Kinyanjui (2019) said since KQ's privatisation in 1996, the Kenyan Government had "never guaranteed" any of KQ's loans, and the airline paid "full corporate tax just like any other private company" and enjoyed no special dispensation when it came to the fuel levy. "In fact," he said, "sometimes they probably apply the screws more on Kenya Airways as low-hanging fruit since they are operating out of Nairobi."

Mugo said KQ negotiated a loan repayment deal with the US EXIM Bank and got "concessions" from former majority shareholder KLM. However, the Kenyan banks were not happy with the proposed conversion of their loans into equity in KQ:

> *The banks were not very happy. We were telling them that we were going to turn their loans into equity, into a share that is not making money anyway. A lot of the work around negotiating that took place because the banks had been adamant that they do not want that deal. The options were either they go for that deal or we file for bankruptcy – and bankruptcy was never an option. Even the Government said it; it was never going to be an option. The part-option was to nationalise the airline and make it completely Government owned. For the banks, that was also a loss.*

Mugo said although the Kenyan banks "completely refused" and went to court, "eventually they came on board ... when the Government agreed to give them guarantees to guarantee the loans in exchange for equity." As a result, the Kenyan Government became the largest shareholder of the airline, with 50,1% equity, followed by the banks at 39% through a special purpose vehicle called KQ Lenders Company, and KLM with 7,95% (MarketScreener, 2020).

Limo Taboi (2019) said KLM was not keen to recapitalise the airline, hence it allowed its shareholding to be diluted from being the largest KQ Shareholder to being a minority Shareholder. He said "the KLM which had invested in Kenya Airways is not the KLM of today," pointing out that the Dutch airline had since merged with Air France to become Air France-KLM. Taboi (2019) believed that the current Air France-KLM leadership "no longer believes in this Africa partnership."

He said the original rationale for the deal was that KLM would bring traffic to Nairobi, with KQ then moving that traffic to onward destinations in Africa and that, likewise, KQ would move traffic to Amsterdam, where KLM would take passengers "further afield." However, the Dutch airline "had a lot of control over KQ" and had since established its own direct routes from Amsterdam to various destinations in Africa, such as Entebbe in Uganda, Kigali in Rwanda, and Dar-es-Salaam in Tanzanzia, in the process undermining KQ.

"Maybe these were things that Kenyans were not happy about because that was against the spirit of what was supposed to happen," Taboi (2019) said.

Bekele (2019) said KQ's privatisation which led to the KLM-KQ partnership held the African carrier back because "KLM made it a feeder airline." He said it seemed to have been the Dutch carrier's intention "to keep KQ as a regional airline that feeds into KLM."

Achola (2019) said KLM brought technical support and market access to KQ, whose staff members "either had a stint at KLM or had some form of training from KLM." He said there was "always the argument around whether the partnership was good for KQ." His own view, as former Acting Commercial Director, was that the Kenyan carrier "could have benefitted more from that joint venture, but I think we did not pull our weight enough."

Achola said the partnership was vital for KQ at the beginning because the airline was transitioning from being "a Government entity into a private entity," hence it needed to change "its outlook and the way it did things."

While he did not believe that KQ was short-changed, Achola (2019) said the airline had experienced "a bit of lethargy" and had not fully taken advantage of the partnership agreement with KLM, while the latter had done so.

Former Marketing Director Chris Diaz (2019) said the partnership with KLM enabled KQ to be a member of the Sky Team, and remains the only African airline to be a member of that global alliance. He said although it may not have been expressly captured in the Shareholders' Agreement, KLM was understood to have had a veto on some important decisions, such as aircraft acquisition and the appointment of a CEO.

"You see, the way the agreement was structured, because KLM was also the big brother, it became like a big brother-small brother situation. You know, when the big brother would say something, the small brother, out of respect, being smaller in terms of shareholding, would go along," Diaz (2019) said.

Although Project Safari's goal was reached, Mugo (2019) said the KQ team still had a lot of work to do: "The business needed to wake up and get aggressive in terms of looking for revenue. That hasn't happened, but then we were always very clear that because of where KQ had been, it was never going to be a sprint. It was going to be a marathon. Therefore, it was going to take time to get it out of the red."

Mugo said Project Safari involved a lot of travelling for Ngunze, who had to negotiate with Boeing and KQ aircraft lessors. She said his extensive foreign travels happened at the expense of day-to-day work at KQ, hence he decided to resign, with the Board retaining him as consultant on Operation Safari "until the end."

Mugo said Ngunze "left at a time when we wished we could clone him." She said the work that he was doing was "very important and took all his time, but then he also needed to run the business with the historical background of what had happened."

She said the success of Operation Pride and Project Safari was attributable to having had "a Board that woke up to the idea that we needed to change things" and to aggressive lobbying of the Kenyan Government that Ngunze and his team had done. She said KQ had hosted a summit on aviation ("the very first one in Kenya") to which Government representatives, Members of Parliament (MPs) and political parties were invited, and had taken MPs to Dubai, Singapore and Ethiopia "for them to see what a cohesive aviation sector looks like."

Mugo stressed the crucial role played by the KQ leadership to manage stakeholders and educate politicians about aviation and its contribution to the economy:

> We were at a point where the Government had woken up to what aviation is … The Government started to realise that even as part of their Vision 2030, there is really nothing that supported aviation. They talked about the airport. They didn't talk about the airline and what support it needed to succeed and to become part of aviation. For a very long time, aviation had been seen as a disjoined sector. Nobody was tying it together.
>
> Therefore, by the time we were doing the external turnaround, the Government was already awake to the fact that we needed to harness the entire aviation industry.

Mugo said KQ's hard lobbying paid off handsomely when Parliament approved the Government guarantees for the airline at 8pm on its last sitting before the August 2017 elections. She said Ngunze and his team had "worked very hard to make sure that we got the buy in because there was no guarantee that the new Government would approve the guarantees package."

Ngunze (2019) said while leadership stability is crucial during a turnaround, he had resigned when he did because he was confident that the operational restructuring "was reasonably well bedded in" and that KQ was "at a point where we could do the financial restructuring." He said the fact that the Board had asked him to stay on as Board Advisor to complete the financial restructuring in November 2017 – five months after his successor had started – was "a mark of confidence of what they saw around the financial restructuring."

Financial Times Correspondent John Aglionby (2016) reported in November 2016 that Ngunze's Operation Pride had begun "to bring results." He said after two years of record-breaking losses, the airline had reduced its net loss to KSh5 billion in the first half of the 2017 financial year, down from KSh12 billion in the previous year, and passenger numbers had risen from 68% to 71%.

However, KALPA continued to be very critical of Ngunze and Operation Pride, and demanded a change in leadership. KQ Chairman Dennis Awori resigned in October 2016, following a threatened indefinite strike by staff members, "particularly pilots," if he and Ngunze did not resign that month. Ngunze announced his resignation a month later (Aglionby, 2016).

Diaz (2019) confirmed that the pilots had embarked on a go-slow and threatened a strike if Awori and Ngunze were not removed. He said pilots would come to work but delay the aircraft from taking off on time, or call in sick at the last minute to cause delays.

Awori was succeeded by former Safaricom CEO Michael Joseph, while Ngunze was succeeded on 1 June 2017 by Polish Sebastian Mikosz, former CEO of Polish national carrier LOT Airlines.

In mid-November that year, KQ announced the successful conclusion of its US$2 billion debt restructuring, with the Kenyan Government having offered $750 million as guarantees for KQ's debt for 10 years. The deal diluted existing KQ Shareholders by 95% and the Nairobi Securities Exchange suspended the carrier's shares for two weeks. Ngunze said the debt restructuring would enable KQ to have time "to reshape the business to pay a bit more on the tail end" (Miriri, 2017).

"We will pay less now to allow us a bit of time to reshape the business to pay a bit more on the tail end," Ngunze said, referring to the debt restructuring (Miriri, 2017).

A high-level summary of KQ's 40-year history and milestones up to 2017 is captured in table 6.5 below.

Table 6.5: History and Milestones of KQ

History and Milestones

1977	1994	1996
• Establishment after breakup of EAC	• Commercialization	• Privatization

2003	2004	2009
• Acquisition of 49% stake in Precision Air	• Delivery of first Boeing 777 aircraft	• ISAGO certification (21st in the World and first in Africa

2010	2012	2014
• Granted full Sky Team membership	• First Airline in Africa to raise capital from investors across the globe through a rights issue	• KQ receives first Dreamliner B787-8 • Westgate Mall attack of 2013 paralyzes tourism sector • Outbreak of Ebola in West Africa

2015	2016	2017
• Posts record-breaking net loss of KES 26.2B	• Implementation of Operation Pride begins • KQ begins sale of aircraft	• KQ marks 40 years in the skies • Launches an unprecedented capital optimization plan dubbed Project Safari

Source: Apex Africa (2017)

Chapter Seven

KENYAN PARLIAMENT VOTES TO NATIONALIZE KENYA AIRWAYS

At a time when clamours were growing in South Africa – mostly from opposition parties like the Democratic Alliance and some influential voices in the media – for SAA to be offloaded, privatised or paired with a strategic equity partner, in Kenya the very opposite development was taking place: Kenya Airways (KQ), which was privatised in 1996 and listed on the stock exchange a year later, was facing the possibility of nationalisation!

Like SAA, the Kenyan national flag carrier was heavily indebted and was a source of much ridicule among a growing number of the business elite in that country. However, unlike SAA, KQ remained firmly under the control of both its Board of Directors and its Chief Executive Officer and his Top Management Team.

Announcing Sebastian Mikosz's appointment as new KQ CEO in May 2017, Board Chairman Michael Joseph expressed hope that Mikosz would return the airline to its former glory as "the 'Pride of Africa'." He pointed out that under Mikosz, LOT Polish Airlines had registered its first profit in years in 2014 and had since expanded significantly, carrying 1,5 million passengers more in 2016 (5,5 million) than it did in 2015 (4 million) (Aglionby, 2017).

Joseph said the KQ BoD had gone "through a long, exhaustive process, looking for someone with the character that would help us turn around KQ to become once more the pride of Africa." He said Mikosz was appointed to make KQ "a profitable airline and operationally a much bigger airline" (Wafula, 2017).

Business journalist Edwin Okoth (2019) said "many people saw the hands of Air France-KLM" in Mikosz's appointment.

In his first media interview 100 days into the job, Mikosz – who was described in the subsequent newspaper article as "a ruthless, no-nonsense executive" – said he had not moved to Kenya to be popular (Wafula, 2017).

Chairman Joseph sat in on that interview (Wafula, 2017).

As Wafula (2017) put it, Mikosz had brought along with him "a team of five Polish executives, all former colleagues at LOT Airlines, as wingmen for the task ahead." Although the decision for Mikosz to bring along his compatriots proved to be unpopular at KQ, Mikosz and the Board defended it.

The new CEO explained the decision thus: "When you know the airline industry, this is like music. You know a good musician that plays a violin in Chicago, so you bring him to Nairobi for a while. This is exactly what I did. The advantage of these guys is that I trust them and I have worked with them and they could hit the ground within three weeks" (Wafula, 2017).

He said he had not yet made up his mind about how long his trusted compatriots would remain with the airline. In the meantime, they were reported to have "joined the Transformation Office" to perform roles identical to those that they had played at LOT (Wafula, 2017).

During that interview, Mikosz informed Wafula (2017) that one of the hand-over reports he had found on his desk showed that KQ had lost "89 pilots and hundreds of engineers" to rival – mostly Middle Eastern – competitors, and had 434 pilots, 10 short of its requirement of 444. He said the Middle Eastern airlines were luring KQ pilots away with "tax-free jobs and loans" which the Kenyan national carrier could not match.

Mikosz said he had inherited "huge challenges in terms of operational excellence, on-time performance, service quality and luggage [tampering]." He said that he would be "open and transparent" as he implemented "some unpopular decisions," and would not pull back because he was employed "to deliver financial results" (Wafula, 2017).

While he was complimentary about the quality of staff members, some of whom had studied abroad and had "the same training and can do the same things that Ethiopian, LOT or United Airlines do," Mikosz was nevertheless worried about the organisational culture: "There is a response I get around here: 'this is the way we do it in Africa'. This is something I do not accept. There is no African way of doing things. There is a good way of doing things or a bad way of doing things" (Wafula, 2017)

Mikosz also bemoaned the existence of "a serious lack of trust, which makes delegation of duties very hard." He undertook to address that challenge and to build "a culture of accountability" (Wafula, 2017).

According to Wafula (2017), Mikosz was not afraid of making tough decisions or mistakes. "Not everyone likes you," Mikosz told Wafula (2017), "but I hope when the financial results come out, there will be a better understanding of [the fact that] this is what we needed to do. It does not mean that there will be no mistakes. Out of the 10 decisions that I am going to make, two might be a mistake."

Mikosz acknowledged that he had benefitted from "a tremendous amount of work" that was done by Ngunze, as part of Operation Pride, saying he had found KQ in the middle of a financial restructuring which was on the verge of being finalised, but said he would bring new ideas, revamp some projects and "close some of them." He said he did not plan to change the name of the restructuring programme because he believed that "Operation Pride is a good name for it" (Wafula, 2017).

Mikosz said he had found "about 650 different projects" that were part of Operation Pride, with some having been completed while others were still pending. Going forward, he said he would change from "a wider approach to focus on five or 10 projects" (Wafula, 2017).

According to Wafula (2017), Mikosz said a five-year plan which he had presented to the BoD was approved, through which he would "prove to the stakeholders that the team can deliver."

"I know that the turnaround will be made from numerous tough decisions, but we also have to compete. The market of Kenya Airways is not just in Kenya, but East Africa and everywhere in the world," Mikosz said (Wafula, 2017).

A week after Mikosz's first interview, four Senior Executives resigned from KQ, reportedly because of Mikosz's hiring of five Polish expatriates. These were Kinyanjui, Head of Internal Audit Chatherine Moraa, Head of Employee Relations Lucy Muhiu and Jet Fuel Procurement Officer Brian Mbuti, all of whom had been with KQ "for more than a dozen years and [had] made important contributions to the airline's operation" under Naikuni and Ngunze (Bekele, 2017).

Mikosz was quoted as saying he had employed compatriots Monka Kietyka-Michna, Edyta Kijewska-Teny, Magdalena Serwach, Marcin Celejewski and Micha Mierciak on three-month contracts not to replace Kenyan Executives, but "to work with the existing team to improve operations." He said the five were tasked with "implementing key objectives throughout the company, including creating, driving and guarding cohesion of KQ strategy" (Bekele, 2017).

Mikosz, who said his top priority was to make KQ Shareholders happy and "comfortable about the airline and their investment," said returning the airline to profitability would "require difficult decisions that might not please everyone" (Bekele, 2017).

At the end of August 2018, Mikosz announced that KQ's long-held ambition of having direct flights to the USA would be realised in October that year when the first non-stop flight to New York would take place, with three new routes likely to be launched to Europe, the Middle East and Asia the following year (Reuters, 2018).

Two years into his three-year contract, Mikosz informed KQ employees via a memorandum that he had decided to resign at the end of December 2019, six months before his contract was due to expire. He said that he had taken the decision on personal grounds and that the Board had accepted his resignation (Genga, 2019). A month later, he insisted to *International Aviation News*, on the sidelines of IATA's AGM in Seoul, South Korea, that he was leaving for personal reasons and that he was satisfied that KQ's turnaround strategy was progressing well.

Mikosz said he had changed KQ from being "an airline [in trouble] into an airline that is fixing itself," and added that he and his team had grown the network and that had allowed them to increase revenues. He said losses had been reduced, revenues increased by 8% to US\$1,1 billion and the loss was reduced by 18%, despite an increase in the fuel cost. Mikosz said although KQ was "going in the right direction," a turnaround such as the airline was involved in "takes a few years" (Bekele, 2019).

Mikosz said while KQ had leased its Boeing 787 and Boeing 777 aircraft to other operators, it had begun to work on a plan to acquire new narrow-body aircraft "because the company needs to grow" (Bekele, 2019).

Kinyanjui (2019) said when Mikosz joined KQ, he terminated McKinsey's contract "and asked them to leave" because he was confident that he would be able to turn the airline around "at a much lower commitment and cost."

Taboi (2019) said that, shortly after his arrival at KQ, Mikosz proposed that the airline be allowed to take over the running of Jomo Kenyatta International Airport (JKIA) after he had concluded "that KQ cannot compete" against airlines like EAL, RwandAir and Emirates which, together with their main airports, were owned by their respective governments which had adopted a Whole-of-State approach to aviation. He said EAL, for instance, was one of seven entities within the larger Ethiopian Airlines Group.

Taboi (2019) said the proposal, which would have seen the airline taking over the running of the profitable JKIA over a 25-year period, was "not quite that radical." However, it was not well received by the country's political leadership, and the Kenyan Parliament took the idea and it "ended up being a different process of nationalisation." He said once Parliament had submitted a report to the Cabinet, the latter would then "push, maybe through a Bill, to renationalise the airline to the early 1990s version."

Mikosz dismissed speculation that his resignation was triggered by the Government's rejection of his proposal that KQ be allowed to run the airport: "That is not true. I made the decision after discussing it with my family. We would be there for three full financial years. There is a good turnaround process going on. It is a good time for me and my family to leave. I am a turnaround specialist and I am leaving only five months ahead of my initial contract [is due to expire]. I think it is enough" (Bekele, 2019).

Mikosz informed *International Aviation News* that the Kenyan Parliament's Transport Committee was still evaluating his private-public partnership proposal to combine all national transport assets under one holding company. He told the publication that it was important to wait for the Committee to issue its report (Bekele, 2019).

A month later, the Kenyan Parliament voted to nationalise KQ "to save it from mounting debts." That followed the Transport Committee's rejection of Mikosz's proposal for KQ to take over the running of JKIA (which has annual revenues of KSh12 billion, half of which is profit) "to boost its revenue" (Reuters, 2019) and its subsequent recommendation – which was debated by the Kenyan Parliament on 18 June 2019 – for the airline's nationalisation (Reuters, 2019).

Transport Committee Chairman David Pkosing said it would take 21 months for the Government to take full control of KQ and 18 months to buy out minority Shareholders at an estimated cost of KSh800 million. He said Air France-KLM would have the option of selling its equity to the Kenyan Government and staying on as a technical partner to KQ (Reuters, 2019).

Pkosing said the balance sheet of the new aviation holding company would be healthier than KQ's alone and would allow the airline to negotiate aircraft leases based on a reduced risk profile (Reuters, 2019).

The recommendation from the Transport Committee, which was approved by Parliament, proposed the setting up of an aviation holding company with four subsidiaries, with KQ and JKIA being among them. The holding company would then be given tax concessions "for a period to be determined" and be exempted from paying excise duty on all goods, including jet fuel (Reuters, 2019). That way KQ, which is more expensive than its competitors, thus "forcing price-sensitive passengers through hubs like Addis Ababa and Kigali," would be able to reduce its prices and be more competitive (Reuters, 2019).

Joseph welcomed the outcome of the vote, saying "nationalisation is what is necessary to compete on a level playing field; it is not what we want, but what we need." He said the airline planned to purchase "nearly 40 additional planes," in addition to its 41, if it can get "the right financial structure" in order to open new routes in an effort to increase profits (Reuters, 2019).

However, Joseph also cautioned that KQ would have to "be run in a commercial way" and avoid having a Board packed "with politically-connected individuals" (Collins, 2019).

In November 2019, Joseph said he would need KSh45 billion to save KQ, describing nationalisation – which he said would not save the airline – as "a charade" (Onyango, 2019).

"Give me $450 million and that is what I need … then we do not need to go through this charade of nationalisation. We will have enough resources on which to grow and change the future of the airline," Joseph said during a TV interview (Onyango, 2019).

He also warned, when appearing before the National Assembly Transport Committee, that KQ would face imminent collapse if the restructure was not concluded within "the next six months." He said if that time frame was not achieved, the Board would be forced to "consider measures that are not going to be very pleasant" (Onyango, 2019).

"The current financial situation of KQ is quite critical and if we know there is going to be a time line, then we can proceed with some form of planning, but right now we have no time line. We do not know when this process (of nationalisation) is going to end. We have seen the result of the Privately Initiated Investment Proposal, which was abandoned," Joseph said (Onyango, 2019).

Speaking in her capacity as Principal Secretary of the Department of Transport, KQ Board Member Esther Koimett said the Government would draw up an implementation plan with clear time lines (Reuters, 2019). She later undertook that by 20 December 2019 the Government would have appointed a transaction expert to draw up an implementation plan that would stipulate clear time lines (Onyango, 2019).

"The Government," she said, "is keen to take a consolidated view of aviation assets of the country in order to make sure they work in a coherent and efficient way to support the Nairobi aviation hub" (Reuters, 2019).

In an interview two months before his exit from KQ, Mikosz hinted at the possibility of politics having got in the way of his running of the airline (Kamau, 2019):

> It (running KQ) came at an extremely high personal cost. It was much higher than I thought. The restructuring of an airline like this is also an energy killer. It sucks all the energy. There were very difficult moments.
>
> I was not hired to attract political attention, but I ended up doing it. With time, my mandate changed from restructuring an airline to include making a case for the change of the airline's mandate. I was hired to restructure the airline, but ended up showing that the airline cannot be restructured if we do not change the environment. Then, of course, you will find people who have made the company toxic when they start attacking you and not your decisions. Maybe I should have been tougher, but I believe I was tough.

He undertook to use his last two months in the job "to prove that KQ is moving in the right direction," saying he was not "walking away a bitter man." However, Kamau (2019) observed that his tenure as CEO had been "nothing short of underwhelming," adding that he was leaving the airline "in no better shape than he found it." His departure came after a net loss of KSh8,56 billion for the six months to June 2019, which compared unfavourably to the KSh4 billion lost during the same period the previous year (Kamau, 2019).

According to Kamau (2019), one of the reasons that Mikosz's Privately Initiated Investment Proposal PIIP) to Kenya Airports Authority, which would have seen the airline running JKIA, was rejected was that, in addition to making losses, KQ was a private company while the former entity is State owned.

Kamau (2019) said Mikosz's "biggest achievement at KQ" was the launch of the airline's direct flights to New York in October 2018, which the out-going CEO felt was "a critical investment" that would, over time, "enhance Kenya as a continental aviation hub." During the interview, Mikosz said the Nairobi-New York route had already attracted a growing number of East African passengers who were taking advantage of the reduced flying time.

However, interview participants like Taboi (2019), Bekele (2019), Mugo (2019), Okoth (2019) and Carol Warui (2019) – who was a public relations consultant to KQ in the run-up to the launch of the New York flight – revealed that what was meant to be a daily flight soon changed to be a thrice-a-week service, which was subsequently scaled back to once a week. Warui (2019) said a mere month after the launch of the inaugural flight, KQ had "reduced by about 10 flights for the month."

In fact, Bekele (2019) described the introduction of the loss-making New York route as yet another KQ attempt to imitate EAL, which had started its own New York route "a few years before."

"When you start a long-haul flight, you should be very, very, very careful. Once you start it, you cannot simply cancel flights because you lose your customers. You have to fly even if you have 10 or 20 passengers on a big plane," Bekele (2019) said.

Writer and researcher Morris Kiruga (2019) said even a once-a-week flight to the US was "too much" when one considered that "Kenyans can't even get US visas frequently" and that "every country except Burundi and South Sudan" in East Africa has its own airline which offers competition to KQ, with governments in those countries investing in airline infrastructure. He said the preceding four years before the New York flight were "very stressful" for Kenya Civil Aviation Authority and Kenya Airports Authority, which had to comply with various US Federal Aviation Authority requirements before direct flights could be allowed from Nairobi.

Former KQ Marketing Director Chris Diaz (2019) said JKIA had to get a Category 1 status for KQ to be able to fly from there directly to New York, and that achieving that goal was "a long process."

Mikosz said among his "three major successes" in the job was having "changed the mindset about KQ as a dying company, despite major financial challenges we continue to operate under." Nationalisation, he said, was the only way KQ would regain its status as "the Pride of Africa." That way, the carrier's mandate would change from a focus on generating returns for Shareholders to being "a strategic asset that plays a bigger role in the economy" and which enhances Nairobi as an aviation hub (Kamau, 2019).

He said it was important for KQ to continue with "what we have started" and that "a political decision" was made to change its mandate (Kamau, 2019).

According to Kamau (2019), at the time KQ's flight schedule required 600 pilots, but the airline had only 414 pilots in its employ, and its route network and fleet acquisition plan for 2019-2020 indicated that it would need 537 pilots by December 2020 if it was "to operate optimally." However, KALPA remained opposed to the employment of foreign pilots for the Boeing 737 aircraft, arguing that foreign recruitment contravenes their collective bargaining agreement. Instead, they wanted Kenyan pilots employed (Collins, 2019).

While flight cancellations reportedly cost KQ an estimated US$50 million a year because of a shortage of pilots, KALPA General Secretary, Captain Murithi Nyagah, said pilots were being blamed unfairly for the airline's poor performance. He blamed "a toxic working environment" for the departure of 150 pilots over the preceding three years to join competitors like EAL, RwandAir, Qatar Airways and Emirates (Collins, 2019).

"It's a diversion tactic to start creating other fires so then people forget about the real issues at hand. Pilots are not part of the problem within this airline; it is the Management we need to ask questions of. Even if pilots were to work for free, they would still make a loss," Nyagah said (Collins, 2019).

As Mikosz got ready to leave Kenya in mid-December, the KQ BoD announced the appointment of JamboJet CEO Allan Kilavuka as Acting CEO with effect from 1 January 2020, pending the appointment of a permanent CEO (Obura, 2019). A LCC, JamboJet is KQ's subsidiary.

Two months later, Kilavuka was confirmed in the position with effect from 1 April 2020 (Kenya Airways, 2020), while Mikosz joined IATA as Senior Vice President for Member and External Relations with effect from 1 June 2020 (Africa Aviation, 2020).

In mid-December, the KQ BoD issued a profit warning for the financial year ending on 31 December 2019, saying that the airline's earnings would be "lower by at least 25%" than earnings reported in 2018. That meant that KQ's loss would rise by at least 35%, from KSh7,3 billion a year earlier to KSh9 billion in December 2019. This, wrote Victor Amadala (2019) in *The Star*, was "despite conducting a massive restructuring plan in 2017 that was expected to shore up the firm's bottom line in five years."

Amadala (2019) said it was the second year in a row that KQ had issued a profit warning, after the 2018 loss had risen by 15% (from KSh5,1 billion in 2017 to KSh5,9 billion in 2018).

In the statement issued by the BoD, Chairman Joseph said although KQ had realised improved revenue, profitability continued to be elusive as a result of increased competition (Amadala, 2019).

For the full 2019 financial year, during which Mikosz was in charge, KQ lost KSh12,98 billion (Maina, 2020; Ombok, 2020).

Highlights of KQ's financial performance between 2015 and 2018 are shown in tables 7.1 and 7.2 below.

On 24 January 2020, the Kenya Association of Trade Agents (KATA) issued a public statement welcoming the pending nationalisation of KQ and urging the airline to focus on improving customer service. KATA CEO Agnes Mucuha said the airline's continued existence was important for Kenya's economy, adding that, if KQ were liquidated, "travel would become very expensive due to decreased load capacity and increased hub operating costs" at JKIA (KATA, 2020).

"Consequently, the Nairobi hub would experience decreased passenger demand for travel, and in the long run the Nairobi hub would cease being attractive in the region," Mucuha said (KATA, 2020)

She added that it had taken the Ugandan Government, following Parliament's intervention in that country, to revive Uganda Airlines after 20 years.

In a memorandum to employees in the last week of January 2020, Kilavuka announced a restructuring plan, as part of Operation Pride, which would include staff retrenchments. He said the restructuring would be handled humanely and in consultation with affected stakeholders in accordance with Kenyan labour law (*Business Daily*, 2020; Ikade, 2020).

"Roles will change; some may be enriched while others are merged. I also want to be clear that as difficult as it is, some roles will disappear altogether, resulting in redundancies," Kilavuka wrote (*Business Daily*, 2020).

The Kenya Aviation Workers Union (KAWU) said it was not officially informed about the impending retrenchments, and called on Kilavuka not to proceed with the exercise until correct lay-off procedures were followed. In a letter to Kilavula, KAWU Secretary-General Moss Ndiema blamed KQ's problems on Management, alleged mismanagement and corruption and said laying employees off would not address the airline's challenges (*Business Daily*, 2020; Ikade, 2020).

Table 7.1: KQ's financial highlights between 2015 and 2017:

PERFORMANCE HIGHLIGHTS
(CONTINUED)

Three year summary of financial highlights

Financial highlights

	2017		2016		2015	
	KShs. Million	US$ Million	KShs. Million	US$ Million	KShs. Million	US$ Million
Turnover						
Passenger	89,845	890.5	94,801	**943.1**	90,408	1,015.3
Freight & mail	7,220	71.6	8,897	**88.5**	9,783	109.9
Handling	2,150	21.2	2,338	**23.3**	2,080	23.4
Other	7,062	70.0	10,122	**100.7**	7,890	88.6
Total	**106,277**	**1,053.3**	**116,158**	**1,155.6**	**110,161**	**1,237.1**
Direct expenditure	(65,356)	(647.7)	(67,861)	**(675.1)**	(76,059)	(854.1)
Fleet ownership costs	(15,524)	(153.9)	(29,578)	**(294.3)**	(25,932)	(291.2)
Overheads	(24,500)	(242.8)	(22,812)	**(226.9)**	(24,503)	(275.2)
Operating loss	**897**	**8.9**	**(4,093)**	**(40.7)**	**(16,333)**	**(183.4)**
Operating margin%	**0.8%**		**(3.5%)**		**(14.8%)**	
Net finance costs	(7,330)	(72.7)	(7,039)	**(70.0)**	(4,581)	(51.4)
Fuel hedge derivatives	312	3.1	(4,155)	**(41.3)**	(7,452)	(83.7)
Other costs	(4,081)	(40.4)	(10,812)	**(107.6)**	(1,346)	(15.1)
Loss before tax	**(10,202)**	**(101.1)**	**(26,099)**	**(259.6)**	**(29,712)**	**(333.7)**
Income tax (expense)/credit	**(5)**	**(0.1)**	(126)	(1.3)	3,969	44.6
Loss for the year	**(10,207)**	**(101.2)**	**(26,225)**	**(260.9)**	**(25,743)**	**(289.1)**
Loss after tax margin%	**(9.6%)**		**(22.6%)**		**(23.4%)**	

Source: KQ Annual Report 2017

However, Taboi (2019) said KQ pilots had negotiated "some very nice perks when the airline was weak," and now doggedly resisted efforts to review those benefits. He said both Mikosz and Joseph often complained about the pilots being lazy, earning "Emirates salaries but not wanting to fly like Emirates pilots." He said while EAL could set the salaries of its pilots, "say everybody will earn $2000 a month and you fly," things were different in Kenya, where things could not be run "by fiat."

"We are not a country where the President can pick up the phone and order things around," said Taboi. "I think that has actually been the challenge that the President had in his early years when he would have seen, in his younger years, past Presidents exercising fiat decisions, and when he came in he found things different. It's a bit like [US President] Donald Trump. Here a judge can over-rule a President."

Taboi was not happy with the airline's impending nationalisation. He said there was not "a very good record of airlines being well run by the State," and was worried about the possibility of "Ministers appointing home boys and home girls to the Boards." He said that used to happen in the 1980s when KQ had two Airbus aircraft and "the President would take them for a trip."

Table 7.2: KQ's financial highlights between 2017 and 2018:

THREE YEAR SUMMARY OF PERFORMANCE HIGHLIGHTS

Financial Highlights

The Group	Dec-18		9 months ended Dec-17 (Restated)		Mar-17	
	KShs. Million	US$ Million	KShs. Million	US$ Million	KShs. Million	US$ Million
Turnover						
Passenger	95,187	939.4	67,613	653.9	89,845	890.5
Freight & Mail	8,468	83.6	5,544	53.6	7,220	71.6
Handling	2,193	21.6	1,546	15.0	2,150	21.3
Other	8,337	82.3	6,096	58.9	7,062	70.0
Total	114,185	1,126.9	80,799	781.4	106,277	1,053.3
Direct Expenditure	(75,030)	(740.4)	(51,719)	(500.2)	(65,356)	(647.7)
Fleet Ownership Costs	(18,929)	(186.8)	(12,535)	(121.2)	(15,524)	(153.9)
Overheads	(20,909)	(206.3)	(15,537)	(150.3)	(24,500)	(242.8)
Operating Profit (Loss)	(683)	(6.7)	1,008	9.7	897	8.9
Operating Margin%	(0.6%)		1.2%		0.8%	
Net Finance Costs	(5,017)	(49.5)	(4,891)	(47.6)	(7,330)	(72.7)
Fuel Hedge Derivatives	-	-	-	-	312	3.1
Other Costs	(1,888)	(18.6)	(2,423)	(23.1)	(4,081)	(40.4)
Loss before tax	(7,588)	(74.9)	(6,306)	(61.0)	(10,202)	(101.1)
Income tax credit / (expense)	30	0.3	(112)	(1.1)	246	2.4
Loss for the year	(7,558)	(74.6)	(6,418)	(62.1)	(9,956)	(98.7)
Loss after Tax margin%	(6.6%)		(7.9%)		(9.4%)	

Source: KQ Annual Report 2018

Taboi said Mikosz's view, which he shared himself, was that KQ could not grow "unless it sits with the Government." However, Taboi (2019) said he thought Mikosz had in mind a situation where the Government would "support the airline the way that other countries are supporting their airlines," but not "full nationalisation."

His understanding, he said, was that Mikosz and Joseph were worried about the degree to which the Kenyan Government has liberally given landing rights to foreign airlines in Nairobi, at KQ's expense. That, he said, was the genesis of Mikosz's thinking that having KQ in control of JKIA would enable the airline to be part of those decisions and help it to improve its balance sheet.

"Mikosz was saying that when another airline comes to Kenya, Kenya is an open space. You can come to Nairobi and you can negotiate with whoever you want. You can say Swissport is the cheapest baggage handler; you give it to Swissport. You give Astral the right to your flowers, and the airline does not benefit. I think this is part of the things they are talking about: some parity and decision making in terms of who gets here," Taboi said.

He said although KQ was on the verge of being nationalised at the time of our interview in September 2019, as he understood Mikosz's and Joseph's position, "nationalisation was not their goal." Instead, they had in mind greater Government involvement, through equity in the airline, with KQ being de-listed.

"Honestly, I think it would be good for the airline to be de-listed. It pains me as an investor, but this model worked from 1996 to 2006. They are not on the same plane. I have tried to look at the annual reports of all the African airlines: Egypt Air, Maroc, Rwanda, Ethiopian, Madagascar, Mauritius. It can work, but again who is the airline serving? Make decisions," Taboi said.

He said Mikosz did not want to be part of an airline which was not growing and which "was not going anywhere."

Taboi said unlike in neighbouring Ethiopia and Rwanda, where the State is a much more potent force in the economy, Kenya was riven with private vested interests which competed aggressively for the kind of opportunities that would be enjoyed by the airlines in those countries:

> *You know, Kenya is not Ethiopia; Kenya is not Rwanda. There are private airlines and private aircraft. There are investors, some of whom are Government officials, former Government officials who are big in airport handling. They are big in airfreight businesses. They are big in hoteling.*
>
> *So, whereas EAL is able to build two hotels in Addis Ababa and push everybody there, in Kenya there are many competing interests. A lot of big things which potentially are revenue in another country are not accessible to KQ here. Cargo is very big for them in those countries, whereas cargo is very liberal in Kenya. If you see the number of [Boeing] 747s which come to Nairobi at night, it's Saudi Air, it's Astral, Singapore Airways, etc, which don't even fly passengers to Nairobi. They do cargo.*
>
> *There is a small town called Eldoret, which is about 320km from here; we have a small airport there served by the KQ subsidiary. These are propeller planes, but you have 747s which come there: Emirates, KLM, Egypt Air, Etihad, and they are bringing in goods to the country. KQ cannot get into that business.*

Taboi said there was a widespread perception – which remained unproved – in Kenya that high-level politicians were involved in some under-handed deals at KQ through, among other things, the leasing of aircraft and ownership of hotels where KQ passengers whose flights were delayed or cancelled were booked. He said there were Kenyans "who still believe that by nationalising the airline, you are going to bury all the past problems."

That meant that the airline's alleged corruption problems would worsen, but have little chance of ever being exposed.

Taboi said KQ's new aircraft were "owned by a different company and leased by KQ." He said the airline's explanation had always been that it was involved in an inter-trade tripartite agreement with, say, JP Morgan and/or City Bank: "You buy this plane, you register it in this name and you pay the loan over 10 years. After 10 years when it is paid off, you transfer it into your books. You see, it's a common thing, but they keep having to go back and explain every year."

Kinyanjui (2019) confirmed that, before KQ's privatisation in 1996, "there was a lot of Government interference and all kinds of shenanigans, with aircraft even taken away for VIPs for all kinds of State trips and whatever." He said that had ended with privatisation, with KQ being run commercially since then. He said former CEO Naikuni was a courageous man who was "known to many parties in the country, including in the Government," and he had resisted any Government attempts to interfere.

Kinyanjui said nationalisation would work only if the Government viewed KQ in the same way that it considered it "as an enabler, [like] infrastructure and other things that are done by government." That way, the Government would have to "sustain the airline no matter what and keep pumping money into it."

However, Kinyanjui saw a disconnect between KQ as a network carrier, which sought to "connect Africa to the world," as opposed to being an airline whose purpose was to connect only Kenya to the world.

Former KQ Communications Manager Wanjiku Mugo (2019) said it would be important for the Government to look at KQ "as a business that is critical for the economy of the country" and to run it professionally, "not nationalise it, but run it in the same way that Ethiopian Airlines is run." She said although EAL was not a private company, it was run like an independent business. She said the Government would have to harmonise the Kenyan aviation sector and place it in a position where it could compete.

Mugo advocated KQ's de-listing, but having the airline run professionally and the haemorrhaging of value stopped. She said that during the partnership with KLM, "every Commercial Director was from Europe and everywhere," hence they did not understand the African market.

"I like the idea that the Government is the biggest Shareholder. Now the Government is able to use its muscle to push some things. Just think about that capital optimisation with the banks. Let's look at Ethiopian Airlines. They don't run it like a State-owned company, but it is heavily State supported," Mugo said.

She said while at Bole International Airport in Addis Ababa EAL was the ground handler, "regardless of which airline you are," at JKIA there were "about four or five ground handlers." That business "which should be going to your national airline is divided into four," she said.

She said the Rwandan Government was protecting its national flag carrier in the same way that EAL was protected in Ethiopia.

Mugo said while the KQ leadership should be concerned about bucking the global trend of formerly State-owned airlines being privatised, it also needed to accept that "when you have reached rock bottom, you might have to go back home to start your journey." She expressed hope that the airline would not be nationalised "for a very long time," but that it would "get its act together" soon for it to be re-privatised:

> *Probably, re-privatisation will require a different skill set because there is also a belief that when it was privatised, KQ got a raw deal from KLM. It has always been hamstrung by the fact that that agreement was not favourable to KQ. If anything, it killed the airline.*
>
> *If it gets re-nationalised and re-privatised, they should probably nationalise it for a period of five years. Like I have already said, it should not become like a Government Department, but it should have Government as a big brother and be run professionally, turn its fortunes around and then look for an investor, probably another airline. Probably KLM will come back with Air France, the bigger brother. Probably look at Asia. Is there an opportunity for an airline in Asia or the Americas that can come in?*

Achola (2019) stressed that, although the Kenyan Government has always been one of KQ's Shareholders, it had "never given money or guarantees" to the airline – "until now when things started really, really going south." He said if the Government chooses to nationalise KQ, "then the airline becomes a public good, in which case it does not need to make money." That would require that the Government would have to "keep pumping money in the name of the airline contributing to the GDP."

While he believed that nationalisation of the airline was "not the right thing to do," Achola said the chances of that happening were quite high because both Parliament "and the guys who are looking for short cuts are pushing for it." The latter reference was to out-going KQ CEO Mikosz and Chairman Joseph.

He said "if a previous set of Management did not do what they were supposed to do," then the right thing to do would have been to replace them with "another set of people to run a profitable airline."

Achola preferred a situation where the Government provided the airline with support through fuel levy and airport concessions. He feared that KQ's nationalisation would make the situation worse because "now you have all sorts of cartels, with tendering interests and employment," which would deprive the CEO of autonomy. In such a situation, he said, "Management will be anybody from God-knows-where and meritocracy will disappear."

"My view is that nationalisation is a wrong thing to do. Nationalisation is not a solution," Achola said firmly.

However, he believed that nationalisation was *fait accompli* because "the current Management has run out of ideas:"

> *Their best idea was to kidnap the airport. They have run out of ideas to grow the top line. The only thing they can think about is to clap and say 'yeah, yeah, we now support nationalisation'. From what I have seen, the pilots' union, for some reason, now supports it. Initially they did not support it. They did not support it because part of the condition was that the Collective Bargaining Agreements (CBA) will be renegotiated. My little understanding of the law is that you cannot take away what you have given by way of a CBA. So, I think they have now sort of settled that idea.*

Achola said in order to come up with a lasting solution for KQ, it was important that the genesis of the airline's problems was understood in the proper context. He said it was important to look at the numbers: "They need to understand the movements. They need to understand, for example, in 2013-2014, what happened to revenue? They need to understand in 2013-2014, what happened to costs? They need to understand what the events were around those years. If people understand some of those things, they can then begin to understand really what ailed the airline," he said.

Ngunze (2019) said he thought that Mikosz and Joseph were not "talking about nationalisation as we understand it," but might be meaning "something else." He chose to refrain from commenting until such time that there was clarity on what they had in mind.

However, he said being privately owned had enabled KQ to "make decisions much easier, much quicker." He said it was "always very important that you have that flexibility," adding that KQ enjoyed it, notwithstanding the fact that the Government was one of its Shareholders.

He expressed the hope that, "if the construct is going to be different" following the Government's majority control, KQ would still "be flexible enough to be able to do its business, without having to be bogged down by the Government public procurement Acts and things like that."

"I rather suspect that those things will be addressed as part of whatever action is being taken today," he said.

Ngunze said KQ remained a commercial airline, despite the capital restructuring which had seen the Government assuming majority control. He said while the airline might be achieving a Government agenda by driving tourism, that was not its "first priority." The carrier continued to consider every route "on its own viability."

Taboi said KQ was not in charge of the way forward because "nationalisation was not their goal." His sense was that all that the airline wanted to accomplish was a de-listing.

Kiruga said nationalising KQ would kill the airline, rather than save it. He said a nationalised KQ would "be a bad headache, a terrible idea actually because we don't have the culture to allow the airline to run as is."

Kiruga said those who looked at EAL and marvelled at what "100% Government ownership can do for you" conveniently ignored the fact that Ethiopia had "a unique culture and a unique history." He said Ethiopia had gone "the Singapore way" and given autonomy to EAL.

"We want to copy Ethiopia, but we are not looking at the kind of culture which this thing is based on, the fact that Ethiopian Airlines comes from a primarily Ethiopian perspective. The Ethiopian perspective of the world is very unique. It was just their New Year this week. Ethiopia is unique in very many ways," Kiruga cautioned.

He said if KQ's nationalisation went ahead, it would be very important to get someone who could run the airline with "full autonomy because an airline does not need Government interference, an airline does not need small, messy things like being involved in Government corruption."

Kenyan-educated University of Sudan academic Athuai Rehan (2019) said a Government-owned KQ would be exposed to much interference. He said continuation of a private-public partnership model would be preferable because the airline would "be messed up" if it were fully owned by the Government.

However, Diaz (2019) was enthusiastically in favour of KQ's nationalisation. He said the decision was "very good" because the Government had already given guarantees worth over KSh77 billion, which meant that about half of the airline was already Government owned. He said that nationalisation would enable the Government to play "a very big role for getting approvals for opening new routes" such as the one between Nairobi and Beijing. That, he said, was because the opening of new routes was a consequence of government-to-government agreements because airlines can't fly over any country without that government's approval.

"Support of the Government is 75% success of the airline becoming profitable, because the Government also gives you the business of passengers. Once a directive has been given that everyone needs to fly Kenya Airways, whether you like it or not, you have to be patriotic. Our revenues definitely went up," Diaz said.

He said having the support of the other governments to whose countries an airline flies also ensures that an airline gets good slot timings and good schedules, and when it launches new routes it gets "Government people creating a lot of attention in the media."

He said the goodwill of flying from country to country, as a result of the government-to-government agreements, was very important.

However, Diaz (2019) cautioned that the Yamassoukrou Decision's open-skies policy would make it difficult – if not impossible – for African governments to protect their national carriers against fellow African airlines.

By September 2020, the Kenyan Parliament was still debating the 2020 National Aviation Management Bill, whose passage into law would pave the way for the airline's nationalisation (Namu & Oniango, 2020).

KQ's consolidated income statement going back to 2012, the last year when the airline recorded a profit, and containing an estimate for the last three years, follows in table 7.3 below.

Table 7.3: KQ's consolidated income statement between 2012 and 2020

Consolidated Income Statement	FY12 KES M	FY13 KES M	FY14 KES M	FY15 KES M	FY16 KES M	FY17 KES M	FY18F KES M	FY19F KES M	FY20F KES M
Revenue	107,897	98,860	106,009	110,161	116,158	106,277	99,900	92,907	85,475
Direct costs	(77,217)	(77,225)	(75,268)	(76,059)	(67,861)	(65,356)	(61,439)	(56,209)	(51,712)
Fleet ownership costs	(9,970)	(11,178)	(12,490)	(25,932)	(29,578)	(15,524)	(16,983)	(14,401)	(13,676)
Gross profit	20,710	10,457	18,251	8,170	18,719	25,397	21,479	22,298	20,087
Overheads	(19,404)	(18,643)	(20,972)	(24,503)	(22,812)	(24,500)	(19,481)	(18,117)	(16,668)
Operating profit/ (loss)	1,306	(9,012)	(2,721)	(16,333)	(4,093)	897	1,998	4,181	3,419
Net finance costs	(1,097)	(486)	(1,601)	(4,581)	(7,039)	(7,330)	(7,185)	(7,216)	(7,184)
Other gains & losses	(1,019)	(1,700)	(1,511)	(1,346)	(10,812)	(4,081)	(2,997)	(2,787)	(2,564)
Profit/ (loss) before income tax	2,146	(10,826)	(4,861)	(29,712)	(26,099)	(10,202)	(7,884)	(6,008)	(6,201)
Income tax (expense)/ credit	(486)	2,962	1,479	3,969	(126)	(5)	-	-	-
Profit for the year	1,660	(7,864)	(3,382)	(25,743)	(26,225)	(10,207)	(7,884)	(6,008)	(6,201)
EPS (KES)	3.58	(6.35)	(2.25)	(17.21)	(17.53)	(6.82)	(5.27)	(4.02)	(4.14)

Source: Company Filings, ApexAfrica Estimates

Source: Apex Africa Capital Limited, October 2017

Chapter Eight

KENYA AIRWAYS AND THE ROLE OF LEADERSHIP

The Probe Commission that was established to investigate why a State-owned KQ performed so poorly had not only recommended commercialisation of the airline, but it had also stressed that KQ could not succeed commercially "unless its State ownership was ended." That marked the beginning of preparations for KQ's privatisation, and of an era when "the best and ablest people in the country" were appointed to run the airline (Debrah & Toroitich, 2005).

That led to the appointment of former Speedwing lead consultant Brian Davies as CEO, with him being given "complete freedom" to review and restructure KQ as he saw fit (Debrah & Toroitich, 2005). Following the death of KQ Chairman Phillip Ndegwa, who was a former CEO of Kenya Commercial Bank, former Cabinet Minister Isaac Omolo Okero succeeded him as Board Chairman in February 1996 (Kenya Cabinet, 2018) and remained Chairman until August 2005 (Njoka, 2005). He was succeeded by Evanson Mwaniki, who was Chairman until October 2015 (*Business Daily*, 2015).

Following Mwaniki's resignation, Toyota Kenya Chairman Dennis Awori stepped in as KQ Chairman for a year, before he was replaced with former Safaricom CEO Michael Joseph in 2016. Joseph's initial three-year term was renewed in June 2019 (*Business Daily*, 2019).

A former Permanent Secretary for Transport (Kiruga, 2019), Titus Naikuni was appointed KQ CEO in January 2003, replacing then out-going Brian Pestbury (Ouma, 2003). He remained in the position until 31 October 2014 (*Business Daily*, 2014) when he was succeeded by Ngunze in November 2014. Ngunze, who stepped down in May 2017, was succeeded by Polish Sebastian Mikosz in June 2017, who also resigned in December 2019 before the expiry of his three-year contract (Volkov, 2017).

Therefore, Okero and Mwaniki each served nine and 10 years respectively as KQ Board Chairperson, while Naikuni – who worked with both Chairpersons – ran the airline for just under 11 years. Ngunze was in the hot seat for two years and Mikosz for two-and-a-half years.

Table 8.1 below shows the leadership picture at KQ between 2003 and 2020.

According to former KQ Information Technology Director Kevin Kinyanjui (2019), Naikuni had "very sufficient authority" to run the airline. He said although the Kenyan Government and KLM had "quite a lot of influence in how the airline was run" because they each had two seats on the BoD, the Board "let Management run the ship." Kinyanjui said Management did a good job and the Board and Shareholders lent their support.

Kinyanjui said Naikuni, who was a great communicator with enviable leadership skills, enjoyed the full confidence of the BoD. He said during the years when he worked at the airline, the CEO of KLM sat on the KQ Board, took "a lot of interest" in the airline and had "a lot of confidence in Titus as the Chief Executive."

"And for us in Management, we enjoyed that because I think you would never have dreamt of interacting with somebody who was running such a large airline, to take an interest in us. So, that was a great honour, a great privilege. These are memories that many people treasure even until now," Kinyanjui said.

Table 8.1: Leadership Stability at KQ between 2003 and 2020:

DATE	2003-2015	2015-2017	2017-2019	2020 - ?
CEO	Titus Naikuni	Mbuvi Ngunze / Sebastian Mikosz	Sebastian Mikosz	Allan Kilavuka (Acting CEO from 1 January 2020, and appointed to the role from 1 June 2020)
CHAIRMAN	Omolo Okero / Evanson Mwaniki	Dennis Awori / Michael Joseph	Michael Joseph	Michael Joseph

Source: Own Composition

He said Naikuni and his Top Management Team (TMT) were fully responsible for making all decisions related to route entries and exits, "enabled by a very deep analysis by the Network Planning Department." He said the Naikuni-led Executive Committee insisted on only profitable routes being flown, or those which had an overall positive contribution to the airline's network.

Kinyanjui said the fact that Naikuni was well known "to many parties in the country and in Government" made it easy for him to resist any political attempts, were they ever to have been made, to interfere in the running of the airline.

Former KQ Strategy Director Thomas Omondi Achola also said the Board was "not micro-managing Management," and that the latter was responsible for making most of the commercial decisions, "with the support of the Board:"

He said decisions on which routes to fly or exit were "110% Management decisions:"

> *I cannot remember any time – and I was in Senior Management for the entire period, 13 years and five months – when we got instructions from the Board that we should operate here. Never. Even when the President went somewhere like Japan and signed a bilateral agreement, of course the Government will come back and say "you guys, we have signed a bilateral agreement with Japan; Kenya Airways should start flying there," we said "that's very nice; we will do a business case analysis." Often the business case did not fly.*

Ngunze (2019) said "there is no question" that power vested in him as CEO and that he was not expected to involve the Board "in driving Management execution." However, he said it was important to understand that "situations are fluid" and that, when a company is "in a fairly precarious situation, the Board tends to be – and was – involved in a more detailed basis than you would expect it to be in understanding the situation where we were because the Board needs to feel the confidence that you are executing the strategy according to where you are."

He said during the Capital Optimisation Process (COP) or Project Safari, the KQ Board met "more regularly" in order to drive alignment and ensure that decisions were made "in a faster pace." However, he said there were moments when he felt that the Board was getting too involved: "There were times, of course, along the way where I felt that the Board was probably a bit too much in the detail, but that was to be expected."

Ngunze said the main KQ Shareholders were briefed "on a regular basis" on Project Safari in order to obtain their buy-in because KQ needed their support in the financial restructuring, and not on Project Pride, which was an operational restructuring. He said while it was difficult to get that Shareholder support in the beginning, the Shareholders supported KQ "very strongly on the financial restructuring once they understood that the operational restructuring was taking place."

Ngunze agreed that leadership stability was crucial during the implementation of a turnaround strategy, pointing out that he had "stayed on until the financial restructuring was completed." Operational restructuring, he said, "never ends."

Kaleyesus Bekele (2019) said Ngunze had tried his best to implement his turnaround strategy, but was not given time to do so because pilots and employees would "often demand a salary increment at a time when the airline was making a loss."

Carol Warui (2019) said "the right leadership can change a lot of things," and added that Ngunze "was committed to the cause" and offered just such leadership.

Writer and researcher Morris Kiruga (2019) said most of the challenges confronting KQ in the last five years had "nothing to do with its decisions in the last five years," but dated back to bad decisions made during the Naikuni era.

While Mikosz listed the opening of the New York route as one of his successes during his tenure, the consensus view among KQ observers in Kenya, but especially participants in this research, was that he had not made much difference at the East African airline. Others blame him for having brought KQ to the verge of nationalisation.

"A man from Europe might not have understood these constituencies as well as he needed to or as quickly as he needed to in order to do something about them. He didn't get the backing he required to follow through," Nairobi-based financial analyst Aly-Kahn Satchu told *Africa Business Magazine* (Collins, 2019).

Long-time KQ observer and Shareholder Limo Taboi (2019) thought Mikosz had supported the introduction of the New York route as some form of quid pro quo for Government support with the restructuring. He said the New York route had been "talked about" even during Naikuni's tenure, but he got a sense that the CEO at the time "did not see the numbers there or did not want to make a commitment." However, Taboi said the subsequent conclusion of code-share agreements between KQ and Delta Airways was likely to open up "a lot more opportunities" for the Kenyan flag carrier.

Both he and former KQ Communications Manager Wanjiku Mugo (2019) said the New York route enabled KQ to claim, in its marketing, that it serves "all the UN cities: New York, Rome, Geneva and Nairobi." Two United Nations agencies, the UN Environment Programme and the UN Human Settlements Programme, are headquartered in the Kenyan capital.

Kiruga (2019) also described the introduction of the Nairobi-New York direct flight as having been "a political decision."

Kaleyesus Bekele (2019) said Parliament's rejection of Mikosz's Privately Initiated Investment Proposal (PIIP), which would have seen KQ run JKIA, followed lobbying by Kenya Airports Authority (KAA) employees. That, he said, left Mikosz frustrated and believing that the airline would then "face a heavy challenge."

Kiruga said he was surprised that Mikosz, who was brought to KQ on the strength that he was "a turnaround maestro," had remained in his job for as long as he did. He said he would have asked Mikosz a few questions, had he had an opportunity to meet him: "I would have asked: 'Do you know Kenya? Do you know Nairobi?' It's not just a pit of vipers; it's realising how powerless you are against people you can't see, like faceless people who don't talk to you directly."

Saying she was responding to the question "very diplomatically," Mugo (2019) – who worked with Mikosz for five months – said she had tried in vain to coach Mikosz about what he needed to do to get the best out of his Kenyan colleagues and to alert him to how Kenyans react to situations. Describing Kenyans as being "very passive-aggressive," Mugo said the expatriate CEO was unable to win over the KQ team and the Kenyan public.

She added:

> *When we got a new CEO – bless him – he had [aviation] background. He didn't have the historical context of what had happened. I feel like he didn't have passion for the brand.*
>
> *I do know that when he came in, he had some ideas. You could tell that he had been fed and given what to expect, but the guy is from Poland. I do not think that he had a lot of exposure to what to expect when he came to Africa, and it was very clear. He wasn't necessarily very open. His management style was also very different, and he came at a time when KQ had had these two CEOs who are Kenyans, who are African, so they understood the nuances.*
>
> *I think it took him … I don't know if he actually got there, but I think it took him quite a while to just even understand the cultural nuances.*

Mugo (2019) said she did not believe that Mikosz had succeeded at KQ. She said he had come with certain expectations "and did not expect the kind of push-back that he received both internally and externally." She said that push-back extended to Members of Parliament, who had summoned him to meetings, as well as the Kenyan Government.

"A lot of things happened. I think, for him as a person, it's not a good thing that you were looking at something you expected to succeed at and you were not making any inroads," Mugo said.

Public relations consultant Carol Warui (2019) was very critical of Mikosz and the way he related to his Kenyan colleagues, but chose not to go on record with her assessment, hence it is not included here.

Kiruga said he thought that Mikosz had had "an experience of a lifetime" in Nairobi. He said the man had been handed "a completely broken thing and was told to fix it, but he didn't have the view and didn't have anyone to help him to do it." He said Mikosz had failed to understand "that the people he has been talking to are deal makers:"

> *Nairobi is run on deals most of the time. It's run on the understanding that I will do something for you and you will do something for me. They had an expectation of him to perform magic, but I don't think he had an expectation of them. He might have said "I want full autonomy," but it's a different thing to say it and another one*

to live it and actually make decisions that you believe are right for the business, even when you are fighting with the Board.

Mugo shared the widely-held view that Joseph, who is celebrated for having built Safaricom into a major telecommunications company in Kenya, may have been too dominant for Miskoz. Mugo (2019) said Joseph's previous success was "buoyed by the fact that Safaricom happened at a time when it was just the right time, so Safaricom was going to succeed any way." She said she got the impression that the complexities of chairing the KQ Board had come "as a shocker" to Joseph.

Mugo said the fact that Mikosz "didn't get up to speed fast enough" opened room for Joseph to be more operationally involved in the business.

"I think that KQ failed to get Sebastian to get up to speed. We warned that we were seeing Joseph in the office more often. I guess another decision that informed the fact that he [Joseph] needed to be the public face is that Sebastian was an unknown and he was a more well-known face that had been successful in the past. He was the assurance to the public that things would work out," Mugo said.

She said that Joseph was "a very strong character" whose presence at KQ was "a bit intimidating even to staff." She said he came across "as being aloof, with not an inkling of understanding the problems."

Kiruga said for most Kenyans, the choice of Joseph as KQ Board Chairman was "a really good decision" because they had fond memories of him building the Safaricom brand. However, he said Joseph was "a builder" and "a hands-on boss" who was "very abrasive and not good at culture." He said in their choice of Joseph, KQ Shareholders had felt that the airline needed "a firm hand to make sure that stuff goes right, but there is no goodwill."

However, Kiruga felt that Joseph's appointment as Board Chairman in 2016 was "wrong for that time because he is self-admittedly a pushy guy." He said the airline found itself at the time "being run by two different white men, with a very different set of experiences:" Joseph was a start-up man who had built Kenya's biggest company, while Mikosz was "actually an airline man." He said even when the two men gave media interviews, Joseph did most of the talking.

"I don't know many companies where the CEO and the Board Chairperson do almost all interviews together. And, you know, the Board Chairman talks more than the CEO," Kiruga said.

Mugo said her friends and former colleagues at KQ informed her that staff morale was low, and this contrasted with the fact that there was "so much optimism" when Operation Pride and Project Safari started. She said that was the situation that Mikosz's successor would inherit and of which he would have to be "very aware."

Kinyanjui said Mikosz's challenge was complicated by the return of some of the aircraft which had been sub-leased to other airlines over a three-year period, which meant that KQ again had "a lot of extra capacity, without markets to take the aircraft into."

In an implied criticism of Mikosz and his leadership style, Kinyanjui said he saw "a very difficult time for the airline again until it gets what I would call the right leadership with pragmatism, being realistic but involving and getting everybody committed to rally behind the right cause." He said it was obvious, judging by "the kind of ways and noise we hear from the airline," that Mikosz and the KQ staff were "not on the same page."

His assessment was that Mikosz's tenure had had "limited success:"

> *You know, if your pilots, your cabin crew or people in ground services – which is the biggest department in operations – don't pull their weight, you will have very limited, if any, success at all. It takes a special kind of man or woman to be able to sometimes deal with things at that level. But, as they always say, with hindsight, it's always like 20-20 vision. Sometimes the things recommended over and over again are the ones that just need the courage to be able to get done.*

Ngunze refrained from expressing an opinion on his successor's tenure, saying he would not "opine because it's important that once you finish a job, you leave."

However, Achola (2019) was not similarly restrained. Firstly, Achola said all the challenges that were cited by Mikosz and Joseph to be confronting KQ (restrictive collective bargaining agreements, lack of Government subsidies and concessions, as well as the liberal granting of landing rights to foreign airlines) and, therefore, to be grounds for the airline's nationalisation were not new. He said the previous KQ leadership had raised those issues over the years, but they suddenly appeared to be gaining traction "because it's a different set of human beings who raise them."

Achola worked with Mikosz from June 2017 until February 2018.

He said he had learned, both from working with McKinsey and from personal experience, that the organisational health index (OHI) had a big bearing on the degree of success that was possible during a turnaround strategy implementation. He said that, from following media reports, it was easy to tell that the KQ Management was "all over the place fighting, fighting the pilots, fighting the other union."

Achola said 70% of the chances of "any transformation succeeding" depended on the OHI. He said the biggest chance of success in a service industry like aviation was through happy employees who felt "appreciated, valued and listened to." He said even if such employees did not feel appropriately remunerated, they would "still be part of the turnaround."

Achola said when they were implementing Operation Pride under Ngunze, they never increased employees' salaries, but engaged with labour. Although they had their own "share of fights with the trade unions" – which ended up "going on strike and exit[ing] some of the Directors" – things did not "get as ugly as they are now in the press."

He said based on both media reports and interactions with people still in the airline's employ, he felt that KQ had become "less consultative." He said eight out of every 10 KQ employees to whom he spoke were complaining "about the working environment, processes not being followed, policies and procedures [not being] followed and not being listened to." He said although he had not heard Mikosz's and Joseph's sides of the story, from a distance his "sense is that the soul of the airline is dead."

"When people are completely disengaged, then you get what you get, what we are getting today. That, for me, is the big thing.

"The aircraft are still there. They are still as new; they have not changed much. The routes are the same, pretty much. The [new] routes that the airline opened are maybe just four, if I remember correctly. The operating procedures and manuals are still the same. What has changed is the leadership," Achola said.

He said although the disconnect with employees had begun earlier – when consequences were visited upon those who were not pulling their weight – and was "sort of repaired," the chasm had since widened during the Mikosz-Joseph era. Therefore, there was a bigger challenge to ensure that the next KQ CEO would have to be somebody who had a different approach to managing people:

> *The next CEO, because the current CEO is leaving, has to be like an Imam or a Rabbi or a Bishop or a Pastor, whatever religion you profess. They have to be actually someone who will heal the soul of the airline. They have to be a people's person. They have to realise that leadership is a conversation. They have to realise that the responsibility of the leader is to create a conversation.*
>
> *They have to realise that the responsibility of the leader is to create loyal followers – and loyalty is not sycophancy, in my view. Loyalty has something to do with the things I talked about, people who share vision, people who feel valued, people who are very clear about where the company is going and people who are very clear about what their role is.*
>
> *Today my sense is, when I meet KQ people, none of those things I have talked about exists. When I picture it, I think Management is on its own and the troops are on their own. I don't know where the two groups are going to end, where they are going. Your guess is as good as mine.*

Achola said during the first "couple of months" of working together, he did not have "serious issues with the current CEO and the current Chairman," but differences developed over time. He said when he was still with KQ, he represented the company in talks with labour, with which KQ had "very, very many runs-in," but it "never got as ugly as it has now, at least not in the press."

He said despite their differences with the unions, KQ had "never on a single day gone to the press and blamed the union for our problems." Instead, they had told the unions "to their faces that some of the issues we were facing in the airline they had contributed to, but they are not the only problem."

He added that when he was still with the airline, they operated "for a whole year without what I would call goodwill" on the part of the pilots in 2015-16, but the airline still made an operating profit. He said that in 2019 KQ was cancelling flights because the pilots had "just decided to operate their normal hours" because they felt unappreciated.

Achola said when he looked at KQ's financial performance, he appreciated the pilots' view that even if they worked for free, the airline would still not have made an operating profit. Therefore, he said, it was neither the pilots nor "the other staff" who were creating problems at the airline. He said on occasions when there was no captain and a flight had to take off within "the next one hour," he could call pilots who were willing to "leave a wedding ceremony (not theirs), to leave a birthday party for their child or to leave an anniversary and come and operate the flight."

Reiterating his view that, based on what he saw when he looked at KQ and what he heard from those who still worked there when he interacted with them, "the soul of the airline is dead," Achola said he was confident that even if the carrier did not have a CEO and was run by a Workers' Council representing the different departments, it could "run on its own:"

> They don't need a busy body creating chaos and messing up the place. If they are to get a CEO, they should get someone who knows what they are doing.
>
> I have so much confidence in the men and women that I left behind – apart from the new ones, whom I don't know. That airline has a very competent workforce. Even the pilots who are being accused of sabotaging the airline, I worked with them for seven years. They are men and women who I know have more than 40 000 leave days. So, for me, when I hear people talking about pilots, pilots, yes, we had our share of fights, but these are guys who are putting in a lot of sacrifice for their airline.

Kiruga shared Achola's characterisation of KQ as being soul-less: "With the kind of [financial] books it has, with the kind of alleged corruption and internal issues, I don't feel like KQ has a soul."

He said that as far as he could tell, there was no shared vision at the airline, with people "pulling for themselves for now [and] staff members being scared." The only shared vision that he could make out, he said, was "probably the Government line that we need to save this company."

"Its problem is that it has no soul. Everyone would jump ship if they had an option, like no-one actually cares about Kenya Airways, except for the Government which needs to come up with the money to look after its assets and, I guess, the people who play with its shares on the stock exchange. There is no goodwill," said Kiruga.

Bekele (2019) said in order to improve the chances of KQ's success, it would be important for the new CEO to be given "ample time because you cannot see the results of a turnaround strategy immediately." He said it was also crucial that the BoD was made up of professional individuals, and not "all those political appointees."

Bekele added:

> They should also be cost prudent. I know it's not easy to reduce their costs; it's a big challenge, but they need to convince labour. The Government should convince the employees that if this airline dies, everybody loses. They can't lose their national pride. It's the Pride of Africa, as they claim. They need to save the airline from going bankrupt. The national interest should be a priority, and not discuss salaries now. This is not time to discuss salaries. Unless the employees and the Management work together, they cannot take the airline back to profitability. Never.

He added that KQ would have to revise or suspend its loss-making long flights and strengthen its route network in Africa, until it has stabilised.

Other Views on Kenya and KQ

A number of the interview participants during this research held a particular view of Kenya and how business is done in that country. Generally, there was a strongly-held view – that was not backed up by any fact – that business decisions like the purchase of aircraft and other supplies inevitably involve some forms of corruption like kick-backs, often involving both those at the business concerned and, without exception, people in political life or leadership.

These not-so-veiled allegations have been levelled against KQ and its leadership, but have not been captured in this chapter because they are not the subject of this study and they are unsubstantiated. However, those allegations' existence is being reflected here for the purpose of completeness.

Referring to Project Mawingu, for instance, business journalist Edwin Okoth (2019) made the following throw-away remark: "You know, in Kenya when you see a big project like that, you don't just look at it and believe that they are buying aircraft."

He added: "It could be some people made good money, and then they don't care what happens after that. It's the same thing that happened with our railways; the big railway we are building, because we didn't think about the business aspect. What are the revenues we are expecting? We just say 'hey, let's build a railway', and in the process some billionaires cropped up. I still believe there were some billionaires who cropped up in the KQ turnaround plan that never worked."

Okoth said whenever there is "a foreign power commanding a lot of influence in Kenyan business, normally you will find a local secret handler, mostly in the name of a big politician or some connected family."

This view is supported by Taboi's (2019) contention that there was widespread perception in Kenya that high-level politicians were involved in some under-handed deals at KQ through, among other things, the leasing of aircraft and ownership of hotels where the airline's passengers whose flights were delayed or cancelled were booked. He said there were Kenyans "who still believe that by nationalising the airline, you are going to bury all the past problems." That meant that the airline's alleged corruption problems would worsen, but have little chance of ever being exposed.

Taboi (2019) said KQ's new aircraft were "owned by a different company and leased by KQ." He said the airline's explanation had always been that it was involved in an inter-trade tripartite agreement with, say, JP Morgan and/or City Bank.

Said Taboi (2019):

> *The KQ leadership has never shaken off the perception that they are people who are milking the airline. Many Kenyans – even in Parliament – think so. They think that Government officials and airline officials are involved in under-hand deals. They have never shaken off this perception that they lease aircraft even from politicians. Over the years, there have always been perceptions of under-hand dealings in terms of corruption.*

Mugo (2019) bemoaned the existence of "a bit of mismanagement," which was "not necessarily as big as people think it is." She attributed this "small mismanagement" to the absence of internal checks and balances.

Okoth (2019) said although KQ has been privatised since 1996, there were still many ordinary Kenyans who perceived the airline as being Government owned. He said whenever he reported unfavourably on the airline, he received calls from members of the public asking him: "Why are you killing our airline? Why do you write bad things about our airline?"

He said the Kenyan Government had given an order that all Government officials had to fly KQ, but the instruction could not be enforced because the airline is generally more expensive to fly than its competitors.

Asked what he would do to ensure a successful KQ turnaround, Taboi said he would go back to Operation Pride and go through the many proposals – many of which he liked – which had come from employees. He would pursue the *matatu* (kombi taxi) model, which would see KQ involved in frequent continental flights.

"They were saying you are serving the African market. Africa is a *matatu* market. When you go to West Africa, people travel with a lot of luggage. You must have maximum luggage capacity. People are going to China to buy things. You must have freight underpinning your passenger decisions," he said.

The challenge, he said, was that the Embraer aircraft, which was ideal for the load factor and the distances involved, did not have sufficient luggage capacity.

Kenyan-educated Sudanese academic Athuai Rehan (2019), who was a lecturer at the University of Sudan at the time of the interview, said both RwandAir and the recently-launched Uganda Airlines were regional competitors to KQ, in addition to the larger EAL. To that list, Bekele added Tanzania, which has also recently revived its national airline.

Rehan (2019) said that left the Kenyan carrier in a position where it would have to "do leaps of change, even in terms of the operations system," or risk going down.

Achola sad some of the things which slowed them down during the implementation of Operation Pride were outside of their control. One of the identified courses of action, for instance, was the need to sign more joint-venture agreements with other airlines. However, progress depended on the willingness of the other airlines to conclude such agreements.

Achola said another challenge was reluctance by some "employees who are completely disconnected" to make required sacrifices, and other Senior Executives who resisted efforts to lay off members of their teams "when they think that they need their people, even when you, as a third party, can see that certain functions we can do away with." Next were reluctance by suppliers to extend KQ's credit terms and failure by the Government to extend concessions to the airline on the basis that it was privately owned.

Kiruga (2019) made the observation that the privatisation of KQ and the companies which met the same fate in the mid-1990s was not decided upon by the Kenyan Government. Instead, privatisation was imposed on Kenya by donors and foreign lenders, as part of a structural adjustment programme (SAP). He said all of those companies, except for Safaricom, had fallen on hard times, with Mumias Sugar Company now "completely gone, eaten by the same things that have eaten the airline."

Kiruga (2019) said at the time of the privatisation, Kenya was broke and going through multi-party elections "on a proper mass" and the Cold War had just ended.

"I don't judge history; history just happens. But now that we seem to have an in-grown need to save Kenya Airways – and this conversation has been going on for years – because it's costing us money, we have a chance to build something. You know, we can rebuild the whole thing, brand-wise," he said.

Kinyanjui (2019) said KQ's challenges were complicated by the fact that some of the aircraft which the airline had sub-leased for three years had since been returned to it, at a time when it already had extra capacity, "without markets to take the aircraft into."

He added that any East African airline was "geographically very well placed" to facilitate travel from West Africa to Central Africa and the rest of the continent, including to the Middle East. However, he said competition with Middle Eastern carriers was tough because those airlines were "fully sponsored by their governments" and are likely to be enjoying a major advantage on fuel cost. As a result, competition for the West African market against Middle Eastern airlines from oil-rich countries was very tough.

Kinyanjui (2019) said even European carriers had been relatively stagnant and "pushed completely to the wall" by Middle Eastern carriers in the past five years.

Asked what he would do to improve the chances of successfully turning KQ around if he had the authority to do so, former KQ Marketing Director Chris Diaz (2019) said he would make sure that customer experience was consistent and that the airline's on-time departure record was addressed, in addition to improving ancillary revenues and having "the best, all-round, cohesive leadership team that is focused on their deliverables and innovation." He would also improve relations with the Government to increase the chances of KQ enjoying rebates on landing charges.

Diaz said while Ethiopian travel agents were required, by law, to ensure that 75% of the tickets sold are booked on EAL, in Kenya travel agents booked seats on KQ only 35% of the time, with the other 65% booked on foreign airlines. Asked why that was the case, he said foreign competitors most likely had "better incentives" in place for the travel agents and were "better priced because they have economies of scale, bigger fleet and favourable fuel prices, among other things." Emirates, he said, had the added advantage that Dubai was "by far one of the best hubs in the world for lay-over connectivity to the rest of the world."

Diaz said when he joined KQ, they started a LCC called JamboJet, which has since become profitable. That decision enabled KQ to remain "a flagship carrier with very strong business class and economy on every aircraft." In addition to flying domestically, JamboJet had since introduced flights to Juba, South Sudan.

Chapter Nine

"OUR HANDS ARE TIED BEHIND OUR BACKS, BUT WE ARE EXPECTED TO WIN A CHAMPIONSHIP"

In order to get the best possible and most comprehensive picture of South African Airways, I spoke to a broad spectrum of stakeholders. These ranged from current and former members of the SAA Top Management Team (TMT), current and former Board Members, current and former Shareholder representatives, through labour representatives and independent experts.

Doing so, as a form of data triangulation, was very important in order to ensure that one has as comprehensive a picture of the airline and its challenges as possible. Altogether, I interviewed 38 individuals on SAA, with the vast majority of them being South Africans. Doing so gave me the kind of unprecedented insights into the airline which have made it possible for me to have full appreciation of the kind of challenges which have beset SAA over the years and, more importantly, to develop a framework for the successful implementation of turnaround strategies in the public sector.

A total of 37 interviews were conducted in person between January 2019 and November of the same year. The vast majority were conducted between January and July 2019, while three took place in November. Among the participants:

- 14 were individuals who were current or former members of the airline's Top Management Team (TMT), with five of them having been former Chief Executive Officers (one of them, Vuyani Jarana, was still CEO at the time);
- nine were Board Members (two of whom had previously served as Senior Executives);
- eight were former Shareholder Representatives (one of whom is still in that position, four were former Cabinet Ministers and one was a former Director-General in the Department of Finance);
- four were employee representatives;
- two were independent aviation experts;
- one was a strategy scholar; and
- one was a long-time SAA observer.

The 38th interview, with Ethiopian Cabinet Minister and academic Dr Arkebe Oqubay, took place in July 2020.

In order to enable the reader to have better appreciation of the strong feelings of the various interview participants, stakeholders' views are captured at length. That enriches the research in a manner that makes "rich, thick descriptions" (Creswell & Miller, 2000) possible and serves the purpose of contextually-informed triangulation advocated by Roth and Mehta (2002:163).

Two of the participants had served as both Senior Executives and subsequently as Board Members on the airline.

The views of the SAA TMT are reflected in this chapter; followed by those of SAA Board Members, employee representatives, Shareholder representatives and independent experts in the subsequent chapters.

Between 1994 and 2020, SAA has had 14 CEOs, half of whom were Acting CEOs (Nico Bezuidenhout had two separate acting stints). At the dawn of democracy, Mike Myburgh was at the helm of the airline. In June 1998 he took early retirement "as part of a management reshuffle which brought turnaround specialist Coleman Andrews" to SAA (Birns, 1999). Upon his departure, Andrews was replaced by Andre Viljoen.

Khaya Ngqula joined the airline in October 2004 and was placed on special leave in February 2009 and was succeeded, in an acting capacity, by former Chief Financial Officer Chris Smythe. In February 2010, Sizakele Mzimela was appointed CEO and remained in the role for two years. In 2013, then Chairman Vuyisile Kona was appointed Acting CEO, and had the briefest stay in the position. Monwabisi Kalawe took over as CEO in the same year, but was out of the job the following year, replaced by Bezuidenhout in his first stint as Acting CEO.

The following year (2015) was the most unstable in the history of the airline – it had three Acting CEOs: Thuli Mpshe, Bezuidenhout and Musa Zwane followed each other in quick succession as Acting CEOs, but Zwane managed to remain in the position until Vuyani Jarana's appointment as CEO on 1 November 2017. When Jarana resigned abruptly at the end of May 2019, General Manager: Commercial Zukisa Ramasia was appointed Acting CEO, but Acting Chairperson Thandeka Mgoduso – who assumed that position when SAA Chairperson JB Magwaza resigned two months after Jarana had thrown in the towel (Mailovich, 2019) –   was appointed Executive Chairperson a few months later (Skiti, 2019).

During this period, the longest time served by an SAA CEO in office was about four-and-a-half years. That distinction goes to Ngqula, followed by Mzimela with two-and-a-half years.

SAA's leadership instability is illustrated in figure 9.1 below and tables 9.1 and 9.2 below.

Between 2012 and 2017, Dudu Myeni – who was in the role for almost six years – was the longest-serving Board Chairperson, followed by Professor Jakes Gerwel, who served five years in the role. Myeni's tenure as SAA Chairperson was also the most unstable for the airline when it comes to its Executive Management.

Zwane (2019) compared the leadership instability at SAA to what obtains at Ethiopian Airlines. The latter, he said, enjoyed "stability of leadership:" in the past 35 years, EAL has had three CEOs, with the current incumbent, Tewolde Gebremariam, having been with the airline for many years before he became CEO. As a result, Gebremariam "had the knowledge of the business and knowledge of how you get the business running profitably."

Having been an Executive Vice-President for Strategic Alliances, Global Sales and Revenue Management at SAA during Andrews's tenure, Bonang Mohale subsequently served on the airline's Board of Directors under Cheryl Carolus.

He said one of SAA's problems was the frequent changes of Ministers responsible for the airline, which resulted in lack of continuity, "where each Minister that comes into the portfolio feels compelled to re-invent the wheel and start afresh." He said that, unlike in the private sector, new Ministers tended "to come with [their] own strategy, [their] own DG, with [their] own executives."

Figure 9.1: SAA leadership instability

For a long period of time SAA has experienced instability at Board and Executive level negatively impacting on company performance

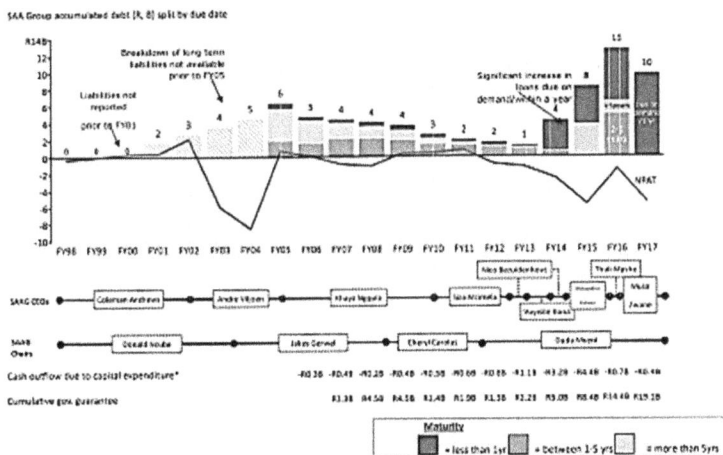

Source: South African Airways (2017)

Table 9.1: SAA leadership changes between 2007 and 2017

Date	2004 - 2007	2008	2009	2010	2011	2012	2013	2014	2015	2016	2017
CEO	Khaya Ngqula	Khaya Ngqula	Khaya Ngqula /Chris Smythe (A)	Chris Smythe (A)/ Siza Mzimela	Siza Mzimela	Siza Mzimela	Vuyisile Kona (A)/ Monwabisi Kalawe	Monwabisi Kalawe/ Nico Bezuindenhout (A)	Thuli Mpshe (A)/ Nico Bezuindhout (A)/ Musa Zwane (A)	Musa Zwane (A)	Musa Zwane (A)/ Vuyani Jarana
Chair	Jakes Gerwel	Jakes Gerwel	Jakes Gerwel	Cheryl Carolus	Cheryl Carolus/ Vuyisile Kona	Dudu Myeni	Dudu Myeni	Dudu Myeni	Dudu Myeni	Dudu Myeni	Dudu Myeni/ JB Magwaza

Source: Solidarity Leadership Institute, amended (2017)

Table 9.2: SAA leadership changes between 2018 and 2020

DATE	2018	2019	2020
CEO	Vuyani Jarana	Vuyani Jarana / Zukisa Ramasia (A)	Zukisa Ramasia
CHAIR	JB Magwaza	JB Magwaza / Thandeka Mgoduso (A)	Thandeka Mgoduso

Source: Own Composition

"Had we been more thoughtful about SAA in the last 25 years, we would have produced at least four CEOs who know how to run a profitable SAA and when Kenya Airways and Ethiopian Airlines are looking for a CEO, they would have found it very easy to come and headhunt from South Africa. Where we are now, unfortunately there has not been a single CEO of SAA that has completed a five-year term; not a single one since we became free. In fact, it's as ridiculous as having had 12 CEOs in 10 years," Mohale (2019) said.

He said the same applied at power utility Eskom, which he estimated had had 10 CEOs in 10 years. Mohale (2019) described the situation as "a tragedy."

Former SAA CEO Vuyani Jarana (2019) – who was still CEO when he was interviewed – said one of the key problems was the apparent belief within the Government that a CEO appointed during a particular Minister's tenure is "that Minister's person." He attributed that to the culture of the governing ANC where, "when a Minister changes, [the new Minister] looks at you through the eyes of the previous Minister."

"The problem with the ANC," Jarana (2019) said, "is that even at its best form, when a Minister is changed, when the next Minister comes in it is as if he is from another party. Now, you can see that flowing through to SOCs. All of a sudden, you've got a position where people are not sure about whether they should trust you or not. The styles are very different."

Mohale concurred. He said: "Primarily, our politicians still think that whenever I get appointed a Minister, I must come with my own DG. That's a problem. Number two, they think that whenever I get into an entity, I must have a CEO that I trust, who is beholden to me, not to South Africa Inc."

Mohale said while the PFMA describes fiduciary responsibility as acting in the best interest of the entity and all its stakeholders and not just that of the Shareholder or the employees, Ministers simply ignored that. The problem, then, has been politicians saying "'but I want my own CEO', not the most competent, the most effective and efficient."

Former Department of Public Enterprises Deputy Director-General Matsietsi Mokholo (2019) said frequent Management changes were a big problem at SAA. To eradicate them, she said it was important to "insulate Management from the political aspect." She said when the President appointed a new Minister of Public Enterprises, it was important to "insulate the entities to say that the Minister cannot come and change the Management." She said it was important that Ministers were confined to "political oversight."

Mokholo said that leadership instability at SAA dated back to the days of Andrews and Ngqula and now needed to be addressed. She said it was important to appoint onto the SAA Board and the TMT "people who understand the business," with some who also have an understanding of how the Government works. She said leadership came with "strong governance tools and instruments," hence it was important for SAA to be allowed space and given time and "adequate support."

Mokholo (2019) said she had raised her concerns, in the form of "a very difficult presentation" to the Cabinet, on 1-2 November 2016:

> *Among the others, the one thing that I left the Cabinet with was that the problems of the State-owned companies are not by design, all of them; others are by default. One of the things by default is how the DPE was created. The DPE does nothing but oversight of entities. So, you created a Department that does nothing. If the Board is doing its job and the Executives are doing their job, frankly, what do we do?*
>
> *I used to be self-critical. I used to say but, guys, let's be critical as DPE officials: what is our role? That structure itself needs to be re-looked at because it adds to the kind of pyramid and bureaucracy. If we deal with that structural*

institutional model, then you are able to start addressing that political interference and insulation.

Mohale said the post-apartheid Government had not thought carefully about how it wanted to use SOEs "as engines to drive economic growth and to drive transformation." He said while the Government's policy – "on paper' – was to create black industrialists through the Broad-Based Black Economic Empowerment policy, "it's not unfair to say the ANC-led Government has killed more black Executives and more black businesses than the whole of apartheid put together."

"And I make that statement provocatively and deliberately," Mohale said.

He said the country had not succeeded, during the first 25 years of democracy, to eradicate the legacy of apartheid, and that State Capture during "the nine wasted years" when Jacob Zuma was in power had taken the country back 20 years. He said "over the past four years" (2014-2017), an estimated R1,5 trillion was lost through State Capture, with a leakage of about R100 billion per annum from the economy "over the last nine years."

Mohale said the problem confronting SAA and other SOCs was the absence of role clarity, specifically when it came to the roles of the Shareholder, the Boards and the Executives. The main challenge, he said, was that "the Shareholder does not know when to get out of the way." He elaborated:

> *First of all, what is the ideal? The ideal is that, if you are a Shareholder, you must appoint a Board that you trust and get out of the way. The Board's role is to understand the Shareholder Compact; what is expected of us? Having understood that, they go and find a CEO who is up to the task – and get out of the way. The CEO's role is to understand this contract that he or she has with the Board and then go and find a team that will help him or her to execute on this timeously, effectively and efficiently. Therefore, the role of the CEO becomes, number one, to create a coherent team; number two, to create clarity; number three, to communicate clarity; number four, to reiterate clarity. If we did only that, I think most of these SOEs would be incredible engines for employment, but also for some amazing economic activity.*
>
> *What did we find at SAA? At SAA we found Ministers who did not even read the Constitution about executive duties and, therefore, what's required of them. Number two, [we found Ministers] who thought that their job is to ensure that their families are looked after first and foremost, not the greatest asset, in the case of SAA, which is employees. At that time, we were talking about 11 000 employees. [We found a situation] where a Minister sees it fit to e-mail you a CV of his wife to say this CV is appropriately suited [for the*

person] to be the VP of Marketing at SAA; and the DG would do the same, and you are caught in the middle.

Mohale said SOEs were also confused about their reporting lines. This related to whether they reported to the Shareholder Minister, the Minister's Department through the Director-General or the relevant Parliamentary Portfolio Committee.

Based on his own experience as CEO, Jarana (2019) said "the mind of the Shareholder is the single biggest obstacle to turning around the SOCs, especially SAA."

Mohale (2019) said it was important to ensure that SOCs' mandates were clear and that good corporate governance, which was "really about the separation of ownership from control," was applied. He said the problem was compounded by the Portfolio Committee on Public Enterprises, which also happened to believe that its members were "our bosses." He said during his time as an Executive at SAA, DPE Director-General Sivi Gounden also believed that "he was our boss."

"So, as the CEO – I worked for Coleman Andrews at the time – who were you reporting to? To Sivi? The Parliamentary Portfolio Committee? The Board? Saki [Macozoma]? Or to the Minister? That confusion was really quite stark. While accepting that the primary role of any successful CEO is stakeholder management, but the stakeholders must not be talking at cross purposes, and they must not be diametrically opposed as to the mandate," Mohale said.

He said he also found the Government itself to be confused about the role that they expected SOEs to play:

They would say these SOEs – Denel, SAA, SABC, etc. – are refusing to transform; therefore, let's go and find a black person who can run them because s/he is one of our own. They find a black person to get in there on the transformation mandate. The first year of posting losses, the DA [Democratic Alliance] asks the question in Parliament, to say why is Denel posting losses, and they forget the mandate they gave you as a black CEO. They say there must be something wrong with the CEO.

At that time, what have you done as the CEO? You have understood the transformation mandate. You have found an Exco [Executive Committee] of eight white men, mostly Afrikaans speaking. You got rid of six of them and, after the first year, you are recalled. They, in a panic, bring in a white CEO who is technically competent because they have forgotten about the mandate. They didn't even give you enough time – I mean, what can you achieve in a year? This white CEO gets given a different mandate by the same Government.

To the white CEO, the mandate is not help us to transform Denel; it is make sure that you turn Denel around.

So, you meet this CEO in a lift and he looks at you and says what the hell did you think you were doing by getting rid of my colleagues? I'm going to get them back because they know what they are doing. So, again it talks to that stop-start that we were doing, and the people get confused because the Shareholder itself is quite confused.

More than a decade later, the challenge of reporting lines identified by Mohale in 2002 continued to exist at SAA. Kalawe (2019) said when he was CEO in 2013/14, he was "never sure whether I was accountable to Malusi Gigaba as my Minister, or Parliament." He said when he and his team had to present to the Portfolio Committee on Public Enterprises, they had to change their presentation to emphasize the developmental mandate "because you are dealing with politicians," but they had to emphasize the commercial mandate when they were dealing with Gigaba.

"So, you must decide: who am I accountable to? I don't want to go to Parliament to present an update on performance. I'm accountable to the Board. If you want anybody to go talk to Parliament or any other stakeholders, it must be the Board, without me. You, as [Board] Chairman, must do that," Kalawe (2019) said.

Mohale (2019) said things would have been different if the Government had planned for a 20-year period. He said SAA, like all other SOCs, were now "bloated by at least a third." He said instead of cost containment, the governing ANC was concerned about cadre deployment. As a result, SOCs had ballooned because they were used "as crucibles for votes [and] for eating now," instead of using them to solve the country's challenges.

Asked where decision rights vested during his time as an executive at SAA, Mohale (2019) said: "All over the show, and sometimes we were unclear ourselves. [They vested] with the DG, with the Minister, with the Board of SAA, with Transnet because they were the ultimate owners, and with the Parliamentary Portfolio Committee."

Mohale (2019) used Eskom as an example. He said former CEO Phakamani Hadebe, who had previously worked for the National Treasury, had joined the power utility "with a demonstrable record of being a banker," but found himself second-guessed by various committees that had been formed to help contain the crisis at the company. He said each one of these committees had to come to him with questions about Eskom's finances and plans. That, he said, was "emblematic of how we run SOEs."

"During a turnaround, that's the time when you need fewer individuals; you need a core of people who really understand so that they look at the whole organisation unhindered, and the financial accountability must be the CEO's. He must not be second-guessed. He doesn't need a lot of help," Mohale (2019) said.

He added that Public Enterprises Minister Pravin Gordhan had erred when he publicly contradicted Hadebe, after he had informed the unions that Eskom would not be able to afford paying salary increases in 2018: "Just by that action, Phakamani's authority was eroded. [National Union of Metalworkers Secretary-General] Irvin Jim said we have a direct line to god, and undermined not only Phakamani Hadebe and his Exco, but also undermined the Board, because they knew that they could talk to the Minister."

Mohale (2019) described SAA's problems to be "of a capital nature, of resources and the bloated staff, and of a global competitive nature." He said while the Government dilly-dallied between SAA's commercial and developmental mandates, Emirates Airways increased its footprint in South Africa by 3000%. He said while SAA had cancelled the Cape Town-London route, British Airways now had two flights between the two cities per day – "and they are making good money."

"So, you can see that it's how we are structured, rather than the route itself," he said.

Mohale (2019) said SAA was expected to compete with newer aircraft that were more fuel efficient. He added that when the price of crude oil went up by 20%, it did not matter what the CEO of SAA did; the national carrier would "never be profitable because 20% of a R15 billion procurement spend was just on one commodity, jet fuel." He said SAA found itself "saddled with hardware that's a fuel guzzler and that's old fashioned," hence it was not "a good value proposition."

Mohale (2019) said the airline, which aspired to be a full-service carrier which excelled at customer experience, had been deserted by business people, who were flying the competition, with the national carrier now "sustained mostly by Government people and black people who are eternal optimists."

Asked if he believed SAA would be able to implement cost retrenchment through staff reduction, Mohale (2019) said it would be "impossible" for the national carrier to do so because of the governing ANC's alliance with the Congress of South African Trade Unions (COSATU) and the South African Communist Party (SACP). He said when an SAA CEO indicated that the number of employees had to be cut by a third in order to reduce costs, "that's where it [the strategy] dies; it will never be implemented under those circumstances."

Mohale (2019) said any good turnaround strategy, like any good merger, was premised on "capital, cost and revenue synergies." He said in SAA's case, the synergies were in scale involving SAA, SAX, Mango and SAA Technical (SAAT). He said it made no sense to have four CEOs, four Boards of Directors and four Chairpersons. He said rationalising the four different business units and reducing costs had to be done first, "having clearly thought out current reality and future vision and how you move from the one to the other, and then right-sizing."

However, Mohale (2019) said SOCs needed more than just right-sizing; they also needed to reduce the number of employees "because they were bloated for wrong reasons." He said a longer-term focus would have seen the airline "given political power and cover" to retrench about 3 000 of its 11 000 employees, with the understanding that when it "is cooking" some years later, it could employ anything up to 20 000 people. The problem, he said, was that the Government was "very short-term focused because our political office is five years."

Mohale (2019) said just as Malaysia adopted Vision 2020 fully knowing that the plan would out-live then Prime Minister Mohamed Malthir's term of office, a SAA CEO would have to drive a 10-year strategy even as s/he knew that s/he only had a five-year contract "and execute it as if your whole life depends on it so that you can hand over to the new CEO to continue with it, or do such a bloody good job that the Board asks you to renew."

Mohale (2019) said South Africa often did the opposite because at times Board Chairpersons, who earned about R1,5 million a year in Board fees, "look at the CEO taking home R5 million and they want the CEO's job." As a result, they focus on frustrating the incumbents so that they would be in the positions themselves.

"Therefore, you can see you are working against each other. The enemy is in your bed, not even in the same room as you," he said.

Former SAA CEO Sizakele Mzimela (2019) said that, to improve the chances of implementing a turnaround strategy successfully, it is important to have "the right people in place." She said while having the right people to implement a turnaround strategy was crucial, being in that position was "pointless if you are not going to allow them the freedom to implement that strategy." Equally important was ensuring that "quick decisions" were made on critical things that would ensure that the strategy was fully implemented.

She said that, during her tenure, she was fortunate to have the right people working with her and she, her team and the Board worked well together to develop their Strategy for Growth, without involving consultants. She said the strategy was drawn up by people who understood aviation and the challenges which confront it.

Mzimela (2019) said once it was presented to the Shareholder, the latter understood the turnaround strategy, "bought into it and understood the need to make quick decisions." She said that continued "for a while, while the Shareholder representatives were a certain group of people" who appreciated the need for agility, but things changed when there were different Shareholder representatives.

Mzimela (2019) said changes in Shareholder Ministers would always be a challenge for SOCs because Ministers tended to have different styles. While some would have a hands-off approach, others would want "to be more involved" than would be expected of a Shareholder, and that slows down decision making. She said it was important for a

Shareholder Minister to understand the aviation industry because aircraft acquisition, for instance, required a minimum of a three-year window period. Other airlines around the world, she said, made fleet decisions for even longer periods like the next 10 to 15 years.

While the Board made decisions expeditiously because it was part of the process of drafting the strategy for change, Mzimela (2019) said delays occurred on those matters which required Shareholder approval. The Board, she said, understood that timing was critical, but "the slowdown actually happened more from a Shareholder perspective."

While she acknowledged that some changes took place at Management level when she was appointed, Mzimela (2019) said having people in acting positions was a blessing in disguise because it enabled her to speed up the process of filling the roles with her appointees. She said she and her team ensured that employees in lower levels within the organisation also understood the strategy and why it had been decided upon. She said the fact that the understanding and buy-in went beyond the Board and the Shareholder was a critical path in the implementation of her turnaround strategy.

"That buy-in came as a result of having delivered very quickly on some of the things that we had said we were going to do, then people said 'ah, there's credibility to this process,'" she said.

Mzimela (2019) acknowledged that her strategy was different from the LTTS: "As of now, when I see what SAA is doing versus what we had proposed back then, it is different. Our strategy was a strategy of growth. That's not what is happening now. Our argument was that you have to grow yourself out of trouble; you can't shrink yourself out of trouble. So, that's where there is a major difference in terms of focus. Obviously, it's a different operating space."

Mzimela (2019) said that, upon her appointment, she was told that SAA had to be run commercially. However, she was also comfortable with its developmental mandate, which she understood to refer to the need to speed up transformation, and not to fly loss-making routes. She said SAA was fully aligned with the Shareholder on this understanding, but acknowledged that another Shareholder Minister's interpretation of the developmental mandate may be different.

Mzimela (2019) acknowledged that the loss-making Johannesburg-Beijing route – which Kalawe (2019) would later try to exit – was introduced during her tenure, but said the decision had nothing to do with political pressure. Instead, its introduction was part of the growth strategy, as a search "for the markets of the future." She said it was merely coincidental that the decision "talked to what tourism was trying to do."

"So, it's not being done because it's being pushed by SA Tourism and so on, but you find that there is alignment, which then helps because you are pushing for a route that they support in terms of tourism," Mzimela (2019) said.

While acknowledging that reducing employee numbers was an important part of cost retrenchment during a turnaround, Mzimela (2019) said the fact that hers was a growth strategy meant that there was no need to consider laying off employees. She said although SOCs' "biggest challenge is always to reduce costs that have a direct impact from a labour perspective," the growth strategy meant that they could absorb those costs in anticipation of future growth.

Mzimela (2019) also acknowledged that reducing employee numbers in an SOC is "the most difficult and always sensitive thing:" "Even when you do want to do it, then you get told 'ah, ah, no', and most of the time it won't be a 'no, you can't do it'. It will be like 'yeah, but timing is important, you know; there are elections coming', or it's this or that. 'We have to manage things before it gets done', but their managing it is three or four months, while you want to get it done in a month."

In her case, Mzimela (2019) said she decided that, in order to grow, she could not employ new people, but would not touch those already employed by the airline.

Mzimela (2019) said the aviation industry was highly capital intensive, which meant that an airline like SAA had "to be properly capitalised."

She said another important factor in this industry was scale, with the bigger airlines being the more profitable. She said that explained why EAL was "the most profitable airline right now on the continent." She said the Ethiopian carrier was the most profitable because it had been "growing, growing, growing," but it was not as profitable when it was still smaller. She said that applied to Emirates, which was focused on weekly finding "a new place to fly to because scale is so important."

"Scale allows them to sell the freedom of saying 'I'm flying via Dubai, but I'm connecting immediately to Australia.' ... So, scale is a very important factor. And, of course, you can only get the scale if you are capitalised properly to grow," Mzimela (2019) said.

In conclusion, Mzimela (2019) said government ownership did not automatically predispose an airline to fail. Again citing EAL, which is fully government owned, she said "it's the way in which the government manages the entity; it's not about the ownership."

Vuyisile Kona (2019) – who, like Mohale, was both a Senior Executive and subsequently a Board Member (and, in his case, also Acting CEO for six months) at SAA – said the only chance of successfully implementing any turnaround strategy at the airline would require the removal of politicians from the picture. He said although politicians made decisions which affected SAA, "they are not accountable for anything."

"Remove politics out of it. Take politics out of it... Get the politicians out. Bring in people who know the business," Kona (2019) stressed.

Also important, he said, was ensuring that the airline had modern, fuel-efficient aircraft.

Kona (2019) said that, during the short period when he was Acting CEO, the Board meddled in operational matters and "started telling me 'don't talk to this Executive; don't employ this one, employ that one'." He said it was important that the Shareholder appointed the Board and then "backs off," and that the Board recommended a CEO and, once that person's appointment was confirmed by the Shareholder, the Board then empowered that CEO.

However, Kona (2019) said it is difficult and "nonsensical ... to empower someone who is really still learning the business in a turnaround time, because during a turnaround there is no time to learn the business." He added: "You need someone to hit the ground running and bring in the right people who understand the business. Now, if the CEO is relying on consultants to tell him, to be whispering while they sit at Exco, that is a problem."

Kona (2019) echoed Mohale's (2019) view that the Government made "a mockery of black people" by appointing them into critical positions in industries which they did not understand, "and then immediately *sihluleka* (we fail), they go for a white person."

While he remained confident that SAA can be turned around successfully, Kona (2019) believed that doing so would be "hard work [and] will take real sweat and blood." He said at least five years would be required to accomplish that goal, based on a new business plan. However, he said it was unfortunate that while SAA "is shrinking [in size], the workforce is not shrinking."

However, Kona (2019) cautioned against laying off employees, saying "retrenchment ... is a very emotionally expensive exercise." He said he belonged to the "old school" that believed in growing the business in order to ensure that all employees were gainfully employed.

"That is a better thing for me to do, than to go through the pain of emotional trauma that you put the organisation through when you come in and retrench people, because we will need these people [when we grow], so don't go through the trauma. Keep these old ladies, or rather work them hard until they themselves decide to leave. They will leave, because you will have to push your productivity. So, you don't have to traumatise the organisation because once you start retrenching, it traumatises the organisation," Kona (2019) said.

Zwane (2019), on the other hand, said reality dictated that, for SAA to stand a reasonable chance of survival, it had to "be lean and mean and reduce [its] costs," but it cannot do so because it is not allowed to retrench employees.

Responding to a question about the Shareholder's disposition and the authority that he had as CEO, Kalawe (2019) said he had "very limited authority; all decisions had to be taken to the Board." He said during his time at SAA, there were two Ministers of Public

Enterprises: Malusi Gigaba and Lynne Brown. He said during his first few months in office, Gigaba had "full confidence in the Board at the time because he had appointed them, and they were the ones who had led the process of formulating the LTTS." However, Browne had no confidence in the self-same Board, and one of her first actions as Minister was "to fire the Board because it was questioning the contribution of Dudu Myeni as the Chairperson."

Zwane (2019) reiterated the view that it was "very critical" to have a Shareholder that believed in and supported the Executive Management team in implementing the strategy. He said that, in his experience, some in Government regarded SAA's plan with "an element of scepticism." He said SAA Executives encountered "that element of scepticism that it probably won't work: 'oh, we've seen this before; oh, it's been around before, we want to check if this time it's going to be successful'," he said.

That scepticism on the part of the Shareholder, Zwane (2019) said, had the effect of making the turnaround strategy "at first not believable and, secondly, not easily implementable."

Kalawe (2019) said that, during his tenure, the SAA Board was not happy with Myeni's performance, and that she had told him that she would use her influence to get the Board fired – "and the guys got kicked out."

To indicate his lack of authority, Kalawe (2019) said Gigaba came to the SAA office "to instruct us to stop the tender process for the planes." He said he had assumed that, as CEO, he could implement the Minister's instruction – until "one of the Board Members who understood how parastatals functioned" advised him to get a Board resolution based on Gigaba's instruction before he could take any action.

"That's a specific example that demonstrates to you that I had no real authority. In a private-sector company, if my commercials show me that I am over-staffed, I don't have to consult; I cut. In that [SAA] environment, I couldn't do so," Kalawe (2019) said.

He said what made matters worse was the fact that, in the case of the new Board appointed by Browne, the people to whom he was accountable on the Board of Directors "had no commercial experience." He said "even if their hearts were in the right place, they did not have commercial expertise to be able to provide support."

Zwane (2019) said that, during his tenure, real power lay with the Board, and not the CEO. He said instead of the Board increasing the level of delegation to the CEO, his power as CEO was cut by 50%. He put it down to trust, saying if the Board was "comfortable with the CEO doing the right things, they would aid the process of change" by increasing his/her delegated authority, instead of "running a parallel Exco structure which eventually leads to a complete failure," as happened during his tenure.

Asked what it would have taken for him to implement SAA's turnaround strategy successfully, Kalawe (2019) cited "stakeholders who are fully supportive of the strategy," a strong balance sheet and a good TMT. He said it was crucial that the Shareholder Minister, his/her officials and other Cabinet Ministers are supportive of the strategy so that the CEO would get "the right support" from them if s/he needed to consult with them on any of its components.

He said it was impossible to run a company with a weak balance sheet like SAA's "and not have confidence that one of the Shareholders will make funding available." He said the airline was living from hand to mouth, and he had to worry constantly about whether he would be able to pay employees' salaries instead of focusing on running the business.

Kalawe (2019) said most of the people in the TMT that he had inherited "were part and parcel of creating the problem that SAA has today." He said terminating their services, "even if it's on the basis of performance," was impossible because he had to consult with the Board's Human Resources Committee. "And if the members of that Board Committee have got relationships with these Managers, you can't touch them," he said.

Kalawe (2019) revealed that even the TMT was divided, with some Board Members being responsible for fomenting those divisions. He said that, on his first day at work, "part of the Management Team was supportive of me, and part of the Management Team was supportive of Managers who had been identified as potential leaders in the new era."

"So, as Managers, we were second-guessing one another. Any information that the guys shared with me, I had to make sure that I was not being set up to fail. You can't operate like that," he said.

Kalawe (2019) said SAA had to decide which of the three markets – domestic, regional and international – it was best positioned to serve. His view was that the airline "was not fit to service the international market" because it was competing against airlines like Emirates, which were funded by their governments and were flying "the latest, fuel-efficient planes." While the bulk of its income was in South African rands, its costs were in US dollars, hence it was "at a disadvantage." He believed that SAA had to focus on South Africa and Africa.

"However, you could not convince the key decision makers to withdraw from the international routes because the SAA flag is national pride – even if you are making losses, the politicians love seeing the tail of an SAA flag on the plane when they do their international travels, even if it doesn't make commercial sense," Kalawe (2019) said.

At the time of the interview, Kalawe (2019) said he then believed that an even more important question was whether the Government should own all or part of SAA. He believed that the airline had to be "off-load[ded] to private parties because they are best positioned to run an airline business like that than the Government is."

"You will never be able to turn SAA around for as long as you have Government as a Shareholder," he said emphatically.

Zwane (2019) said having a political Shareholder made things "problematic because most things are not necessarily directed by sane, commercial attributes." Instead, there was always "a political overtone that encompasses everything." He said there were times when signals and instructions that were conveyed to the Board and his Management Team were "confused."

He added that having a political Shareholder was "playing one of the most crucial roles in ensuring that nothing happens:"

> There are two things you must remember. At the time, you have a lot of changes. You have changes to the Ministers, so you have [Nhlanhla] Nene, [Des] van Rooyen, [Pravin] Gordhan and Malusi Gigaba: four Ministers [of Finance] in a short space of time. In the company, each Minister drives a different agenda. You also have a Chairperson [Myeni] who is driving her own agenda.
>
> You are in that situation of instability. You have to take some crucial decisions, but because of all these changes on one side, those decisions are not forthcoming, and because those decisions are not forthcoming, it's difficult for you to act in a certain way.

He said political influences had a bearing on the running of SOCs because what was experienced by SAA also happened at other SOCs "because they all report to this one Shareholder, the Government."

Kalawe (2019) said, in an echo of the dominant views in the turnaround literature, that "a turnaround can never be a turnaround if you don't restructure the asset, if you don't restructure people." However, he said the Government would "never allow" a minority Shareholder to retrench people. He said that was one of "a number of decisions" that a minority Shareholder would not be able to make if the Government remained a majority Shareholder – unless the minority Shareholder had "veto rights over key decisions in the business."

He cited the example of Aeroporto di Roma, which had a 25% shareholding in the Airports Company South Africa, but had "the final say on key decisions."

Kalawe (2019) said an ideal equity partner for SAA would have to be one that had "a very strong balance sheet because SAA needs money," and which had "solid experience in the aviation industry" because "most of the SAA Executives who understand the industry [have left]; the guys who are there now are pen pushers."

Kalawe (2019) said during his tenure, he brought Silvain Bosc, a commercial specialist from Air France, to run SAA's commercial portfolio "because it is the engine making money in an airline." However, he said the South African Police Service harassed Bosc until he left, and a South African who had the required expertise could not be found "to be able to help us extract value from all these routes."

Kalawe (2019) said the Government had to decide if it wanted SAA to drive a developmental mandate or to succeed commercially. If it wanted the airline to succeed commercially, then they would have to "offload it to parties who are skilled in running an airline;" and if it wanted the carrier to drive a developmental mandate, "they must set aside a budget to make that happen."

Zwane (2019) said it was important for the country to have SOCs in order to be able to drive its policy agenda. However, for the system to work, the Government as a Shareholder would have to adopt a hands-off approach and concern itself only with returns on investment and, if capitalisation was necessary, providing the required capital. He said the Government would then have to hold the Board to account to ensure that "whatever investments they make yield the desired returns."

Kalawe (2019) pointed out that for as long as foreign airlines like Emirates were allowed to fly out of Cape Town and Durban, in the process undermining Johannesburg as an international hub for SAA, the national carrier would struggle. He said when SAA flew to the United Arab Emirates, it was "not allowed to do that." Therefore, it was imperative that the Department of Transport, which is responsible for aviation policy and granting landing rights, created a regulatory framework that would be supportive of SAA.

Kalawe (2019) said a Boeing 787-800 aircraft operated by SAA generated losses, but when it was moved to Mango it made a profit. The reason, he said, was that, unlike their SAA counterparts who accounted for "40-45%" of the airline's people costs, pilots at Mango Airlines were normally retired SAA people who were paid a third of what SAA pilots earned. He said he had tried to tackle the challenge posed by SAA pilots' "huge salaries" but, like Ngqula before him, he had failed and "Vuyani is going to try and fail dismally." He said that was because SAA pilots had done their homework and had "signed an agreement with SAA that is untouchable."

That, said Kalawe (2019), was a conundrum to which a solution would have to be found if SAA was ever to be turned around successfully.

Zwane (2019) said SAA employees have had "a number of CEOs and all sorts of turnarounds." As a result, the workforce was "battered" and had "turnaround fatigue," which led to them not being supportive of the strategies:

> *After a while, you're turning around, losing balance and falling. Now we've got all of these employees who really are doing their best to ensure that the company is afloat. They are doing their best to ensure that the strategy is*

implemented, but because of this fatigue that I'm talking about, you find that it's hard for people to really give it their best shot.

Zwane (2019) added that buy-in from other stakeholders like labour, SAA customers and suppliers would also have made a difference in improving the chances of successfully implementing the turnaround strategy. He said that the Board also lacked the willpower to ensure that the turnaround strategy was implemented.

Zwane (2019) said that, in addition to employees' "turnaround fatigue," the fact that most of the Executives were acting in their respective positions during his time as Acting CEO did not help matters. "I'll use the analogy made by the current Chairperson [JB Magwaza], who said that when you are the actor in the position that I was acting in, you are like a castrated man. There's nothing you can do," he explained.

Zwane (2019) identified the fact that SAA and the Airports Company South Africa (ACSA) reported to different Shareholder Ministers as being part of the problem, as was the Department of Transport's decision to grant landing rights to Emirates in Cape Town and Durban. He said such a situation was not allowed in Ethiopia, for instance, whose airline was thriving. He said EAL enjoyed policy coherence because all aspects of air travel – including the granting of landing rights to foreign airlines – fell under one Ministry.

"You have all these guys now landing all over the place. Now, why do you need the domestic airline, then, because you are making it compete unfairly with other airlines from around the world? So, when you compare Ethiopian Airlines with SAA, that's one serious flaw in the system for us," he said.

He said the national carrier was also negatively affected by decisions taken by other Government Departments, such as the decision by the Department of Home Affairs that travellers to and from South Africa who had minors with them needed to have unabridged birth certificates containing the details of both parents, which hindered travel.

Zwane (2019) concurred with Kalawe (2019) that the national carrier would "never be profitable … because its ownership structure is not geared for profitability." He said "within a year or two," SAA would be liquidated if the Government stopped bailing it out financially, and that its inevitable liquidation would be delayed if "the Government keeps pumping in money and then you have incremental changes taking place in the company." The airline's future, he said, lay in private hands.

When the interview started with him, Jarana (2019) was eager to get a number of things off his chest. In particular, he was keen to talk about his deep sense of frustration at SAA. At first, in response to the initial question about how he had settled into the job, he spoke for a minimum of 15 minutes uninterrupted, before he could take any subsequent questions. One got the sense that he was keen to use the opportunity presented by the interview to offload or unburden himself.

He bemoaned the fact that he spent so much of his time dealing with "liquidity and balance sheet issues." He said the banks had "walked away" from the national carrier, and he had to "win them back into the system." When he spoke to them, they asked for "a path to debt reduction" because SAA was "over-geared," in addition to "a path to profitability." He said he had given the banks "that path" and asked them "to plug" into SAA's financial system to check for themselves every month.

Jarana (2019) said while the banks were growing increasingly confident and were again supporting the business, it was "painful that the Government is not coming through on their part of the bargain." He said he had made it clear to the Government that SAA would need a capital injection of R21,7 billion to be turned around. That amount would cover the airline's old and current debt and provide working capital. Although Pretoria had bought into the plan and approved the Agenda for Change, it was not honouring its part of the bargain.

He said if the Shareholder "came to the party," he would not be spending so much time engaging with the banks.

"Unfortunately, if you own something, you can't wish it away. If you want to continue owning it, you are going to have to fund it. Capital costs are normal in business. Maybe at SAA there have been too many of those, where people did not implement and turn it around.

"So, we asked that that must happen, but the Government is not fully coming through in terms of its side. That's the picture we are in," a frustrated Jarana (2019) said.

Jarana (2019) said what was even more frustrating was the fact that the National Treasury, which was the Shareholder Ministry at the time, had signed off on SAA's corporate plan, which included the R21,7 billion that would be required to implement the turnaround strategy. He said then-Deputy Finance Minister Mondli Gungubele was with the SAA team when it presented the plan to the Standing Committee on Appropriations and to the Portfolio Committees on Finance and Public Enterprises, all of which knew the strategy chapter and verse. He said the Standing Committee on Public Accounts had even said it was the first time that it had been given "a very clear plan and a sense of what is going to happen and a trail of execution, therefore give these people money."

"My view is that if you sign off on a Corporate Plan, you are not only signing off on the nice things; you are also signing off on the painful side of issues.... So, this is the issue. Commitment was made by virtue of National Treasury signing off on the Corporate Plan, but what I'm finding difficult is that it would appear to me that there's not 100% alignment within the Cabinet," he said.

Jarana (2019) said if the Government informed him that it no longer wanted SAA and the airline had to be wound up, he would do so; and if the view was that he was not the right steward, he would step aside and "say find the right steward that you'll give money to support; we are as clear as that."

Giving a review of progress made during his 18 months in office at the time, Jarana (2019) said some progress had been made, especially domestically and regionally where SAA was experiencing "positive gross profit margins." The international network continued to be a challenge and would need a review of the SAA fleet and fleet economics, as well as a change in timing for some of the routes. Part of the problem on the international network, he said, was that they did not fly the aircraft long enough. Upon landing in London in the morning, for instance, the aircraft remained on the ground for 11 hours before it took off in the evening, and that had cost implications.

Jarana (2019) said in order for him to succeed in turning the airline around, he would need skills at executive level ("I'm talking about really, really, proper, heavy-lifting skills"), among other things. He said unlike the telecommunications industry where he had worked before joining SAA, the national carrier was under-resourced at executive level: "Leadership capacity is too thin. Skill sets, especially commercial skills, are almost non-existent… If you don't have senior leadership teams who have seen the bigger picture, you will not succeed in turning the business around."

Part of the problem, according to Jarana (2019), was that SAA was not an attractive proposition as a prospective employer. SAA, he said, was "not an employer brand – it is damaged, with all the history of instability." He said efforts to recruit hard-working men and women "who are strong executives" from companies like Unilever were unsuccessful because "they can't stomach the uncertainty about the future because this thing is known to be unstable."

Jarana (2019) said people with valuable skills had long left the airline. Among those who remained at SAA were "good people who have got good hearts and like the brand, but some of them don't have the prerequisite skills to make the turnaround work."

He said SAA desperately needed funding to provide certainty about the future. He said if the Government gave the national carrier money "grudgingly, after making all sorts of statements in the public, effectively they undermine the plan." Jarana (2019) said an airline was like a listed a company: people who booked seats on SAA six to nine months before they were due to fly were "effectively shareholders in the brand." Nobody, he said, bought shares in a company whose future they doubted.

That is why, Jarana (2019) explained, statements like those of Finance Minister Tito Mboweni in New York in November 2018 that SAA should be sold, and one by Reserve Bank Governor Lesetja Kganyago "yesterday who said don't bail out SOCs," were irresponsible. Mboweni had told the investor conference: "It [SAA] is loss making; we are unlikely to sort out the situation, so my view would be to close it down. Why I say close it down is because it's unlikely that you are going to find any private-sector equity partner who will come join this asset" (BusinessTech, 2018).

Jarana (2019) described Mboweni's (2018) statement as reckless:

> *He is quoted as having said so in the media, which I find very reckless because what is happening now is that you have a Government that is not cohesive. There is no accountability. Everyone goes and shouts. We don't need critics; we need people coming with solutions.*
>
> *You can't disown your kids; you can't disown them because you feel they are on drugs, are you with me? You can't. You need to take responsibility for your role as a parent. In the case of the Government today, and the ANC Government in particular, they* **have** *to take accountability.*
>
> *Even Tito [Mboweni], when you appoint these people who are appointed as Board Members and CEOs, they are appointed by the Cabinet, and not by one person. Now, if you appoint people who are of good will but are not making sure that they have got the requisite skills, then you can't come, when they have got it wrong, and say 'well, then kill the SOC'. If you are going to kill it, then make a decision to do so; don't shout on the streets. For some of us who have made a sacrifice to come and make it work, effectively you are pulling the capital under our feet.*

Jarana (2019) said it was strange that, until then, "the reckless statements" were made by senior politicians from the governing ANC, and not opposition parties like the Democratic Alliance, the Economic Freedom Fighters, the United Democratic Movement or the Inkatha Freedom Party. Instead, those statements were made by Cabinet Ministers, "which means there's no cohesion at the Cabinet level."

He added, tellingly: "Now the Shareholder has lost his mind, in a nutshell."

As one listened to Jarana (2019) expressing his frustrations, still in response to that first question about how he had settled into his job, it was clear that he had reached the end of his tether. He continued:

> *So, in a nutshell, the Government doesn't want to fix the airline. I can say it unequivocally, because if they wanted to, they would be consistent and make sure that there is a line of command that is clear. You can't have Pravin saying this, Tito saying that, Lesetja Kganyago saying this, but the President is quiet about it. He is not chaperoning his Ministers in one direction.*
>
> *We didn't break the airline; we came to fix it. Now, to the extent that we are good stewards, then we need support from them because we didn't break it. We don't get any benefits from the airline better than we would do elsewhere.*

So, I'm crystallising the issue of consistency. I'm saying it's skills, it's funding, it's the mind of the Shareholder.

The single biggest thing [holding us back] is the mind of the Shareholder. If the Shareholder doesn't know what to do with the asset and the Shareholder is not consistent with its own ambitions, then as a Board and an Executive you sit in limbo because the sense of urgency, the sense of direction is not there. You say you want a strategic equity partner, but there's no conversation that says 'okay, guys, here's the time line; this is the enablement.' On the one hand, it will not happen; on the other, sell it today – but all these things are shouted on the streets.

So, the mind of the Shareholder is the single biggest obstacle to turning around the SOCs, especially SAA.

Like Zwane (2019), Jarana (2019) said comparisons of SAA with EAL were unfair. He said those who indulged in such comparisons "actually don't want to compare the real truth." At EAL, he said, the Board was "given space to operate," but in SAA's case in South Africa, "the Government wants to control, but they don't have the mind to control correctly."

Jarana (2019) said in addition to "the mind of the Shareholder" being "the single biggest danger" to SAA, another challenge was that the Government lacked "skin in the game." Asked what he meant, he said the Government was driven by political ambitions and would not make a decision on the airline "if that decision is going to undermine or affect their own political careers." As a result, decisions would be postponed because "the objective is not commercial." Since in reality SAA belonged to taxpayers and not to the Government, Pretoria was more concerned about "social, political management, which is not consistent with a commercial enterprise which is not a monopoly."

"You see," he said, "if this was Cyril's [President Ramaphosa's] company, he would know he is losing his own wealth. He would have intervened yesterday. He would not have allowed Tito, all of them, to make the shouting."

SAA Chief Restructuring Officer Peter Davies (2019) said the national carrier's suppliers followed the local and global media "and all they see is that it's doom and gloom." He said Mboweni's statement about SAA had sent a wrong message to those suppliers – including travel agents – and potential customers (passengers). He said everybody had to recognize that 70% of SAA's business comes from abroad, and was not generated in South Africa. He said in the case of the revenue generated by SAA on its routes to Washington DC and New York in the USA, those two routes generated "more revenue than the entire SAA domestic network."

Davies (2019) said people tended to forget that airlines were "a commodity, a fast-moving consumer good," saying there was "nothing more perishable than an empty seat on take-off; you'll never sell it again."

Josua Du Plessis (2019) said existing uncertainty about SAA was a major drawback in the implementation of the turnaround strategy:

> *A part of your successful turnaround is also the perception of the country. The one big, big ticket item is as long as there's uncertainty about SAA's future, and as long as there are statements being made that SAA is going to go under and the Minister is not going to help us, people do not want to invest R100 000 in a ticket if they are not sure they will get their money's worth when they fly the airline. If you have a family of four and you fly business class from New York to South Africa in a once-in-a-lifetime holiday, are you going to invest a few hundred thousand rands in an airline that you read the other day is in financial troubles?*

Turning to the Board of Directors (BoD), Jarana (2019) said its members were concerned about protecting their own integrity. Some of them, he said, wanted to avoid upsetting the Government because they were keen to remain on the Board or to be considered appointable on Boards of other SOCs.

A former social footballer during his youth, Jarana (2019) used the analogy of that popular game when he said a match was won "through man-marking and 50-50 tackles," and not through zonal marking. He said football players felt emboldened to go for 50-50 tackles when they knew that victory would also benefit them personally and that if, in the process, they got injured, the team would look after them and if they got red carded "the coach will not say 'I will never play Vuyani again'."

Added Jarana (2019):

> *The only thing that the Boards are there to say is, well, the PFMA says you must walk this way. So, invariably, 50-50 things that need to be done and things that need to be said to challenge the Shareholder, the Board is not prepared to do because they want tenure and also there's a bigger ecosystem, so no one wants to ruffle the feathers since they have a downside exposure. That's why there's no skin in the game.*

He said it was frustrating to be told, when "competition is fighting you back to back," about the rules and what the Shareholder said. He said even when the national carrier needed to make critical decisions on an urgent basis, they would be told to give the Minister 30 days to make a decision. When that 30-day period expired, the Minister would ask for another 30 days before he could respond to the airline. He said during those

60 days, "they push back to you a number of questions on something that is a commercial response."

Explained an exasperated Jarana (2019):

> *Invariably, when I said [there is no] skin in the game, this thing is not meant well because no one is losing money in a true sense. People are protecting their political and social egos. The danger to this is – and this is the model for SOCs – if you want to make an SOC like SAA work, give it to a competent Board, cut them loose, make sure that you hold them accountable, and you bring personal liability not in terms of the PFMA, but in terms of the performance of the company. So, that's what you try and push for. The model of a PFMA-based company is not meant for a commercial enterprise.*
>
> *Therefore, you can sit with a situation where you are burning cash and you need to intervene, but you can't make a decision because the Board will tell you "no, to make this decision, you are going to be in breach of the PFMA; you need Treasury to approve for you." When you go to the Treasury, the official there is not interested. He's interested in making sure that all the rules are ticked, but there's no fraud, there's nothing. It's purely a rule that says you need to go through this process, but you are burning cash at the time.*
>
> *It's almost like you are going to hospital in an emergency ward; there's a doctor there. Somebody is dying, but you don't have medicine. You say, look, there's a trolley that comes; there's a guy who says "by the way, I have medicine for this guy." You won't take it; they would rather have you die because they will say how did they take medicine from you? The PFMA doesn't allow it. That's the issue.*

Jarana (2019) said the Government had to keep in mind that SAA was a commercial enterprise and "not Home Affairs; even Home Affairs needs some agility."

He cited two concrete examples. He said that when he learned that South American carrier LATAM was planning to use an A350 plane on the Sao Paolo-Johannesburg route, thus doubling its capacity, he knew that prices were going to fall and SAA's Johannesburg-Sao Paolo route was going to turn negative. To counter LATAM's move, he wanted SAA to start a Buenos Aires, Argentina route to "siphon" the 30% of LATAM passengers who fly to South Africa via Brazil in order to undermine the Sao Paolo hub. However, he knew that "it's going to take me six months to respond."

The second example he cited was that of Guangzhou in China. Seeing that SAA was "burning cash" on the Johannesburg-Hong Kong route, Jarana (2019) said he wanted to divert four frequencies from Hong Kong to Guangzhou as a tactical response, but it took six months before permission was granted for him to proceed – when SAA was losing

R750 million a year on the Hong Kong route.

He said Government officials asked "all textbook questions" in order to "cover their backs." He asked, rhetorically, why the Government was involved in route decisions, as a Shareholder, when it had a Board for the airline.

"So, you either have a Board or no Board. You either say, well, I don't want a Board; I want to manage it [SAA] myself as a Shareholder. Then we know we're dealing with a single entity that sits with us in the room as Executives. You know your Board approves today, but you get questions back to the same Board," Jarana (2019) said.

He said he had no problem with the market, policy and regulation, but SAA's problems were internal, between Management and the SAA Board on the one hand, and the Government as Shareholder on the other hand.

Jarana (2019) said although it was an SAA subsidiary, Mango Airlines was very different. It was "agile [and] set up as a private enterprise." He wanted to replicate the Mango culture within SAA because the LCC was both agile and entrepreneurial, with its remuneration structure based on low salaries and high bonuses based on meeting performance targets.

The culture at SAA, however, was different: "Here the culture is 'Ahh, this is my uncle's place; the Government will help us. Somebody owes me a living. This is my company. I am a national. I am a comrade. I am a socialist. I am a resident. I am a citizen. Therefore, I am owed a living.'"

Jarana (2019) said, given the shortage of people with aviation expertise in South Africa and SAA's non-attractiveness as an employer brand, he was relying on Seabury to source the right people from abroad for the national carrier, for six to 12 months, while SAA was recruiting. These expatriates would be required to help develop local talent.

He said he had spent much of 2018 dealing with the National Treasury on a capital structure for SAA, but it was an ongoing battle. However, they had finally reached a compromise on how they could find each other. The challenge, however, was the frequent changes of Ministers.

"You see, I would say I am on the fourth Minister within a 12-month period, and I guess it's the nature of politics. When you change Ministers, it's painful because each Minister has a view, and you need to allow him to test your logic and you find each other around the strategy. When you change Ministries (from National Treasury as Shareholder to the Ministry of Public Enterprises), it's even worse because you change administrators plus the politicians, so we have a double problem," Jarana (2019) said.

Asked what he would do differently if he were the responsible Minister and wanted the airline to be commercially viable, Jarana (2019) said he would appoint a Board that he trusted, which he would give full authority to run the airline and hold accountable, but would not second-guess it. He would require that the Board appoints a competent CEO and delegates appropriately to him/her. He said once the Board presented to him a strategy that he believed in, he would not tie "their hands at the back and expect them to win a championship." Therefore, he would move the airline out of the PFMA so that it would compete fairly with other airlines, but would unleash the country's law enforcement agencies on the Directors in the event of fraud.

"BA doesn't have a PFMA; they act quickly. Emirates doesn't have that. They are State owned, but they are run like a corporate entity. Ethiopian Airlines, similar; Kenya Airways, similar. By and large all State owned, but they are enabled by being released from a very cumbersome piece of legislation where you have had to talk to so many people to be able to achieve success," Jarana (2019) said.

He added that he would also secure funding for the airline from the banks so that SAA would be debt-free and appropriately capitalised.

SAA Interim Chief Financial Officer Deon Fredericks (2019) – who was seconded to the airline from Telkom – said Telkom was exempt from the PFMA. He said the listed company, in which the Government has 40% equity – had an independent Board which was empowered to take binding decisions. When the situation required, Telkom was also able to lay off 8 000 employees, but merely informed the Government as an interested stakeholder, and did not seek its permission.

Responding to a question about whether a similar dispensation could be extended to SAA, Fredericks (2019) revealed that initial discussions had taken place with the Shareholder, and said they were in the process of "working on a document that we want to present to the Shareholder," which he hoped would "definitely help."

Fredericks (2019) said it was important to get "the red tape" out of SAA in order to improve agility. He said its continued existence slowed the company down and provided people who do not do their work with "a place to hide" because they point at the bureaucracy as the sole reason for the carrier's poor performance, rather than their own ineptitude.

Du Plessis (2019) said the PFMA had "a very big impact" on the airline. He said that, in terms of the PFMA, if a Manager made a decision, s/he can go to jail for a long time. As a result, "decision making starts becoming decisions by committee, with 50 signatures."

Du Plessis (2019) said Government procurement processes in a commercial entity like SAA were "really painful." The PFMA, he said, was "one of the biggest stumbling blocks" and considerably slowed down decision making. He said "a document written for the management of a Government Department is very difficult to apply in a commercial entity."

However, former SAA Board Member Swazi Tshabalala (2019), who chaired the Board's LTTS Committee during her time on the BoD, was not as worried about the

PFMA. On its own, she said, the PFMA was "not that constraining." She said it was "all the other things that they add around the PFMA that are constraining," but felt that the Government was "entitled to at least a set of some rules about how" public money that it provided was used.

Instead, Tshabalala (2019) said there was room for "certain provisions in the PFMA" from which SAA could be exempted, that would allow the airline to enter into strategic partnerships without requiring Government approval, "as long as the Government maintains a majority shareholding" in SAA.

Jarana (2019) said he would also insist on reciprocity of policy on aviation. As the Minister, he would ensure that South Africa did not have "open skies to a point where you kill your domestic air transport mechanism" because if the country were too open, international carriers would siphon traffic from Durban, Cape Town and maybe even Port Elizabeth in future.

Jarana (2019) bemoaned the absence of "policy logic in Government" on aviation. He said there was so much fragmentation, with the Government having "no strategic position on aviation." He said there was a transport policy, an aviation policy and a tourism promotion policy, "all running in parallel." He said Ethiopia, on the other hand, had aligned policy to ensure that people – including the Chinese – "go to Addis Ababa before they come here."

Jarana (2019) revealed that SAA was planning to initiate and sponsor a Government discussion on aviation policy, which would involve the Departments of Transport, Tourism and Home Affairs.

Mokholo (2019), who was previously a DDG at the DPE, said the Government realised, in hindsight, that liberalising the skies created problems for South Africa. She said there was a realisation that the Cabotage Rules (allowing foreign airlines to pick up passengers within a country, instead of confining them to one hub) had to be changed. She acknowledged that having three domestic airports (excluding the private Lanseria International Airport in Johannesburg) becoming international points of entry and departure placed the national carrier at a disadvantage.

"So, we said we need to stop Cabotage. We need to allow BA to fly directly into OR Tambo, and that's it. We allow Mango, Kulula, Comair, the ones that would fit domestically, to compete with SAA or to compete with Mango. On competitive neutrality, we are not saying there must not be competition with SAA, but we are saying close it (foreign airlines landing and departing from Cape Town and Durban) so that you can be able to allow this economic fairness," Mokholo (2019) said.

Jarana (2019) concurred with the dominant view in the literature on turnaround strategy that, during the implementation of a turnaround strategy, a CEO should be sufficiently empowered to make decisions. He said the chemistry between a CEO and the Board, and between the Board and the Shareholder, was "very important." He said a CEO needed to be given "the space and good-enough guard rails to operate in, because your ability to respond and combat issues, especially with SAA in its current form, is important."

Proactively comparing the disposition of the Ministers under whom he had served for a decent period, Jarana (2019) said Gigaba "was more liberal about saying 'listen, combat this thing and make sure that you take it out of pain; respond to the issues'," while Nene was "a little bit conservative" and Gordhan was "extremely conservative." He said even when he faced difficult challenges to which he had an answer, he would not be comfortable to approach Gordhan with a proposed solution because "you would be pressed for answers, and some of those answers the Shareholder may not like or believe they are correct."

He said he found it extremely frustrating, for example, that, as SAA Group CEO, neither her nor the Board could appoint the CEO or Chief Financial Officer (CFO) of subsidiaries SAAT or Air Chefs without the approval of Minister Gordhan. He said that he and the SAA Board waited for six months for the Minister's permission to appoint a CFO for SAAT – and a day before the interview with me, the preferred candidate had informed him that he had got a job at one of SAA's competitors.

Jarana (2019) explained:

> Now we have to start from square one. This is the issue that people don't understand. SAA is an ailing company; you need to enable the Board and the CEO to execute quickly. If you don't trust them, get rid of them. Get rid of them because nobody is going to take you to court.
>
> The problem we have is that there's distrust and, therefore, you don't enable people; so, it's a lose-lose because ultimately we won't turn around the airline. The long and short answer is simple. It's that I don't feel as enabled as I would be in a private-sector context – which is still full of governance, by the way.

Davies (2019) shared Janara's (2019) concerns. He said the rules and regulations under which SAA operated had to be relaxed for two reasons: unlike a Government Department, SAA has competitors "breathing down our neck" and the airline was "in intensive care." He said there had to be appreciation of the fact that the aviation industry was "a dog-eat-dog business, a nasty business;" SAA needed to be able to make decisions quickly, hence it had "to be treated differently in that sense."

SAA Chairman Johannes Magwaza (2019) said while the BoD made decisions quickly, it then had to refer those decisions to the Shareholder. SAA had lost the designated SAAT CFO and he was "now sitting at Comair, in an office without a proper job description."

"I sign these letters that go to the Minister and they sit there; they sit there, and I phone him. I personally phone him. You know, we lost him [the SAAT CFO designate]," Magwaza said.

He also revealed that a candidate chosen by the SAA Board for the position of CFO of Mango was turned down by Gordhan, who said "no, no, no, look at somebody else." Asked what reasons were given for the Minister's decision, Magwaza said: "They just felt that he was not the right person to be the CFO of Mango."

Davies (2019) said he did not think that SAA had a Shareholder that wanted to take decisions. He said at previous government-owned airlines where he had worked, the Boards were entrusted with decision making. However, at SAA they had to go through the Board process, "which is simply a replication of the Government process, and then having gone through the Board process, we have to do exactly the same through the Government." He said he could not but wonder why SAA had a BoD at all. He said this elongated decision making had a potentially detrimental effect on SAA.

"We don't make these things up. We don't sit here thinking 'how can we upset the Board? How can we upset the Shareholder?' These are fairly obvious facts, and it is frustrating," Davies (2019) said.

Jarana (2019) said there was sufficient delegation to him from the BoD, especially because "the Chairman is very supportive." However, he said there were some political dynamics, as tended to be the case with "SOC Boards," hence "some of the things that ought to be sorted don't get sorted because politics comes in the way." He likened the BoD dynamics to "a jungle," with some Directors having "some brief from somewhere." He said the politics of the Shareholder played itself out in the BoD: "While you are enabled, you can say it [the politics] is proxified and happening at the Board level."

Vuyiswa Raseroka (2019), SAA General Manager for Human Capital, said her observation was that the level of delegation to the CEO was insufficient. "Honestly, I think it could be better. It can be improved a lot," she said.

Davies (2019) said the airline's leadership had "a long way to go in terms of being allowed to make our decisions quicker." He said while he could understand the reasons based on what had previously happened at SAA, he did not think it made sense for the Board and the Shareholder to recruit trustworthy, experienced leaders and then deny them the right to make important operational decisions.

"So, why do you go to all the effort of making sure that you get the best, independent, well-experienced, passionate, track-proven Management Team and then say 'ahh, but we're going to treat you like the previous Management Team'? In other words, the perception is we don't trust you."

Davies (2019) warned that if the SAA leadership was "not allowed to do what we want to do, in the time that we are given to do it, then we won't succeed; it's as simple as that."

He said the SAA TMT had recently made a decision about aircraft, and what would normally take "weeks, if not months" to be approved internally had taken him less than one month to have it submitted to the Minister in terms of Section 54 of the PFMA. At the time of the interview, he was awaiting the Minister's response.

"What he needs to do now is to react as quickly as we have. Intellectually, it's a no brainer. Intellectually, it has gone through the processes within the company, so I'm hoping that he's going to make the decision quickly," Davies (2019) said.

He said that was a defining moment for SAA, and revealed that he was accused by one Board Member of trying to "drive a coach and horses through due process." He said that he had said, in response: "I'm not trying to drive a coach and horses through due process. I'm on the coach and the horse, but I want to drive it quicker through due process. I don't want to ride a donkey."

Davies (2019) added: "In a competitive environment which is fast changing, it's quite difficult for an airline to make commercial decisions when you are being treated like a Post Office ... I think it's a fact that SAA has never been allowed to operate as a normal commercial airline because of restrictions placed by the Shareholder. I'm being brutally honest."

Fredericks (2019) said while he understood that the Shareholder's and the Board's involvement in operational matters were a consequence of SAA's history of losses going back to 2012 and the fact that Management in the past had not covered itself in glory, the current status quo deprived the airline of agility at a time when it needed it most. He said the Section 54 determinations that required Ministerial approval for route changes delayed implementation of important decisions.

"You can't operate a normal company like that, even more a company in distress. Ultimately, the Shareholder and the Board need to make sure that a Management Team is appointed that they trust and, based on that, you can then say these are the delegations that we will give you so that you can operate the organisation in an efficient manner," Fredericks (2019) said.

He said because the airline was "a mess," the Board needed to be more supportive of Management, instead of "just beating up Management every time, beating up the CEO." He said given the fact that SAA did not have the right skills, most of the responsibilities fell on the CEO's shoulders, and the Board needed to be more understanding of that situation:

> *It's like in a war: if there are no more soldiers to fight there, ultimately the*
> *generals will need to get off the truck and get into the trenches. That's what*

needs to happen. By that, I'm not saying that they don't need to keep Management responsible and accountable, but they need to be able to understand certain situations.

Asked if he believed that SAA would be able to cut costs through reducing the number of its employees, Jarana (2019) said if the airline did not do so, it would not succeed. Therefore, retrenchment was part of the turnaround strategy, as was the sale of non-core assets like Air Chefs. He was worried, however, that the Government had an "obsession about owning an asset, even if it gives you nothing."

He said in his home village of Qunu in the Eastern Cape people valued cattle and kept them until they were old, but did not sell them. If a cow or an ox died, they felt as sad as if they had lost a family member. "This is how the Government is thinking. Even if the asset is draining resources, some people want to keep it," he said.

Jarana (2019) said SAA had about 9 500 employees at the time. If he retrenched 1 500 of them (with the proviso that they would be re-employed when the airline grew), he would save the remaining 8 000 jobs, instead of losing all 9 500 of them if SAA were liquidated. However, when he raised the subject for discussion, "there's this thing of kicking the can down the road, as if ultimately you are not going to get there."

Jarana (2019) said it would not be possible to turn SAA around "without reducing the workforce" and "without taking away some of the benefits that are crazy, like those of pilots" which were part of the agreement signed in 2002.

"That's why the issue about a joint conversation with the Shareholder is critical so that the Board can have not a father-and-child relationship with the Minister, but a strategic discussion of equals. The Minister cannot come to the Board with a father-and-child type of attitude, because then you kill debates. There has to be transformation in attitudes and in the minds on that side," he said.

Davies (2019) said when benchmarked against the global norm, SAA was overstaffed, especially if one looked at the number of employees per aeroplane. He said that the Government had to appreciate that the airline had to be "a lean and mean machine."

He said while "a certain headcount reduction" was necessary, including through offering voluntary severance packages, it was also important to keep in mind that SAA did not have "the right product at the right place that should charge at the same rate" as its competitors.

Fredericks (2019) and Raseroka (2019) revealed that the national carrier had begun to second spare SAA pilots to other airlines, with others having chosen to take early-retirement packages. Those seconded to other airlines over a five-year period would be able to return to SAA when their contracts at those airlines expired, when the national carrier hoped it would have turned around and would be in a growth phase.

Fredericks (2019) said that, as part of its cost-containment exercise, SAA no longer purchased newspapers, flowers, cold beverages like water "and other peripheral things" for its Executives. He pointed out that he had personally paid for the water on his table, which he had offered to me at the beginning of the interview.

Jarana (2019) said he was "aware" that some of the important things that he felt needed to be done to save SAA would be "almost impossible to do within my tenure." Asked why he held that view, he said while he believed that "workforce reduction" would take place because it was "not optional," he thought acquisition of a SEP would be stuck indefinitely in Parliament. Therefore, he was readying himself to enter into quasi-equity deals that would see partners participate in SAA, without selling equity in the national carrier. He believed that option was possible because it was "a soft way of crowding in private sector participation."

Jarana (2019) had in mind alternatives like a Metal-Neutral Joint Venture, which was "a lot more complex" and would require global anti-trust immunity. He said that he knew that the traditional mergers and acquisition option would not happen during his tenure at SAA.

Jarana (2019) expressed hope that, after the May 2019 general elections in the country, there would be better coherence in Government "not just on SOCs, but on a number of things." He said unless there was that much-needed alignment in Government and Pretoria spoke with one voice, South Africa would not succeed.

In concluding the interview, Jarana (2019) had advice for the Government:

> When we speak about SOCs, accept that they have been in a hole for a long time and are the children we don't like, but to get rid of the children you need a process. That process must be bought into by everybody else; or rehabilitate them, take them to a rehabilitation centre. You need to actually work on a rehab programme with everybody. It doesn't help to complain and say 'hey, my children are on drugs', and so on. It helps no one. At the end of the day, they are your children.
>
> By the way, you parented them. You chose them a nanny; you chose what they eat; you chose which school they went to; you chose who was a minder. Now you can't, therefore, throw them up in the air. If you want to kill them or send them somewhere in the North Pole, you must agree and take them to the North Pole. So, if you want to rehabilitate them, you must commit to the rehabilitation programme, painful as it is. This is where I see lack of cohesion. We need to do that.

Two months after the interview, Jarana resigned from SAA. In his resignation letter, which found its way into the media, he echoed the concerns that he had raised during the interview with me, mostly related to "uncertainty about funding and bureaucratic processes delaying decision making needed to turn around the airline" (Omarjee, 2019).

Omarjee (2019) culled the following 10 "key quotes" from Jarana's resignation letter:

- Uncertainty about funding – "From 2018 to date, we have had no less than three incidents in which the company was almost unable to pay salaries due to a lack of funding."

- No Government buy in – "We have not been able to obtain any further funding commitment from Government, making it difficult to focus on the execution of the strategy. I spend most of my time dealing with liquidity and solvency issues. Lack of commitment to fund SAA is systematically undermining the implementation of the strategy, making it increasingly difficult to succeed."

- Delayed decision making – "One of the areas of concern is speed in decision making. It is impossible to succeed in the turnaround with the current level of bureaucracy we have to go through to implement [the] strategy."

- Blurred lines of accountability – "Lines of accountability are becoming increasingly blurred about what operational decisions are in my domain, which are in the Board's domain and which are in the Minister's domain."

- Lack of trust – "Trust levels are very low, impacting [on] ways of working. [When] implementing a turnaround strategy for a company in crisis as SAA, clarity of command structure, alignment of purpose and high levels of trust are critical elements of success."

- Depleting funding – "The R3,5 billion [emergency funding] facility will be depleted in June 2019."

- No budget allocations to SAA – "You would know that we negotiated a specific dispensation with lenders to continue funding SAA going forward. This was predicated on SAA being mentioned in the Minister of Finance's budget speech, which did not happen."

- Rising debt levels – "We have always maintained the SAA debt levels are unsustainable. However, instead of reducing debt while aggressively implementing the LTTS, we have increased it, thus attracting additional interest charges, which all undermine the plan."

- Long-Term Turnaround Strategy at risk – "The strategy is being systematically undermined, and as the Group Chief Executive Officer, I can no longer be able to assure the Board and the public that the LTTS is achievable. A lot has to change to enable the accelerated implementation of the LTTS. To date, I am not convinced that we can make the required changes both in terms of process and how we coordinate ourselves as a team comprising Executives, a Board and two Shareholder Ministers."

- Internally created problems – "Sixty percent of the problems at SAA are internal (within the control of Management and staff, the Board and the Shareholder), whilst 40% are market challenges."

Writing in the national newspaper *City Press Business* a week later, academic Khaya Sithole (2019) said decision-making autonomy was fundamental "to all CEOs operating within an openly competitive market, as SAA does." He said the decision to "cripple" the airline's decision-making process "with the type of bureaucracy that its competitors do not have to contend with directly compromised its competitive ability."

When he joined SAA in December 2017 as Chief Restructuring Officer, British pilot and turnaround specialist Peter Davies had impressive credentials. Among the key positions he had held in the aviation sector were being Regional Director for Europe for Australian carrier Qantas Airlines; Managing Director of KLM Cargo; he had worked in "key turnaround positions" in the United Kingdom, Europe and the Americas (North and South) at DHL; and was founding CEO of the Caribbean Airlines (formerly known as British West Indian Airlines). He had also occupied senior management positions at SN Brussels Airlines, which was the successor to the Government-owned SABENA, and had launched a new airline in Oman. He had also served on the Board of Governors of the International Air Transport Association (IATA).

Davies (2019) said when he was approached to join SAA, he had felt that "here was an airline that, from a Key Performance Indicator point of view, can be fixed." He said that, when he looked at it holistically on paper, he believed that "you can create a profitable airline out of SAA." He said what appealed to him, when he was first approached, was that the Board representatives who engaged with him told him that "they wanted to make sufficient and significant changes by bringing in people who would lend their expertise from a business point of view," supported by people like him to turn the airline around.

"I got the impression that they meant it. Bear in mind, of course, that they had had 10 CEOs in 11 years. I thought, perhaps, this was a change. I saw it as an opportunity to see if I can help what is obviously clearly a significant global airline in terms of South Africa," Davies (2019) said.

Davies (2019) said that, in his experience, leaders spent most of their time trying to convince people of the need for a turnaround. He said the same applied at SAA, where Jarana as CEO spent time creating an environment in which people could work to the best of their ability.

Davies (2019) said SAA's turnaround efforts in the past had been frustrated both "by not having the longevity and sustainability in the Management" and poor capitalisation. Equally important was the need for a leadership team to enjoy the full confidence of the Shareholders.

"In my experience," Davies (2019) said, "to do a turnaround, you need to have a clear path forward. You need to have the confidence of the Shareholders. You need to have the money available that allows you to make those changes."

He said while the finances at SAA were not "as robust as they should be," which forced the airline to rely on bank loans, some progress had been made in implementing the LTTS, but "more tough decisions" remained to be made.

Davies (2019) said one of the challenges facing the national carrier was that "SAA is way out of date in terms of technology and taking advantage of it." Another challenge, he said, was that those in the SAA TMT who were there when the decay set in at the airline were still around, together with those in Middle Management:

> *The problem is that normally in a turnaround situation the Senior Management is gone; the Management Team that took the company into bankruptcy is perhaps not the best to take the company out of bankruptcy. The grassroots people – the pilots, the loaders, the customer service people, the cabin crew, the accountants and clerks, etc. – basically don't change, except in numbers.*
>
> *For that environment to be successful, Middle Management has to change. Therefore, it's Middle Management that's immune to the problem. They hold the conduit; they manage the lines of communication. They can be vicious, they can be nasty, they can be positive, they can be like damn right telling lies. It's a bit like a ball of wool that has been played with by a cat. It's normally a complete mess.*

Davies (2019) said wherever he has worked in the world, regardless of culture, he has "always found exactly the same thing: Middle Management operating in their own individual fiefdoms." He said people in this layer of leadership within an organisation tend "to duck their heads when things have gone wrong" and often blame those lower than them in the organisation, which was something he found to be "grossly unfair." That, he explained, was the reason why it was important for the new TMT to "go straight to the grassroots, often through the unions" – and said that was what Jarana was doing.

Davies (2019) said unions were "part of the solution" and needed to be taken along.

He said Middle Management tended to blame everybody else – Senior Management, the Government, Shareholders, "even Boeing or Airbus" – but themselves. To deal with them, he got them worried and nervous "because you're not going to create a turnaround without spilling some milk; I am not saying blood, but certainly milk." He said to get the required change, it was important to "send not a tsunami, but to raise some ripples in terms of making people sit up and think 'umh, hmm'."

Davies (2019) said that, in order to implement a turnaround strategy successfully, first it is important to have the right Management Team "that allows you to do that, that's practical, that understands the vision, that has no axes to grind and that just gets on to do the job." Next is having a delegation of authority framework that would enable the TMT to be operationally agile, "as opposed to waiting for some bureaucracy to tell you three months later 'no, you can't do that'." Fleet-footedness, he said, was paramount.

Davies (2019) said according to his analysis, SAA found itself in its current situation not only because it was more expensive than its competitors, but for a number of other reasons. These included the fact that the airline had "buried its head in the sand and ignored what was happening in the world." Among the things that Davies (2019) believed the SAA leadership had ignored were:

- Competition;
- technology in terms of the aircraft and the engines; and
- distribution of technology and how millennials were going to buy seats going forward.

"It knew about it, but ignored it and did nothing about it, which is the responsibility of Management, not people at grassroots. It was the failure of Management," Davies (2019) said.

He said it was because the SAA leadership had ignored all those factors that the airline was now lumped with "a higher cost base than we should."

Du Plessis (2019) said the average cost per seat-kilometre in the aviation industry had been decreasing for many years. While SAA had been able to reduce it by 15%, "the only problem is that when we reached our goal, we were where the rest of the industry was four or five years ago – and they have reduced it further."

Du Plessis (2019) said while the number of air passengers had increased from 10 million to 12 million in South Africa over the past four years, the total revenue in the domestic market had remained the same. That, he said, meant that "the only way you can survive is by changing your operating costs."

Fredericks (2019) agreed that SAA's "systems and processes" were antiquated. He said the airline was still using a SAP system of 2005, which had "never been upgraded." As a result, they could not "do the new things and new products that we want to address."

Davies (2019) said if SAA's debt was not taken over by the Government, the national carrier would not make it. He said when Margaret Thatcher was British Prime Minister in the early 1980s, British Airways was heavily indebted, as were the airlines in Australia and New Zealand. He said Thatcher's Government took over BA's debt and "the Management of the day had to make sure that the inefficiencies were eradicated so that they didn't pile up more debt."

Fredericks (2019) said SAA's debt was one of the major challenges hobbling the airline and making it difficult for it to implement the LTTS. He said while the airline used to have payment terms of 40 days on fuel with its suppliers, one of the companies had pushed the terms down to seven days. When SAA protested, the two parties eventually settled on 10 days. That, he said, wreaked havoc with SAA's cash flow, especially as it paid R1,3 billion in interest per annum on a turnover of R27 billion.

Asked what he would do differently if he had carte blanche to do anything it took to turn the airline around, Davies (2019) said he would not do things differently, but would "do things quicker because the implementation plan that we have is the right implementation plan." Instead, he would ensure that there was agility in decision making. He said he would also ensure that SAA employed the best available international talent "to fix the problem in the short term," given the shortage of aviation expertise in the country.

Davies (2019) echoed Jarana's (2019) view that, over the years, SAA had lost "a lot of good expertise," with many frustrated South Africans having left to join mostly Gulf airlines. He said international experience had to be brought into SAA, while being mindful of the country's history:

> I believe in bringing in people with different expertise. I think the country of South Africa is unique in its history and, therefore, we've got to treat that with respect and manage it in such a way that we don't appear to be going back a hundred years or so. I think we've got to be sensitive but firm in terms of what needs to happen, and you can only do that by your management style and personality, and understand and listen.

Fredericks (2019) concurred that SAA had "limited expertise," and that people who had something to offer did not want to work for the airline. He said he had agreed to be seconded to SAA only because he was at the end of his career, hence all he could lose was his reputation, "which I try not to lose by doing the right thing at the end of the day."

Fredericks (2019) said there were people at SAA who were not adding value, but getting them out of the company would be "another difficult challenge at the end of the day."

Davies (2019) said Ethiopian Airlines, Emirates and Etihad were all government owned, but were successful because their governments allowed them operational autonomy. Most of these airlines, he said, saw "SAA as a coffin." He said they followed the media and could tell that SAA was struggling and the Government cannot support it.

"The question is, and the conclusion I've come to is: what is the strength of that coffin? How many nails can it take? In other words, how much money has the Government got to fix it? Or, if it is not fixed because we've failed and moved on, at what point does it crumble?" Davies (2019) asked rhetorically.

The fundamental question, he said, was whether South Africa could afford its own airline. While he believed that SAA could be saved ("otherwise, I wouldn't waste my time"), Davies (2019) felt that it would be imperative for the Government to allow the carrier to operate unhindered. However, he was not optimistic that that would happen.

Fredericks (2019) said that in order to improve the chances of successfully implementing a turnaround strategy, it was important to have at least three things: support from the Shareholder, a good BoD which "works well and can provide guidance," and "a good-working Executive Committee (Exco)." Equally important was a good working relationship among those three, accompanied by alignment among them. He said if any one of those three groups did not work well, then it would be difficult to achieve success.

Fredericks (2019) said while progress may still be possible, discord among the three stakeholders would "delay processes, delay approvals and make it very difficult for the organisation to operate efficiently." He said if the Shareholder, the BoD and the Exco were not aligned, progress would be hindered because "then you are going to spend time just spinning the wheels and not moving forward."

He said a company going through a turnaround could not afford to have passengers on either the BoD or the Exco.

Asked if he believed SAA had the required level of support from the Shareholder, Fredericks (2019) said that was not the case. He said the fact that SAA reported to the DPE, but has to go to the National Treasury when it needs financial support, was frustrating.

"As you've seen in the newspapers, we are always begging. You can't operate a turnaround strategy like that. So, you need to address that. Ultimately, when it comes to a turnaround strategy, if you have agreed on it, you need to fund it," he said.

Fredericks (2019) said it was vital to give certainty to SAA's creditors, lenders and customers. He said during his four months at SAA at the time of the interview, he had spent most of his time "engaging with creditors and lenders," and that happened at the expense of him working on things that needed to be addressed to turn the carrier around.

Like Jarana (2019) and Davies (2019), Fredericks (2019) was also aggrieved by Mboweni's comments on SAA, saying they worked against the airline. He said negative comments on SAA by a Cabinet Minister had a deleterious impact on the airline because it dealt with forward bookings.

"Somebody sits in London or New York and sees this newspaper article. That agent says 'Sir, let me not book you on SAA; it seems they have trouble and may not be flying in six months' time or a year', which means that suddenly you have an immediate negative impact on your cash flow as well as your bottom line. That's why I say overall there's support, but there needs to be alignment between the Minister of Finance and the Minister of Public Enterprises – they need to speak with one voice," Fredericks (2019) said.

He said, owing to SAA's financial position, the BoD could not sign off SAA's March 2018 financial statements "because there's no clarity on us being a going concern." He said the national carrier found itself stuck between lenders on the one side and the Shareholder on the other side, like "ham in the sandwich." In the absence of an alignment between the Government and lenders, the airline would "struggle on a continuous basis at the end of the day."

Fredericks (2019) said it was not helpful that the unions at SAA were not fully coming to the party. He said that when he told the unions, at one meeting, that the airline was "in big trouble," the rejoinder was "we have heard this before." He said at another meeting, one of the unions threatened to down tools if he did not address an issue that they had put on the table. He said there was not as much appreciation of the fact that everybody at SAA had to come to the party:

> The people don't understand we are in so much trouble, and people need to own up and say "what do I contribute?" It's not only the Shareholder that must contribute; I must contribute. We have called everybody to order to say "what contribution do you make?" I made the example to them that Telkom was making a profit, but we had a zero-percent salary increase. To do it here, they would probably strike tomorrow.
>
> So, it's just a mind-set of people, and I think it's entitlement: "I'm entitled to this. I don't have to contribute; everybody else must, but I don't have to."

Fredericks (2019) said that those in management positions at SAA were not managing. Instead, everything was "managed from the top." "Management needs to manage," he said.

Asked what lessons could be learned from the Telkom example, Fredericks (2019) mentioned three things: "Get a good Board; the Shareholder needs to empower the Board, and then get the right people on the right seats."

Acting Chief Commercial Officer Pumla Luhabe (2019) said to improve the chances of successfully implementing the turnaround strategy, capital funding would be required to implement the initiatives identified in the five-year corporate plan, followed by an "overhaul of the culture of the organisation in terms of its people."

Luhabe (2019) believed that leadership stability was crucial to ensure a successful implementation of the LTTS. She said Jarana, who had been CEO for just over a year at the time, had prioritized filling executive positions – and had "fairly succeeded in doing that." She said leadership stability would help entrench a new culture and ensure that the next tier of leadership was motivated and coached appropriately.

"When people don't have a leadership head, they are bound to be aimless and not to have proper direction. So, leadership stability is also very crucial," Luhabe (2019) said.

She said cost retrenchment was "a big challenge" at SAA, with run-away costs being part of the reason the airline has struggled with profitability. She said the national carrier had "notoriously struggled with its cost structure over the years," and pointed out that the airline would continue to be unprofitable for as long as costs were not reigned in "because we do not operate in a vacuum or an environment where we are a monopoly." Luhabe (2019) said it was imperative for SAA to find a way of reducing its cost structure because, when compared to network competitors like BA and Singapore Airlines, its cost structure was "way above the benchmark in the industry."

Luhabe (2019) said ancillary revenue represented six percent of SAA's income, but the airline had plans to continue to grow it.

Luhabe (2019) said it was important that SAA worked to reign in those costs that were within its control, such as those incurred by the number of days that a flight crew spends in a destination. She said the national carrier would have to benchmark itself against its competitors, and work to reduce the amount of time an aircraft spent on the ground abroad.

She said the CEO and the General Manager for Human Resources, Vuyiswa Raseroka, had been in talks with "the pilot body and the cabin crew management and the cabin crew themselves" to relax some of "the ultra-generous" benefits that they enjoyed. These included pilots' rights to displace a fee-paying passenger in order to accommodate a family member.

"That's just unacceptable in my personal view, and I think that's the view that the company holds as well," Luhabe (2019) said.

She said a series of engagements had taken place with the pilots' association to relax those strenuous conditions, and she was confident that "they have made very good progress."

Raseroka (2019) said the organisational design (OD) was intended to "build an organisation that's fit for the future." She said while an operating model was developed for the LTTS, it was important to redesign the SAA structure to align with the operating model. Key among the design principles, she said, was that they wanted to "commercialise the airline."

Raseroka (2019) said the new structure would ensure that there was clear accountability for the profitability of different parts of the business throughout the airline in order to avoid the situation which obtained at the time, where there were people responsible for revenue, sitting in the Commercial part of the business, and others looking after costs, siting in the Finance Department.

"What happens is if you ask them, in the case of an income statement, who is responsible for gross profit, or ultimately profit, you won't find a single person who owns it. ... So, the OD, therefore, is going to contribute to the commercialisation of the airline to really drive the P&L of the organisation to make sure that we have the right capabilities, the right people, the right rules, making sure that we have a structure that is fit for purpose, but that is efficient as well. That's our contribution," Raseroka (2019) said.

She said SAA needed to commercialise in order to ensure that every route was profitable. She said the domestic routes had "not been making money for five years, but no one has ever asked that question." The OD would ensure that there was accountability for route profitability in future.

Raseroka (2019) said the OD was approved by the Board's Remunerations Committee and she was due to take it to the BoD that week and, thereafter, to the Shareholder. She said sharing the new structure with the Shareholder was important because SAA's Shareholder Compact stipulated that Shareholder approval was required if more than two percent of the workforce was going to be retrenched. However, she conceded that ordinarily approval of an OD would fall within the purview of the BoD, and not the Shareholder.

In terms of the existing Shareholder Compact, her engagement with the Shareholder on the OD would be meant both to inform the Shareholder and to obtain the necessary approval to proceed. She also conceded that this requirement had the effect of slowing down decision making at the airline:

> To be honest with you, it's a big hurdle and a setback. I always make the example: BA wants to recruit someone, it wants to change its structure, it will do it now. Here you have to go through processes; you have to make submissions; you have to go to the Board; you have to go to the Shareholder.
>
> So, you talk about agility, about being nimble and agile – we don't have it. The PFMA is there for a reason, but it's how it's implemented. It really

becomes so cumbersome to navigate your way through all the PFMA requirements. There are issues of how people interpret it; there are issues of how people tend to create empires around the PFMA. What it does is that it stifles efficiencies; it stifles creativity because now we are boxed in: you can't do this, you can't do that.

I had said when I joined here that I think SAA needs to be at least carved out of the PFMA, but build in very stringent processes to make sure that there's no fraud in procurement processes. We can do that; the private sector has got that, instead of saddling the airline with the PFMA, but, yeah …

Raseroka (2019) cited the example of getting a consulting company on board to work with her on the OD. She said the process had started shortly after her joining SAA a year earlier, but the initial tender was turned down by the BoD. When the BoD eventually approved the preferred bidder, there was a change of Shareholder Minister and the process had to be started afresh. Raseroka (2019) said she had lost some of the savings to which she had committed for SAA through the OD.

"So, I have lost time; I have lost about 10 months. That means that every month I am losing a certain saving, whereas if I was able to do this much earlier, I would at least have spent some of the savings, but not only then because this is two-fold: it is about cost rationalisation, but it is also about increasing your profitability by getting the right people into the right roles," she explained.

She conceded that, if she were in a private company, she would have long completed the organisational restructuring process.

Raseroka (2019) said as part of her contribution to cost retrenchment, she had already offered willing flight-deck crew, cabin crew and pilots sabbaticals, voluntary severance and early retirement packages and realised savings. In that case, she needed only Board approval, and not Shareholder approval. As a result, she had managed to reduce the number of pilots "to the desired number," but she was not as successful with the cabin crew.

Raseroka (2019) said she was at a stage where Section 189 notices had to be issued in terms of the Labour Relations Act to begin the consultation process for retrenchments. For that she needed Shareholder approval, and "that's where we are stuck then, meaning, therefore, that we are carrying excess costs every month," she said.

Asked what would happen if the Shareholder turned the Section 189 request down, Raseroka (2019) replied:

If the Shareholder wants this airline to succeed, the Shareholder should say yes. If the Shareholder says no, then the taxpayer is going to continue to pay for employees who are in excess, who are not doing much. The productivity levels at SAA are quite low.

We are going to drive performance across SAA through the OD. We are going to drive performance; there is going to be consequence management for non-performance. You need to have fewer people doing more, whereas currently, if you look, we are over-staffed in certain areas. People don't come to work; there's just laissez-faire in terms of performance.

So, if the Shareholder doesn't approve – because we have got more staff than we need – we'll continue carrying excess people, but who is going to fund that? It means the taxpayer is going to continue to fund the non-productivity of SAA. It's a consequence that's going to come as a result of that, so I'm sure the Shareholder will not be foolhardy.

Raseroka (2019) was mindful that, even if the Board and the Shareholder gave her the required approvals, she would not be able to start with the Section 189 consultations with labour on 1 May 2019, as was planned, because of the general elections that were due to take place that month. However, she said part of the OD had created new roles, which she would then seek to fill as a matter of urgency.

She said "the biggest area" that was not properly capacitated was Commercial, which was "the heartbeat of this organisation because that's where most of the business is happening." Therefore, she would want to be allowed to "capacitate that area" first.

Raseroka (2019) said she had begun to see some green shoots in the other areas of the business, because they had managed to bring in "people with right commercial skills, who've been in the airline industry and have really done large-scale turnaround projects."

She said that, once the new structure was approved, not all SAA employees would need to apply anew. She said that, in terms of the structure, there were roles that would have changed materially, there would be new roles and others would continue to be what they were. Those employees whose roles would not have changed would not be required to re-apply, but those in roles which had changed materially and those eyeing the new positions would have to re-apply.

Raseroka (2019) said that, in order to arrive at the new OD, workshops involving 250 people were held throughout SAA, during which questions were asked about the culture of SAA and various work practices were looked at "in terms of what are the standards, what are the processes and what are the people aspects of it." From the workshops, they had come up with five culture themes, for which there would be sponsors, tribes and ambassadors.

Raseroka, for instance, was going to own "Responsible" as a culture theme.

She forecast that it would take three years to embed the new organisational culture, but said low-hanging fruits would have to be identified as soon as possible. Those would be about "how your Exco shows up, how it talks about the cultural themes, how they own them and how you walk the talk as a leader." She would have to live the "Responsible" theme, which would form part of her Performance Contract.

Raseroka (2019) said labour was aware that "there's this OD happening." However, she was concerned that there were some Managers who were said to threaten employees with whom they were not happy by saying "I'm gonna OD you."

Raseroka (2019) said organisational stability was "absolutely crucial, especially in an organisation that is limping like SAA." She said that it was important to have a leadership that would see the turnaround through.

She said leadership instability was "one of the reasons why SAA is where it is now because every new CEO comes in, starts the LTTS, half way that CEO is gone, Exco is gone and a new CEO comes and starts the process all over again." Raseroka (2019) said when she and the CEO joined the airline, "people said we are giving you two years and then you will be out of here:"

> *I was joking the other day, saying "oh, I've been here for about 14 months now; that means I have a couple of months left." So, people don't believe that what we are doing we will see to the end. There is a lot of scepticism about it. … If I leave now and another GM for HR comes in, s/he is going to have to understand where this came from. It's going to be another six months down the line. They may not even believe in it and want to change it, and that means resources, and it will have been a waste of resources.*
>
> *So, I think there's anxiety if we'll see this through, but I'm living for today. Tomorrow will take care of itself.*

However, Raseroka (2019) said she sensed growing "understanding and appreciation," on the part of the Board, "of the need to make quick decisions, move quickly and turn around." She said she was "seeing that the Board is coming to the party," and said she got the impression that the BoD realised that "if the CEO leaves now, that means all this work that we have done – the resources, the costs, the time that has gone into it – obviously will fall flat."

Raseroka (2019) – who had worked at BP, Telkom, MultiChoice and Vodacom as HR Director for Africa, Group Executive: Human Resources, Vice President: Human Resources Africa and Managing Executive: Human Resources respectively – was recruited to SAA by Jarana. She said she found it frustrating that "something that I would get done in a day or two, here it takes me months to do."

"Procurement is frustrating. Everything is a drag," she said.

She said there was a low staff turnover at SAA, sitting around five to eight percent of the staff complement. She said employees did not leave "because there's brand affinity, and people believe in the story."

She said it was crucial that the SAA TMT was freed up to do what it was employed to do:

> *I believe that if leadership is given the latitude to do what it needs to do, this airline will turn around. Less Shareholder involvement, less Board involvement – I'm saying build boundaries and empower the leadership to drive the agenda. But there's this bungee-jumping, I call it, where the Board wants to move in there and move back, the Shareholder gets in and moves back. You can't bungee-jump in a situation like this because time is of the essence.*
>
> *... And I understand why; there's an element of mistrust as well. Things have happened in this organisation in the past, where people were given latitude to do certain things; obviously the wrong things happened. So, one understands, but it's a question of how do you build trust, put those boundaries and empower? If you are not going to do that, you may as well shut this airline down because here it's about agility. Empower the CEO and trust that the CEO will do the right thing.*

Five months after the interview and four months after Jarana's resignation, Raseroka was mysteriously placed on suspension, without any reasons being given (Skiti, 2019).

Based on what SAA Chairman JB Magwaza (2019) told me during the interview with him, it was, perhaps, an inevitability that reasons would be found to get Raseroka out of SAA after Jarana's resignation. Magwaza (2019) said some members of the Board wanted to get involved in appointments of SAA Executives, and would often have a fight with the CEO on the issue. He said they did not respect the operations-governance line and sought to involve themselves in operational matters. The main source of friction with the CEO, he said, was "about people that you bring into the organisation."

Magwaza (2019) said some members of the BoD would treat Raseroka unfairly at meetings – just because she was appointed by Jarana:

> *I mean, the poor lady at Human Resources, really; I would sit and I would scream at some of my fellow Board Members and I would say don't, you can't do this – because they didn't like her, but Vuyani liked her. As far as delivery is concerned, she is delivering to the organisation. Turnaround time is short, right people she is bringing in. On the OD work, yes, top of the game, but she can never be enough for some of my Board Members.*

Du Plessis (2019) said the frequent changes in leadership led to a situation where new CEOs had to start from scratch to earn the Government's trust, hence the Significance and Materiality Framework (SMF) which stipulates decisions requiring Government approval and the Delegation of Authority "tend to be extremely restrictive." He said when he spoke to suppliers who had worked with EAL, they told him that "the two parties sit in a boardroom opposite each other, the Management negotiate, they sign the deal, they walk over to the Minister, he signs it off and 24 hours later everything is complete."

Du Plessis (2019) said it was imperative that the SAA leadership team was allowed the necessary "freedom to make the decisions required, within the framework, but with far faster turnaround times in terms of getting stuff approved, getting it in place – far more like a commercial entity."

Speaking on the basis of his experience at SAA over three decades, Du Plessis (2019) said the biggest challenge for the airline was "if the President, the Shareholders, the Board, the CEO, the Executive and the staff are not aligned, you don't get anything done."

Du Plessis (2019) said that, over the years, SAA had experienced "a lot of in-fighting at some stages between the Exco, the CEO, the Board, the Minister and the Chairpersons of the Board," and that had brought about a form of stasis in the organisation. He likened the situation to children caught between warring parents:

> What happens is if your parents are fighting, the children sometimes become undisciplined. If Treasury and the DPE are not 100% aligned between developmental strategy versus fiscal control, it causes a problem. Are we there to develop the country or are we there to make profit? Is the mandate very clear?
>
> So, what would happen if we do what Mom wants and you still are creating jobs, but Dad is refusing to give you money for the jobs? You are stuck between a rock and a hard place.

Du Plessis (2019) said he could remember one period, when Bezuidenhout was Acting CEO for the first time and he had a 90-day plan, when there was "total alignment among the Minister, the Chair, the CEO and the Exco." As a result of that alignment, there was "a lot of action and positive results in a short period of time," with employees on board and "everybody running in the same direction."

Du Plessis (2019) said management instability was "the biggest reason we have not been able to fix SAA." He said successful airlines like EAL have been far more stable, with the latter having had two CEOs in the past decade, compared to 10 for SAA. He said it was deeply frustrating that just as the SAA team had finally managed to "get someone [a CEO] at Airline 101, when they need to be at Airline 301 for the airline to be able to be profitable, you have a change in guard."

He said having people in acting positions for an extended period was debilitating for the airline. He said people in acting roles could not make binding decisions, and this confirmed the need for "management stability."

Du Plessis (2019) said apart from the fact that the culture at SAA was prone to get "totally toxic," high performers also got frustrated when they were appointed into senior positions, only to find that their hands were tied. "People," he said, "do not want to be associated with failure because of a lack of ability to implement what is required."

He cited the example of a former General Manager: Commercial, who was "a great guy" and had come from a commercial airline where he could open and close routes as the situation demanded. However, he got very frustrated when he got to SAA and "it takes him a year to get the same decision made."

Du Plessis (2019) said the absence of performance incentives was another challenge. He said "high achievers want to take risks, but get rewarded for it." He said while he understood that there could be no rewards when the airline made losses, nevertheless he believed that some reward had to be considered for reducing the quantum of annual losses from, say, R4 billion to R1 billion.

"Nobody wants to wait for four or five years and be totally dependent on someone else," he said.

To ensure SAA's success, Du Plessis (2019) said it would be important that the Government adopted a Fly South Africa Act, similar to the USA's Fly America Act, which would require everybody in the public sector to fly the national carrier: "You do not undermine your State-owned airline by subsidising other airlines. You have Americans flying on American airlines, but our Government officials also fly on them [American airlines]. You do not have a level playing field," he said.

Du Plessis (2019) said to improve the chances of successfully turning SAA around, it would be important to "address some of the [existing] labour agreements." He said while doing so would cause short-term unhappiness, in the end it would yield long-term sustainability.

He also strongly advocated the sale of equity in SAA. He said doing so would not only enable the airline to move away from the PFMA, but it would also enable SAA to create "a very strong footprint in southern Africa for the region to feed into their network" to help the national airline to realise growth. It would also provide SAA much-needed capital and place it in a position where it would gain from knowledge transfer.

Du Plessis (2019) said SAA was disadvantaged by the Government's requirement that, when it made large-scale purchases like those of new aircraft, it had to contribute a certain percentage of the value of the purchase towards the National Industrialisation

Participation Programme (NIPP), when its competitors like Emirates did not have to do the same in the UAE.

"So, we pay the money that went into building the aviation village in Centurion, and we must compete against our competitors with more expensive planes. So, you've got that unfair playing field that I have mentioned, like the Fly America Act and a few others," Du Plessis (2019) concluded.

In an interview with the *Sunday Times* in September 2020, Bezuidenhout stressed the importance of agility in decision making at SAA, saying an airline could not be run as though it were "a government department" (Barron, 2020).

Chapter Ten

FRACTIOUS BOARDS OF DIRECTORS HAVE LEGAL LIABILITY, BUT LIMITED AUTHORITY

During interviews with SAA Board Members who were in office at the time (in 2019) and those who had gone before them, a very clear picture emerged: the Boards of Directors (BoDs) tended to be fractious; some of their members did not respect the operations-governance divide and the Shareholder Ministers exercised much of the authority. In the meantime, Board Members carried the full legal liability for the airline, and yet they did not enjoy the requisite authority to make unfettered decisions and to mitigate the risks, as they saw them, which confronted the airline.

Just as the CEOs and their Top Management Teams (TMS) complained about the Boards' interference in operational matters, Board Members also complained about an all-powerful and intrusive Shareholder who would not leave them alone to carry out their fiduciary duties.

There was also mutual distrust among Board Members, especially before November 2017, and some believed that their fellow Non-Executive Directors were less concerned about good corporate governance at the airline, but sought to advance the interests of the factions to which they belonged in the governing party. These dynamics are laid bare in this chapter, which is based on interviews conducted with the Board Members in 2019.

The Board Members covered in this interview were those appointed by Pravin Gordhan, as Finance Minister, in September 2016 and those appointed by Malusi Gigaba, also as Finance Minister, a year later.

Mzimkulu Malunga and Bajabulie Swazi Tshabalala were among 11 individuals appointed by then-Finance Minister Pravin Gordhan onto the Board of SAA with effect from 1 September 2016. Myeni was the only member of the out-going BoD who was retained, and continued in her position as Chairperson. Former SAA Chief Financial Officer Tryphosa Ramano was appointed Deputy Chairperson (GCIS, 2016).

Gordhan met with the new Board Members on 31 August 2016, before their appointment was made public, "to share with them the status of the airline and

Government's expectations of the Board." The Minister took the Board through its mandate and informed it that its "primary focus" was to return SAA to financial sustainability, "while also delivering on other important Government objectives" (Ministry of Finance, 2016). The "other important Government objectives" were not listed in the press release issued after the meeting.

Gordhan also used the opportunity to stress "the roles and responsibilities and the separation of powers between Non-Executive Directors and Executives, in line with the Protocol on Corporate Governance which applies to all public-sector institutions." During the meeting, Gordhan also informed the incoming BoD that SAA's application for a guarantee that would enable it to remain a going concern had been approved, with a series of conditions (Ministry of Finance, 2016).

The conditions were the following (Ministry of Finance, 2016):

- The Board's primary focus had to be to return the airline to financial sustainability;

- SAA's strategy had to be strengthened, with "alignment with other State-owned airlines ensured;"

- SAA had to implement "more aggressive cost-cutting initiatives" in a number of areas, namely fuel, aircraft ownership, labour, maintenance, repair and overhaul, as well as procurement;

- SAA's network and fleet plan had to "be refined based on a sound business case so that the airline takes advantage of opportunities to scale back [its] operations to focus only on operating routes which positively contribute to [its] profitability, closes routes that have been making losses for longer than one year and ensures that the network plan is aligned with the other State-owned airlines;"

- SAA's strategy had to "better differentiate the airline, enabling it to continue to compete effectively, *inter alia* through addressing the customer value proposition;"

- SAA had to work with the National Treasury and the DPE "in giving consideration to the possible merger of SAA with SAX and the potential introduction of a strategic equity partner;"

- The Board had to "start a new process of appointing the CEO, the CFO and other key executives, *in consultation with the Minister*" (emphasis mine);

- SAA had to secure funding "to meet the airline's liquidity requirements;"

- The Board had to "ensure that the AFS for both 2014/15 and 2015/16 are finalised;" and

- SAA had to "report progress on a regular basis to National Treasury."

During an interview with me three years later, Malunga (2019) – who was one of six Board Members who were dropped when new Finance Minister Malusi Gigaba reconstituted the Board a year later – confirmed that the LTTS was "one of the main deliverables of the Board." He said there was already a LTTS Board Committee in existence when the new Board took office, and said the LTTS was a continuation of the SAA Business Restructuring Process work done by Ngqula's team – with Seabury's help – in earlier years. The strategy, Malunga (2019) said, was "formalised as the LTTS under Gigaba" during his tenure as Minister of Public Enterprises in 2013.

Tshabalala was then appointed new Chairperson of the LTTS Committee. Malunga (2019) said the role of the LTTS Committee work "was big,... especially because there was no permanent Management at SAA." He said out of the 11 SAA Executive Committee (Exco) members at the time, "eight were acting."

"The Board basically took it (the LTTS) over. The Management was just implementing: Acting CEO, Acting CFO, acting this one, acting that one," Malunga (2019) said.

He was complimentary about the LTTS which, he said, "touched on all the key drivers, all the components of that business." Malunga (2019) said in addition to identifying things that were working well, such as SAA's great safety record, the LTTS had honed in on the things that needed to be fixed.

"On the negative side, the costs are high, the revenue is declining, market share is declining, there hasn't been consistency of longevity at the top, like the core Management, even the Boards. Where SAA's biggest problems are is the iteration at the top; in no time there is a new Board. One of the key problems with SAA was iteration at the top and the financial structure in terms of a weak balance sheet because of the debt," Malunga (2019) said.

He said that he had suggested that, in addition to closely monitoring costs and seeking to reduce them, the Board should also establish "a Revenue Committee whose role is how to increase revenue." He said at the time the airline had revenue of about R31 billion, but its costs were about R34 billion. "So," Malunga said, "a business like that is dead in the water."

However, he could not "win the debate on this one."

Malunga (2019), who chaired the Board's Marketing and Communications Ad-hoc Committee, recalled a moment when the British Broadcasting Corporation (BBC) ran a story saying "SAA only had three months to live and will not be there in December." He said that he had suggested that the Board should get Gordhan to issue a public statement declaring that "this airline is not going anywhere; it will be around for a long time." He said not a single one of his fellow Board Members supported him, but some of them phoned him after the meeting to say they agreed with him. In the meantime, SAA lost "almost R100 million in bookings."

"Then I realised that there is politics here; maybe I came to the wrong place. It was then that I realised that this thing is actually much bigger than I had anticipated in terms of the dynamics. In fact, one of the things that I thought let the turnaround strategy down is that many people seem to have come to the Board with mandates from all and sundry, maybe from the private sector and others from this section of the ruling party. Some of us didn't get those e-mails, so we got there to say what can I do to put my best foot forward. That, basically, troubled me a lot," Malunga (2019) said.

A former journalist and former CEO of a media publishing house, Malunga (2019) said some people in the media would tell him which Board Members and Executives were leaking information on SAA to the media.

Malunga (2019) said while he could not tell exactly what the respective agendas were, a clear pattern emerged in that BoD where suggestions were supported or opposed based on who made them:

> *I felt that the mandates were conflicting in the sense that, perhaps, Dudu felt that she had a mandate from the President [Zuma] and Tryphosa and others maybe felt that they had a mandate from Pravin [Gordhan] and other interests, while some of us didn't get a mandate from anyone. We were caught up in no-man's land.*

> *It's not clear to me what exactly the mandates were, but I could see there were people there who came with mandates – just the way they behaved and their mannerisms, what they prioritized and what they did not prioritize clearly showed me that this one came with a particular mandate.*

Malunga (2019) said Gordhan, as Shareholder Minister, was "actually quite good," but the relationship between the latter and SAA Chairperson Dudu Myeni was "definitely bad; they just disliked each other." He said Gordhan, who generally had a good relationship with the rest of the BoD, often held meetings with the SAA Board, that Myeni would send an apology at the eleventh hour and Gordhan would "make a snide comment in her absence and, of course, she would get that information."

Malunga (2019) said then-Deputy Finance Minister Mcebisi Jonas was "calm, never showed emotions." He said the impasse between Myeni and Gordhan ended in March 2017 when the latter was fired and replaced with Gigaba as Finance Minister.

Malunga (2019) said he disapproved of the way in which the Board related to the SAA Management:

> *The Management – I felt sorry for them because most of them at the time were acting. They were treated badly, even by the Board. Nobody really saw them, if you ask me. I felt that the Board didn't think that Management mattered that much. So, people on the Board seemed to have come with the idea that you can't find good people at SAA. Therefore, they are not worth being taken seriously. That's why people would phone them in the middle of the night and harass them.*
>
> *When we were there, my worry was that our Board was getting too close to operations to a point where the LTTS Committee had a sub-committee which was meeting every week with the Management, almost like driving the LTTS, which is something that the CEO should have been doing. I think that was a mistake, if you ask me, which is why I was always hoping that when the new captain of the ship comes, it would be better.*

He said even though he understood that most of the people in the Management Team were acting, hence the Board's lack of confidence in them, he thought the Board's operational involvement "at some point became too much." However, Malunga (2019) was of the view that the SAA TMT had "a good working relationship" with the National Treasury team, but he could not attest to the strength of that relationship.

He said it worried him deeply that "the relationship between the Board and Management was non-existent; the Board was just dictating." Malunga (2019) said: "They didn't think anything could come from Management. If Management came and made an input, for instance, I don't think the Board took it seriously. Some of us did, but I didn't think that the Board took Management seriously at all."

Asked why it was that eight of the 11 Exco members were acting, Malunga (2019) said he thought that it "conveniently suited" the SAA Boards "because with acting appointees, you can come into the operations and make decisions." He said "acting people have no legitimacy, so if you are a Board that wants to interfere in operations, it becomes easier" to do so.

Malunga (2019) said the LTTS Committee even developed an SAA organisational structure which it presented to the Board for approval. He said he cautioned against a Board Committee developing an organisational structure, arguing that it was the CEO who needed to do so. The response? Malunga (2019) said he was told "no, we don't have the time."

"Of course, when the CEO came, he changed the structure," Malunga (2019) said.

He said that instead of "spending too much time on the LTTS itself," in retrospect he felt that the Board should have prioritised the appointment of the CEO "and let the leadership come back to us on how they are going to turn the organisation around."

Asked why it took so long for the Board to appoint a CEO, Malunga (2019) said the previous Board had recommended a CEO to the Shareholder for appointment, but neither the new Board nor the Shareholder was keen on the recommended candidate. He said Myeni, "being the surviving member of the old Board, still felt that we had finished the process," when Gordhan's clear mandate to the new Board was for it to re-open the process and recommend a preferred candidate to him.

Malunga (2019) said decision making at SAA lay at Board and Shareholder levels, and "Management didn't make any decisions." He said at the beginning Gordhan gave the Board "a bit of space," but a new Shareholder Compact subsequently "took a fair amount of the decision-making powers to the Shareholder."

Malunga (2019) believed that the national carrier can be turned around "if there is a strong leadership at managerial level, a cohesive Board with a single mandate, a non-interfering Shareholder and quick decision making from the Shareholder level to make the organisation agile because it is operating in a highly-competitive space." He said while its competitors are agile and make decisions swiftly, SAA, on the other hand, "needs to get concurrence from the Shareholder for some decisions – and the Shareholder can take months to give you concurrence, whereas if you are Ethiopian Airlines, that decision does not go to the Shareholder."

Malunga (2019) said while "the Shareholder can take months" to give concurrence about proposed route exits in terms of Section 54 of the PFMA, the self-same Shareholder "can also say: go and fly this route because it is strategic to do so, but the Shareholder doesn't give you money to fly this uneconomic route."

According to Malunga (2019), SAA's "biggest problem is structure." The airline, he said, "is hamstrung by its structure because decision making does not reside where it should." Explained Malunga (2019):

> You've got a Shareholder – I suspect because it is putting in so much money – that says we must make decisions how that money is spent. I can understand the rationale, but it does not obtain in the practical sense.
>
> And then you've got a Board to which people come with different interests, mandates and stuff like that. They are appointed by one person, but I think often people pull in different directions either as individuals or because it's just the way human beings are, or because of the contestations that South Africa is about. South Africa is a contested territory – and then, of course, the disempowerment of Management.

I think if you've got good Management there that knows what it is doing and you give them power to move, SAA could move.

Malunga (2019) said the Board's role should be confined to oversight, "but mostly stakeholder stuff" because the airline needed "a lot of stakeholder stuff to be done to reach out to society." In particular, he believed that the Board could help in managing the expectations of provincial politicians, most of whom would like the national carrier to fly to their respective provinces and foreign airlines like BA, Virgin and Emirates to land and take off from their main cities, at the expense of Johannesburg as a regional hub.

However, Malunga (2019) said even such work would require prior approval from the Shareholder: "You can't do that engagement without the Shareholder sanctioning you to do that. The Shareholder wants you to stay away. You can't go to the DA or the EFF, as a Board, to say that we need your support to talk this airline up instead of hitting it up every time you are on television and calling for it to be privatised. You can't do that because that is the domain of the Shareholder – and the Shareholder is not doing that, but the Shareholder is pumping money into SAA."

To turn SAA around successfully, Malunga (2019) said the Shareholder should allow the BoD space to play its oversight role, and the Board should appoint "competent Management and then give it management space, devolve some of the power to them and have strong oversight, but give Management space to move."

Malunga (2019) shared Vuyani Jarana's (2019) and Vuyiswa Raseroka's (2019) view that, if SAA were privately owned, the Shareholder would not be as interventionist and that the Shareholder was not directly invested (what Jarana called having "skin in the game") because the money repeatedly pumped into the airline belonged to taxpayers, and not to the individual Ministers or, indeed, those constituting the Government. A private Shareholder, he said, would "know that if you don't meet your targets, no taxpayer is going to come and bail you out – you either swing or go belly up."

Malunga (2019) said SAA was one of three African airlines with commercial potential, with the other two being Kenya Airways (KQ) and Ethiopian Airlines (EAL). He said if those who ran the national carrier kept that in mind, there would be "much better decision-making taking place at SAA than is the case at the moment and a lot less politics being played."

Tshabalala (2019) said during her time on the SAA Board, the focus was on returning the airline to profitability. She said one of the factors which are responsible for SAA's losses "is the fact that they were trying to do everything, fly everywhere." She said the national carrier was not focused and adopted a strategy that may have been sensible "maybe 20 years ago when you didn't have Emirates, you didn't have Ethiopian Airlines," when Africa was still "a captive market" for the South African airline. She said that changed "as soon as KQ and EAL decided that they wanted in."

According to Tshabalala (2019), SAA did not respond to the threat posed by KQ and EAL.

Secondly, Tshabalala (2019) said SAA's lack of capital muscle to enable it to acquire the latest, fuel-efficient planes meant that it could not compete effectively with KQ, EAL and other airlines, coupled with its ultra-generous working conditions for its pilots and cabin crew. She said SAA had planes which were "20, 25 years old," which were expensive to maintain.

She said that, although SAA had lost "a lot of very skilled people" during Myeni's tenure as Board Chairperson, the carrier still has "too many people." She said the national carrier was also not efficiently organised internally, and the information technology system that it used was not "the best of class."

Tshabalala (2019) said there were many things that needed to be fixed, and SAA did not have the money to fix them. She said to turn SAA around and make it profitable, the airline would have to be properly capitalised to the tune of "just under R22 billion" to cover its debts. Tshabalala (2019) said the best way to "rescue SAA is to get it partnered with one of the major airlines," which would provide the required capital injection.

Tshabalala (2019) confirmed that the LTTS Committee that she chaired "had been in existence for a very long time." She said the Committee had registered "some good wins" when it was first established, especially when it was looking at costs. That, however, was "until Dudu's influence got greater and greater and eventually the Committee wasn't even operating at all."

Asked why the Committee was no longer operating, Tshabalala (2019) replied rhetorically: "Well, was she [Myeni] listening to any ideas? Was she listening? Was she prepared to consider the drastic changes that were required? She wasn't. She wasn't. I don't know what her priority was."

Asked if the Board deferred to Myeni as Chairperson, Tshabalala (2019) said "before we arrived, absolutely." She said there were four members of that Board remaining, and they all resigned until Myeni was the only member of the old Board remaining. She said she believed that Myeni "basically ran the show after Cheryl Carolus, Siza Mzimela and those people had left," and some "senior operational staff left as well."

Tshabalala (2019) explained:

> We had so many people suspended and nothing was happening. They were
> sitting at home, earning salaries. There was just absolute chaos. It just wasn't
> working. The Board was just one person. All the Committees effectively were

non-functional, including the Audit Committee, which is madness in terms of the Companies Act.

Tshabalala (2019) said the remaining SAA TMT – including Acting CEO Zwane – was "terrified, absolutely terrified of" Myeni. She said one of the first things that Gordhan did, as the responsible Minister, was to reconstitute the LTTS, and she was appointed to chair it.

Tshabalala (2019) said there was a time when the Board met "over 20 times" in six months. Over time, that became untenable for her because she was based in Abidjan, Ivory Coast, where she was Vice President and CFO of the African Development Bank.

Commenting on the locus of decision rights at SAA during her time on the Board, Tshabalala (2019) said "Dudu had taken all of the authority" and it was "very difficult [for the Acting CEO] to focus on anything." She said the new Board wanted a CEO whom it would empower, and ask him/her "to put together a delegation of authority framework that makes sense for what needs to be done." An approach would then be made to the National Treasury to "make them understand, appreciate and approve" so that the document forms the basis of the delegation to the CEO.

Tshabalala (2019) said once that was done, it would then free up Management "to get on with things like selling aircraft, leasing aircraft," all of which "should not be decisions that sit with National Treasury." Otherwise, she said, "in a way they [SAA] are being asked to compete with their hands tied."

Asked if the Board or its LTTS Committee raised the matter of an appropriate delegation framework with the Shareholder and, if so, what the response was, Tshabalala (2019) replied: "Usually nothing. Usually nothing. A part of it, of course, is that they are trying to micro-manage an airline themselves, without aviation experience. Who is sitting there with aviation experience? Nobody."

Tshabalala (2019) said when other airlines approached SAA about a possible partnership, Management would be required to get Shareholder approval before even engaging in exploratory talks with the potential suitor. She said National Treasury would first have to consider the approach "and, as usual, they never come back to you … because that's their thing, if they've got something which is a conundrum, then they simply do not respond." Such conduct by a Shareholder Ministry, Tshabalala (2019) stressed, "is fatal for a business like an airline."

Tshabalala (2019) was part of the Presidential Review Committee (PRC) on State-Owned Enterprises appointed by Zuma in 2011, and chaired its Business Case work stream. She said the PRC recommended that SAA should be sold "because all you are doing now is watching its value erode:"

In fact, our view was that sell SAA, sell Telkom because, what are you doing?
As Government, you are not in a situation where you are dealing with market
failure, where something must be provided and the private sector is not willing
to provide it. So, what are you doing exactly? What you should be doing is to
try and maximise the amount of money that you would get out of that asset so
that you can redeploy it elsewhere. Otherwise, there is no market failure. That
need is well serviced.

Tshabalala (2019) said upon its submission, the PRC's report on State-Owned Enterprises was approved by the Cabinet and published on the Presidency's website.

Gigaba (2019), who was twice SAA Shareholder first as Minister of Public Enterprises and later as Minister of Finance, said the PRC's recommendations "were neglected, completely ignored." That, he said, was because the Government "has lacked vision for State-owned companies." As a result, he felt that "any turnaround strategy, whether for SAA or anyone else, will not succeed."

Tshabalala (2019) said there was a time when a partnership among SAA, KQ and EAL would have made sense, with the three airlines agreeing to "divvy up Africa among themselves." She said although EAL has since grown phenomenally, she still believes that a three-way partnership remains an option for the three African carriers.

Alternatively, she said implementation of the Yamassoukrou Decision might help SAA because then there would be "no need for Ethiopian Airways to feel they must go to Durban, Cape Town and Johannesburg" since they will have many options in East, West and Central Africa. That way, EAL would "leave SAA with Southern Africa, with SADC [Southern African Development Community]."

Tshabalala (2019) said it was important for the BoD to "delegate fully" to the CEO and the TMT: "Me, I come from the school that says delegate fully. My view was that, yes, we have different experiences and we bring certain expertise into Board positions, but we don't run the airline. I feel very strongly that we should not run the airline; we should not attempt to run the airline. All we do is to provide guidance, to provide strategic guidance on those major decisions."

She said while it made sense for the BoD to have a view on aircraft acquisitions, which typically involved "a huge amount of money," she did not believe that the same applied to ordinary Management decisions. However, Tshabalala (2019) said that she knew that some of her fellow Non-Executive Directors did not share her views on the need to empower Management. She said that was where the Shareholder Ministries, the National Treasury and Public Enterprises, had a duty to set the right "tone at the top."

Tshabalala (2019) said entities like SAA got moved to National Treasury only because they were in financial trouble so that the latter would focus on how to minimise the cost to the fiscus. The National Treasury, she said, was not equipped to manage SOEs and "should not be running any SOEs."

She shared Gigaba's (2019) view that, ideally, there should be one Ministry looking after SOCs. She questioned if the Department of Public Enterprises – which was created in order to privatise SOCs and was not meant to out-live the interim Government of National Unity which was formed in 1994 – was equal to that task.

Tshabalala (2019) said she and the Directors who were appointed at the same time with her put SAA's developmental mandate "on the back burner" and focused, instead, on its commercial viability. She said they knew that "the Treasury would not be willing to fund any losses in the delivery of that developmental mandate."

Tshabalala (2019) said while SAA had "too many assets that were not making money and it was also very, very clear that we had too many people," she did not think that the answer to reducing the airline's losses lay in retrenching people. She said turnarounds were impacted by the environments in which they occurred, and did not have a template. She believed that opportunities for cost containment at SAA lay elsewhere, including in eradicating corruption and renegotiating existing contracts.

She said one of the candidates who were interviewed for the position of CEO was an American man who was "a ruthless, ruthless turnaround leader." She said: "If you close your eyes and forget where you are, that's probably the guy who would get you from where you were to being profitable in no time flat, but that's probably the guy who would result in operations ceasing completely because there would be outrage over there."

Tshabalala (2019) said the BoD had decided on Briton Peter Davies as Chief Restructuring Officer because he had worked in the Caribbean and Asia, hence he had "that experience of working in complicated environments in terms of that racial dynamic." She said the Board wanted somebody who, in addition to knowing what it took for an airline to be successful, also understood "that the journey from where you are to there involves a lot of negotiations in the middle."

Tshabalala (2019), who also chaired the Air Chefs BoD, said she believed that particular SAA subsidiary "should have been privatised a long time ago" so that it would not be reliant on SAA alone. She recalled, from her Transnet days, that Air Chefs was corporatised "in preparation for sale, and all of that was subsequently reversed." She hoped that the subsidiary's sale would soon take place.

Tshabalala (2019) said SAAT, on the other hand, was important and should be retained within the SAA Group, provided it was run "well and competitively" and an appropriate partnership was concluded for it.

Asked what she would do if she were given carte blanche to turn the airline around, Tshabalala (2019) said she would advise the Government to get the Yamassoukro

Decision "done and dusted because it's important," and would sell 49,9% of equity in SAA to raise capital. She said SAA desperately needed "more efficient aircraft," even if they were not brand new.

Next she would sell "all the bits and pieces" of SAA that were not core to the business and immediately enter into talks with KQ and EAL "about carving up Africa." She would also focus on the Southern African Development Community as SAA's immediate catchment area, as well as Australia, South and North America, and reduce the number of SAA flights. In Asia and the Middle East, Tshabalala (2019) would "concede ground" because she believed it would be tough for the national carrier to compete in routes to those regions.

Tshabalala (2019) said that, in order to improve the chances of leadership stability, she would "fully support" the development of an incentive plan to reward SAA employees as important milestones were reached on the LTTS journey:

> *People must, first of all, visualise the goal that they are headed to and must be rewarded for meeting very tough thresholds. That does two things: obviously it motivates them, but it also ties them in because every time they meet those thresholds, there's more money. You don't have to pay them all of it; there can be a portion which is retained in order to make sure that through that entire period there is a big pay-off when they deliver the turnaround.*

Tshabalala (2019) said the Board would be "failing in its fiduciary responsibility" if it did not support the proposal of a staff incentive plan. She said she would ask any Board Member who had a problem with that proposal to "step aside."

Aviation expert Ahmed Bassa was one of six individuals who were appointed by Gigaba, then as Finance Minister, onto the SAA BoD in November 2017. The other five were new Chairman JB Magwaza, Nolitha Fakude, Geoff Rothschild, Tinyiko Mhlari and Martin Kingston. They joined Tshabalala, Peter Tshisevhe, Thandeka Mgoduso, Peter Maluleka and Akhter Moosa to complete the SAA Board, and replaced Myeni, Ramano, Malunga, Siphilile Buthelezi, Nazmeera Moola and Gugu Sipamla, who were released from the Board.

Bassa (2019) is a great proponent of the concept of a national airline. He said in addition to providing employment to about 10 000 people and a livelihood to 55 000 people (assuming that each person working there has 5,5 dependants), SAA made a direct contribution to the country's economy in various unquantifiable ways. He said these ways included providing important transport links, "theoretically contribut[ing] to tourism," providing training and education and "giv[ing] a sense of pride." According to Bassa (2019), "a country without a national carrier is a nation without pride."

Bassa (2019) said at the dawn of democracy in South Africa in 1994, the country had "fewer than 20 Bilateral Air Services Agreements," but today has "about 150." He said only 12 international airlines flew to South Africa in 1994, but there were 60 carriers flying to the country in 2000.

Bassa (2019) said most of the Bilateral Air Services Agreements (BASA) that the Government concluded with other countries were at the expense of SAA as a national carrier. He said most international passengers from South Africa now travelled on Emirates, "the single largest foreign carrier" in the country, with eight flights per day originating from South Africa. He said Emirates had 50 flights a day from India, 30 a day from the United Kingdom and 30 a day from Australia.

Former Department of Public Enterprises Deputy Director-General Matsietsi Mokholo (2019) said policy incoherence was responsible for the wholesale liberalisation of the skies, at the expense of SAA. She said the way the Government allowed "new entrants, especially foreign airlines, into our space was creating problems for our domestic airlines." That, she said, led to valid questions being asked about why the Government wants "to own these entities if we are not going to support them from a policy point of view."

Mokholo (2019) said the idea of developing a Whole-of-State approach was intended, among other things, to "look at how we license foreign airlines coming into the country and how we allow them to operate within the two principles of Competitive Neutrality and Cabotage Rules." She said, from the perspective of the Principle of Competitive Neutrality, the Government took the view that State-owned airlines "will pay taxes like everybody else, they will be subjected to everything else, but there should be certain things that we do or legislation to give them that added advantage." One of the ways of giving SAA an advantage, she said, was not to allow foreign airlines to land in the country "and still even carry passengers through domestically."

Bassa (2019) said South Africa should have taken a leaf out of Thailand's book and aggressively promoted itself as an international tourist destination, using SAA as an asset, instead of generously granting landing rights in the country to many foreign carriers. As a national carrier, SAA would then have had to fly principally on the basis of trade, political links, "colonial seriality," tourism, as well as sports and culture.

He said that, since SAA was a national carrier, the airline would have to understand that "the Shareholder exercises his right to tell you where to fly." However, Bassa (2019) did not know how those unprofitable routes would be paid for or who would pay for them. Asked how much of SAA's mandate was meant to be commercial viability and how much of it was developmental, Bassa (2019) said: "Being a non-operational person, I would say it is 60-40% commercial and developmental."

He said in addition to flying to a number of smaller, domestic towns and cities, through SAX and SA Airlink as feeder airlines, in order to keep politicians happy, SAA also had to "keep alive certain routes as recognition for those countries in Africa that used to support us during the apartheid days." Specifically, he mentioned Nigeria:

> *One of the places we used to fly to politically was [Nigerian capital] Abuja, but you don't go to Abuja because nothing happens there, so you go back to Lagos. The Nigerian Government said "please fly to Abuja." This Government says "please fly to Abuja," but our commercial figures say fly to Lagos. When you are a national carrier, sometimes you are told, in very harsh tones, that you have got to fly there.*

However, Bassa (2019) added that the Board needs "to do some very unpleasant things" by exiting some routes that were not viable commercially.

Bassa (2019) said in order to turn SAA around, CEO Vuyani Jarana and his TMT would have to reduce costs, increase revenue and "innovate in trying to ensure that the revenue base expands without adding an additional cent." While he was effusive with praise for Jarana, Bassa (2019) was very critical of the Management Team at SAA in terms of its skills and expertise ("Vuyani, if I have to stand him up against 20 white men, I'll pick him because he has got it. I can tell you personally because I engage with him, but below him there is zero," he said).

SAA Audit Committee Chairman Akhter Moosa (2019) shared the generally widespread concern about the quality of the SAA Executive Team, saying that, as a result, Jarana was "carrying a load which is unbearable." He thought that Jarana, who had "a good man in Deon [Fredericks]," was "working unhealthy hours" because "the rest of his team is not at a level that can give him less to worry about."

Asked where decision rights lay at SAA, Bassa (2019) said it was "a very clouded place." He cited, as "an example which shocked me," the fact that the SAA Board could not "appoint a CFO or a CEO of the Divisions without the Minister approving it." He also cited another example where SAA proposed a business partnership with Heynad, which he described as "the largest Chinese government-owned holding company" which owns Swissport and Gatecom, but, once it was submitted to him, "the Minister sat on it for weeks and only gave us a decision last week."

"I'll give you another example," Bassa (2019) said. "I'm the Chairman of SAA Technical. We recommended a CFO at the end of November, beginning of December 2018. We only got the approval three weeks ago. You can't work like that."

Akhter Moosa (2019) also referred to significant delays experienced when making the Mango CEO appointment.

The interview with Bassa took place on 23 April 2019, so "three weeks ago" would have been at the beginning of that month.

"You know, we create these layers, Kaizer, and we slow things down. Sometimes I don't know why we do that, where we don't see a commercial rationale for moving things fast, and we get bogged down in processes and law and all of that. We just miss the bigger point. I wonder if we add value," said a despairing Moosa (2019).

In a response which had an echo of the SAA Business Restructuring Plan, Bassa (2019) said in order to improve the chances of successfully turning SAA around, it would be important to "shrink the size of the business, but make it more efficient." He identified "three types of places where you can clean out:"

> *Number one, we have dead wood here. We have people who come to work so that they can go home. They come to work to go home. Find out who there are.*
>
> *Number two, we have people who have been appointed and promoted because of their connections with the previous Board. We need to find out who they are and get rid of them.*
>
> *Next, we have a lot of duplication of work. If you put a fine tooth comb, you'll find that three people are doing the job of one person, whereas one person, if you get the right warm body, if they are sufficient and smart and if you pay him a little bit more, you can get him to do the work of three people at the cost of one-and-a-half persons. We need to do that.*

Bassa (2019) said the OD led by Raseroka would "allow us to retrench, but it also allows us to become smarter, slicker and sharper." Asked if the Shareholder would approve a reduction of warm bodies, Bassa (2019) said the Shareholder had "said don't talk about it until after the elections." However, a workshop had already taken place with "the Shareholder's people to explain to them" as a form of a progress report on the OD process.

Bassa (2019) had no doubt, though, that the unions would oppose the OD and the process that would accompany it to populate the new and substantially-changed positions on the structure:

> *Let me tell you, labour will scupper it. Labour will challenge it. Labour literally runs this company. I'm sure they run other companies as well, which is a sad thing because, at the end of the day, we're going to end up with people who are palatable to labour, but are not good enough for the business.*

Asked how the Board would respond to that situation, Bassa (2019) said the challenge posed by labour to SOCs was "a national issue." He said the Government had to decide if it wanted "to be the custodian of the tripartite alliance" or to "wear a pseudo-capitalist hat with a social democratic leader to say 'listen, you guys have to go your separate way and I'll meet you on the shop floor'." He believed that "once contestation within the ANC is done and dusted, I think there's going to be contestation between labour and Government."

Asked what the Board and Management would have to do to improve the chances of successfully implementing the LTTS, Bassa (2019) said "the Board is great" and Jarana was "a very good CEO." The challenge, he said, remained the "dead wood" below the CEO.

He also disclosed that he had recommended, "on more than one occasion," that the Minister appoints "one or two members of his Department" onto the SAA Board "so that he is kept updated on a daily basis." To his regret, that recommendation was not acted upon.

Martin Kingston (2019) said the LTTS which the Board inherited when it was appointed in November 2017 – starting on the same day on which Jarana started as CEO – was not much different from the previous turnaround strategies. He said when the Board reviewed the previous strategies, it realised that "they are all variants on a theme; they're broadly consistent strategies with a couple of caveats." The first caveat, he said, was that the strategies were not implemented, "so they stay there, gathering dust."

To improve the chances of successfully implementing the turnaround strategy, Kingston (2019) said SAA would have to have "the right fleet and the right route network." At the time, he said, the airline did not have the right route network and had "the wrong fleet for the route network."

Kingston (2019), who took over the chairmanship of the LTTS when Tshabalala resigned from the Board, also emphasised the importance of a "capital structure that enables you to implement the strategy so you can't be teetering on the verge of insolvency all the time and live a hand-to-mouth existence." He said it normally took "two to three years" of implementing a turnaround strategy "before you see green shoots."

Just as important, Kingston (2019) said, was the need to have "the right revenue and cost structure," with revenue being "a function of route and pricing." SAA, he said, had neither.

"Then you need to superimpose upon that the need for an Executive Team with the requisite skills and experience, overseen by a Board which comes with objectivity, authority and experience, and with a Shareholder who provides passive support and acts as a Shareholder rather than a Shareholder who seeks to either block or interfere. We don't have any of those things – or we didn't. Now it is impossible to implement any coherent, consistent, viable strategy in the absence of one of those factors," Kingston (2019) added.

Asked how he perceived the Shareholder's disposition towards the airline, Kingston (2019) replied: "The Shareholder is confused." He said SAA had "shuttled between Finance and Public Enterprises" and both Ministries had been "denuded of experience and resources." He said although the DPE was the Shareholder of record, SAA continued to rely on the National Treasury for funding, hence "we need to sing for our supper," while the Department of Transport enjoyed "regulatory authority."

Kingston (2019) said he had joined the Board on two conditions: that his fellow Board Members were not "the sort of people who were there previously in the past regime" and that there would be no political interference. When the interview with him took place in January 2019, he was comfortable that there was no political interference and that there was "a high level of attentiveness" by the Shareholder to SAA's financial challenges.

However, Kingston (2019) was uncomfortable with one of the main pillars of the LTTS: that the Government's aviation assets should be integrated under the SAA Group. He described SAX as "a disaster," saying the Board had "enough work on [its] plate at SAA, without having to worry about SAX, that ends up being the tail that wags the dog." He said the BoD had been "quite robust about interrogating the rationale for such a thought process."

He was emphatic that it was the Board – and "not the Shareholder or the Executive" – which had responsibility for strategy. He said while the Shareholder understood that, the Shareholder still had a problem with SAX, which it believed could be solved by housing the feeder airline under SAA. Kingston (2019) said he did not share that view. Instead, he believed that a solution lay in closing SAX, saying that did not mean that the routes serviced by SAX would not be considered.

Former DPE Director-General Dr Andrew Shaw (2019) said seeking to combine SAA and SAX was "a red herring." He said putting two "poorly-run entities" together in the hope that they would cover their costs and "will suddenly work" was unrealistic.

Kingston (2019) said SAA was "in dire need of skills and experience, capital and technology" and would benefit from a strategic equity partnership (SEP) with an established airline which would "have all three of those in spades relative to SAA." He believed that "the biggest and quickest and easiest way to transfuse human, financial and strategic capital [into SAA] was with a partner who understands the stuff."

However, apart from being concerned about the regulations which did not allow for more than 20% of SAA to be owned by a foreigner and for more than 49% of it to be owned by anybody other than the State, Kingston (2019) was also not sanguine that such an airline would be interested in the SAA of 2019.

Speaking without his SAA hat on, Kingston (2019) said the most under-performing sector of the local economy was tourism. He said if South Africa had "a fully-integrated strategy for tourism" and SAA was a component element of it, then it would be different. It would be legitimate then, he said, to consider the role that the airline played towards delivering on that strategy.

Speaking again as an SAA NED, Kingston (2019) said he was content that the Board on which he served was largely made up of professionals, and not constituted on the basis of ANC cadre deployment. He said it was important that people were appointed into positions on the basis of "requisite skills and experience for the job," and not because of their membership of or support for the governing party.

Kingston (2019) said retrenchment was one of two important elements to cost containment, with an improvement of productivity levels being the other. He said SAA had held "progressive discussions" with labour, with the latter beginning to appreciate the nature of the challenges confronting the airline. However, he was worried that, given intense competition in what was "a completely open-skies environment," SAA did not have time on its side. He said if it was going to take three to five years to implement the turnaround strategy, "there will soon be nothing left by the time we finish."

Kingston (2019) said the SAA team had to worry more about the unions rather than the Shareholder, with the latter serving "like a proxy for the unions." Another concern, he said, was that it cost money to retrench people, and would potentially "cost more than running the airline."

Kingston (2019) said whereas KQ could employ Polish expatriate Sebastian Mikosz as CEO because its Board believed he was the best person to turn the airline around, in South Africa the appointment of Daniel du Toit as CEO of State-owned armaments company Denel had caused a major uproar because "this guy is white, not that he is a foreigner." He said it was very important for the country to embrace the need to employ "the best qualified people for the job," while simultaneously continuing with "our transformation journey."

Kingston (2019) said there was "absolute clarity as to where decision rights vest" at SAA, including on the levels of authority. He said "the vast majority of decision rights vest in the Board," even though some Board decisions required the approval or concurrence of the Shareholder, and there was appropriate delegation to the CEO "and those that he delegates to."

Kingston (2019) said there was "an ongoing discussion – others might call it a debate – about whether there is scope to delegate more to the Chief Executive." Personally, he was "pretty uncomfortable about that not because I think Boards should run companies, but because I think that you need to have appropriate checks and balances."

He was also unhappy with the fact that there were decisions that the Board could make only with the support of the Shareholder. These, he said, included the appointment of a CEO, the opening and closing of routes and financial decisions above a certain threshold.

Kingston (2019) added:

> *Last time I checked, the Chief Executive doesn't report to Shareholders. He reports to the Board, so there is a learning exercise because it is very clear that he doesn't report to the Shareholder, but South Africa has perfected a behaviour which is contrary, by the way, to not just the Companies Act, but the MOIs of most of these companies. That's behavioural. It's not because it's statutory. That can only be changed by interaction, by education, but I think they were making progress in that regard.*

Kingston (2019) said the view, in the literature on turnaround strategy implementation, that a CEO should have more authority delegated to him/her because swift decisions need to be made during a turnaround would be "the Chief Executive's view." The Board, on the other hand, was more aligned to his own view.

Kingston (2019) said nobody that he knew had unfettered authority. Instead, everybody operated within a certain environment. More important, in his view, was "how efficient the environment is, how competent the people are and how capable they are to understand the issues and take decisions."

"The truth," he said, "is that we have an organisation at SAA that is in crisis. So, it's not just a turnaround; it's actually worse than a turnaround. It's a turnaround in crisis where all the laundry list of issues that I have rehearsed to you (and I didn't just rehearse it off the top of my head), all of those things weren't working and it's going to take time to fix them. How, in that environment, can you give a Chief Executive unfettered authority? Who is he going to delegate to, because he won't do it all himself; he still has to have an Executive that is competent and capable, but also you've got to still have the same checks and balances?"

However, fellow Board Member and Chairman of the Audit and Risk Committee Akhter Moosa (2019) felt that SAA needed "a CEO who is significantly more empowered." He said the Board needed to be more aligned to Management, which he did not believe to be the case "in some instances." He said "sometimes the Board can also be an obstacle" and acted in a manner which showed lack of trust in Jarana as CEO.

Moosa (2019) said there was "endless contestation" during Board meetings, when there was "the Executive to implement." He said that "endless contestation" showed lack of trust in the CEO:

> *From the Board, I think the lack of trust in the CEO at times hampers the turnaround. I think we have conflict. I think there should be more trust placed in the CEO to execute, and I think that sometimes the Board doesn't give the CEO the necessary comfort because he feels threatened at times. On the other hand, the CEO could engage differently to win over the Board. So, I've got a feeling that we need some kind of workshop to iron out the differences because that hampers the implementation.*
>
> *What I am saying is there are pockets of unhappiness from both the CEO's side and from some Board Members with the CEO. I get that impression....and it seems evident in the Board meetings. So, I think that hampers [implementation of the LTTS] because you are not comfortable in your role. I think that is one part of it.*

Department of Public Enterprises Acting Deputy Director-General Avril Halstead (2019) had some sympathy for the BoD which, she said, was "in a really difficult position." She said the fact that Board Members were "literally sitting on a knife's edge every day," worried if they were allowing the airline to trade recklessly, made it "difficult for them to delegate authority to Management as much as they may want to, under the circumstances."

"I don't know how frequently, but I've seen, every three months, legal opinions that they are seeking that they are still on the straight and narrow and haven't stepped off. When Board Members are feeling like they are close to the edge, they get nervous and want to make sure that they've got control of the sort of risks that may result in them stepping over," Halstead (2019) said.

Moosa (2019) said he had "a lot of time" for Jarana, but expressed concern that "he works abnormal hours and takes on a load that is going to crush him." He expressed great frustration with the Board-Management dynamic, which he said was far from ideal. He said while robust discussions were to be welcomed, "endless contestation and not looking at the bigger picture" – something which had come to be "the hallmark for a while now" – was holding SAA back.

"When you get into a ship like this," Moosa (2019) said, "you have got to trust the captain. You've got to trust the captain completely, and he has got to know that you trust him. He has also got to know that he has to listen to you."

He said while some NEDs had since "softened up," the situation had not improved "sufficiently to create a dynamic Board." Describing himself as being unhappy, Moosa (2019) went as far as saying "short of the entire Board being replaced, I think there has to be a re-appointment of other members," preferably appointing "people who really bring aviation knowledge into the scheme of things." He said the Board needed the

Shareholder's intervention.

Board Chairman JB Magwaza (2019) concurred with Moosa (2019). He said the Board undermined Jarana to the extent that he got "terribly frustrated because he sees a Board that is second-guessing him." He said in addition to agility, SAA needed "a Board with balls," which was something that Jarana did not enjoy and which had led to his resignation.

Magwaza (2019) said he had written to Gordhan to suggest a reconstitution of the Board, but a member of the Minister's team at the DPE informed him that "the Minister needs a Board resolution."

"I have written to him [Gordhan] three letters, with one letter sent to him two weeks ago. He says that letter is not clear; I don't know what is not clear in the letter. He says we must attach to my letter a resolution from the Board that we believe, as a Board, the Board needs to be reconstituted and be given fit-for-purpose Board Members," Magwaza (2019) said.

Moosa (2019) said South Africa, as a country, had slipped and needed "much more decisive leadership and action right from the top, right from the Government and from the major SOC levels." He said although "more gutsy leadership" which did things differently would "cause a bit of upheaval," that was what the country required to confront its challenges head on.

Kingston (2019) said SAA's past turnaround strategies were not implemented because the Shareholder was either incompetent, incapable or unsupportive. "They certainly had an interfering Shareholder, as we now know," he said.

The second reason, he said, was that the Boards and the Management were "not fit for purpose," while the third was that the required funding was not provided:

> *We operate on a drip-feed mentality in this country; I don't mean at SAA, but there, too. If you're worrying about how you pay next month's salaries, how on earth do you commit to overhauling your fleet, for the sake of an argument, which is a long-term financial commitment, and ensuring that your fleet is appropriate to route network with an underlying or underpinning cost structure that enables you to be competitive, because that's what it's all about? You can't do it. It never happened.*

Moosa (2019) said when SAA had a serious financial challenge in December 2017, the Board approached Gigaba, who was Finance Minister and SAA Shareholder at the time, with a request for urgent funding, otherwise the BoD would have had no option but to file for business rescue or the airline's sequestration. He said Gigaba gave SAA R10 billion, with half of it "appropriated correctly" and the other half coming from the Emergency

Fund, which was subsequently challenged by one of the opposition parties. Gigaba then gave the Board a letter confirming that it would receive another R5 billion appropriation in the following year's budget.

Moosa (2019) said the Board had told Gigaba, Nhlanhla Nene and Tito Mboweni, during their respective tenures as Finance Ministers, that it was planning to place SAA on business rescue or even get it liquidated because it was insolvent. He said the Board had written "at least eight or 10" such letters to the Ministers, and "each one of those letters were responded to in a politically-correct version to say the Government is committed to SAA, that there is a sovereign guarantee."

Moosa (2019) said the Board was "not permitted to put the entity into business rescue without the consent of the Shareholder, whereas you could do it with another company."

Magwaza (2019), who was also very critical of Mboweni's public statement that SAA should be wound up, said the Finance Minister "could be right." He said the Board had "already arrived at that position a number of months before he uttered the statement that we needed to wind this thing up and fold it up, but were informed by his predecessor that that was not an option." That was because the Board could not make such a decision on its own, without the Shareholder's concurrence.

Referring to Mboweni's statement, Magwaza (2019) said SAA needed a Shareholder "who is not going to be making irresponsible statements, which then begin to scare the Board, scare the Executives and, worse of all, scare all the other stakeholders such as suppliers that maybe this thing is going to be folding up first thing tomorrow morning if there is this kind of statement." He said in addition to making suppliers jittery, Mboweni's statement led to cancellations of international ticket bookings on SAA and had the effect of undermining the LTTS.

Magwaza (2019) said even previous SAA Boards had reached the same conclusion, but were told by the Shareholder not to place the airline on business rescue, let alone liquidate it. He said the Board was in the process of seeking legal opinion to establish how exposed Board Members were. He said he considered it important to have "a paper trail because somebody from outside is going to say that this Board acted irresponsibly and then take me to the cleaners as a Board Member."

He said the Board had not taken steps to liquidate SAA for two reasons: because SAA's Memorandum of Incorporation contained a clause which said such action required the consent of the Shareholder, and because historically the Government has come in to bail the airline, "so you work on that hope."

"You close one eye and say *Nkulunkulu wami* [my God], they must come to the party," he said.

Kingston (2019) said when he joined the Board in November 2017, the previous Board "had imposed a stricture which was that SAA couldn't enter into contracts that went beyond six months." He said no business could be run like that and, following their intervention, SAA was again able to conclude long-term contracts, like its competitors. That was because long-term contracts are "more efficient and give you more flexibility and greater bargaining power." In the case of a six-month contract, however, one is "on the receiving end of every single bargain."

Kingston (2019) confirmed Jarana's (2019) view that the new Board and Management had taken the LTTS announced by Gigaba in 2013, fine-tuned it and started implementing it. He also shared the concerns raised by Jarana (2019), Fredericks (2019) and Bassa (2019), among others, that SAA did not have the required skills to turn the airline around.

Kingston (2019) said while Jarana was "particularly good at and focused on customer interface aspects," many in the next tier of leadership were "clearly not fit for purpose." He said such people needed to be removed and replaced with "individuals with the requisite skill set and then you need to pay the right market price for those people." The challenge, however, was that "removing people isn't very easy in South Africa."

The Board, he said, was "not only aware – but also supportive – of the need to ensure that we have a fit-for-purpose Management Team." Kingston (2019) said he believed that the SAA Executive Team needed to be "not comprehensively, but pretty meaningfully re-organised." That, he said, meant that there was likely to be ongoing management instability at the airline.

"I suppose the challenge is: do you do this in one fell swoop or do you take your time? There are pros and cons," Kingston (2019) said.

Moosa (2019) said the SAA TMT was "partly capable," and that impacted negatively on the airline's agility because "agility demands that the Board entrusts it [the LTTS] to a capable Executive."

Magwaza (2019) said the Board had come into an organisation that was "seriously depleted in terms of Executives," where some "very senior people" had been in acting positions "for something like four years." He said those individuals were not the most capable: "I mean, you get a paper written by an Executive and when you look at it you say 'ohh, gosh, what happened to this person?'"

Kingston (2019) said Jarana, as CEO, was the person best placed to prevent the instability from "having a disproportionate impact" on the airline. He expressed the hope that Jarana, who enjoyed "the support of the Board and the Shareholder – about that there is no doubt," would feel emboldened to take the necessary steps, but "even he needs to have the reassurance that the other ingredients are in place."

Asked why, when both Jarana and the Board took office in November 2017, there were still people in acting positions at the airline, Kingston (2019) said that reflected indecision. He said it was important for decisions to be taken and "you have to live with the consequences of the decision." However, "the majority of the Board want[ed] to review every option," instead of letting the CEO do his job.

"I think that is a particularly South African problem," he said; "we look at anything a hundred different ways, rather than taking a decision. I mean implementation – or lack of implementation – is our biggest problem."

Kingston (2019) said SAA was technically insolvent because the Shareholder was drip-feeding the airline instead of providing the full R21,7 billion required to turn SAA around. That, he said, was because if the Government committed the full amount at once, then it would have to account for it accordingly in its budget. While repeatedly assuring the Board that it would not let SAA fail, the Government would also not guarantee that the required amount would be provided over the three-year period, preferring that SAA asks annually what it needs for the following year. That, Kingston (2019) said, raises a question mark about the airline being a going concern because it needs "to look 18 months into the future, at least."

Kingston (2019) said "a drip-feed, hand-to-mouth approach to providing or securing capital support" did not make it possible for the Board take long-term decisions as it implemented the turnaround strategy. He said the Board has had a series of engagements with Finance Ministers Gigaba and Nene and, subsequent to its return to the DPE, with Gordhan on this matter, and he believed that there was "a higher level of appreciation now than there has been before."

He said while the LTTS was viable, provided it was implemented, it could not be implemented if the required human and capital resources were not available. He said there needed to be political will "not just at political level, but also at the level of the Board and the Executive," to take tough decisions.

Kingston (2019) concluded:

> I'm in a camp that says the numbers don't lie; I don't mean just at SAA level, but also at a sovereign level. We need to grasp the nettle. Now there is a consequence of grasping the nettle; but there is no country that digs itself out of the hole that we are in without going through an austerity programme. There is none. So, we're not going to turn SAA around without taking difficult decisions; nor will the country.

Mokholo (2019) said consideration had to be given to assuring SAA of funding through ring-fenced annual allocations that would not be used for other purposes. She said it was important for the Shareholder to sit with the Board and Management and require them to commit, with their "heads on the block," to a time frame within which they would realistically turn the airline around. She said once the Board and Management had committed firmly to a time frame, "you can even consecutively buffer it [the airline]: if they say it will take three years, give them five years; subsidise them consistently, but have terms of ring-fenced areas of that subsidisation because if you keep giving them bulk amounts of money, they may use it for other things."

Moosa (2019) said implementation of the LTTS was slower than was necessary to turn the airline around. He said there had been some successes, though, such as the fact that most routes were positive in terms of gross profit, with the exception of Entebbe, Hong Kong and Port Elizabeth. He added that there had also been "some successes at HR" because voluntary severance packages had been implemented for the flight-deck crew and the cabin crew.

Moosa (2019) said the delay in implementing the OD side of the strategy was a challenge. He said SAA "bleeds cash at the rate of about R250 million a month," and that the savings that would have resulted from "a timely implementation" of the OD was "in the order of R50 million a month" and R600 million in total.

Gigaba (2019) said forensic reports revealed that SAA lost about R1 billion a year "on the salary structure of pilots," "another billion-plus rands on uncollected seat fares from third parties." He said if SAA were efficient, it would be collecting "close to R3 billion" due to it per annum.

Mokholo (2019) said over-staffing at SAA and other SOCs was "one thing that has to be looked into." She said SAA and most of its sister companies had "appointed people because we say that part of their mandate is to create jobs."

Using the example of an aircraft, Mokholo (2019) said each aircraft was regulated to carry a certain number of passengers and baggage. She said it was common cause that if an aircraft exceeded its weight limit, it stood a chance of crashing, especially upon take off. The same, she said, applied to SAA in case of its surplus employees:

> *Once you have identified that you want to turn this airline around, ask yourself: this human capital that I have, how much weight is it adding? Can I risk taking off with this weight, when I know that on air I might have a problem? That's why the relationship with the unions is important. They realize that this makes sense, but they don't want it, then they go to the Shareholder.*

Continuing with that aircraft analogy, Mokholo (2019) said one solution lies in SAA having to "leave some [of the employees constituting the extra baggage] behind," while another may lie in the creation of a start-up air cargo company to which extra employees can be shifted. She said while the South African Airways Pilots Association (SAAPA) was "very, very difficult," it was important to have "those tough discussions" with it.

Moosa (2019) said the capacity within the airline was "not optimal," that SAA was "not agile enough" and that the need to obtain Shareholder approval on some decisions led to unnecessary delays.

He said SAA had not submitted its annual financial statements for March 2018 because it was not certain if it would have enough money for the following 12 months to be a going concern. He said the airline survived "on a quarterly basis," had a net equity deficit of R14 billion, which was funded by borrowings, and debt interest of R1,5 billion a year.

"I am not unmindful of the challenges the national Government has because there's a budget and it's limited and there are so many demands on the State, but if you want to run an airline, you can't run it on that grand deficit," Moosa (2019) said.

He said SAA did not get "the right level of assurance" that it would be recapitalised to the level agreed upon, in terms of the LTTS, and the timing of the funding made it "very difficult" for the national carrier to engage meaningfully with lenders and suppliers. He said organisations like IATA were worried about SAA's going-concern status and were demanding cash deposits or guarantees

"I think recently we gave IATA $20 million in guarantees, which eats into the available guarantees that the Government issues to us," Moosa (2019) said.

He said SAA required "greater agility from the Shareholder and less bureaucratic approaches," with "the right level of skills" seconded from the Shareholder for the purposes of oversight "and better timely decisions." Moosa (2019) said his experience was that, when matters got to the Minister, "they are addressed immediately."

Moosa (2019) said that, apart from getting an equity partner, a solution to SAA's capitalisation challenge would have to entail the Government taking over the airline's debt onto its balance sheet to enable the airline to start with zero debt. If the Government could not do so, he said for it to take at least half of SAA's R14 billion debt would make a big difference. "You can't run SAA with a R14 billion net equity deficit," he said.

Like Jarana, Magwaza (2019) knew exactly what he wanted to talk about during the interview and was raring to do so. Asked how things were going in terms of the implementation of the LTTS and what he thought would improve the chances of getting the turnaround strategy implemented successfully, he spoke for at least 20 minutes, uninterrupted, making a series of important points. Held on 24 June 2019, the interview took place a month after Jarana's resignation.

First, he said, he would "start from a perspective that is not conventional." He disclosed that he had reluctantly accepted his appointment as SAA Chairman, "much against my will." He said he was warned by people close to him that it was "a poisoned chalice, as if I didn't know that." However, he discovered, within two weeks of his assumption of the SAA Chairmanship, that the information that had been given to him about the airline "was not even 10% of what is wrong with the airline."

Magwaza (2019) said he had researched the previous "nine strategies" that were intended to turn SAA's fortunes around and had received reports on them. Like other participants in this research, he said "there was nothing wrong with the strategies *per se*," except for the fact that they were not implemented. However, Magwaza (2019) said the strategies were "very good academic papers, but lacked gravity in terms of being fulcrumed on the organisation."

Magwaza (2019) said when he and the CEO looked at the LTTS, they concluded that, "with the best will in the world, we are not going to be able to implement it, unless we sit down and actually develop an implementation strategy, procedure and processes." He said those who had developed the strategy had picked up on those factors, but they had not captured it in a manner that would "be meaningful and useful to the person who implements the strategy."

Magwaza (2019) said the first thing that was not right and which would not work for any strategy was having a Shareholder "who understands this thing, is anxious that it happens and it happens now" and then starts over-reaching. He said in such a situation, "then the strategy would flounder because if you are not sitting there every day and you are merely basing [your action] on what you read and your own anxiety – and you are not even managing your own anxiety – you put so much pressure on an already over-pressurised environment and people end up trying to make you happy, rather than doing the job that is required in the organisation."

He said the role played by Gordhan as a Shareholder was not helpful to the airline:

> You need a Shareholder who is going to understand that this is a sick organisation and, therefore, you need to allow the people whom you have brought in there, first the Board and then the Executive, to be given space to implement the strategy. Don't breathe down their throats every other week and every other minute. The first issue is about understanding what is happening and giving the Board and the Executive the opportunity to do what you would require.
>
> Secondly, you need a Shareholder who is prepared, when it comes to decisions, to make major, major decisions, and not run helter-skelter because of the pressure he has from other politicians. If you can't get a Shareholder who is going to say to the other politicians "please give me time, don't come here and tell me what to do," you are going to flounder. He must be a strong Shareholder who is able to manage his own politics and not allow that politics to come and affect the organisation.

Just as he reflected on the kind of Shareholder required to enhance the chances of a successful implementation of the turnaround strategy, Magwaza (2019) also spent some time talking about the kind of Board that SAA needed. Ideally, he said, a Board should be constituted such that it has "a good mix of skills, expertise and gravitas so that they will have a lot of respect firstly from the Shareholder himself," and then from the Executive and the general public. He said where "the Board mix in terms of skills, expertise and gravitas is not up to scratch, they will flounder even trying to understand the strategy; they will flounder in terms of dealing with all these other stakeholders and they will start to interfere."

In a direct reference to the SAA Board that he headed, Magwaza (2019) explained further:

> *You want a Board that draws a thick line between the role of a Board and the role of the Executive. You can't have a Board that now transgresses and steps over the line in terms of what it should do and what the Executives are supposed to do.*
>
> *I have a very crude expression that was given to me by my father, who said you don't buy a dog and then you do the barking yourself because the dog will be confused in that situation. So, you need to get a Board with that kind of understanding.*

Magwaza (2019) said the SAA Board, which needed someone with "a serious understanding of aviation and skills and expertise and repertoire," had only one such person, Bassa. He said it was a handicap that even he, as Chairman, did not have aviation experience, saying he had found "that to be quite a serious disadvantage in terms of implementing the very same strategy that you have agreed upon."

More importantly, Magwaza (2019) said SAA needed "a Board that is going to be pulling together" so that there would be no time wasted on containing "intra-Board conflicts and intra-Board issues." He said the national carrier needed Board Members who were prepared to spend time on SAA matters "because the thing is sick, very, very sick." Therefore, the airline needed "a Board that has perspective and is able to deal with people," and not "professional Board Members who sit on a number of Boards" because they would not have adequate time.

Magwaza (2019) said it was also important that SAA had a Board which understood organisational dynamics "so that if a union shouts, you are not going to jump and think the world is going to fall over."

Magwaza (2019) said SAA could not be turned around "with one or two Executives." That situation, he said, was "what actually gave Vuyani serious burnout in the organisation."

He said SAA needed a CEO who would be able to command the respect of the Shareholder, the Board and people inside the airline. Describing Jarana, Magwaza (2019) said: "Vuyani was a very, very good person. I still have to come across a person who works so hard. I still have to come across a person who is so smart, very smart; very, very smart. In a short space of time, he came from a different industry and he understood the aviation industry quickly. When he talks, you can hear, you can see that he is talking about something that he knows. He is very passionate."

Magwaza (2019) said if a company had people who were not passionate during a turnaround strategy, it would not succeed. The starting point, he said, was having a CEO "being given space within which to operate."

Magwaza (2019) said there were people at SAA who had made it a habit to keep digging a hole:

> *This place would have been liquidated 15 years ago, and all this time people have been digging the hole deeper and deeper and deeper and deeper. So, when you come to turning around an organisation in a situation like that, you need to say to people: "Stop digging the hole. At least, stop digging the hole."*
>
> *To get people to stop digging the hole, it means you must be robust. You must be prepared to be unpopular. You must be prepared to fire people who are digging the hole.*
>
> *Turnarounds, by their very nature, are robust processes, and you need a person who is brave, who can really get in and do it, become unpopular in doing so. But here we expect that the Board is the one that is going to turn around the organisation. It's not going to happen that way. No, it's not going to happen that way. It must be the Executives who do it.*

Magwaza (2019) expressed doubt about SAA still breaking even in financial year 2021, as is forecast in the Agenda for Change, given Jarana's resignation. He said it would take up to six months to get a new CEO for the airline, and that person would need "four or five months to understand what is happening before he can contribute meaningfully." He said the national carrier's strategy plans had "been undermined seriously" by Jarana's exit.

He said SAA found itself at the time with an Acting CEO, an Interim CFO and an Acting CEO of SAAT.

Magwaza (2019) said the Shareholder had to be prepared to capitalise the airline, or shut it down. He said he had sent the turnaround strategy to Gordhan, when he was appointed Minister of Public Enterprises in 2018, and asked him to read it and sign off on it with the Board, but the Minister had not got back to him:

His predecessors, Malusi Gigaba, understood the strategy and said "okay, go ahead, guys, and make it work." We then had Nhlanhla Nene; he wasn't even there for six months. We were able to present to him the turnaround strategy and he understood it and said "now it makes sense; even the way you conceptualise it and talk about it, it's going to work."

We have not even had an opportunity to present to our Minister this turnaround strategy.

A verbatim transcript of this part of the interview follows below:

Me   : *You have not? Since he became Minister of Public Enterprises?*

Magwaza   : *No.*

Me   : *What explains that?*

Magwaza   : *He received it, but he has not sat down with us for us to take him through it.*

Me   : *Not even with you as Chairman?*

Magwaza   : *Not even with me as the Chairman. I mean, I can't, within an hour … get an hour's meeting. I can't do it. You need somebody who is going to come in and sit, which is what I think he has done at Eskom. I think he has bothered to go in and sit with those people and understand their strategy. Whether they are happy with his interference or not, I don't know.*
Our Minister has not had that opportunity to look at our strategy. He keeps on saying that we are missing the plot. Maybe I agree; maybe we are missing the plot, but he doesn't understand our strategy because he has not been told by the Board what the strategy is.

Magwaza (2019) said SAA's lenders understood the strategy "better than our Shareholder, by the way."

He said it was "only now" that a team made up of some SAA Board Members and some of the Executives met regularly with a team from the DPE to discuss "the aviation strategy for the country, which is a different thing from turning around what is wrong here."

Asked if he or the Board had ever tried to engage directly with President Cyril Ramaphosa on SAA matters, including the LTTS, Magwaza (2019) said they had not done so because, "rightly or wrongly," the Board believed in following protocol. He said he wanted to have "the moral high ground for me to say go to hell; I can go to your boss now."

"Have we reached that point?" Magwaza (2019) asked rhetorically. "Maybe we have reached it, but we didn't act because politicians are politicians. You close one eye and look at what is happening. The current Minister of Public Enterprises, for instance, is held very highly by the President, so you need to be very careful when you go to the President. We have not asked the President for an audience to say to him this is what is happening."

However, Magwaza (2019) said the Board's inability to go directly to Ramaphosa was "exactly what frustrated Vuyani."

He said while he believed that Gordhan was doing his best, he was doing so "in a vacuum because he has not been able to sit down with us and look at the strategy itself." He said the Board sent Gordhan quarterly reports giving him updates on the implementation of the turnaround strategy, including "in terms of what is still to happen." Asked if they heard back from the Minister in response to their reports, Magwaza (2019) answered with one word: "No."

Magwaza (2019) said neither he nor the Board had had an opportunity to present SAA's quarterly reports to Gordhan. He said it was only after Jarana's resignation that they had managed to "engage quite seriously" with Gordhan on the airline's financial challenges.

The SAA Chairman said he wished that the national carrier had not been removed from National Treasury as its primary Shareholder. He said the airline was then talking directly to National Treasury about financial issues, and not through an intermediary like the DPE:

> We were at a calamity when Nene was here. We went to him and sat down with him and said Minister, listen here, we need R5 billion – and he had enough courage to say alright, I am not going to wait for the appropriation thing in Parliament. I am going to give you R5 billion, and we were able to take that letter to the lenders and the lenders were prepared to give us money on the back of that letter.

> We have now been wanting the same kind of letter from the current Minister for four months. He has to go and talk to his colleague at Treasury, and time goes on. We spend a lot of time doing that.

On 2 June 2019, the day on which the news of Jarana's resignation was reported upon in the media, the *Sunday Times Business Times* published an interview with Sipho Maseko, CEO of Telkom Limited. In the article, headlined "Any SOE's success begins with the Board," Maseko attributed his success in turning around the privatised Telkom – in which the State holds 40% equity – to "a strong, supportive Board that shielded him from Government interference." That, Maseko informed the paper, had "allowed him to make the unpopular decisions without which [Telkom] would have gone down the tubes" (Barron, 2019).

The article followed Telkom's release of its results for the previous financial year, which indicated that earnings had grown by 22,6%, with the news leading to a 13,6% rise in the Telkom share price to R98,20.

Journalist Chris Barron (2019) said Telkom's story had "an important lesson for other State-owned entities." He reported that key to Maseko's support was "the right Board," which had "interceded firmly between Management and its biggest Shareholder." Barron (2019) reported that until then, the Government had "disastrously interfered with executive decisions."

Barron (2019) said Maseko told him: "I had a gift. The Board gave us the right support, the right air cover so we could make the kind of decisions we've had to make, some of them very difficult."

Barron (2019) reported that Telkom had cut more than 2 000 jobs in 2018 and reduced the number of permanent employees by 12,5%. Those interventions had come "on top of retrenchment cycles that [had] reduced the head count in its main consumer business, Telkom Company, from more than 21 200 people in 2013 to 9 952 last year [2018]."

Maseko is reported to have informed Barron (2019) that it was not easy to cut jobs, but it had to be done because Telkom was "staring down the barrel of a gun." Telkom, according to Maseko, was "in terminal decline," was "losing revenue on a compounded rate of 2% per annum" and its costs were "out of control." Like SAA, the company had been "left behind" by its competitors, but, unlike SAA, Telkom was "never going to get a bailout from anyone" (Barron, 2019).

According to Barron (2019), the biggest challenge which had faced Maseko when he was appointed Telkom CEO in 2013 was "State interference, which had sabotaged the efforts of his predecessors." He was fortunate to have had a Board which "shielded him," without which, Barron (2019) wrote, the chances of other State-owned companies emulating Telkom's success were "minimal."

Maseko told Barron (2019), in the course of the interview:

> *You need the full support of your Board, which must be able to intercede between Management and Shareholder. The role of the Board is important; it's not ceremonial. It helps to secure the right alignment with Shareholders on an ongoing basis.*
>
> *… If you have been brought in as CEO, the Board must absolutely trust your decisions. If the Board second-guesses you, or if the Board wants to decide, or let the Shareholders decide, then the Board or Shareholders must run the company.*

... It's all about governance, the right Board, the right Board support. Even if you have the right public-private partnership on paper, if you don't have the right Board support, it's not going to happen.

Barron (2019) reported that while Telkom's success was built "on the back of its burgeoning mobile business," its intention to launch a mobile operation had "met with considerable Shareholder resistance, especially when it was going well." As a result, Telkom had come close to exiting the mobile business some years ago. That explained Maseko's view that "people don't realise how easily we could have taken the wrong decisions, done the wrong things, without the Board support we had." However, since the Government could not "overrule the Board or the CEO," the company was able to persist with its strategy and succeeded.

According to Barron (2019), Maseko contrasted his experience at Telkom with that of Eskom CEO Phakamani Hadebe, who was serving notice at the time after announcing that he would be stepping down prematurely. When Hadebe announced a zero-percent increase for Eskom employees in an effort to contain costs, he was publicly overruled by Gordhan.

Maseko disapproved strongly of such action by the Minister, telling Barron (2019): "Back your man, don't gainsay him publicly. If you don't agree with him, pull him into a room and talk, but don't gainsay him publicly. It undermines the entire structure."

In the interview with him on 24 June 2020, Magwaza (2019) referred to Barron's (2019) article on Maseko. He told me: "I read the article on Sipho Maseko in the *Sunday Times*. I was from church, and I said 'Sipho, were you doing us as a case study?' All the elements that Sipho talked about there are not found here."

Magwaza (2019) said some SAA Board Members believed that "they should be the ones making the decisions." He said they wanted to get involved in the appointment of the Chief Commercial Officer and in the appointment of the CEO and the CFO of subsidiaries SAAT and Mango and were involved in the appointment of the General Manager: Human Resources.

"For me," Magwaza (2019) said, "that's the CEO's job. Of course, when you do that to a person like Vuyani, het gets terribly frustrated because he sees a Board that is second-guessing him."

At the end of the hour-long interview, Magwaza (2019) stressed the need for a turnaround strategy to be implementable; the need for an empowered, passionate CEO who enjoys the support of the Board; the need for skilled, hard-working Executives and the need for the Shareholder not to interfere with the work of the Board:

Nyatsumba, fundamentally the strategy must be implementable. It must not be a turnaround strategy because it worked somewhere else and there and there. That's one.

Two, you must have a passionate CEO. It's so fundamental, but someone who is passionate with brains and is prepared to work, and you must also have at least the Executives that are going to work for him. If you don't have them, get them in immediately.

Board, don't interfere with the work of the CEO. Shareholder, don't interfere with the work of the Board.

You need agility. You need agility, and you need to move quickly; but you also need a Board that has balls. That's what we didn't give Vuyani. I didn't give Vuyani that.

In an interview with the *Financial Mail* in August 2020, in her capacity as CEO of Transnet SOC Ltd, former DPE Director-General Portia Derby (formerly Molefe) echoed some of the views that were expressed by Maseko in his *Sunday Times* interview a year earlier. She emphasised the importance of alignment between a BoD and a company's Executive Management, and between the BoD and the Shareholder (Talevi, 2020).

Derby told the journalist: "You can tell if it's not going to go somewhere healthy quickly when you watch the relationship between the Board and the Executive. The minute that relationship breaks down, you are in trouble.

"And then you also watch the relationship between the Board and the Shareholder representative: if that relationship is tight and it's working, you're fine. The minute it falls apart, it's a hiding to nowhere and, unfortunately, it's not just individuals who suffer in the process, it's also the entity" (Talevi, 2020).

Efforts to interview Myeni, SAA's longest-serving Chairperson, were not successful. There was no reply to communication sent to her at least twice, via both WhatsApp and an e-mail, requesting an interview with her.

On 27 May 2020, the North Gauteng High Court declared Myeni, who was taken to court by the SAA Pilots Association (SAAPA) and the Organisation Undoing Tax Abuse (OUTA), a delinquent director for life following her actions during her tenure as SAA Chairperson. Judge Ronel Tolmay also referred the judgement to the National Prosecuting Authority for it to determine if an investigation regarding "possible criminal conduct" should take place (Thamm, 2020).

In a media statement following the ruling, Myeni vowed to appeal against the judgement (Ndaba, 2020). On 22 December 2020, Judge Tolmay dismissed her appeal and ordered her to pay SAAPA's and OUTA's legal costs (Child, 2020). When she finally appeared before the Commission of Inquiry into State Capture (colloquially known as the

Zondo Commission of Inquiry) in November 2020, she refused to answer most questions for fear of incriminating herself.

According to the Institute of Directors in South Africa (2019), Boards of SOCs in South Africa face certain "specific challenges," with the main one being that "there are no clear lines of accountability amongst the various levels of governance role players." Another challenge, according to the Institute, is that the Shareholder often makes appointments to the Management Team or the Boards "without due consideration for their skills, experience or independence."

The Institute (2019) said as the sole Shareholder, the Government "holds overwhelming power and influence, which sometimes leads to interference." That leads to the dilemma where SOCs are required to be financially viable, "while also implementing Government policies." These goals, argues the IoDSA (2019), "are frequently incompatible."

"Because governance is not its primary responsibility, and because it is the sole or majority Shareholder, [the] Government is essentially able to influence Boards in a way that private-sector Shareholders are not," said the IoDSA (2019).

Chapter Eleven

ONE GOVERNMENT, BUT DIFFERENT APPROACHES, DEPENDING ON WHO IS THE MINISTER

Although only one party has governed South Africa since the country became a democracy in 1994, the Government's approach to State-owned companies (SOCs) in general and South African Airways (SAA) in particular has differed from time to time, depending on who was the responsible Minister at the time. Altogether, South Africa has more than 700 SOCs, mostly reporting to the different Ministers responsible for policy in the areas in which they operate.

Therefore, all Ministers in the Cabinet are Shareholders for some SOCs and are responsible for appointing the Boards of Directors (BoDs) and even the Chief Executive Officers (CEOs) of those SOCs. However, the Ministry of Public Enterprises is the only one whose sole responsibility is overseeing the functioning of a selected number of SOCs, but does not itself play in the policy space for those SOCs. Its exclusive role is to be the Shareholder representing the Government's interests in large SOCs like logistics company Transnet, power utility Eskom, armaments company Denel and national carrier SAA, among others.

As its financial challenges worsened, SAA was transferred from the DPE to the National Treasury in December 2014, with the Minister of Finance becoming its new Shareholder Minister, and was returned to the DPE on 1 August 2018. Between December 2014 and December 2019, the airline had six Shareholder Ministers, as shown in table 11.1 below.

Former Finance Minister Nhlanhla Nene described the airline's transfer from the DPE to the National Treasury as placing it "under administration." As a result, his approach as Shareholder Minister at the time centred on SAA's financial survival.

Barbara Hogan was appointed Minister of Public Enterprises when President Jacob Zuma came into office in May 2009. She was in the role for just under 18 months and was succeeded by Malusi Gigaba in October 2010. Asked what factors would have impacted positively on the implementation of SAA's turnaround strategy, Hogan (2019) said the quality of the Board and the Top Management (TMT) would have been "the most important things," especially given the fact that SAA had recently become a stand-alone company after being bought by the State from Transnet two years earlier. She said she was not certain of the extent to which SAA's financial sustainability as a stand-alone airline would have been considered at the time, given the fact that it had benefited from cross-subsidisation in the Transnet stable.

Table 11.1: List of SAA's Shareholder Ministers between December 2014 and December 2019

Shareholder Minister	Portfolio	Period
Nhlanhla Nene	Minister of Finance	23 May 2014 – 9 December 2015
David van Rooyen	Minister of Finance	9 December 2015 – 13 December 2015
Pravin Gordhan	Minister of Finance	13 December 2015 – 31 March 2017
Malusi Gigaba	Minister of Finance	31 March 2017 – 27 February 2018
Nhlanhla Nene	Minister of Finance	27 February 2017 – 9 October 2018
Pravin Gordhan	Minister of Public Enterprises	1 August 2018 – to date

Source: Own Composition

Hogan (2019) said by 2009 it was clear that SAA needed "some form of intervention," hence she had appointed "a strong Board of people who were fairly independent minded." Former South African Ambassador to the UK Cheryl Carolus succeeded Gerwel as Board Chairperson, with the following individuals appointed at the same time with her: HR professional Cyril Jantjies, Johannesburg Stock Exchange CEO Russel Loubser, Shell SA Chairman and Vice-President Bonang Mohale, Advocate Lindi Nkosi-Thomas, marketing professional Margie Whitehouse and Skills Dynamics CEO Duduzile Myeni.

A consulting company which was "involved in social development projects in Richards Bay for government," Myeni's Skills Dynamics was launched that same year (Pather, 2016).

Hogan (2019) said Zuma was "very angry" that she had appointed that "very strong Board" when he was not watching her "to that extent." She said one of the important factors to improve the chances of a successful implementation of a turnaround strategy was the appointment of a Board "with particular skills and expertise," while bearing in mind the importance of Board continuity. She said "messing around with corporate governance and the managerial experience, which happened to most of the SOEs," meant that there was no continuity.

"You would have one strategy after another, dissolution of Management, interference with Management, and a Board which doesn't have an eye on the ball," Hogan (2019) said.

She said when the Board was replaced in September 2012, it had managed to stabilise the airline, which was "beginning to get some stabilities in the organisation." Hogan (2019) said she would attend some of SAA's strategic planning sessions, and her staff would evaluate the plans.

She said she considered her role, as Shareholder Minister, to be "appointing Boards, when it was necessary, which had the requisite knowledge and experience to handle multi-billion-rand corporations and which were given the authority to exercise their roles as a Board properly." She said that was easy to do when the SOEs were operating well, but difficult when they were "floundering around."

Hogan (2019) said the role of the Government Shareholder was not clear:

> *So, then, what is the role of the Shareholder? Injections of capital? Really, what powers do you have? You know, you can go in there and insist that they sort things out. You can rant and rave, but ultimately the power lies with that Board and the company itself. What the Shareholder's role then becomes is that you have got to develop an intimate understanding of the operations and the problem at hand, and not just believe the stories that the Board is giving you, but invite other opinions.*

She said that, to deepen her understanding of the sector, she accepted an invitation from Comair for a meeting, and the latter had "some very significant criticisms of the way SAA was operating" – and she thought that criticism was "still valid." She said it was crucial that a Shareholder Minister had "deep understanding of the business at hand," and she felt that was something that the Government did not have "the capability as a Shareholder to do."

Hogan (2019) said during her tenure decision rights at SAA vested with the Board, "but a Board that trusted the CEO." She said there was "a good relationship between the CEO and the Board."

She said it was important for a CEO also to understand that s/he was accountable to the Board "in every possible way." There were times, she said, when she did not think that was the case at some SOEs, but felt that "sometimes a CEO would act with impunity and just overwhelm the Board."

Hogan (2019) said SAA had fallen on hard times because of "the most massive failure of corporate governance," and the fact that the airline had not recovered from the global recession of 2008/9. She said she could not see the airline "getting out of this mess" unless it acquired "at least a minor equity partner" because the Government would not be able to bail it out all the time.

In a segue, Hogan (2019) remembered sitting in a Cabinet meeting where two Ministers argued at length – against each other – about an individual who had been recommended by one of the Ministers for appointment as Chairman of an SOC. "We sat for three hours and argued about one person that no one knew," she said.

Hogan (2019) said "politicians and Government Departments are not the ideal entities to be getting involved in the running of major corporates." She said that, during her tenure, she had found the Shareholder's Agreements that the DPE had with SOCs to be "quite a mess."

"To what extent," she asked, "do you impose on a State-owned company Government's latest fad, and to what extent do you impose on that SOC the priorities of the country? And sometimes those get confused with each other."

Asked to what extent she believed SAA would be allowed to implement staff retrenchment as part of cost containment, Hogan (2019) – who said she did not herself like downsizing – said that would require "a very powerful Minister, a non-ideologically inclined Minister and a Cabinet that would endorse that." She said "intensive engagement in the [ANC-led] tripartite alliance" would have to precede any possible retrenchment.

Hogan (2019) said the country can no longer afford endless Government bailouts of SOCs because "there are too many demands on the fiscus these days." She said that was a political question that had to be settled, and it was "probably going to take some time to settle it." The alternative, she said, was going to be wholesale failure of the SOCs, which would lead to much higher levels of unemployment.

Hogan (2019) advocated massive "re-skilling in a very serious way" of those who would lose jobs, instead of "just doing the traditional retrenchment packages."

Hogan (2019) identified, as "a big, serious inhibiting factor" when it comes to the implementation of SAA's turnaround strategy, "the corporate governance framework, in particular the Shareholder's role." She said if corporate governance and the Shareholder's role were not sorted out, SAA would "go under, even with equity injections."

She said South Africa had put "a very clunky system in place for corporate governance and it's stuffing these poor SOEs." She said it was important that the airline was allowed to be agile in its decision making.

Hogan (2019) said another challenge was the role of Parliament. She said that as a Minister, she was accountable to Parliament, and yet "there is also the linkage from SAA straight to Parliament."

During Hogan's tenure, Dr Andrew Shaw was the Director-General in the DPE and was exposed to all SOCs falling within the Department. Before that, he was DDG responsible for the transport portfolio. Long after he had left the Department, he continued to follow SAA from a distance at the big consulting firm where he works because doing so is part of his responsibilities. In that capacity, he has continued to have engagements with SAA CEOs and CFOs.

Shaw (2019) said his personal view was that the SAA Board and Management were constrained, in their efforts to implement any turnaround strategy aggressively, by the Government and the unions. He said if SAA were privately owned, the unions would "very quickly understand the space that you are in and they will come to the party." However, at SAA the unions were confident that the Government would step in to bail the airline out if they put sufficient pressure on it.

He said SAA's inability to act quickly to exit unprofitable routes was another one of its big challenges. He said "this long, odious process" that required the national carrier to test such decisions with the Shareholder placed it at a disadvantage when compared to its competitors, which did not have similar constraints.

Shaw (2019) shared the concern raised by Magwaza (2019), Moosa (2019) and others that the governance structure at SAA "doesn't work very well." He said the Board "essentially wishes to take on some of the operational duties" and allows itself to be "pressured by the Shareholder to become involved in what are essentially management issues." He said even Carolus, as Chairperson, "played a very strong role in devising a strategy around network expansion."

He said the Government wanted to influence what SAA does and union pressure uses "the Shareholder as a conduit to communicate." Shaw (2019) said in such a situation, a CEO finds himself/herself "more constrained than if you are in the private sector."

Shaw (2019) said on the contrary, a company undergoing a turnaround requires a supportive BoD:

> *I think if your company is in a turnaround, the Board generally is very supportive of the Executive driving that strategy, and normally holds them to a set of metrics, and those metrics are "reduce costs, look for additional market share and take forward certain structural initiatives like sell certain parts of the business, restructure how you contract with others." Those would have been identified in the turnaround and the Board should be measuring you on*

each one of those, and the Board should be held accountable itself to those measures. The Executives should largely be left alone to drive those out, and come back to the Board if there are issues that require some changes.

Matsietsi Mokholo joined the DPE on 1 March 2007 as Chief Director: Legal, as part of the Legal, Governance and Risk Unit. Her responsibilities included "assisting with the appointment of Boards and CEOs" for entities which fell under the DPE and developing guidelines, tools and frameworks. Five years later, she was appointed DDG: Legal.

Mokholo (2019) said the Department went through "a transition and an evolution that was quick" after the ANC's 52nd National Conference which took place in Polokwane, Limpopo. Public Enterprises Minister Alec Erwin resigned when President Thabo Mbeki was recalled in September 2008, and was succeeded by Brigitte Mabandla, who was the incumbent until 10 May 2009. Hogan took over as Minister of Public Enterprises in May 2009, and was succeeded by Gigaba in November 2010.

In two years, there were four Ministers of Public Enterprises. Mokholo (2019) said Director-General Portia Molefe left shortly after Hogan's dismissal, and was replaced with Tseliso Matona. Mokholo herself was appointed Acting DDG for a while, before being confirmed in the position in 2012.

Mokholo (2019) said these changes at the DPE "had a major impact on the entire portfolio of DPE." She said Hogan believed in an arm's length relationship with SOCs: "She would really allow Boards to run entities and CEOs to do their own thing and stick to the framework of the PFMA in terms of the role of the Executive Authority."

Gigaba, on the other hand, "changed the tempo a bit because he came after the resolution by the ruling party at the Polokwane conference that now we are a developmental state."

Mokholo (2019) explained:

> *When he came, he said what does this developmental state mean? He said it means that we are a developing country; we need to grow the economy, but growth must start within. And what are the tools of this developmental state? He said the major ones are State-owned companies. He said, therefore, the arm's length relationship that we are having as a Shareholder Department of these entities – and some of them have big and huge economic drivers – that relationship is not going to allow us to achieve what we want with a developmental state.*
>
> *Therefore, we moved from an arm's length relationship with the entities to an interventionist approach as a Shareholder.*

Mokholo (2019) said "it is inevitable that every Minister, when they come, looks at the whole portfolio." She said while Hogan wanted gradual changes which would follow

SOCs' Memoranda of Incorporation and the Companies Act, Gigaba "said look, our whole model is not right."

Mokholo (2019) said she "marvelled at the idea of having an interventionist approach." She said during her foreign travels with Erwin to look at models of how other Shareholder Ministries approached their duties, she had found that "most of them were very close to their entities." Specifically, she cited China as being "very close to its entities."

"We loved the fact that now we can have the entities and be able to use them strategically," Mokholo (2019) said.

In retrospect, she said the changes were both good and bad:

> So, the changes were good, but also the changes were not so good. What was not good about the changes is that they did not allow the entities to adjust to the strategic intent statements. They were too frequent. They were too constant and sometimes they were driven not entirely by the operational needs of the entities; they were driven from the political side, more than anything. So, they did have sometimes unintended consequences for the entities.

Mokholo (2019) said that, on the positive side, the interventionist approach enabled the Department to get SOCs to collaborate more closely with one another. She said SOC-to-SOC collaboration would not have been possible "if you did not have a close relationship with your entities."

Mokholo (2019), who was working at the Presidency at the time of the interview, said she had been part of the development of the LTTS and the Whole-of-State Policy, whose aim was to get the Government's aviation assets – Air Traffic Navigation Services, Airports Company South Africa, SAA and SAX – working closely together. She said the policy was "so well-developed and crafted," but the different Ministers could not agree to it when it got to the relevant Cabinet cluster:

> I still believe the shareholder model in South Africa is wrong. You have a Department of Public Enterprises that does nothing but shareholder management, and then you have a Department of Transport that does three things: it develops policy, it has its own entities that it is managing, and it also has regulation. So, with that incongruity, they can easily cherry-pick where this policy should be.
>
> That's why, with the Whole-of-State Policy, it became a debate, and a debate and a debate, but the policy was developed, well documented and it made sense. It was also benchmarked against all these other countries. You go

to Heathrow [Airport in London]: we land, we park, period – and they are not apologetic about it.

Gigaba (2019) said there was a disjuncture in the Government. He said while "the DPE was building SAA, the Department of Transport is destroying SAA." He said it was only now that there was "a common understanding that this opening of the skies must stop." He said the Minister of Transport was supposed to present a new, integrated air transport policy framework which would "reverse the liberalisation, cut down on foreign airlines, withdraw the Fifth Freedom rights, and all of those things," to give to foreign airlines "the same regime they give us in their own countries."

Gigaba (2019) added:

We say no decision must be taken which impacts on SAA by [the Department of] Transport without consulting and taking into consideration the interests of the State as represented by SAA. No decision must be taken by [the Department of] Energy on the Energy Policy which impacts on the interests of the State as represented by Eskom.

That's basic. At the end, when we take a policy decision, it's because we know it advances our interest in this way: commercially and developmentally. It can't just be a broad, ambiguous policy decision which is going to sound good when it is announced, but at the end of the day we know it's going to impact on us.

However, he said making policy decisions was one thing, but implementing them another altogether. He said the Government habitually spent "too much time pontificating" and was "more federal than we even make ourselves to be." He said "the fights among Ministers and Departments are huge, which makes [policy] implementation difficult."

Gigaba (2019) found the Government's position, as carried out by the Department of Transport, absolutely incomprehensible:

It's unbelievable. It was as if here you have an air space that you don't believe in and you allow others to destroy it in some bizarre belief that somehow you are going to save your own asset by destroying it. This belief that "oh, no, competition is good for SAA." If it is, why do the Emiratis not think so, the Qataris and the British, and so on? Why don't they think about the same thing?

I mean, these are supposed to be the champions of the free market, liberalisation and free competition. They don't allow it in their own countries, but we're supposed to let it happen here.

Gigaba (2019) said South Africa lacked the "type of a cohesive, developmental state that existed in South-East Asia or in China and Dubai (the UAE) where, once a decision is taken, you implement it or face consequences." He added tellingly: "No, here you can afford not to implement it and get away with it, depending on which faction in the ruling party you associate yourself with – and people are allowed to do so."

Coming to SAA, Gigaba (2019) said ways were often found to undermine collective Cabinet decisions:

> So, we take a decision that, look, guys, we need to implement a turnaround strategy for SAA; we pilot it, we run with it, we go with it. The biggest problem would be that you take decisions and then too many structures must implement, too many people must still discuss and debate, too many people have the power to overturn, to over-rule and undermine, stuff like that. It makes it really very difficult.

Asked if he believed the Government will ever get to a stage where it excelled at implementing its plans, Gigaba (2019) said that goal was attainable, provided that there was Government rationalisation which would see the role of the "Government Shareholder Manager grow in capacity and stature to be able to do what it needs to do." He said the Government would benefit immensely from the SOCs "if it managed them well."

"I think in the course of that, we can be able to define better what we mean by developmental mandate of State-owned companies, and I think we need to move beyond the cluster organisation of Government which was introduced by President Mbeki," Gigaba (2019) said.

He said while it worked well "to organise and shape the agenda for Cabinet," the cluster system did not lead to coordination in decision making and implementation. He said Ministers tended to use their respective clusters "to pass through their draft policies and legislation to get them approved by the Cabinet as quickly as possible so that they go and execute."

Gigaba (2019) said Ministers tendered to see their Cabinet Clusters as mechanisms to rubber-stamp their policies, without their interrogation: "It's not to say when you get there, if the Department of Transport says we want to do that and the Minister of Public Enterprises says but we can't do that, that's wrong for x and y reasons, then it is not done."

And what about robust engagement among Ministers?

"Even if it is there – and at times there is – but the person who is piloting the policy or legislation, *uphuma lapho ayo-implementa leya lakhe* [leaves there and goes to implement his or her own policy]," Gigaba (2019) responded.

He said that he had suggested that the Presidency had to play "a greater role." He said Mbeki had attempted to do that trough his Presidential Advisory Committee, which was headed by Joel Netshitenzhe, which had "some little success." He said Mbeki was "onto something there, but it didn't go far enough."

Mokholo (2019) said if the Government wanted SAA and other SOCs to be successful, it had to be willing to make "trade-offs that are necessary." To do so, certain things would have to be done: "If you want them to provide quality service, give the Board authority; appoint good people onto the Board; allow them sufficient time to do their work; put in place proper Shareholder Compacts. Let them know how you, as the Shareholder, will drive that quality. Secondly, give them sufficient Shareholder support financially and then say these are my terms for that, and then identify the KPAs [Key Performance Areas] and the KPIs [Key Performance Indicators]."

Asked what factors would impact positively on the implementation of SAA's turnaround strategy, Gigaba (2019) listed visualisation of the desired end state of the airline, good leadership and Government support. He said it was important for all stakeholders – particularly the Government – to have a good idea of the desired state of SAA that they had in mind, and then to work diligently towards realisation of that vision.

Good leadership, he said, was required at Board and Management levels at SAA, as well as at Shareholder level. "You need good leadership there," Gigaba (2019) said. "You need stability at that level; it gives us that much more space to implement the plan."

Thirdly, he said the Government had to "be prepared to provide support to SAA, both economic and non-economic." He said the Government had made the mistake of focusing too much on providing financial support, without paying "any attention to non-financial support." Specifically, Gigaba (2019) said a quick reversal of the policy of freedom of the skies "and its negative impact" was crucial, together with a swift implementation of "a comprehensive plan to make OR Tambo International Airport an international hub."

It was very clear during the interview that Gigaba, who had twice been SAA's Shareholder both as Minister of Public Enterprises and as Minister of Finance, had done a lot of thinking on these issues. Spelling out the details of the "comprehensive plan," Gigaba (2019) said:

> *You say to the Department of Home Affairs: introduce e-gates, introduce visas on arrival, introduce e-visas. You say to the Department of Police, to State Security: no crime – make OR Tambo International Airport a crime-zee*

zone. You say to the Department of Telecommunications: wire the whole area, the whole airport.

And then you say to [the Department of] Transport: link OR Tambo Airport, more efficiently now, to Sandton. The link is there; there's not much that you can do. The Gautrain is there. Nobody complains about the 15 minutes of travel, but the issue is if Home Affairs introduces e-visas, e-gates, visas on arrival, you basically make it easy for any person who is on transit for five hours, for half a day, to say "argh, let me go to Sandton and chill out there; I've checked in any way. I'll be back for my flight."

Introduce efficiencies at OR Tambo Airport that you find in Singapore or Dubai. Introduce proper shopping; develop the infrastructure because if I have five hours, I may not want to go to Sandton, but I have five hours to kill. I will not be sitting on a steel bench. Let me walk around; let me do some shopping; let me have eateries and stuff like that.

Every Department that is relevant to creating that hub must now be called in and told: "I'm not asking you how long you need; I'm telling you. I give you 12 months. Within the first month, I want you to come back to tell me what you would have achieved; in three months, in six months, in nine months and in 12 months, when the full plan roll-out happens." In that way, you make OR Tambo Airport and SAA a choice. Because you are competing with Kenya Airways and Nairobi Jomo Kenyatta International Airport; you are competing with Ethiopia. They are up north, within the traffic hub. We are outside the traffic hub.

You need to create a hub and then, with time, you look at what are the best cost factors of SAA which, if you reduced, you will reduce the price of SAA. Because for all the patrons that SAA has lost, you need to help them to regain that patronage.

Mokholo (2019) said it was important for the Shareholder to be clear about the degree of focus that it wanted SAA to achieve and what it wanted the airline to be:

We cannot have it all. We need to make decisions about what we want SAA to be. Do we want it to have a successful restaurant? Do we want it to become a hospitality company when it comes to the issue of Voyager miles? Do we want it to have a cargo division? Do we want it to have a technical service division?

What are the things that support the entity that we want? Others can support it, whether being out-sourced; others need to be in. So, we need to make decisions around those things. We can still maintain it like that, but then invite others to participate at different levels.

Gigaba (2019) said when he was appointed Minister of Public Enterprises in October 2010, "SAA's financial health was quite weak as a result of long-standing reasons." These were mainly structural. The airline's challenges, he said, were not "so much" about the fact that it is owned by the State, but its problem "lay more on the approach of the Shareholder to the airline, which was not clear." Gigaba (2019) said the Government's approach to SAA remains "not clear even now."

"It's a bit fuzzy," he said. "We are trying to say the Shareholder needs to clarify its standpoint on SAA and be very clear because that informs how, then, SAA structures itself, how it is supported, how it operates and what are the goals that we set for it."

Gigaba (2019) said the fact that SAA was not properly capitalised and had "huge overheads, a lot of routes and an ageing fleet" when it was taken out of Transnet led to a situation where new leaders coming into the airline did not "want to take decisions" and tended "to defer decisions downwards while the bottom structures were deferring decisions upwards."

"Any leadership that came in looked at this as an opportunity for them to make as much money as possible out of the airline and run away, without finishing their term. As a result, we've had a huge turnover of CEOs and CFOs, and many turnaround strategies," Gigaba (2019) said.

In essence, his words had the effect of absolving both the Shareholder and its Boards of Directors of any responsibility for the high leadership turnover and the resultant instability at SAA. Instead, avaricious CEOs and CFOs – most of whom had their reputations tarnished when they left under a cloud – were to blame for the leadership instability which has characterised the airline since 1998.

Gigaba (2019) listed a series of instructions that he believed the Shareholder should have given the airline. He said the Shareholder needed to set SAA a series of objectives, spell out how it was going to support the airline to reach those objectives and then instruct it to come up with a strategy. He listed a number of examples:

For example, you say to them: "Okay, first we want you to be commercially viable. We want you to take over the routes that are going to bring in money. Secondly, we want you to dominate the African air space. Thirdly, we want you to take us to every capital in BRICS. Fourthly, we want you to keep employment at this level and, within that range, we want you to bear in mind that these are the transformation objectives that we want you to achieve in terms of your pilots, your captains and your senior officers, in terms of your cabin attendants, your management and all of that."

When you have said that, you then say to the airline: "To keep you afloat, we need to take several decisions. One, we need to keep your overheads manageable. Two, we need to keep your fuel levy affordable. Three, we need to subsidise you on routes which are not profitable, but which we need for strategic purposes as a country because we must fly to [New] Delhi or Mumbai, we must fly to Beijing, we must fly to Sao Paolo, we must fly to Moscow, and then the African routes.

Gigaba (2019) said the Government was "the weakest" when it came to implementing its own decisions. He said the decision "to rationalise the three airlines into one group was taken years ago," but remained unimplemented. He foresaw a situation where "by the end of the decade, we'll still be sitting in small task groups that are not yielding results," which would be discussing the same issues.

In summary, Gigaba (2019) said, SAA's challenges could be traced to "historical problems and the lack of vision for SOEs." He said things were not helped by the fact that the recommendations of Zuma's PRC into SOEs "were neglected, completely ignored." Therefore, he said, "any turnaround strategy, whether for SAA or anyone else, will not succeed."

He added grimly: "The same will happen with Eskom. The push for the unbundling of Eskom is going to fail because, ultimately, you are providing a Grandpa for a headache, without taking the full diagnosis into consideration so that you arrive at a correct treatment plan."

Gigaba (2019) said a successful implementation plan requires a solid team "with sufficient autonomy to take bold decisions," provided everybody understood that "autonomy carries with it both the courage to take bold decisions and the courage to take responsibility when those decisions fail." He said when a decision failed, a team should not "turn around and say the Shareholder did this."

"In this country, we have become so accustomed to scapegoating," Gigaba (2019) said. "[We tend to say] this thing didn't happen because *loya wenze ukuthi* [this one did that] and, therefore, hunt that one down; it's not my fault." SAA, he said, needed "an Executive that is streamlined, lean, but also bold enough and autonomous enough to take decisions," with the Shareholder providing "a clear vision."

Gigaba (2019) reiterated his view that the Shareholder was responsible for SAA's problems:

The biggest problem, I think, for SAA has been the Shareholder, and the reason why you have had the turnaround strategies not succeeding has been because the Shareholder lacks vision, continuity and persistence. So, in the middle of implementing one turnaround strategy, you change everything, and the people who come in are not given an instruction to pursue the reform.

Instead, they come in and they are told: change everything. Or, if they are not told, they do it themselves because they presume that to be their mandate, otherwise why has everybody been changed? If you were happy with the political and administrative plan, you would have left the people in charge to continue. If you change all of that, uproot them, you are sending a message to us who are coming in that you were not happy, so change everything – and then they do. You then have to spend more money on consultants, doing more consulting, coming with new plans, which are also not going to be implemented because by the time they need to be implemented, there is a new leadership and there are changes.

Gigaba (2019) said China's success was based on consistency. He said China did not depend on electoral cycles. Continuing to speak about China, he said: "The leadership knows: this is a 50-year vision. If you are appointed into this position, you don't come with your own plans. You come in here to implement the vision and plans of the party – which is what I keep on referring to as an organising philosophy."

He said in South Africa, the Government, as SOCs' Shareholder, lacks that "organising philosophy," and that has been "the driving force behind the failures."

Gigaba (2019) said the Shareholder was "confused as ever" about how it should handle the national airline. He said while there were views – including among some within the governing party – that SAA should be sold, he had always argued that selling SAA would be "very short-sighted." He said given South Africa's geographic location on the southern-most tip of the southern hemisphere and far from "the main, dominant traffic routes," selling SAA would expose the country to unimaginable risks.

Gigaba (2019) said:

If you had a war or a pestilence breaking out and other airlines decided, as they did with the Ebola outbreak a few years ago, that we're not travelling to Africa, we are cutting our flights, what happens to our travellers? How does an economy like this one afford to have travellers cut out like that?

We need metal on air, able to take people from one point to another. Our own people, at least, and those from the African continent who, when all else fails, must rely on SAA. So, that argument for me that we don't need SAA is extremely short-sighted.

Later that year, the Corona Virus Disease 2019 struck in China and spread to different parts of the world, including South Africa. Most countries – including South Africa – closed their air spaces to international flights. Indeed, as Gigaba had indicated, the

Government relied on SAA to repatriate thousands of South Africans who were stranded in different parts of the world, including China.

During the interview, Gigaba (2019) said there was no previously-disadvantaged South African who would be able to purchase "an operating share in an airline," hence the sale of SAA would not even advance Black Economic Empowerment.

He said it was the Government's confusion about what to do with SAA that had led to conflicting public statements from some Cabinet Ministers, with Mboweni "making what to me was a heinous statement against our SOEs." He said statements like Mboweni's created "uncertainty in an environment where he, as Finance Minister, must plan."

Gigaba (2019) said the question which the Government had to answer was not so much what percentage of the airline it wanted to sell, but what it wanted to do with the airline. He said Telkom, where the Government is the biggest Shareholder with 40%, could not be used as a model for SAA because "the environments are not the same."

Asked what factors worked against a successful implementation of SAA's turnaround strategies, Gigaba (2019) cited "leadership instability at Board level, at Executive Director level and at Ministerial level." Quickly adding that he was "not bidding for any position," he said stability helps by creating "that long-term outlook." He said even that stability at Ministerial level should "focus on the work at hand, not witch-hunts and other things which are beside the point." He said the absence of leadership stability and skills would "be a huge hindrance" in the implementation of any turnaround strategy.

Another hindrance, he said, was "a bloated Management." He said the Management Team had "to be cut down to a manageable size where decisions are taken, plans executed efficiently and effectively and you have people who can take responsibility."

Gigaba (2019) said it was crucial for the Government finally to come up with "a feasible financial plan" for SAA, in addition to acquiring a SEP for the airline:

> I think the Government needs to come up, ultimately, with a feasible financial plan. Hobbling from one plan to the next doesn't help at this stage. We need one that is feasible, comprehensive, where we bite the bullet and say "this is what we are going to do." Part of that, obviously, has to include getting, at the right time, a proper partner who is going to come in with skills, with finances and with influence because, without those, the airline is going to fail.

Gigaba (2019) was confident that, "realistically speaking, SAA can overcome its cost drag and get on top of those challenges." He said although it would take some time to get there, nevertheless that goal could be achieved fairly quickly and, "within the next two or three years," SAA could break even "and start recording good results." In the process, the airline would reduce its debt "and that which is linked to the sovereign."

He said for the airline to accomplish this goal would "require huge decisions," which would include renegotiating its pilots' contracts and the benefits enjoyed by the cabin crew, and collecting money due to SAA from Angola, Congo and other countries on the continent. He said he had never understood why SAA flight and cabin crew members had "to spend four days abroad when they have been flying, staying at five-star hotels." He said if the stay-over abroad could be reduced to two to three days, it would have "a huge impact on the airline."

"Those are unnecessary losses," Gigaba (2019) said.

He said the fact that findings of studies conducted in 2012-13 – and recently reconfirmed – had revealed that SAA's African routes were lucrative meant that it was important for the national carrier to seek to establish dominance on the continent to deny space to African and foreign competitors. Head office costs would also have to be reduced through retrenchments, early retirements and natural attrition. Gigaba (2019) said that was done in the past, but the SAA leadership became "undisciplined again" and allowed staff numbers to grow.

He said the airline needed disciplined Senior Executives – the HR Manager, the Chief Operations Officer, the Chief Restructuring Officer, the CFO and the CEO – in order "to ensure that it sticks to the plan, as they are supposed to."

Gigaba (2019) said he did not know whether Jarana and his TMT were "sufficiently empowered," but the Board that he had appointed in 2017 was made up of "people with sufficient skills and credibility, who are not going to allow their credibility to hang in the balance for nothing." That, he said, was "a good Board." He said that, when he appointed it, he had "acted swiftly, under difficult conditions, to ensure that there is a new Board," and he had brought in "people with good expertise and market depth to be able to exercise their responsibility."

"I think that those people understand the role of the CEO and Management and, therefore, give the CEO good support, arm's length support for him to be able to run the airline. For me, I would say I'm quite happy so far, but this is me watching from the distance," Gigaba (2019) said.

The former Minister also believed that there was the will, on the part of the Government, to capitalise SAA properly, "both directly and through finding an equity partner." He said the Government's plan was to build SAA's value up before calling for an SEP so that it would get "good revenues."

Former Finance Minister Nhlanhla Nene (2019) attributed SAA's poor governance to the BoD and loss of skills by the airline. The former challenge, he said, led to a high turnover of CEOs and other Senior Executives and led to a situation where "nobody in his sober mind would want to be associated with that situation that obtained at the time."

He said during his tenure, the SAA Board was dysfunctional and "interfering in a big way in the manner in which the Executive was working." He said the Board Chairperson (Myeni) "was a very strong character" who, in addition to not understanding the industry, "had certain agendas and would be able to push the Board in a particular direction."

"When you have a dysfunctional Board, that's not a governance structure which should oversee the Executive in the discharge of its duties. Even the relationship between the Board and the Executive was at its lowest during that time," Nene (2019) said.

As a result, the Executive Committee was also divided, with some of its members deciding "to work with the Board, even though the Board has lost its way" so that they would remain in their jobs, while others tried to stand up to the Board Chairperson.

Nene (2019) said the fact that SAA flew "unsustainable and unprofessional routes for a considerable period of time" exacerbated its situation.

He said while Mango, as an SAA subsidiary, was profitable, the mother airline itself was not sustainable. He said Mango employed "people with the right set of skills who were actually doing what they were supposed to do," while at SAA "things had gone completely off the track."

Asked what the Shareholder did to resolve the Board crisis, Nene (2019) said "the Shareholder was in a very difficult position to try and deal with the matter." At the time, the Minister of Public Enterprises was SAA's Shareholder and the National Treasury had a dedicated team trying to assist the DPE to deal with issues. The challenge, he said, was that the National Treasury advised the Shareholder, but the DPE had to take responsibility for the implementation of the proposed interventions. That led to the Ministry of Finance being seen to be attempting to impose its will on another Ministry.

"So," Nene (2019) explained, "there would also be tensions now, even between Ministries. As a result, whatever guidance and directives that would be given to Public Enterprises would not be implemented properly because the person who was supposed to do that is actually the Department [Minister] of Public Enterprises. That was until such time that SAA was transferred to the National Treasury."

Nene (2019) said by the time SAA was transferred to the Ministry of Finance in December 2014, "the National Treasury's focus and interest was not on the business side of it, but on the financial side of it" because the National Treasury had provided both guarantees and "hard cash for the airline to run."

Nene (2019) explained the dilemma which confronted him:

> *Now you are caught up in a situation where, if you don't give cash, the airline has either to submit to business rescue or you have liquidation. When you have thrown such amounts of money at a public entity, either you pay for the burial,*

as I would put it, or you pay for the recuperation of the patient. You put the patient in the ICU; you get the patient back to life because you actually want to recover what you have put into the enterprise. Also, the issue of attracting a private equity partner to come in became such an issue for ideological and political reasons that we would be selling family silver, and what have you.

He added that in order for SAA to be attractive to a potential equity partner, it would have to be "in good shape or showing signs of recovery because nobody wants to put in money into an entity that is not going to rescue itself." As the Shareholder, he said he did "a number of things" trying to fix that challenge.

Nene (2019) said "the fact of the matter" was that although the LTTS made sense, it was not implemented.

Dealing with the issue of SAA having a number of Ministries (especially Public Enterprises, National Treasury and Transport) whose decisions impact directly on its fate, Nene (2019) pointed out that the national airline was not the only SOC to find itself in that situation. He said Eskom found itself in the same boat, with the Ministers of Public Enterprises, Energy as well as Finance taking a keen interest in its work and impacting on its fate in some way.

He said while it would help for SAA to have one responsible Ministry, the fact remains that the Ministers of Public Enterprises, Finance and Transport represented not only the same Government, but also the same political party. He said the situation should not pose a problem "as long as those Departments are talking to one another and they share a common view and objective of running these enterprises."

"If we have a common objective of actually getting these public enterprises working, and we as Government are actually working together in tandem, there shouldn't be such a big issue, but the issue comes when those are not pulling in one direction," he said.

Nene (2019) conceded, however, that "there will always be personalities." He said "if other people feel that the other Ministry is playing Big Brother in the stable, they would want to flex their muscles in a particular direction." He said if this dynamic played itself out to the detriment of SAA, "then those people don't share the interest of the country for the airline."

He said one of the things that the National Treasury would be told was that SAA needed to be bailed out "because it flies the national flag." Nobody, he said, "would want to destroy that."

"We would want the flag carrier to be a sound and solid business," Nene (2019) said, "but if it is not delivering in that regard, why are you allowing somebody to carry the flag and that person is not a good ambassador for the country?"

Responding to the criticism regarding the need for the Shareholder to approve decisions made by the SAA Board in terms of the SMF in accordance with Section 54 of the PFMA, Nene (2019) said the airline's transfer from the DPE to National Treasury was akin to putting it under administration:

> *When you are under administration, you actually do operate under a very different environment where, indeed, the thought that you can invest requires the approval of the Shareholder because you put money in here and these people have been put under administration precisely because of the things that happened in the past.*

> *So, I would imagine that once that part is over, it is important to return to normality and set up new governance rules and be able to operate the company and allow the Executives to perform their functions without the interference of the Shareholder Representatives. So, during my time it was a completely different environment. I am not too sure what the situation is now, but it was because of that that there was that a strong arm from the Shareholder Representative.*

Responding to a question about why the Government could not give SAA the kind of operational latitude that the Ethiopian Government gives EAL, Nene (2019) said the KQ and EAL examples worked "precisely because there is one common thread that runs through them, unique as they are." That was the fact that at those two African airlines "they have allowed the Executives to run the business without interference from the Shareholder."

Nene (2019) said he had had conversations with former EAL CEO Girma Wake a number of times, and once Wake told him that when the Ethiopian President appointed him to turn the airline around, he had asked for non-interference:

> *He said that's what he asked for. Then he actually delivered. He delivered, and I do think that if we have a Board that understands its limitations and its role, and also an Executive that understands its limitations and its roles, with the entire delegation of authority to the relevant structures, it's possible for the airline [SAA] to do well.*

Nene (2019) said the Government will have to understand that SAA is a business enterprise that it would have to support financially for a period of time until it could stand on its own, "or turn it around and then allow for private participation through a strategic equity partner," which was an option that the National Treasury had placed on the table. That, he said, would have to be informed "by the state in which the airline is and what the end state is." He said the Government would have learned from the Telkom example that holding a stake in a profitable enterprise contributes positively to the fiscus through dividends.

Asked what he would do to ensure a successful implementation of the LTTS, if he were given carte blanche to do so, Nene (2019) said the "the turnaround strategy that is on the table needs implementation and the buy-in of everybody." Therefore, he would establish how much of that strategy has been implemented and then ensure that the rest of it received urgent attention.

Next, he would ensure that "the required expertise" was brought into the airline and that a SEP was brought on board.

Nene (2019) said SAA and ACSA, which are both owned by the State, should work more closely together to ensure that OR Tambo International Airport was turned "into the Dubai of Africa," with SAA being "the proud beneficiary of such an activity." He said that was what was beginning to happen with Nairobi, Kenya, and said South Africa was better placed to establish an African hub than the East African country.

"But if you are not quick in grabbing that opportunity, it's going to disappear in front of your eyes," Nene (2019) cautioned.

Lungisa Fuzile (2019), who was Director-General in the Department of Finance from May 2011 until December 2017 (Reuters, 2017), worked under four Finance Ministers: Gordhan, Nene, Des van Rooyen and Gigaba (Omarjee). During that period, he had dealings with SAA both as the most senior public servant at the National Treasury, and later as Shareholder Representative after the airline was moved to the Finance Ministry.

Fuzile (2019) said the National Treasury team "spent a hell of a long time" being close to SAA because of the various guarantees that the national carrier has had from the Government "for a very long period of time." He said the Finance Ministry wanted SOCs "to be able to stand alone on the strength of their balance sheets" and to be able to raise money in the capital markets, "preferably without any Government backing, and be able to operate on the strength of their balance sheets and their own cash flows." That approach, he said, was "informed by the desire to expose them to the discipline that the markets impose."

Fuzile (2019) said the Finance Ministry was acutely aware of the fact that the Government might not always have "all of the capacity needed to make these calls and assess the business, its health and governance" to ensure that SOCs were "on the right path and trajectory." The National Treasury, therefore, wanted SAA and other SOCs "to operate like any commercial business."

He said during the period when SAA was under the National Treasury, there was "a lot of paralysis" at the airline. Not only did SAA not have a full Board "most of that time," but the Board was also divided. He said the divisions continued even after a full Board –

"which was largely functional" – was eventually appointed. He said Chairperson Dudu Myeni "ran her kind of show" and would sometimes not sign, as she was required to do, communication from the Board to the Government. In the end, Fuzile (2019) said, the BoD "learned to find a way to work around her," with the Deputy Chairperson stepping in to sign that communication.

Fuzile (2019) said once the full Board was appointed, it played its fiduciary role and the Shareholder Ministry "tried to play its own role and tried to let the CEO play his role." However, difficulties continued to be experienced "because the Chair would work around all of these people and issue instructions to the CEO, sometimes illegal instructions." He said notwithstanding efforts "to bring a semblance of normality," governance remained "messed up."

Fuzile (2019) shared Tshabalala's (2019) view that Acting SAA CEO Musa Zwane was "petrified by the Chairperson."

Asked what factors would enhance the chances of SAA's turnaround strategy being implemented successfully, Fuzile (2019) expressed doubt that the airline could ever be turned around "while it is still in the hands of the Government fully." That, he said, was because the Government tended to put political considerations "ahead of everything."

"They may mask – and mask they do – what is a political decision and try and present it as an economic argument," Fuzile (2019) said.

The second challenge, he said, was that the Government did not have the resources required by SAA; and, thirdly, governance would always remain a challenge for as long as politicians were involved.

Referring to developments at Eskom and the South African Broadcasting Corporation (SABC), where the Government had stepped in to prevent retrenchments from being implemented, Fuzile (2019) said the Government did not understand that the fact that it had job creation as a stated goal did not "mean that you must use your own entities to employ people." As a result, the Boards and CEOs of those two entities "can't take the right decisions – and they have wanted to do so."

Asked why he thought the Boards and CEOs at KQ and EAL were allowed operational autonomy but SAA was not given the same leeway here at home, Fuzile (2019) again said politics was the difference:

> *Those countries have got a longer history [of independence] than us. They have had time to be sentimental about things, and they have realised that they have burnt themselves in the process. At different times, they have had bad leaders. If you take Kenya, for example, they have had bad leaders for a very long time, so the economy and the entities get battered and you reach that*

point of desperation where, if you like, you sober up and you accept that this we can't do.

In South Africa, knowing what I do, you are used to good politicians. They sometimes want to do the right things, but politically doing the right thing may be suicidal for them.

Fuzile (2019) said that, unlike South Africa, neither Kenya nor Ethiopia has had "a history of unionism like we have had, and a government with a relationship with a union and a Communist Party like the ANC has had." He said in South Africa there were times when there was not "even the right space to have the right conversation on, for instance, State participation or ownership versus privatisation." He said COSATU, the SACP and left-leaning individuals within the ANC had been "victorious in making sure that you don't even allow the debate truly to take place."

Referring to the fierce – and sometimes personal – criticism of Mboweni whenever he has expressed unfavourable views on the economy and SOCs, Fuzile (2019) said: "You saw how they mauled Tito [Mboweni], right? Because they suspect that once you go down that path, they may not have sufficient argument to motivate for what they want, so avoid the argument from taking place."

Fuzile (2019) said, contrary to the views of turnaround scholars that during a turnaround period a CEO should have more authority delegated to him or her, that has not been the case at SAA. He said there were attempts to delegate more authority to Jarana, even though he was aware that even then there was haggling within the Board about whether Jarana had to be allowed to "have authority to take decisions."

Fuzile (2019) said he knew for a fact that, before his resignation in May 2019, Jarana (2019) had previously tendered his resignation – and was "persuaded to withdraw it." He said it was important that, to improve the chances of success, the BoD allowed the CEO space within which to manoeuvre and that the CEO, likewise, accorded the BoD the necessary respect:

What you want is that there must be proper governance. There is a Board. So, the chemistry, the delineation of roles between the CEO and the Board must be the right one, between the Board and the Shareholder Minister must be the right one. It just takes the kind of mentality and maturity, and you want to be able not only to know these things, but you must live them. People within the business must feel that Jarana is an empowered CEO, but he is not a bull in a china shop. I'm saying that we don't have that balance, unfortunately, at SAA.

Fuzile (2019) said when SAA was under the National Treasury, the Shareholder Minister was "acutely aware that you can't fix the thing with an Acting CEO, an Acting CFO, an Acting Head of Strategy" and others like that, or with a three-member Board with "only one person with proper qualifications." He said while having a number of vacancies and people in acting positions undermined the turnaround strategy, the problem was that "the people who ought to change that preferred it that way because it served them well."

Fuzile (2019) said he thought SAA had reached a point where, short of headcount reduction, it would not survive. He said the airline had two options: either it reduced everybody's salaries, which was "a very hard thing to do," or reduced the number of employees. Simultaneously, he said every other cost would have to be adjusted commensurately, without changing the quality of the service provided and the client experience in the process.

Asked what he would do to turn SAA around, if he were given carte blanche to do so, Fuzile (2019) said his first action would be "to look one more time at the Board" to establish if it was sufficiently cohesive and worked as a team:

> And when you get the people, you almost would want to sit with them and say to them: "You know, guys, I hope you understand that the day you have a kind of disagreement that makes you feel you are 'enemies', let me know so that we re-set. I make the decision who has got to leave the Board, or whether all of you should leave, because the key thing is that there must never be a story about you fighting when the airline has not been turned around. So, you must get out of the way, or we get the one or two persons who are a problem out of the way."
>
> Once they get that, I would ask them: "Do you think Jarana is your man? Jarana, do you think you can work with these people? They are your bosses; it's not the other way around." I mean, if it's true that one day he said "it's either you or me," once a CEO reaches that point where he can talk like that to a Board, it's either the Board leaves or he leaves. It's dysfunctional, because you can't have the wrong balance of power. Then if he thinks he can work with the Board and the Board thinks that it can work with him, then you say to them: good, let's turn the airline around.

Fuzile (2019) said he would then insist on SAA getting an equity partner, with priority given to preparing the airline "for privatisation as quickly as possible, because what you want is to get it out of the Government's books."

"When I talk of a private-sector/strategic equity partner, I have in mind Kenya Airways, Ethiopian Airlines, Emirates, Lufthansa. You would look at those things as a package where you say: what do we bring in that gives this thing a chance? If it is about getting all of it into the private sector, we would do that. If it is about private-sector-plus participation with another airline, which may not even be a private sector-owned airline, so be it," he said.

Avril Halstead dealt with SAA from her time as Chief Director responsible for SOE oversight at the Department of Finance. Subsequently, she moved to the DPE as Acting DDG: Transport Enterprises, with her responsibilities including oversight over SAA. As she put it, that meant that she has "sat on both sides of the table, but being the Shareholder representative from both angles."

When the interview with her took place on 15 February 2019, she disclosed that SAA was in the process of making some adjustments, "basically very small refinements" to the LTTS, "basically looking to execute what was put on the table late in 2017."

Halstead (2019) said that, from a Shareholder perspective, "strong management capacity" was considered to be vital for a successful implementation of the turnaround strategy. She said the depletion of senior management capacity at SAA over the past five years or longer, especially in critical areas like Finance and Commercial Operations, had affected the airline badly. Commercial operations, she said, was "the heartbeat of the airline."

Also concerning to the Shareholder was "depletion of capacity" at SAAT, an area of the business which had been "more plagued by fraud and corruption," Halstead (2019) said. Therefore, "beefing up management capacity" was an urgent priority. That was why the Shareholder had appointed Vuyani Jarana as CEO, facilitated the employment of Peter Davies as Chief Restructuring Officer and the appointment of Deon Fredericks as Interim CFO.

Halstead (2019) said in order to fix supply chain and procurement issues, two individuals previously employed at the Chief Procurement Officer's Department at the National Treasury had joined SAA about a year earlier "to strengthen their procurement."

She said SAA had Boeing and Airbus aircraft in its fleet, but had since transferred all its Boeing aircraft to Mango and flew only Airbus aircraft, which improved operational efficiencies. She said the airline had closed a number of loss-making routes on the regional network and all its domestic and regional routes, bar two, were profitable.

Halstead (2019) said given the fact that liquidity was "a big challenge for SAA," the Government had committed to "a phased recapitalisation" of the airline. She said bringing in an SEP was an option, but only once SAA's own financial performance had improved to make it an attractive proposition.

Halstead (2019) acknowledged SAA's complaints about "the extra-bureaucratic requirements that are placed on them as a result of being a State-owned enterprise," largely related to the PFMA and the SMF, which require them to obtain Ministerial approval for a number of decisions, including route openings and closures. She said the difficulty for the Shareholder was that, as much as it understood that SAA was in a fiercely competitive space, South Africa had "just come out of an era of huge corruption, mismanagement and so on."

She said during her time at the National Treasury, she had seen "many, many CEOs, not just at SAA," asking for special dispensations and promising that they would behave differently from their predecessors. She said it later transpired that "they are not that different and special," and that made it difficult to relax "a lot of the internal controls and delegation of authority, without seeing a building of trust."

She continued:

> Even if you see a building of trust, you've got to bear in mind that this might be a good Management Team who are compliant, ethical, have integrity and are doing things the right way, but tomorrow somebody else can come in who is not ethical and does not have integrity, and we need to make sure that checks and balances are there.

Halstead (2019) said the DPE wanted to strike a balance between "looking back and cleaning up and going after all the people who did bad things," while simultaneously "looking forward and saying 'how are we going to be making sure this airline is profitable?'" She said the Shareholder prioritised "get[ting] the bad people out of top management levels" first because, if that was not done, "you get very little traction in implementing the strategy." Instead, much anger and resistance take place "from people on the ground."

She said the DPE held weekly, monthly and quarterly monitoring meetings with SAA Management, with the Minister having "regular meetings with the Board and the Executive."

However, both Magwaza (2019) and Jarana (2019), as Chairman and CEO respectively, disputed that the Minister had "regular meetings" with them. In fact, Magwaza (2019) said he had struggled to get an audience with Gordhan.

Halstead (2019) said one of the DPE's responsibilities was to facilitate resolution of policy issues that impacted negatively on SAA. She acknowledged that there were "a lot of different policies that affect the aviation sector," with the approach by different Government Departments being "very fragmented," and said the DPE was "looking to have a more holistic approach" to the aviation sector.

Halstead (2019) explained that it was the Minister who was the Shareholder, and not the DPE. She said their role, as Departmental officials, was "to do a lot of the technical leg work so that the Minister is focused on solving the key strategic issues and navigating through the political space these policy proposals."

On operational costs, Halstead (2019) said while she did not readily have the numbers, she believed that SAA had gone up "from something like 9 500 employees to 12 000." That meant that the airline has an excess of about 2 000 employees. She said while she did not think any retrenchment would be authorised before the May 2019 general elections, she did not know what would happen after the elections.

However, Halstead (2019) acknowledged that the national carrier had struggled not only because of things that it had done, but "also because of things that the Government does to them." She said SAA could not possibly implement a turnaround strategy successfully when it is "like R17 billion insolvent; they are not going to dig themselves out of the hole by themselves."

She said that, regrettably, there had been "very poor recognition" by the Government that SAA could not dig itself out of the hole by itself; instead, the airline needed to be properly recapitalised.

Enoch Godongwana, Head of the ANC's Economic Transformation Committee, was Deputy Minister of Public Enterprises when Hogan was Minister. He echoed the views expressed by Hogan (2019) and Mokholo (2019) that, during Hogan's tenure, the SAA Board and Management were given "power to run the institution, free from interference." Godongwana (2019) said he and Hogan concerned themselves with "the policy environment and, therefore, a set of KPIs for them, as a Shareholder."

Godongwana (2019) dismissed as "a moot point" the argument that SAA was not properly capitalised when the airline was taken out of the protective clutches of Transnet. He said during Ngqula's tenure, the Government provided money for SAA to use to effect staff retrenchment so that the airline would be more competitive, but unions later complained that "Management ended up paying themselves bonuses out of that money."

Both Ngqula (2020) and Kriel (2020) denied that allegation. Kriel (2020) said the only money that SAA received from the Government at the time was to cover once-off costs for the SAA Business Restructuring Plan. She said: "We did not receive any money from the National Treasury, but a guarantee which was taken to the banks to raise the money for once-off costs (including the voluntary severance packages). The latter was a relatively small number – the large once-off costs numbers resided in the onerous contracts we needed to renegotiate (including the Boeing leases that were done by Transnet when SAA still formed part of Transnet)."

Godongwana (2019) said he would accept the criticism that frequent changes of Ministers at Public Enterprises have had a negative impact on SAA, and that the Ministers each tended to have different expectations of the airline. He pointed to other portfolios, especially Communications, where frequent changes of Ministers have had a similarly negative impact on the sector.

Godongwana (2019) revealed that Mboweni had told him that, following a meeting with Jarana during which the latter took him through a presentation on SAA, he [Mboweni] was happy to consider transferring SAA's debt to the Government in order to enable a debt-free national carrier to improve its chances of being successfully turned around. Godongwana (2019) said it was unfortunate that Jarana resigned shortly after Mboweni had agreed to the proposal.

To improve the chances of successfully turning SAA around, Godongwana (2019) said it was crucial to confine the BoD to oversight and to ensure that appropriate authority was delegated to the CEO and the TMT:

> *You must allow Management the opportunity to run an institution – if it means restructuring to cut costs and retrenching, so be it. If Management is not given that leeway, therefore, they are not going to be competitive. The starting point is to give Management authority. There is nothing that prevents them, in terms of the PFMA, from delegating as much authority as you can. That's the first thing.*

> *For me, the starting point is to get Management to have operational decisions. If they can't change the institution, fire them; but you must give them sufficient time and autonomy to make the right decision to turn the institution around. There is nothing that says you can't do so at SAA.*

Equally importantly, he said, only individuals with "the requisite skills" should be appointed onto the BoD. He said these had to be "people of integrity, whose primary concern is the success of the airline and, therefore, who will understand they have a fiduciary duty to SAA."

Godongwana (2019) said he did not share the view that there was a shortage of black skills in the country. He said there was no shortage "of people who are probably sympathetic to the ANC who understand the industry."

Thirdly, he said it was important to take a long-term view and get a SEP that would complement the airline. He said the ANC's policy on the sale of State assets had not changed, and that the Framework Agreement which was concluded between the Government and the unions in 1995 remained unchanged. In terms of that Framework Agreement, the unions only insisted on "genuine consultation."

What had changed, however, was the political will on the part of the relevant individuals in Government.

Mokholo (2019) said the National Treasury gave SAA money in 2012 to deal with retrenchments, but the airline used that money "for operational requirements" because of opposition to retrenchment from labour.

Numerous requests for an interview with Gordhan, as the incumbent SAA Shareholder during this research, were unsuccessful. The first request was sent to him in December 2018, and was followed by a number of others until July 2019. All elicited no response from the Minister. Eventually, when attempts were made to get people close to Gordhan – including Fuzile and Halstead – to intercede on my behalf, Halstead responded on 31 July 2019 to say "it will not be possible to schedule a meeting with him" because he was "extremely busy at the moment, resolving challenges at various SOEs, in particular Eskom, as well as having to deal with legal issues, primarily relating to the case with the Public Protector."

Similar requests for an interview with Mboweni were also unsuccessful, and no responses were received to letters sent to him by e-mail asking for an interview.

To get these Ministers' views, I had to rely on their reported media statements. Speaking in Parliament in June 2019, Gordhan said the situation at SOCs required special measures, which "shall include greater intervention from the Shareholder if the Boards and Management do not take the steps needed to deliver on the outcomes expected of each company." He argued that such threatened Shareholder intervention was "in keeping with the Companies Act and the PFMA" (Du Toit, 2019).

During the same speech, Gordhan attributed SAA's poor performance to State capture, being caught in a debt trap and its inability to service its debt, an unsustainable cost structure, an incorrect fleet configuration and red tape. On the last point, specifically, Gordhan said the national carrier was "hobbled by many cumbersome approval processes" (Smith, 2019).

Writing in the *Sunday Times* in November 2019 after the Government had placed SAA in business rescue, in an effort to pre-empt Solidarity's High Court application for the airline to be placed in business rescue after its financial situation had deteriorated following a week-long strike by the National Union of Metalworkers of South Africa (NUMSA) and the South African Cabin Crew Association (SACCA), Gordhan (2019) said SAA had reached "an untenable state." He said the business rescue practitioner (BRP) to be appointed would have "total control of the company" and that the Government, like other interested parties, would "make inputs, should the practitioner invite these."

Explaining "the decisive announcement" made by Ramaphosa, Gordhan (2019) wrote: "[SAA] had reached an untenable state. At some stage, it was likened to a patient experiencing multiple organ failure. Something had to be done, and done quickly, to stop the decline and uncertainty. Under the conditions that presented themselves – of urgency, financial distress and the rapid deterioration of revenue exacerbated by the strike – there were only two options left: liquidation or business rescue."

Gordhan (2019) said notwithstanding "many attempts" over the years to reposition SAA and "many turnaround strategies," there was "failure of effective implementation by successive teams" and that had put the airline in "increasing difficulties." He said short of going the business rescue route, many of SAA's employees "of around 10 000 would have been affected, without the normal protection of the Labour Relations Act."

Gordhan (2019) made plain the fact that the appointment of a BRP was a recommendation from the SAA BoD, and said the Government had agreed with it. He said the appointed BRP, Les Matuson at the time, would "take decisive actions." The process, he said, was "the best chance of retaining viable parts of SAA and transforming the airline into a stronger company that can attract an equity partner."

Gordhan (2019) said many lessons had to be learned from the SAA experience. One of them, he wrote, was that there was a need "to be more diligent about governance." "Public enterprises need capable and skilled leadership teams that are knowledgeable about the sectors in which they operate. Also, we have to manage the relationship between cost and revenue because no business can succeed if costs are higher than revenue," he wrote.

A few weeks later, Carol Paton (2019) argued that the SAA Shareholder's behaviour was "bizarre." Although the Shareholder had signed off on SAA's LTTS, which was very clearly predicated on a need for R21,7 billion to cover the airline's debts and running costs, the Government "never came up with the money." Instead, the Government had waited until the airline was in business rescue before promising the full amount, "even then spread over the next three years."

Paton (2019) accused the Government of having intervened "constantly and inappropriately" at SAA. She said when Gordhan (2019) wrote that attention had to be given to governance, he meant that the "Government should have stepped in earlier, not with money, but to run the show."

Despite having said in November 2019 that the BRPs (Siviwe Dongwana was subsequently appointed to work with Matuson) would "take total control of the company," in February 2020 Gordhan changed tune, when he did not like the decisions taken by the BRPs. He announced that the BRPs must still get his permission for fundamental decisions related to the restructuring of the airline because, "in terms of the PFMA, the Accounting Officer is accountable to the Executive Authority" (Paton, 2020). That, said Gordhan, meant that the BRPs could not take decisions on the disposal of SAA's assets without permission from himself (Paton, 2020).

Eric Levenstein (2020) was among those who differed with Gordhan on the matter. The Companies Act, he wrote, "makes it clear that the business rescue practitioners are obligated to act independently and, like a Director, must act in the best interests of the company." He said the business rescue plan that they would produce would ultimately reflect the extent of the independence they enjoyed when they finalised SAA's restructuring.

Writing in *Business Day* in August 2020, new DPE Director-General Kgathatso Tlhakudi (2020) – who was appointed into the role a month earlier – revealed that SAA had had nine turnaround strategies over the years and attributed the airline's failure to implement those strategies successfully to internal and external challenges. Among internal challenges, he cited "lack of stability at Board and executive level," under-capitalisation and the fact that "key roles were filled by ill-intentioned, temporary or inappropriately skilled individuals." External challenges that he mentioned were South Africa's slow economic growth, foreign exchange fluctuations, oil price volatility and the labour strike which had taken place at the national carrier in November 2019.

Tlhakudi (2020) said the Government wanted "the new SAA" which would emerge after the business rescue process to succeed because it wanted to "leverage the airline to ensure affordable air travel and improve connectivity in a country and region with large distances between economic hubs." The Government, he said, wanted the airlined "to remain a catalyst for wider benefits in its role as a critical component and facilitator of business and tourism."

A few days later, the DPE issued a press statement in which it indicated, for the very first time, that the Government no longer wanted to be the majority owner of SAA, but merely wanted to "maintain a certain level of presence" in the ownership of the new SAA which would emerge after the conclusion of the business rescue process. The Department said the Government looked at Telkom Limited as a model, where it has a 40% stake, in addition to the 14,2% owned by the country's Public Investment Corporation (Paton, 2020).

Despite having said in November 2018 that there was no way SAA could be fixed and that it would be better to close the airline down and start a new one (Whitehouse, 2019), on 25 February 2020 Mboweni announced that, in addition to having its debt and interest payment taken care of, the national carrier would also receive additional support to fund its restructuring. SAA would receive R16,4 billion to cover debt and interest repayments, in addition to an emergency loan of R3,5 billion received from the Development Bank of Southern Africa in January 2020 (Paton, 2020).

Delivering his Medium-Term Budget Policy Statement in Parliament on 28 October 2020, Mboweni allocated R10,5 billion to SAA as post-commencement finance to finalise the airline's business rescue. The money, which had been awaited since SAA's business rescue plan was approved by the airline's creditors, labour unions and the Shareholder on 14 July 2020, came from re-allocations from a number of other Government Departments' initial allocations in February 2020.

A day later, Public Enterprises Minister Pravin Gordhan issued a media statement in which he welcomed the R10,5 billion allocation to SAA, saying the money would "pave the way for the finalisation of the business rescue process and [the] restructuring of the airline." He said "a new national airline," which would have a strategic equity partner, would be established by the first half of 2021 and would be run "in a professional and sustainable manner to support key economic sectors, including tourism, and solidify South Africa as an African gateway to international markets" (Mkokeli, 2020).

Chapter Twelve

LABOUR POINTS FINGERS AT SAA MANAGEMENT AND BOARDS OF DIRECTORS

Just as members of the SAA Top Management Team (TMT) pointed accusing fingers at the Board of Directors (BoD), the Shareholder and labour, unions active at the national carrier, pointed their own fingers primarily at the other three stakeholder groups. SAA, they said, found itself in the trouble it was in because of its past leadership, those who had served on its BoDs and the Shareholder's failure to make decisions timeously.

However, although there was a great degree of distrust of both those who had been part of the SAA TMT over extended periods and some of those who had served on the airline's BoDs, there was a lot of goodwill towards Vuyani Jarana, who was held in high regard during his time as CEO between November 2017 and May 2019.

Solidarity is one of the unions which are active at SAA, and represented about 750 employees – the vast majority of them at SAA Technical (SAAT) – at the time of the interview in May 2019.

When SAA's results for the 2016/17 financial year were finally released, showing yet another big loss, Solidarity – through its Solidarity Research Institute (SRI) headed by Connie Mulder – initiated a process of establishing if a State-owned company (SOC) can be placed in business rescue. With SOCs covered by the Companies Act 71 of 2008, which provides for business rescue, Mulder (2019) said SRI then conducted an in-depth study to establish if SAA could be said to be likely to be a going concern over the next 12 to 18 months.

As part of that study, Mulder (2019) said the SRI team spoke to former SAA Acting CEO Nico Bezuidenhout and former Chief Strategy Officer Barry Parsons, who were involved in putting the LTTS together. He said they concluded that the airline can be saved, provided that it follows the LTTS closely. The problem, he said, was not the LTTS, but the fact that it was not rigorously implemented:

> *The problem that we find at SAA is not the Long-Term Turnaround Strategy.*
> *The turnaround strategy is actually good. It's closely modelled on Air New*

Zealand's turnaround strategy. Air New Zealand faces the same geographic challenges that SAA has. The only problem that we have is that our implementation got side-tracked. It got side-tracked severely due to corruption and influence, with one person coming to mind, Dudu Myeni, who torpedoed several deals that would have taken place.

Mulder (2019) said their study revealed that Air New Zealand's strategy was implemented "almost flawlessly" because the politicians in that country allowed the Management Team to run the airline: "They stepped out of it. Even though they still own it, they are not involved in the day-to-day management," he said.

Part of SAA's challenge, according to Mulder (2019), is the fact that it has to operate in accordance with the PFMA, when its competitors have no similar strictures constraining them. He said ideally SAA would have to be exempted from the PFMA, "which is not necessarily a smart idea, given South Africa's history of State capture."

Mulder (2019) said the fact that a number of SAA CEOs had tried to implement the LTTS but failed indicated that "there's something wrong with the way that the CEOs are handled." He said it could not be argued that the CEOs were incompetent because most of them had "achieved successes elsewhere." He said every former SAA CEO that SRI spoke to had experienced "massive frustration with quite simply not being able to do the work."

Mulder (2019) echoed the view that SAA was "really struggling with skills and a massive recruitment problem." He said the airline found itself in "this weird situation, which Eskom also has: with a lot of staff, but not enough skills." He said in order to improve the chances of the airline being successfully turned around, the Government would have to sell up to 51% of the national carrier to an established network carrier.

Mulder (2019) said Air New Zealand was also government owned, had "about the same staff complement as SAA" and had "bigger geographical challenges," but it was profitable. He said SAA's problems could be solved "in five years" if the airline were privatised either fully or partially.

He said once the SRI had finished its study, it shared it with Jarana and Public Enterprises Minister Pravin Gordhan, as the CEO and the Shareholder respectively, and got its court papers ready to apply for SAA to be placed in business rescue. However, when Jarana committed to implementing the LTTS, the SRI resolved to stay its court application in order to give the CEO a chance. He said Solidarity also agreed to Jarana's request not to publicise its plans to launch court action to get the airline placed in business rescue.

"At Mr Jarana's request, we said that we were not going to publicise it for the simple reason that then you give them no chance. They had already hit a massive deep in long-term ticket sales just when there were rumours that liquidation was coming, because no one wants to be stuck with an SAA ticket eight months from now and they can't use it," Mulder (2019) said.

He said Solidarity's experience was that SAA was "very, very top heavy," with authority heavily centralised, thus depriving the airline of the ability to be fleet-footed. To compound matters, he said, there was heavy Shareholder involvement:

> *Obviously, one of the main problems is that decision making primarily takes place mostly at Shareholder lever because at Board level there is always the shadow of the Government owning 100%. So, the Board is the Shareholder; they are completely beholden to the Minister, who then decides. So, a lot of the critical, strategic decision making regarding the LTTS was done at Shareholder level – meaning no decision making.*

> *They just didn't make the decisions; that paralysed the company downwards, with several instances of guys trying to make decisions and then getting stopped because they need to comply and they [the Shareholder] need to check, those sorts of things. It's not a conducive environment for running a fleet-footed company.*

Mulder (2019) said while Solidarity accepted that cost and asset retrenchment had to take place at SAA, the union believed that more cost savings could be made in procurement "and those spaces where they are spending way too much." He said Solidary was "obviously not happy with getting [staff retrenchment] done," but agreed that savings needed to be made in procurement and maintenance costs.

Mulder (2019) said "most of the time" business rescue was embarked upon in order to save jobs, after having paid debtors. He said it was crucial, therefore, that SAA Management took labour along, even if it needed to retrench staff, to explain "why you are retrenching." He said alignment among the different stakeholder groups was very important:

> *The first thing, if you want to implement a turnaround successfully, is to get stakeholders around the table – that's Shareholders, labour, Management – and make sure everyone is aligned, and that you communicate that we are going to have some pain for two or three years, but then we are going to turn around. The reason for turnaround strategies is that if we don't do this, then everyone goes down – and that's what we have seen at SAA. If you don't turn around, we are going into liquidation and then 11 000 jobs are gone. That's one of the main issues. So, labour is absolutely critical in this process.*

Mulder (2019) said while Jarana's predecessors "did not really consult, Mr Jarana has a much better, much more open channel." He said Solidarity felt that Jarana was readily accessible and that he took its views seriously. "So, it's not just a tea-and-sympathy meeting," he said. "It looks like Mr Jarana and Management are really serious about turning SAA around; they are just facing massive restrictions regarding the Shareholder and those types of things."

Mulder (2019) stressed that labour also had a responsibility "to come to the party." He said unions had to realise "that if we continue with these demands, if we put them on strike action, we are going to kill this airline, which is going to be tricky for us all." He said it was unfortunate that South Africa had "a history of a lot of tension between labour and management," often characterised by "massive distrust and *mala fides* on both sides."

Mulder (2019) said SAA employees were "paid quite well in terms of the market." That, he said, meant that below-inflation increases or even wage freezes should be possible as part of cost containment.

Mulder (2019) said COSATU's alliance with the governing party had led to the situation where South Africa has "a problem with the public sector being way over-staffed," with Government expenditure representing 33% of the country's Gross Domestic Product. He said the Government was unable to "stop this train because they are beholden to the unions."

At SAA, he said, the Government's special relationship with labour created "a massive problem for Management" because, when the airline needed to cut costs, labour leaders would talk to the Shareholder "and put pressure from that side." As a result, "normal decision making is interfered with because the labour union can use external leverages that you as Management don't have a lot of power over."

The COSATU-affiliated South African Transport and Allied Workers' Union (SATAWU) represents just over 700 employees at SAAT. Representing the union during the interview were Tinyiko Mashele, Provincial Chairperson for Aviation; Lucas Moatshe, Provincial Secretary for Aviation, and Xolile Zonke, SATAWU SAA Chairperson. Mashele and Moatshe were full-time SATAWU representatives at SAA, while Zonke was an aircraft engineer.

Mashele (2019) said both Jarana and his predecessors had presented the various iterations of the turnaround strategy to labour, with "numerous consultation processes" having taken place "to advance the strategies."

Collectively, the three men had 52 years' experience in aviation: Zonke and Mashele each had 20 years' experience as aeronautical engineers, while Moatshe had 12 years' experience with SAAT in the same capacity.

Zonke (2019) said SATAWU tended "to view things differently from Management" because its primary goal was "to hold Management accountable for the decisions that they make to make sure that they are in the interest of all role players, which are the Government, SAA Management and the employees." He said whenever the different turnaround strategies were presented to the union, "obviously we engage; we consult; we solicit accountability; we solicit responsibility."

However, Zonke (2019) expressed reservations that the views of internal subject-matter experts, especially at SAAT, were not properly canvassed in drawing up the LTTS. He said that, as a result, he and his fellow aeronautical engineers felt undermined.

Zonke (2019) said SATAWU had no problem with the turnaround strategies presented, but was frustrated by their non-implementation:

> *But as we consult, obviously we have no access to the Board, to a certain extent, and the decisions which are taken. From where we sit, we feel like the strategies were somehow 80% or 90% promising in terms of turning the airline around, but not the other end of consultation, which is at the Board level; we don't know the dynamics there. We feel like a lot of responsibility lies with the Board and Upper Management to make sure that the strategy which they consulted on with us is implemented.*

He said SATAWU was not comfortable that the Board was fully supportive of the LTTS. He could not tell whether that was a result of "lack of total buy-in" or if there were internal factions within the Board.

Zonke (2019) said during Management's consultations with labour, "certain things we okayed as labour, certain things we still needed to be consulted on." Particularly, the union placed on the table the practice of SAA employees being suspended for periods of up to "two or three years" and receiving salaries, at a time when the airline is losing money. He said these suspensions suggested that Middle Management had not bought into the LTTS "because the decisions that they make are undermining the strategy."

He said turning the airline around would require "total commitment" from Management. He said SAA's challenges were compounded by the fact that some Managers who had been with the airline "for very many years" were "contaminated." Instead of fully embracing the LTTS and vigorously implementing it, such Managers were concerned about "coming up with solutions which eliminate them as being guilty:"

> *The strategy is dependent on the honesty of those Managers to give input into the strategy. Now if there is no honesty and integrity from those Managers, that is the first step that we take towards the failure of the strategy because there is no commitment and no guaranteed participation in the strategy. All these things happen at lower levels in Departments, but in reality the outputs of those Departments are feeding into the main strategy.*
>
> *So, if these components at the bottom are not supporting what the strategy needs, the strategy is going to crumble down because those are the building*

blocks of your strategy. That's what's going to determine if your strategy is successful.

Zonke (2019) said it was time that those Managers against whom there were allegations were held to account and, if found guilty, removed from the airline.

He said although Jarana's strategies enjoyed labour's support, nevertheless employees were demoralised and exposed to "a lot of turmoil" because of the high leadership turnover at the airline and the failure to implement the strategies.

Mashele (2019) said the only aspect of the LTTS that SATAWU did not support was its "projection of close to 2000 retrenchments."

He said it was unfortunate that Jarana – who enjoyed SATAWU's support – had resigned and that the Board had decided not to allow him to serve his three-month notice period. He said SATAWU found itself unable to support him because he had voluntarily walked away from his job.

"We find ourselves in a difficult position to say, yes, we thought he was actually turning the company around," Mashele (2019) said. "He has complained about support that he was not getting from the other role players. Unfortunately, he has actually voluntarily stepped down. How do you then protect such a person?"

Moatshe (2019) said one of the things which had expedited SAA's decline was the fact that the airline was "one of the SOCs that were surrounded by State capture." Specifically, he said there "was looting of spares at SAAT."

Moatshe (2019) also blamed the Government's failure to take steps to eliminate the abuse of Black Economic Empowerment, of which "most of our Management" took advantage by ensuring that suppliers charged inflated prices from which they benefitted through bribes. Also to blame, he said, were "some of the Board Members who played a role in us finding ourselves in this difficult position financially."

To improve the chances of SAA being successfully turned around, Mashele (2019) said "the full support of the Shareholder, in terms of finances," would be crucial. He said SATAWU shared Jarana's (2019) concerns that SAA was not mentioned in Finance Minister Tito Mboweni's budget speech in February 2019.

"Where," Mashele (2019) asked rhetorically, "does that put SAA's future when we are not assured of whether we will have the company tomorrow because of funding? We need the support of the Shareholder."

He commended Jarana as having been "very good" at insisting on being allowed to run the airline as CEO, saying "the previous CEOs were actually micro-managed by the Shareholder as to what should be done and how they should do it." Jarana, on the other hand, was "actually trying to apply his own mind to whatever he was doing, because he had a business mind and was not politically inclined."

"That is what we actually need," Mashele (2019) said.

SATAWU, Mashele (2019) said, agreed that it was imperative for the CEO to be "given the powers to run the business." He said it was instructions from the Shareholder that had led to SAA flying routes that were not commercially viable.

"A person with a business mind would not have allowed that to happen. It shows that this person was being micro-managed. We need a CEO who is going to be given authority to run the company," Mashele (2019) said.

Speaking about Jarana, Zonke (2019) said:

> We believe that, as the CEO, he should have had authority, but we don't know the terms of his contract. We don't know the extent to which politics played a role. We don't know the extent to which sabotage played a role. We don't know all these issues, but we would like to believe that he had the powers. We didn't know his Delegation of Authority and his jurisdiction.
>
> We ask ourselves so many questions. We were convinced that he is the man and we were convinced that all these strategies will go through. Why is this guy losing momentum after the spirit that he came into the organisation with? How he spoke to us, how he consulted with us, how he gave us his commitment, and a year after he joined us he resigns. It raises a question. Did he fail? Was he failed? We can only know if we are privy to his area of jurisdiction or his Delegation of Authority.

Mashele (2019) said SAA has had "strategies one after another" because of the high turnover of CEOs at the airline. He said before a CEO could implement any strategy, "already you are out, and whoever comes to take over brings his own strategies."

On the question of the Government getting a strategic equity partner (SEP) for SAA, Mashele (2019) said SATAWU did not see the need for one because it believed that SAA "can be sustainable and generate a profit by 2021, as projected by the out-going CEO." He said South Africa had one "of the highest unemployment rates" in the world, hence SATAWU did not want a SEP that might insist on retrenchments which would "affect the very same 10 000 employees who are here." Instead, he said SATAWU would want SAA's "ever-green agreement" with the South African Airways Pilots Association reviewed to save costs.

However, expressing his own "personal view" and not SATAWU's, Moatshe (2019) said:

> Looking at the current state of the business and how the Government is struggling to finance SOCs, it's inevitable that at some point a strategic partner will have to be brought on board. Obviously, that being an inevitable position

that you are faced with, you need to think of a strategy of how you are going to manage them as your partners because at some point it will happen, whether we like it or not.

For me, it's not a matter of whether I want or I don't want [a strategic partner], because it's going to happen either way. So, for me it's more a question of how do we manage them when they come through.

Zonke (2019) said the union was "amenable to any process that puts the best interests of the Government, the public, SAAT as a business and its employees" first, provided that the partnership – "whoever is the role player there" – restores SAA to "its position as the best airline in Africa."

Pointing to their collective 52-year experience in aviation, Zonke (2019) said they were qualified to "give input in terms of the potential of the organisation." He said they believed strongly that the national carrier can be sustainably profitable and "grow even more than it was prior to this period" if it was properly capitalised and had support from the Shareholder.

"Therefore, we do not believe that the Government should let go of SAA," he said. "We know the strategic role that SAA plays for the Government. We should just come up with strategies to harmonise those interests of different stakeholders. We believe SAA has got potential."

The South African Cabin Crew Association (SACCA) was also consulted by Jarana on the LTTS, according to the organisation's Deputy President, Christopher Shabangu (2019), who proceeded to give a high-level summary of the turnaround strategy as being "basically about shrinking costs, cutting unprofessional [uncommercial] routes and new businesses, which may include a joint venture."

Shabangu (2019) said SACCA was optimistic that Jarana "could implement the strategy because it's his plan as a businessman." He said his association had no problem with the turnaround strategy at all, even though SACCA knew that it entailed "a need to shrink the staff complement." He said the process of reducing employee numbers had already begun "in a systematic way."

"In December [2018], in all reality, we as a union were supposed to be served with Section 189 notices, but we were able to speak to him [Jarana] and came back with different strategies which include giving people longer sabbaticals during which the company is not carrying a cost, but people can still go out and look for a job somewhere else while they still have the comfort of a job here. So, that was an innovative way of dealing with job losses," Shabangu (2019) said.

He said SACCA understood that among the sacrifices that would need to be made were job cuts. He said the union was keen to ensure that employees were "systematically let go" because that would make things easier for them to find jobs elsewhere "because then it is almost planned."

He said although Jarana had not formulated the LTTS, which was an iteration of previous SAA turnaround strategies (he said there had been "between seven and nine" such strategies), he had taken the one that he had inherited "and worked on it and tweaked it." He said SACCA was happy with Jarana's performance as CEO, which was why the association was defending him.

Shabangu (2019) said it was important that the BoD was "an enabler and not an inhibitor," and called for the airline to be removed from the clutches of the PFMA: "As much as we are talking about the Shareholder, saying there are PFMA requirements, you cannot talk about billions of rands that are wasted and people's jobs, and yet you are still stuck to the PFMA as if it's God's law."

Saying he was talking as "a lay man," Shabangu (2019) said it was important to ensure that, in the event of the PFMA being relaxed for the national carrier, that was not done "for the purposes of privatising the same SAA."

Asked what needed to be done to improve the chances of successfully implementing SAA's turnaround strategy, Shabangu (2019) responded:

> *Have the right people; that's all. Have the right people who will understand business. I didn't say airline business. People who, first of all, will understand simple business. We will get to the point that they need to understand the airline industry, yes, but they need to understand business first. Simple things like I buy and sell and what is involved in that, and then people who have the skills, like Jarana. We believe he had the skills.*

> *Then the international part of it is that you have to be exposed to airlines; that's just an extra. Otherwise, if we are going to be thrown all those things, we are basically saying all our African airlines must be run by Europeans. It makes no sense.*

SAA's pilots have come up in almost every interview that I have conducted as part of this research. In all those instances, the pilots have been mentioned proactively, by the various participants in this research, as having favourable working conditions which are so rigidly in their favour, regardless of whatever challenges the airline may be going through.

What do SAA's pilots themselves think?

Captain Grant Back, Chairman of the SAA Pilots Association (SAAPA), begged to differ. During an interview which lasted for about two hours, Back (2019) expressed great frustration – and even unhappiness – with the SAA BoD and the TMT, which he held jointly responsible for the hard times on which the airline had fallen. He said whenever the association came forward to negotiate in a spirit of give and take, often it encountered a situation where it was expected to give up some of its benefits, without others within the airline coming under similar levels of pressure.

Back (2019) started with a history of SAAPA's "ever-green" agreement with the airline. He said the association had been around "for a long, long time and [had] looked after the interests of the pilots from an industrial relations level." He said South Africa had "a large excess of pilots around in the late 1980s" because of poor remuneration levels and terms and conditions of employment. He said perks which routinely came with the job, which were "a norm in the industry," were "fairly non-existent" for SAA pilots at the time.

"The remuneration wasn't great. Times were tough," he said.

That was the time, Back (2019) said, when SAAPA looked at conditions of employment for pilots "at various other airlines around the world and put together a Regulating Agreement" containing pilots' terms and conditions of employment, which was accepted in 1988. The association's approach, he said, was "to negotiate the best terms we could at the time."

Back (2019) said that, in putting together the Regulating Agreement (RA), SAAPA leveraged the fact that SAA pilots had "always been held in high esteem around the world." He acknowledged that there was "a lot of negative perceptions about the RA, [which had] been bandied around in the press and in Parliament, even by Dudu Myeni when she was here," with the pilots presented as "the problem at the airline."

"It has been a great way of subterfuge, smoke and mirrors to point fingers at the pilots and our terms and conditions of employment. That was a negotiated agreement. It was not gifted to us, as it has been discussed in the past. It was a hard-won agreement," Back (2019) said.

He said the description of the RA as an "ever-green agreement" created the impression that it never expired. On the contrary, he said, since it was signed in 1988, the RA had been amended a number of times. He said just as SAAPA can put certain issues on the table for renegotiation in terms of the RA, so, too, can SAA.

"And we have," he said, "we have negotiated on many of the topics. The agreements make provision for that."

A member of the Executive Committee of the Association of Star Alliance Pilots, Back (2019) said his American counterparts informed him that they also did not have agreements without expiry dates, but they negotiated each year on specific items, as has SAAPA. He said when Bezuidenhout was Acting CEO, SAAPA "had so many side agreements" that it asked that they be incorporated into a new, revised RA, and Bezuidenhout agreed.

Back (2019) said a restructuring which had taken place in Operations, when Sizakele Mzimela was CEO, had given rise to serious concerns on SAAPA's part. He said to be found within the Operations Department were important divisions like Operations, Flight Operations, Operations Control Centre, Crew Movement Centre and others. He said the new structure, headed by former cabin crew member Zukiswa Ramasia, disempowered pilots at SAA. He said SAAPA had proposed a different Operations structure and submitted it to Jarana, who promised to give it to Accenture, which was working with Raseroka on the OD.

Although he had not seen the final OD at the time of the interview, Back (2019) said he understood that SAAPA's proposed structure had been "diluted to 40-50%" because it was feared that it would "give too much power to the pilots."

Back (2019) said SAAPA contained "an incredible amount of expertise among the pilot body." Some of its members, he said, were "doctors, engineers" and held up to three degrees:

> Now if you look at any successful airline around the world, the pilots are involved in decision-making processes. Not only that; they can also be at Board level because they understand the industry.
>
> And, you know what? To make an industry work, not only do you need understanding for it, but also passion for it. It makes a significant difference between success and failure.

Back (2019) said SAAPA had three main demands, which would make a difference in the airline's sustainability. The association, he said, demanded the appointment of a Director of Flight Operations who reported to the CFO, and who met criteria that would be set by itself; "a seat on the Board" and "a CEO of SAAT with the criteria [to be set by SAAPA]."

Back (2019) described Operations as "the heart and soul of the airline," which was a part of the business where Jarana had made no changes:

> We say this constantly to the CEO that the same people that got us into this mess over the last 10 years are still here; there has been no change. It needs to change, otherwise you are kidding yourself if you think there is going to be significant overall change in the way things are managed within Operations, which is the heart and soul. That's pilots; that's cabin crew; that's ground staff; that's technical ...

Back (2019) said pilots' areas of expertise were "flying aeroplanes, looking at routes, making those routes efficient, making decisions on how best to operate those routes, how to have a reporting structure that works and uses the resources that are available to make the best decisions on the day."

He said the position of General Manager (GM): Operations, which was occupied by Ramasia, did not exist "in any other airline around the world." Instead, the position was called Director of Flight Operations, with the incumbent required to be a pilot.

Back said the Operations team at SAA was made up of former cabin crew members: Ramasia as GM, Lindy Jordaan, Michelle Kemp and Sean Pillay. He said there was "not one pilot in there:"

> There is a faction within the cabin crew who have always disliked the pilots because, you know, pilots get paid a certain salary and pilots have certain terms and conditions, and there has always been this professional jealousy that exists between the two. At every turn, it seems as though there is an agenda at play: let's disempower the pilots as much as we can.

According to Back (2019), "the vast majority of successful airlines around the world" – such as United Airlines and American Airlines in the United States and Lufthansa in Germany – have pilots at both Management and Board levels. He said he had spent sleepless nights trying to think of what needed to be done to get SAA sorted out because SAAPA had "this incredibly large vested interest."

Back (2019) said he had been at SAA for 25 years and wanted "new guys coming in to have 25, 30 years here as well." He said unlike SAA CEOs who "come and go" after four to five years, together with "other Senior Managers at Executive level," SAAPA had "the interest of the airline at heart."

"It's not about sole benefit," he said, "but without the pilots' participation, this airline will not be nearly as close to what it could be."

Back (2019) spoke about the amount of passion that people who work for airlines tend to have:

> To make something really work very well, specifically an airline where you have got check-in staff, you've got aeroplane engineers, service levels on the aeroplanes, those are all the key people who make the operation work. Do you know why they choose to do those jobs? They do it because of their inherent love for this industry. That's what they love to do. They love to fly; they love to work on aeroplanes; they like to be engineers. They want to be involved in the industry. That's something that's here (puts his hand on the chest). That's why we choose to do what we do.

Like most of the participants in this research, Back (2019) blamed Government meddling and poor Board appointments for SAA's problems. He said the airline found itself in a situation where "there have been agendas from the top down."

Back (2019) said he was planning to take his members out on strike, "for the first time in 80 years," in order to "force change because nothing seems to work," just as KQ pilots had forced change to the Board of the East African airline. Back said the threatened strike was about being "a responsible party who is affected by the business and future of SAA," but not "about salaries or better perks and terms and conditions." He added that the pilots were also "very concerned about the state of SAAT and the servicing of our aircraft."

Unlike SACCA's Shabangu, Back (2019) said the CEO of SAA had to be somebody with aviation experience and understand the business. However, if the successful candidate did not have aviation experience, that person would have to surround him/herself with people "who are the best in the business, such as the best networking guys and the best revenue management guys."

Back (2019) said SAA had been unfortunate to have "CEOs that are questionable insofar as their knowledge and understanding of the aviation industry" in the past. He said the pilots' association has tried, in the past, to get involved in efforts to bring maladministration to the attention of the relevant authorities. In the process, SAAPA had sought to defend itself and its members by drawing attention to "the gross mismanagement and the large exodus of skills" from SAA during Myeni's tenure as Board Chairperson. That, he said, was the reason SAAPA had joined hands with the Organisation Undoing Tax Abuse to take Myeni to court to have her declared a delinquent director.

"Under Dudu Myeni, there was very little accountability," Back (2019) said. "Everyone was beholden to her… She created this type of beholden-ness to individuals in the company. We've got a couple of bad apples that are still in the company."

Back (2019) commended Jarana on his accessibility, and said he had made time to meet with a SAAPA delegation even before he assumed his role as CEO on 1 November 2017. Back (2019) said he felt that Jarana "has integrity" and that "his heart is in the right place," although he did not think that he "had any idea how mammoth a task" he was taking on as SAA CEO.

However, Back (2019) felt that Jarana was hamstrung by his lack of experience in dealing with unions, which was something that was "a huge stumbling block in a State-owned entity and can really muddy the water and make it difficult to get things done." He said he also suspected that there were "forces within SAA" that wanted to see Jarana fail.

"I think he is trying his damnedest and I think he is so frustrated. I think he has very few people he can trust. I think that the type of stuff I am talking about would need a new operational structure," said Back (2019).

He said he believed that Jarana was "being undermined by the people that he is working with," and that he was dealing with "a Board that is split down the middle."

Back (2019) said he had since lost faith in the CEO:

> *I was a staunch advocate and supporter of Vuyani Jarana when he was appointed. I like him as a person and the engagements that we have had. I have really appreciated his openness and his candour. Once or twice we have had our differences, but that's to be expected, but I have lost faith in him.*
>
> *Not in him as a man of integrity – though I did say to him that I thought he has been captured and he thought it was funny and he took a bit of umbrage, but I didn't mean in a corrupt manner. I meant by the forces within SAA that will undermine him in every turn.*
>
> *You know, he had death threats when he first joined. I don't know how much truth there is to it, but I think there was. There's a lot of evil within this company. When I say evil, it's like the forces of darkness who will do whatever to undermine and to further their own agendas.*

Back (2019) said Jarana hated the pilots' RA ("he calls it the 'radio-active agreement'") and wanted to "put it away in a safe for three years." Back (2019) said Jarana told him the agreement was onerous on SAA, and he had responded by saying "it wasn't onerous on the company when it was put together and when the company last made money."

While he said the pilots were "very fortunate in the travel perks" they enjoy, Back (2019) said SAAPA was "happy to look at those specifics if they are too onerous for the company." He said business-class travel at an airline's expense was an industry norm for pilots, but added that SAAPA remained willing to work with SAA "on productivity issues, on terms and conditions such as travel; whatever can help make a difference."

Back (2019) said when SAAPA sat down with Management "to make real changes" to the agreement, SAA Management focused on "who was going to be offloaded in front of whom" when the flight was full. He said the RA gave pilots "a very high status – and we said fine, we will go as normal passengers." However, the SAA leadership required that SAAPA agrees that pilots will "go below Management level:"

> *We were like hang on a second. The optics, as we were told by the CEO on this particular issue, was that it doesn't look good when pilots and their families are travelling, offloading fee-paying passengers. So, we said we will address that, but it's not about that. There are so many agendas every time we come to the table to offer something, it's thrown back on our faces, and you'll see that there is a common thread: it's all about their empowerment and our disempowerment.*

Back (2019) said that at a meeting in January 2018, Jarana had insisted on transparency and the pilots' involvement, but when he walked out of the room, "the very people who have been there for the last x number of years, and the very people who don't want us there," were in charge of the meeting.

He said 20 months into Jarana's tenure, they were "exactly where we were at that first meeting: there is very little sharing of information; there is no open, honest dialogue, it seems." He said the pilots were being asked to make concessions, but the negotiations soon became "one-sided bargaining:"

> *Let's say you and I are on opposite sides of the table and you say to me, "look, we need to look at productivity" and I say "okay, great, here's our recommendation," and you go "thank you" and you go scratch, scratch, scratch. "This is what I want; there's my proposal." Then we go: "Hang on a second. This is not mutual-gains bargaining."*

> *And where do we land up? At an impasse. We are not going anywhere – and that is what is frustrating him, and that's the type of negotiations that are ongoing within the company at the moment, and we find it so frustrating; which is pushing us closer and closer towards drawing a line in the sand and saying "no more."*

Asked if Chief Restructuring Officer Peter Davies, who was himself a pilot, was able to help the two sides to bridge the divide, Back (2019) said: "The problem with Peter Davis is this, and this is going to be brutally honest: he is a foreigner. He is a white man. He has been brought into an entity where he can see the problems and he is trying to call the shots. He is not fitting into the agenda of others, so he's being disempowered and side-lined. Peter doesn't have the power and authority that he used to have."

Back (2019) alleged that there were "powers within the airline that are trying to side-line him [Davies] and his team so much that he doesn't have a work permit here." He said Davies's team, which understood the aviation industry and could "make recommendations to get us back on track," had shrunk in size. "They can only be here twice or thrice a week, and then they have to go back to London, and then they come back. So, there's no continuity," Back (2019) said.

It was not possible to verify this allegation with either Davies or anybody else at SAA.

Back (2019) said SAA needed "strong, decisive leadership that brings people together, and not divides." He said SAA needed to have a company ethos of "who are we, because we don't know what we are right now." SAA, he said, was "this fragmented, chaotic, rudderless, no-one-makes-decisions entity."

Back (2019) said the national carrier needed "an open, honest, trusting environment" which would enable all issues to be put on the table and discussed, "and not based on false rhetoric and this whole anti-pilot sentiment where you say this whole Regulating Agreement is rubbish and a cost to the company."

SAAPA, Back (2019) said, was ready for genuine, mutual-gains bargaining:

> *Well, let's talk about it. Show us where you think we can make changes that can work, and we'll come to the party. If we, as an association, felt there were really the right people on board, with the right acumen and had the mandate to make decisions, and not waffle about like we do, like a leaf in the wind, we would be right on board – and the members would, too.*
>
> *Because, what do we want? We want an airline that survives. We want growth, not only because of our careers. Imagine, in a shrinking company we have gone from 800 pilots to 650. That means guys are waiting 22 years to become a captain. We want growth so that more can become captains. We want growth so that we can meet our transformation agenda – and SAAPA has been very proactive on the transformation agenda – which, of course, the company won't say anything about because it doesn't serve their needs because they like to see us as this white majority, male organisation.*

Back (2019) explained that the reduction in the number of pilots had occurred after Michelle Kemp, who is responsible for planning for pilots, informed SAAPA that, based on SAA's plans, the airline had 22% too many pilots. He said to avoid a furlough, SAAPA encouraged its members to take unpaid leave and go work for other airlines over a period of four to five years. That way, they can come back to SAA with a 90-day notice period.

Back (2019) said 122 pilots took that option, but SAAPA was told that the number "could be as high at 200." He said the pilots were seen to be top-heavy at the time. He said even though "the airline is significantly top-heavy in all the other areas, nothing was done there."

However, Back (2019) said SAA subsequently found itself to have a shortage of pilots and incurred overtime pay "in excess of R4 million" in the last quarter of 2018.

Chapter Thirteen

A VIEW FROM INDEPENDENT EXPERTS AND LONG-TERM SAA OBSERVERS

Terry Markman, a member of the South African Airline Deregulation Committee which led to the passage in 1991 of legislation deregulating the industry, is a civil and transportation engineer who has worked in South Africa, Namibia, Botswana, Zimbabwe, Swaziland and the United Kingdom over the past five decades, during which he has been a transport consultant at Arup in Johannesburg. A long-time SAA watcher, Markman has been responsible for numerous transport policy projects.

Although he has followed the national carrier closely over the years and has written on it, primarily calling for its privatisation, Markman (2019) says he is not an aviation expert, but somebody who, in his words, is "fairly knowledgeable about the policy side of things." A free market proponent, Markman (2019) also describes himself as being "very biased, not against this Government, but against any government," and proceeds from the premise that "every single government in the world should not be running their own airline."

Markman (2019) argues that whenever governments have privatised their airlines, "nine out of every ten times they have done very well," and cites, among the examples, BA, Lufthansa and Air France. He said that SAA would not be turned around for as long as it was owned by the State.

Markman (2019) said for SAA to stand any chance at all of potentially being turned around, it would have to be "de-politicised." He said political interference at the national carrier was "horrific" and would not allow the CEO "to do all the unpalatable things" like reducing the number of employees.

Markman (2019) said every year that the Government waited before "getting rid" of SAA was "another R5 billion because that's what they are chewing up at the moment." He said he could see no reason why the Government would spend "R5 billion of taxpayers' money supporting an airline, as opposed to providing houses, health, education, university degrees, whatever."

Saying he was aware that some held the view that SAA served an important developmental purpose, Markman (2019) argued: "If you can destroy wealth and call it development, it's a very strange type of development."

Markman (2019) said he was particularly worried about the fact that Public Enterprises Minister Pravin Gordhan was the person in charge of the Department of Public Enterprises (DPE). That, he said, was "worse than before" for South Africa because Gordhan was widely acknowledged to be honest:

> *Why do I say that? I don't know him at all. I think he is honest, I think he is honourable; I think he is a decent guy, but he is in his mind convinced that the State has to run the airline. Now if you have a person whom you know is crooked and he is running the airline, you say "oh, well, clearly he doesn't know what he is talking about."*

Markman (2019) said a viable option would be for the Government to create a new airline company "called the South African International Air Company," to take the place of SAA, and put it out to tender for international airlines to bid for it. He said the international carriers would bid for the name and all the landing rights and bilateral air services agreements that SAA currently enjoys.

Professor Kobus Jonker (2019), Director of the Tshwane University of Technology Business School, said more than political interference, SAA's problem was, above all, "leadership failure." He contrasted SAA to Ethiopian Airlines (EAL), where people were taken through the organisation and trained to ensure that they have "competent leaders who know the industry and who can take it [EAL] forward." He said "the leadership failure" at SAA started at Board level and affected much of the airline's leadership structures.

Jonker (2019) said SAA had lost its competitive edge because it focused too much on "this thing of just surviving until next year." That, he said, explained why EAL was stealing a march on the national carrier by "creating other hubs in Africa, in East Africa, in Southern Africa and Malawi," in the process posing an even bigger threat to SAA.

Jonker (2019) said it was important for the Government to think of the funding provided to SAA as an investment, and not a bail out. He said a change in the Government's thinking would force it to bring in an equity partner in order to improve the chances of generating a return on investment. He said it was important to keep in mind that the fact that BA was privatised "didn't make any difference to the British Government or to the image of British Airways." Instead, the airline went on to be profitable.

He said in addition to ensuring that only people with expertise were appointed onto the Board of Directors (BoD), it was important to ensure that "a lot of power" was delegated to a capable CEO with his/her Top Management Team (TMT), who should make decisions on which routes to fly or exit. He said SAA's problem was that the Government viewed State-owned companies (SOCs) in the same manner in which it viewed Government Departments:

> *I think the paradigm that we have in South Africa is that a State-owned company is the same as a Government Department. A Government Department is just a department; it has a certain role in the country and has a certain budget. Although the money must be used efficiently, the Government has no choice but to finance it because we need that function in South Africa. I think a State-owned enterprise is actually a business, and there is a huge responsibility to run it like a good business. I think we have lost that plot.*

Aviation economist Dr Joachim Vermooten (2019) said it was important for an airline implementing a turnaround strategy to have "a realistic restructuring plan" which quantifies the costs of initiatives that need to be implemented and the revenue to be generated. He said as these plans were put together, it was important for those who run an airline like SAA to remember that a carrier that is in trouble will not retain the same traffic volumes because "people will shy away from it." Therefore, in such a situation, optimistic assumptions should not be made about traffic volumes "because you are in a weaker financial position and everybody knows it."

Secondly, Vermooten (2019) said it was important that "realistic assumptions" that were made as part of the turnaround plan had to "become viable within a reasonable time frame." These assumptions would have to be accompanied by "significant cost reductions" related to capacity, employees, fleet and the operating network.

Vermooten (2019) said even successful airlines always have demands for capital that exceed accumulated profits. The funding of this capital expenditure, he said, explained why most formerly government-owned airlines have been privatised over the years since governments had numerous social needs to meet.

Vermooten (2019) traced the beginning of SAA's troubles to 2012, when SAA embarked on a market-share growth strategy. He said "the whole growth story" focused on more aircraft and routes, with the leadership unmindful of the fact that "if you have capacity ahead of demand, you can't ever make any profit."

He said to increase the chances of successfully turning SAA around, the current leadership would have to emulate the Ngqula team by reducing the scale of operations, taking out some aircraft (whether leased or owned) and reducing the route network. He said these efforts would have to be accompanied by similar reductions "in all functions" across the airline.

"We demonstrated that in the past with the previous restructuring programme. The National Treasury has published that in 2009, 2010 and 2011 SAA actually became profitable. The cost of restructuring was isolated from the ongoing cost and it was very transparent. There were a few things that were not done that could have been done, but the finances were stabilised within 18 months and it remained so until I left," Vermooten (2019) said.

Said Vermooten (2019), in an echo of Vera Kriel's (2019) views:

> *SAA has been growing in size, in scope and in people. In people, it has grown much too fast even for its size. Now the idea of restructuring for Government is that you tinker with a little bit and suddenly a miracle happens and it is profitable. That's a fallacy because if the airline has to be different, it has to look different.*

Vermooten (2019) said it was impractical for SAA to seek to offer a combination of international services, regional services as well as "two or three branded domestic services." He said airlines owned by governments tended to be good "with long-distance formations."

He also stressed that for as long as the national carrier had a dual mandate – which he described as "an excuse for people to raid SAA" – no turnaround would be successful.

Vermooten (2019) said he was currently consulting to a southern African government whose national carrier was allocated budgets at the beginning of each financial year so that it can carry out its developmental mandate. That way, he said, the funding is certain and the airline can plan ahead, unlike in the case of SAA where "two Ministers go to banks and issue guarantees *ex post facto*" and the funding was "always patching up something in the past."

Asked if he believed SAA could be rescued, Vermooten (2019) said the airline could be turned around only if the Government absorbed its past losses and debts so that there could be a return "to normal budgetary processes where you can look at the future and some funding for that," and develop a plan for SAA which would look different from the one that currently exists. He said it would be important to decide on a narrower focus and to ensure that non-core subsidiaries were sold off.

Vermooten (2019) stressed the importance of marketing activities in the countries to which SAA flies. He said on the Germany-South Africa route, 70% of the traffic originated in Germany, a market where "most of those people are already frequent-flyer members of Lufthansa." SAA, he said, got "the dominant part of the smaller market that is from South Africa, where the tariffs are must less than in Europe."

"In Johannesburg, if the bulk of your market is in Europe, your marketing decisions should be made there," Vermooten (2019) said. "You will either win or lose there. You won't win with a guy with a set of rule books here in South Africa, x thousand miles away from Europe, and think that he can control and do innovative things over there."

He compared it to a wise fisherman who throws his net where the fish are. He said it was the marketing activities "in the market where it matters" that are a key enabler. That, he said, was "where you win or lose … at that point when the guy has to decide which airline to choose."

Leading international independent aviation analyst and advisor Chris Tarry founded CTAIRA in London in 2002. According to his profile, "he has served as special advisor on aviation policy issues to the UK Government, to Parliamentary Committees and to the Civil Aviation Authority, and has also advised a number of airlines as well as major airframe manufacturers and aircraft lessors on strategic development issues" (CTAIRA, 2020:online).

Tarry (2019), who met SAA CEO Jarana in Johannesburg in 2018, following an introduction arranged by Chief Restructuring Officer Peter Davies, said the first thing to do when seeking to turn an airline around is to establish which routes make money and which ones make losses, and then to adjust capacity accordingly. He said such a process of route adjustment "might involve shrinking," although an airline would have to guard against "shrink[ing] too far."

He said he came to South Africa "over 20 years ago" for a meeting with Transnet and the Government to discuss SAA. He said he had indicated even then that "more money" would be needed to get SAA through its challenges to "become self-sustaining, with or without a strategic partner."

Tarry (2019) said the assessment of profitable and loss-making routes had to focus not only on routes that were making or losing money at that particular moment, but also at "those which could make money, for other reasonable changes, in the near or medium term."

Tarry (2019) said a situation such as SAA found itself in, where decisions regarding routes require Shareholder approval, "makes it exceptionally difficult." He said, during his days as a sales analyst in the City of London over a 20-year period, when he was involved in efforts to float airlines on the London Stock Exchange or to sell them, the first question that he asked of a government-owned airline was how much the government in question interfered operationally.

He said it was crucial that there was "a separation between ownership and Management," with the latter being able "to do the best thing for the company." SAA's situation, he said, was "very difficult."

"The ideal is actually to ensure that the owner signs off on the plan that the Management has put in place and that Management is able to implement that plan so that they don't, every time they make a decision, have to go back to the Shareholder for approval," he said.

Tarry (2019) said implementing a turnaround strategy required "a Management Team that is strong enough to run the business and not get diverted from turnaround or transactions or anything else, because if they compromise their ability to run the business, then they compromise their ability to generate cash – and it all falls apart." He said he had experienced situations during turnarounds or planned business acquisitions where "everybody gets very excited and they take their eyes off running the business." The result, he said, is that "that damages the business severely."

He said it was vital, therefore, to ensure that a company implementing a turnaround strategy, like SAA, had not only "enough Management resource, but an appropriate Management resource." He echoed the view in the literature on turnaround strategy implementation that "the capabilities and requirements for turning businesses around differ from those needed in normal conditions."

Tarry (2019) said based on information available to him from a distance, SAA's TMT was trying "to stem the losses and put SAA in a position where you have a core of routes that are profitable and it will have a size and a scale which is likely to be smaller than now." He said inevitably there would be "employment consequences" that go with that decision, followed by acquisition of a strategic partner for the airline.

"And, I think, if we are looking at it from a point of view of value, there should be significant strategic value in SAA, which is not shown through its trading value at the moment," Tarry (2019) said.

He said SAA was "not different from any other airline, and any other state airline" when it came to the high degree of union activism. He said there was "a battle" when BA – which was "a hugely loss-making company" – was privatised, but "Management won and BA was able to be floated." As a result of that loss by labour, the "union practices" changed.

Tarry (2019) said the same happened at Aer Lingus in Ireland and at Air France, with the latter having been "almost unmanageable before it was privatised." He said when Air France was due to be privatised, France hosted the 2002 FIFA World – "and the unions went on strike and there was all sorts of pressure." However, "the Government backed Management to make the change."

Tarry (2019) said airlines have "always been unionised, unless they have been private airlines when they started out." He said unions have traditionally been "very aggressive at state-owned carriers, until those behaviours are changed.

Quoting William Walsh, CEO of BA owner International Consolidated Airlines Group (IAG), Tarry (2019) said it was very important to ensure that employees at state-owned airlines got to a stage where they believed that the government would not fund them:

> *What was very interesting was when William Walsh, who now runs IAG – he ran BA and before that ran Aer Lingus – said you have to get to a point where the workforce knows or believes that the government is not going to continue to support the business. I call it precipice management. So, you march everybody to the edge, you look over and they say "ahh, there's no support." It's actually when the workforce believes or has sufficient belief that they are not going to get supported by the government that they have to change their behaviour. It's the same all over in airlines.*

Tarry (2019), who has worked with many state-owned airlines, said there was "no reason why, from a financial performance point of view or whatever, a state-owned airline should have different objectives from a privately-owned airline." The difference, he said, was that "some state-owned airlines are not particularly efficient because they have been allowed to get into that position."

He said it was important to give turnaround efforts ample time and to ensure that airlines undergoing a turnaround were properly capitalised:

> *The issue is how long it takes to turn them around, and what you expect is a reasonable number. Sometimes there's an expectation that a turnaround can happen too quickly. They need cash; they need a lot of management time and they need a reasonable expectation. Even when you've got to that point – so, let's say you've turned the airline around and you break even – that's not the end of the story. You then need to make sure that it generates enough cash for it to be financially sustainable.*
>
> *Once it's got to break even or clearly on the path, it becomes more attractive to attract an investor, a trade investor or a financial investor, but again you have to be clear what returns they may generate from their investment.*

Tarry (2019) said it was important that areas of responsibility were clear: the Board had to sign off on a strategy and Management had to implement it, accounting for performance against the strategy approved by the BoD. The Shareholder, on the other hand, had to decide whether or not the strategy and its promised returns were worth supporting and what they stood to lose if they did not support it.

On the CEO's role, Tarry (2019) was categorical: "He should be able to run his business, and he should be held to account for not running it. He shouldn't have to run off to the Shareholder to ask for permission. The CEO should run the business, without interference. He is the Chief Executive Officer."

Tarry (2019) said he had briefed airlines in India and was asked by the Board of Air India if the Government should continue to capitalise the airline. His response, he said, was that any funding provided had to be conditional and given "in such a way that it can be drawn from when they meet performance targets." He said providing an open cheque would not make the airline profitable.

According to Tarry (2019), SAA and any other state-owned airlines had to "become as profitable or have to have as best performance as possible against the constraints of their local economic importance." He said providing unconditional funding to such airlines would not lead to "the behavioural changes you need in terms of work practices because the view and the belief is that the government will always bail them out, always provide the amount of money that they perceive they need."

Added Tarry (2019): "So, it's how you have to break that cycle, and the only way you break that cycle is almost to take it to the edge, and then you will still have people say 'no, no, no, the government will continue to invest in us'. They have to believe that the government won't. It's pretty hard, but once you get that and there is a coherent plan, it works"

He said when an airline was acquiring a new fleet, it was important for it to talk to the manufacturers, who were often willing to make lines of credit available and to provide money to help with a turnaround programme. He said both public and private sources of capital had to be considered to implement a turnaround.

Tarry (2019) said it was vital for Management to set "very clear objectives" for the business and to do everything possible to "take the workforce along with them." He said employees had to understand "all the elements of the business," and should not be given false hope. They have to be told that "it is tough, but we have to make all these changes and this is what we are going to do."

In an echo of former SAA Chairman JB Magwaza's (2019) views, Tarry (2019) said: "Any management strategy has to be coherent; it has to be credible and it has to be capable of implementation." He said that he had come across airlines whose strategies were based on "assumptions [which are] too optimistic:"

> *They place too much emphasis on how much cash they think they will generate and how little they need. My starting point for a business plan is always to halve the amount of cash they think they will generate and double the amount of cash they think they will need.*

He cautioned that Management had to take care to ensure that turnaround strategies were not visions, but were "very clear, spelling what their objectives are going to be and how they will realise them." He stressed "that anything to do with strategy has a financial cost and a financial consequence," and Management had to be "very clear what they [those costs and consequences] are."

Tarry (2019) said during the process of developing a turnaround strategy, Management also had to "take a view not only of what your competitors are doing now, but also of what they are likely to do by the time you have implemented your strategy." He said although it was "very, very important" for that to be done, "a lot of people" did not do it.

In what he called "shrink, survive, grow and prosper, then compete and grab," Tarry (2019) said SAA would have to consider carefully how much of its back-office support, with all the costs involved, it wanted to be part of the airline going forward. He said it was important for SAA to establish what costs it had control over and which ones were subject to external negotiations. Without having researched SAA, Tarry (2019) said labour and administered costs related to air navigation and airport taxes should be things about which something could be done "locally in South Africa," while nothing could be done about fuel costs.

"If you look at all the cost lines, then it comes back almost to what we said before: shrink, survive, grow and prosper, the four things. How much is it going to cost me to shrink?" Tarry (2019) asked.

In an interview with me in July 2020, Dr Arkebe Oqubay (2020), Deputy Chairman of the EAL BoD and a Senior Minister in the Ethiopian Government, revealed that he had had a number of exploratory meetings with Public Enterprises Minister Pravin Gordhan and that EAL CEO Tewolde Gebremariam had done the same with his counterparts at SAA. He said EAL was keen on a commercial or strategic partnership with SAA and had offered the South African national carrier the use of its world-class MRO and other facilities in Addis Ababa. That partnership could include South Africa's use of Ethiopia's e-visa software.

Oqubay (2020) said SAA and KQ were wrong in viewing EAL as their competitor. Instead, the main competitors to all three African airlines were the Middle Eastern carriers and Turkish Airlines, whose footprint on the continent had grown phenomenally. He said the African carriers had to target the Chinese market. China, he said, had "more than 150 million tourists," with Africa only getting 2% to 3% of that share. He said South Africa was particularly well placed to attract Chinese tourists, given its attractiveness as a tourist destination.

Oqubay (2020) said EAL was originally open to purchasing a stake in SAA to become the airline's strategic equity partner, but backed off when it realised, following a preliminary due diligence, that "it is far too late" because of the extent of SAA's challenges. More importantly, EAL was scared off by the lack of alignment between Gordhan and Finance Minister Tito Mboweni and by SAA's history of corporate governance failures.

"South African policy makers are not guided by one policy. Mboweni wants to privatise the airline and Gordhan wants to have SAA State owned. The Government should have one position, but there is no coherent policy. There is conflict," Oqubay (2020) said.

Oqubay (2020) revealed that, during his discussions with Gordhan, the latter had asked him if EAL would be open to managing SAA. However, Oqubay (2020) said while the Ethiopian flag carrier – which already has equity in airlines in the region, in countries such as Malawi and Mozambique – would have been keen to consider that request, it felt that it would not be easy to manage SAA for at least three reasons: rampant Government interference, the unions' radicalism and the airline's corporate governance failures.

SAA, he said, had three times the number of employees when compared to EAL, based on the money-staff-aircraft ratio. If EAL were to manage SAA, "the turnaround would have to be surgical" in terms of labour retrenchment, and he was not certain if the Government would allow that to happen.

"Our feeling is that the major problem of SAA is political intervention. The Management Team and the Board are not appointed on the basis of merit. They are put there because of political connections," Oqubay (2020) said.

Oqubay (2010) said SA Express had approached EAL with a proposal for a partnership, and the latter was more favourable to that request because "the depth of its crisis is much better than SAA's."

Chapter Fourteen

WHAT SUCCESS IN AFRICAN AVIATION LOOKS LIKE

 $\mathcal{I}$ n most of the interviews conducted on SAA's and KQ's implementation of their respective turnaround strategies, Ethiopian Airlines (EAL) came up repeatedly, without any prompting. It was clear from the interviews that both sets of interview participants considered the Ethiopian airline to be the main benchmark for airlines on the continent – with good reason. In Kenya, participants who had worked for KQ mentioned EAL almost reluctantly, or referred to it indirectly as "the competition."

Given the indirect centrality of EAL in this research, coupled with the fact that EAL is now the largest and most profitable African airline (Mills & van der Merwe, 2020; Oqubay & Tesfachew, 2019) which benchmarks itself against leading global airlines like Singapore Airlines, United, Lufthansa and Emirates (Oqubay & Tesfachew, 2019), a synopsis of that airline is presented here.

This chapter is meant to illustrate what success looks like in African aviation and what factors contributed to that success.

Not only did EAL come up spontaneously during the course of the interviews conducted for this research, but its success also attracted the attention of the African Development Bank (AfDB), which featured it as a case study in its "How They Did It" (HDI) series. The AfDB HDI series is described as "a new line of publications from the Vice-Presidency for Economic Governance and Knowledge Management," which seeks to profile "interesting economic transformation experiences and discuss how some countries have addressed various development issues" in an effort to help member countries to achieve the bank's "High-5 priorities."

To compile the EAL case study, the AfDB commissioned Dr Arkebe Oqubay, EAL Vice-Chairman and an Ethiopian Cabinet Minister and Special Adviser to the Prime Minister, and Dr Taferre Tesfachew, a development economist who has served as a Senior Director at the United Nations Commission for Trade and Development for over 25 years.

The early years of EAL, going back to the management agreement concluded by the Ethiopian Government with TWA in September 1945, have already been covered in chapter 3. This chapter picks up from the background information provided in that chapter.

While the period from 1975 to 2000 was tough for EAL, given the political upheavals mentioned in chapter 3, things changed considerably in the 2000s following the return to EAL of Girma Wake and Tewolde Grebremariam in 2004 from Gulf Air and New York respectively to assume the positions of CEO and Deputy CEO. Gebremariam had headed EAL operations in New York (Mills & van der Merwe, 2020). Oqubay and Tesfachew (2019:8) say the appointment of Wake, Gebremariam and other "highly experienced insiders began to turn the fortunes of EAL from managing crises to pursuing growth and upgrading capabilities."

Wake was CEO until 2011, when he was succeeded by Gebremariam as CEO (The Africa List, n.d.). Wake, who joined EAL at the age of 22 when he was still a second-year student at Addis Ababa University, said he was inspired, during his time with Gulf Air, by "how visionary they were" on that airline: "They are not afraid to push; they are not afraid to go forward. So, when I came back to Ethiopian Airlines as CEO, I had seen how other countries and organisations work and that gave me an opportunity to look at things differently" (The Africa List, n.d.).

Former South African Finance Minister Nhlanhla Nene (2019) told me that Wake, with whom he had spoken "a number of times," told him that when the Ethiopian President appointed him "to turn things around, the first thing he had asked for was non-interference." Nene said Wake had accepted the job on that condition, and he had gone on to deliver.

Oqubay and Tesfachew (2019:8) said a new EAL Board and Wake's Management Team "unanimously decided to develop a fundamental new vision and long-term plan for rapid growth." In 2005, they adopted Vision 2010, a five-year plan to increase the EAL fleet, to double its number of passengers and to triple its cargo volume. By 2010, EAL had accomplished all goals: its fleet had grown by 60% to 41 commercial aircraft, it had doubled its passengers to 3,2 million per annum and its cargo volume had tripled (Oqubay & Tesfachew, 2019:8).

Gebremariam told Mills and Van der Merwe (2020) that Vision 2010 was intended to reposition EAL and to increase its turnover from US$400 million in 2005 to US$1 billion in five years. By 2010, EAL's turnover stood at US$1,3 billion (Mills & Van der Merwe, 2020).

Inspired by its performance on Vision 2010, that year EAL adopted an even more ambitious, 15-year strategy called Vision 2025, which "laid out a fundamental new trajectory for the company." In terms of Vision 2025, EAL planned to increase the number of aircraft in its fleet to 120 by 2025, with this number to go up to 200 aircraft by 2030 to take advantage of bulk-purchase discounts, to fly to 90 international destinations (Mills & Van der Merwe, 2020) and to double its target of US$5 billion in revenue to US$10 billion by 2025-30 (Oqubay & Tesfachew, 2019:4).

Five years later, the Ethiopian carrier had "become the largest African airline." In 2018 it transported "more than 12 million passengers (a four-fold increase since 2010) and half a million tons of cargo," and its fleet size comprised "more than 100 new-generation aircraft (a three-fold increase since 2010) and it flew to 115 international destinations, among them Los Angeles in the USA and Tokyo, Japan. Its China-Africa routes alone were expected to carry one million passengers in 2018, making EAL "the major airline linking Africa with China" (Oqubay & Tesfachew, 2019:8).

In 2018, EAL was voted the Best African Airline and globally ranked 40th in customer service and 24th in size by the World Airline Awards (Oqubay & Tesfachew, 2019: 4).

The growth in EAL's fleet size, number of destinations and profit is shown in figures 14.1, 14.2 and 14.3 below.

Figure 14.1: Growth in EAL's fleet size between 1946 and 2018

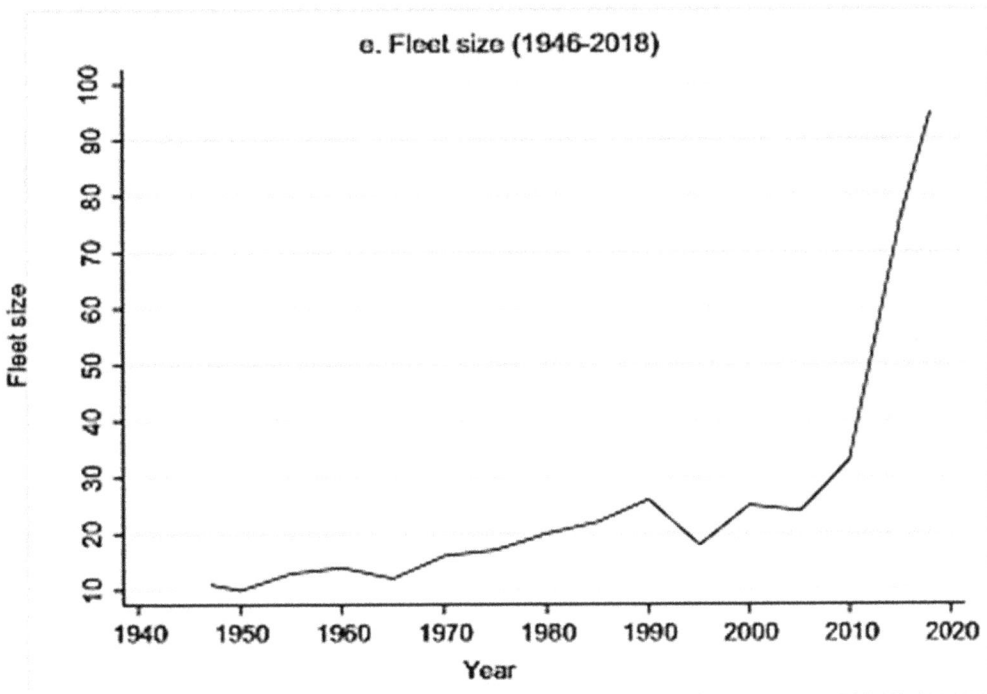

Source: Oqubay & Tesfachew (2019)

Figure 14.2: Growth in EAL's number of destinations between 1946 and 2018

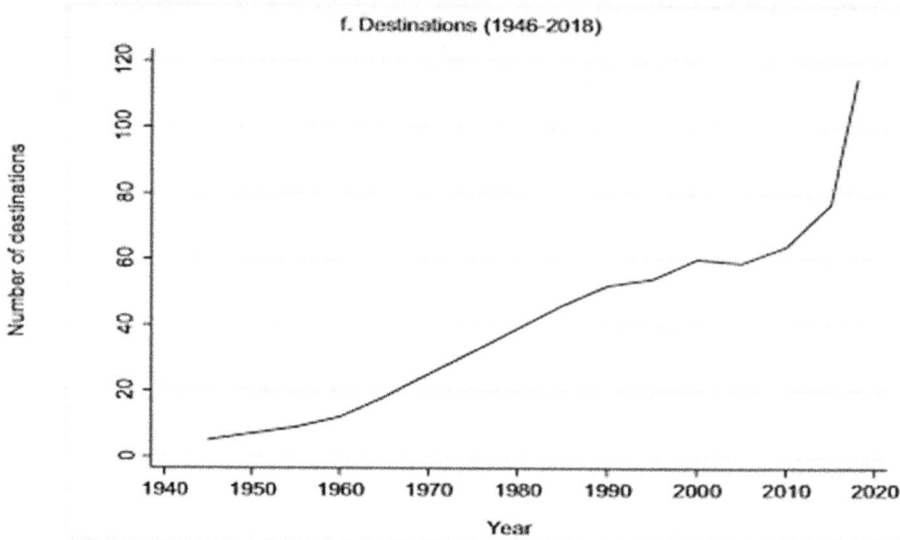

f. Destinations (1946-2018)

Source: Source: Oqubay & Tesfachew (2019)

Mills and Van der Merwe (2020) said Grebremariam told them early in 2020 that the previous year EAL was flying to 127 destinations, with a turnover of US$2 billion, and its fleet size stood at 117 aircraft.

Oqubay and Tesfachew (2019:3) attribute the fact that EAL today serves that many international destinations and services "more cities in Africa than any other airline" to its use of cutting-edge technology and its "modern organisational and management techniques."

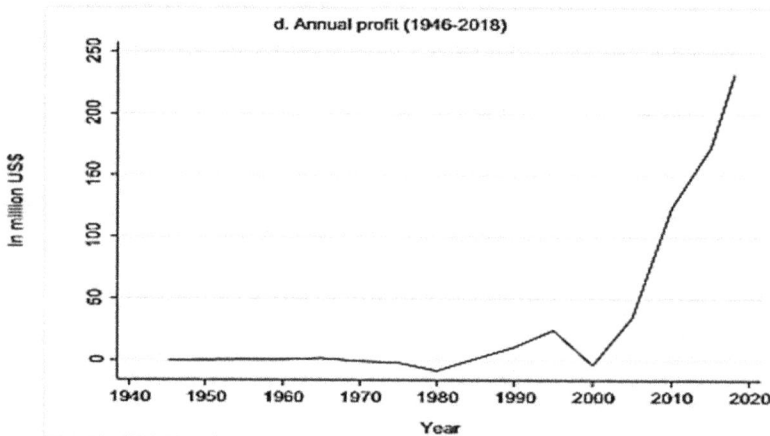

d. Annual profit (1946-2018)

Figure 14.3: Growth in EAL's profits between 1946 and 2018
Source: Oqubay & Tesfachew (2019)

Oqubay and Tesfachew (2019:8) summed up: "This rapid overall expansion has made EAL the most profitable aviation company in Africa, while other African airlines (including EgyptAir, Kenya Airways and South African Airways) have struggled. Progress has been achieved in the face of intense competitive pressure from Gulf and Middle Eastern carriers, which enjoyed economies of scale and large direct and indirect subsidies. Competition from Middle Eastern state-supported airlines remains EAL's most formidable challenge."

Mills and Van der Merwe (2020) point out that there are many international competitors "capable of outspending Ethiopian Airlines" to gain a foothold in Africa. Turkish Airlines, for instance, has "an increasingly active African network," while Emirates handles "more than five million African passengers annually." They add that African carriers' share of the continental market "has fallen from 80% to 20%," even as the number of passengers had increased to 88 million by 2019.

Oqubay & Tesfachew (2019: 9) point out that, as part of its upgrading and catch-up strategy, EAL committed to expansion and modernisation of its fleet by introducing "the latest aircraft to secure first-comer advantages." As a result, EAL was "the first airline in Africa to order the most modern aircraft – the Boeing Dreamliner B787 – and the longest-range commercial aircraft, the Boeing B777-200 LR."

Following a lengthy internal discussion, EAL (which had until then only used Boeing aircraft) decided to diversify its fleet through the purchase of the Airbus A350, "the latest and most environmentally sound aircraft" (Oqubay & Tesfachew, 2019:9).

Oqubay and Tesfachew (2019:9) say organisational capability and continuous process improvement have been central to EAL's Vision 2025, while Mills and Van der Merwe (2020) say it is good governance and the Ethiopian Government's habit of leaving technocrats "to get on with their jobs, free from political interference" that have accounted for the airline's success.

Oqubay and Tesfachew (2019:9) say given EAL's phenomenal growth, a new organisational structure became necessary to facilitate a strategic shift from an airline to a fully diversified aviation group, called Ethiopian Aviation Group (EAG). They revealed that before the formation of the EAG, various services and operations were structured "in seven autonomous strategic business units, each operating as an independent profit center" (sic). These units were International Passenger Service, Domestic Express Service, Cargo Service, Technical Services, the Aviation Academy, Ground Services, as well as Catering and Hotel Services. The airline's growth meant that EAL "needed a more integrated structure that allowed strategic planning, coherence, performance monitoring and accountability" (Oqubay & Tesfachew, 2019:9).

According to Oqubay and Tesfachew (2019:10), the new EAG structure required "a fundamental shift affecting all functions," including EAL's strategy of acquiring equity shareholding and providing operational and management services to other African airlines. As part of that strategy, EAL had acquired:

- 40% shareholding in AfricanSky Airline in West Africa, which EAL is also managing;

- 49% shareholding in Air Malawi to strengthen its Southern African hub;

- 49% shareholding in Guinea Airlines;

- 49% shareholding in Chad Airlines;

- 45% shareholding and management contract in CEIBA Intercontinental in Equatorial Guinea; and

- 51% shareholding of a joint company with DHL Logistics to enable EAL "to move beyond conventional passenger air services to become a leading logistics provider in Africa."

According to Oqubay and Tesfachew (2019:10), EAL has also started a new programme "to develop and manage African airports, including air traffic control."

They add that while EAL had previously benchmarked itself against "leading African airlines," its Board and Management have since "decided to upgrade its benchmarking standards to compare its performance with leading global airlines – Singapore Airlines, United, Lufthansa and Emirates" (p.10).

EAL joined Star Alliance in 2011, "following almost two years of mentoring by Lufthansa" and five years after SAA had joined the same global alliance. Employing 15 000 employees, EAL has also invested $500 million in upgrading its aviation academy and MRO and another $500 million in hubs infrastructure (Oqubay & Tesfachew, 2019: 10).

According to Oqubay and Tesfachew (2019:10), the Ethiopian Government's ownership of the airline has been of great importance. It has provided EAL with stability and growth opportunities and enabled it to pursue "a long-term strategy rather than short-term profitability." The Government's inability to subsidise EAL "has clearly provided the discipline to EAL to ensure fiscal responsibility" (Oqubay & Tesfachew, 2019:11).

Crucially, Oqubay and Tesfachew (2019:11) said the Ethiopian Government's ownership of the successful African carrier "defies the notions that ownership determines performance and that public ownership is inferior to private [ownership]." EAL, they said, has performed "considerably better than many privately-owned airlines," and this has demonstrated "the advantages of long-term strategic orientation rather than the short-profit orientation dominant in the Anglo-Saxon corporate world."

Argued Oqubay & Tesfachew (2019:10-11):

> *Technological learning and catch-up in Ethiopia's aviation industry would have been impossible without the Government's strong commitment and support. EAL was established by the State at a time when no domestic private company had the required capacity, and it was nurtured by the State as a major industrial policy instrument for several decades. From the beginning, EAL was built into a national champion by the Government, which maintained self-discipline in its relationship with the airline while playing a developmental role.*
>
> *Even during the 1975-2000 phase, when Government interference posed major operations challenges, it was clear that ultimately the Government of the day had no interest in jeopardising the survival of EAL, which has always been regarded as a flagship State enterprise with unofficial corporate independence. During the 2001-18 phase of EAL's development, the Government used the airline as an instrument of industrial policy and offered it new growth opportunities by pushing it to serve the export sector.*

Mills and Van der Merwe (2020) point out that Gebremariam joined EAL in 1984 at the age of 18, and returned to EAL in 2004 from New York, where he had headed the airline's operations. According to Mills and Van der Merwe (2020), Grebremariam attributed EAL's success to "the strong foundation laid by its management contract with TWA" and its "government-owned, commercially-run" model, which enabled the airline to be run "for the long term, not just one quarter." That, Gebremariam told Mills and Van der Merwe (2020), was particularly important because the new technology of aircraft like the Boeing 787 and the A350 required "a longer-term horizon."

Ethiopian-based international aviation journalist Kaleyesus Bekele (2019) told me during an interview in September 2019 that when EAL went through a challenging period at a time when the oil price was high, the CEO met with labour and "they sat down and cut back their allowances." He said EAL staff – including pilots – "even work free of pay on Sundays and some extra days."

Bekele (2019), who lives close to the Bole International Airport in Addis Ababa, said that he regularly saw the EAL team going to work "even on Sundays." He said EAL employees' salaries were "very minimal when compared to the salaries at SAA and KQ," and that Gebremariam once told him that "we don't work for a pay cheque; we have a national obligation."

Bekele (2019) said Gebremariam gave him a lift "some years back ... [and] was driving himself in a simple Toyota car." He said it was only recently that Gebremariam had got a driver, adding that EAL had "only one Mercedes-Benz that they use when Senior Executives from Boeing or IATA come for a visit."

In a confirmation of Bekele's (2019) version, Mills and Van der Merwe (2020) wrote that Gebremariam drove "a modest, 15-year Honda" when they visited him at EAL headquarters, which they said were "true to the Government's mantra about keeping overheads low." EAL, they wrote, had a serious commitment to cost management.

"Cost is critical for the airline business," they report Gebremariam as having told them, "since it is very difficult to make profits. We are very prudent and very frugal. You cannot be as lavish as South African Airways and expect to survive."

In an interview with me in July 2020, Oqubay (2020) revealed that the Ethiopian Prime Minister and the President do not have their own aircraft. Whenever the Prime Minister or the President travels abroad, they charter an EAL aircraft, which gets modified accordingly, "and the Government pays for it through the Ministry of Finance."

Bekele (2019) said the one important lesson that SAA and KQ can learn from EAL was about the need to be "cost prudent:"

> The lesson that KQ and SAA can learn from Ethiopian Airlines is that, first, it's not your personal interests that should come first when you work for a national carrier. When you work for an international carrier in other parts of the world, I don't know, the case can be different, but when you work for a national carrier, if you are looking for money, you should go somewhere else where you can make better money, get a better pay. When you work for a national carrier, of course you have a life to live, you have a family to take care of, but you should also think of your national flag, your national interest. So, what should come first is your national interest.

Chapter Fifteen

FINDINGS AND DISCUSSION

The findings of the research into the implementation of turnaround strategies at State-owned companies, which focused primarily on South African Airways (SAA) and Kenya Airways (KQ), with Ethiopian Airlines as a benchmark, have already been presented in detail in the previous chapters. In this chapter, those findings are discussed.

This research followed the observation that not all efforts to implement turnaround strategies succeed (Bibeault, 1999; Hopkins, 2008). Once developed and approved, some turnaround strategies are implemented and result in the desired or anticipated successful outcomes, while in other instances chosen turnaround strategies are implemented with equal vigour, but fail to result in the desired outcomes. The research sought to establish what factors impact on or determine the outcomes of chosen turnaround strategies.

Once the determinants of a turnaround d strategy implementation outcome were established, this study sought to develop a framework for a successful implementation of turnaround strategies in African business, with SAA and KQ as case studies.

The study's secondary objectives were:

- To investigate the determinants of turnaround strategy outcomes for the selected African airlines;

- to establish the barriers of the turnaround strategy implementation process for the selected African airlines;

- to establish the enablers of the turnaround strategy implementation process for the selected African airlines;

- to determine what difference, if any, the ownership pattern of the airline makes in the possible successful implementation of the turnaround strategy for the selected African airlines; and

- to determine the key elements of a successful turnaround strategy implementation for the selected African airlines.

A qualitative research methodology was used, with constructivism as a paradigm. According to Guba and Lincoln (1994), that paradigm accepts the existence of multiple realities and the need for interaction between the enquirer and the subject of one's study, with the researcher as "a passionate participant."

The chosen research design was a case study. According to Welch, Piekkari, Plakoyiannaki and Paavilainen-Mantymaki (2011:740), case studies are the most popular qualitative research strategy because of their potential "to generate novel and ground-breaking theoretical insights," and Yin (2014) argues that a two-case study can offer a considerable opportunity for direct (literal) replication, thus leading to analytic generalisation.

Data were collected primarily through semi-structured interviews. Other sources of data used were company documents and publications such as annual reports, archival records, reports and presentations to the relevant Parliamentary Portfolio Committees, media articles and relevant physical artefacts.

Summary of the Results

SAA last made a profit in 2011 (Whitehouse, 2019). Although the airline often did not publish its results because of concern about its going-concern status (Kingston, 2019), various estimates indicate that SAA's losses over a 13-year period totalled R28 billion (Planting, 2020), with cumulative losses of R26,1 billion having been made between 2015 and 2020 (Maeko, 2020).

Since 2004, SAA has had four turnaround strategies. These were:

- *Bambanani* – Let's Join Hands Together, championed by then Chief Financial Officer Tryphosa Ramano during Khaya Ngqula's tenure as CEO in 2005;

- The SAA Business Restructuring Plan (SAA BRP), implemented by Ngqula and former Head of Corporate Strategy and Planning Vera Kriel in 2006;

- The Growth Strategy implemented by Sizakele Mzimela in 2011; and

- The Long-Term Turnaround Strategy (LTTS) which was championed by then Minister of Public Enterprises Malusi Gigaba and made public in September 2013.

Focused on cost savings and financial efficiencies, *Bambanani* was "not good enough" and did not make much of a difference (Ngqula, 2019). The SAA BRP was implemented actively and led to the airline recording an operational profit (Ngqula, 2019; Kriel, 2019; Vermooten, 2019), although a net loss of approximately R1 billion was forecast for the 2007/8, 2008/9 and 2009/10 financial years (SAA Business Restructuring Plan, 2007).

However, SAA registered a profit of R581 million in 2009/10, a profit of R782 million in 2010/11 and a loss of R1,25 billion in 2011/12 (SAPA, 2012). The R782 million profit of 2010/11 was the last positive result posted by the airline in the last 10 years.

Considerable progress was made in the implementation of the SAA Business Restructuring Plan because the Top Management Team (TMT) and the Board were fully aligned and the Shareholder was supportive: "The Board was very committed. We had fantastic support from the Board. You can't do this without the Board's support. The Board was so committed that it established a Special Restructuring Sub-Committee for that period," said Kriel (2019).

As CEO, Ngqula (2019) enjoyed the full support of then-Public Enterprises Minister Alec Erwin, with whom he had a great personal relationship and to whom he had ready access, and the Minister made funding available to the airline for the purposes of the restructuring. The quality of Ngqula's TMT was also good (Ngqula, 2019; Shaw, 2019; Vermooten, 2019) and there was leadership stability during his tenure.

Mzimela's Growth Strategy, on the other hand, was ill advised and increased SAA's costs at a time when the airline should have been making savings (Shaw, 2019; Vermooten, 2019). Former Department of Public Enterprises Director-General Dr Andrew Shaw's (2019) view then was that previous SAA strategies by McKinsey and Seabury "had shown that that [expansion] was an unlikely strategy to work with." Until then, he said, "everybody had said the network should be more constrained."

Strangely, although it was based on previous turnaround strategies like the SAA BRP, the LTTS was actively championed by Gigaba as Shareholder Minister. At the October 2012 SAA Annual General Meeting (AGM), Gigaba (2013) gave the new Board very specific instructions to come up with a long-term strategy to turn the airline around. He informed the Board that it was appointed "primarily to turn the airline around to a position of financial independence and operational efficiency." He said for that goal to be accomplished, it was imperative for "a long-term vision and strategy" to be developed to get SAA to become competitive and well run, "with clear plans and targets for the future, including on such issues as fleet procurement." He said the process of stabilising the airline would see his Department, the SAA Board and the airline's Management Team collaborating to review the carrier's business model, structure and strategy.

Gigaba (2013) said the envisaged Long-Term Turnaround Strategy (LTTS) had to be drafted in collaboration "with all stakeholders."

In September the following year, Gigaba (2013) informed the Portfolio Committee on Public Enterprises that a task team comprising SAA, SA Express and the Department of Public Enterprises (DPE) was established, "under the leadership of a special SAA Board Sub-Committee," to draft the strategy. He said work done or commissioned by previous

SAA Boards, the Management Team and third-party consultants was considered and revalidated. That included an SAA business overview that was commissioned by the DPE to Mott MacDonald and Spectrum Capital.

Although the drafting of the LTTS included the three stakeholder groups, it was clear that the brain behind the strategy was the Minister. In his address to the SAA Board at the 2012 AGM, Gigaba (2013) was not only very clear about the fact that the airline needed to have a turnaround strategy, but he was also specific about the elements that strategy had to feature. It follows, therefore, that the LTTS was more the Minister's project, rather than that of the SAA TMT and/or the Board.

It was odd that a company's strategy was developed at the instance of the Shareholder, and not the CEO and his/her TMT and the Board of Directors (BoD). The norm is for a company's CEO and his/her TMT to develop or commission a strategy and then sell it to the BoD and obtain approval for it, whereafter the Shareholder/s would then be briefed in order to ensure alignment.

Gigaba's actions were consistent with his view at the time, as articulated by former DPE Deputy Director-General (DDG) Matsietsi Mokholo (2019), that after the ANC's 51st national conference in Polokwane, South Africa was meant to be a developmental State, hence the Shareholder Ministry had to adopt "an interventionist approach."

Efforts by Monwabisi Kalawe and Vuyani Jarana, as CEOs respectively at different times, to implement the LTTS encountered various challenges. Kalawe (2019) experienced great frustration when it came to implementing the four main pillars of the LTTS: withdrawal from loss-making routes, getting an equity injection from the Government, reducing headcount and procuring wide-body aircraft. On all four pillars, he could not register success:

- He and the BoD were not allowed to exit the non-profitable Johannesburg-Beijing route because such a decision did not enjoy the support of all interested stakeholders in the Government, in particular then Minister of Tourism Marthinus van Schalkwyk;

- The promised R6 billion capital injection from the Government was not forthcoming, with the best that the National Treasury could do being an undertaking to give SAA a guarantee – provided the airline stopped flying loss-making routes;

- He could not implement employee retrenchment, which was another pillar of the LTTS, because the country was on the verge of national elections at the time; and

- A tender to procure 23 new, fuel-efficient wide-body aircraft was cancelled because "there were two camps in the Cabinet at the time: some guys were supportive of Airbus and some were supportive of Boeing."

"All the key pillars that were supposed to drive the strategy did not get support from the key stakeholders. If an environment had been created for us to implement those pillars, SAA would be better today," Kalawe said (2019).

Kalawe's (2019) exit from SAA, "at the behest of Board Chairperson Dudu Myeni," was followed by a series of Acting CEOs who had absolutely no authority (Malunga, 2019; Tshabalala, 2019) and were micro-managed by the BoD. According to former SAA Non-Executive Director Swazi Tshabalala (2019), the longest-serving Acting CEO, Musa Zwane, was "absolutely terrified" of Myeni. It was not until the appointment of Vuyani Jarana in November 2017 that yet another serious effort was made to implement the LTTS.

Like Kalawe before him, Jarana had his own frustrations when it came to implementing the LTTS. Jarana's (2019) biggest sources of frustration, as he catalogued them, were:

- The Shareholder's failure to provide the R21,7 billion funding – to cover SAA's debt and working capital – on which the LTTS was premised (despite the Shareholder having signed off on the LTTS);

- Lack of operational autonomy and agility, with most important decisions requiring Shareholder approval, which was often late or not coming at all;

- Lack of Shareholder support for employee retrenchment; and

- A non-cohesive BoD which operated like "a jungle," with some Directors having "some brief from somewhere."

KQ, on the other hand, has had four restructurings: These were:
- The Probe Committee's commercialisation recommendation, which led to the airline's privatisation and listing on the Nairobi Stock Exchange in 1996, with Dutch airline KLM emerging as the majority Shareholder with 26%;

- The Kenya Airways Turnaround Plan (KATAP) in 2004/5;

- Project Mawingu in 2011; and

- Operation Pride and the Cost Optimisation Plan (COP) or Project Safari from 2015/6.

Among these turnaround strategies, the Probe Committee's recommended commercialisation and KATAP were great successes, and each saw the airline making profits for a number of years in a row.

Although KQ continued to be profitable in the years after its listing on the Nairobi Stock Exchange, the quantum of its profits grew progressively smaller between 2000 and 2003. According to former KQ Information Technology Director Kevin Kinyanjui (2019), then CEO Titus Naikuni and his TMT became worried that if the airline did not change course, it would find itself "in loss-making territory" within a year or two. As a result, Naikuni introduced KATAP, which focused on cost containment and revenue generation.

KATAP involved all KQ employees and focused on a critical examination of all aspects of the airline which involved costs, ranging from "each core area of the operations," through to "those who were working in cargo and ground handling." Staff members were encouraged to come up with suggestions to increase revenue generation and to contain costs (Kinyanjui, 2019).

According to Kinyanjui (2019), KATAP resulted in "around 30-40% of the costs being slashed in one year alone," with many opportunities for revenue generation identified. He said the pilots chipped in with "pilot techniques" which saved fuel consumption upon take-off and landing in order to reduce costs and, in the process, impacted positively on the bottom line. As part of cost containment during KATAP, 800 people were retrenched (Mugo, 2019) and KQ was profitable "all the way up to 2010" (Achola, 2019).

The success of KATAP emboldened the KQ leadership to dream big. On the back of KATAP's success, Naikuni and his team launched Project Mawingu, an ambitious, 10-year growth strategy which included aggressive route expansion and fleet acquisition. Through Project Mawingu, KQ aspired "to become Africa's largest and one of a few airlines to serve every inhabited continent in the world." The ambition was to grow the airline's fleet from 42 aircraft in 2011 to 115 aircraft by 2021 and to increase KQ's international destinations from 58 to 117 "in 177 countries in six continents" (Amollo, 2015; Thiong'o, 2015).

To acquire the new fleet and grow its routes, KQ needed an estimated US$3,7 billion in financing cover during the first five years, with much of it provided through "cash flows and traditional sources of finance such as debt and capital markets" (Amollo, 2015). KQ issued 1 477 million shares at a price of KSh134 per share and raised KSh20,7 billion (US$250,1 million), which formed part of the airline's initial pre-delivery payments for aircraft acquisition in the 2014 and 2015 financial years. According to Amollo (2015), KQ described the rights issue as "the largest of its kind in East Africa" at the time.

The airline also took out a hedge against the fuel price (Mungai & Bula, 2018).

The first phase of KQ's fleet renewal programme, which involved acquisition of 10 Boeing Dreamliner aircraft and the exit of the Boeing 767 fleet, was completed successfully in 2015 (Amollo, 2015).

However, owing to a variety of factors – among them terrorist attacks in Nairobi and a fire at Jomo Kenyatta International Airport (JKIA) in 2013, coupled with an outbreak of the Ebola Virus Disease in West Africa in 2014 – KQ found itself heavily indebted and unable to service its loans. Consequently, unlike KATAP, Project Mawingu was a disaster which burdened KQ with costs and led to the challenges which necessitated Operation Pride in 2015 and the COP or Project Safari in 2016.

Subsequent to the adoption of Project Mawingu in 2011, KQ recorded a profit in 2012 only, with losses of different magnitudes registered until December 2020.

Operation Pride saw KQ's fleet reduced by almost a third, non-core assets like land sold, the airline's Heathrow International Airport slot in London sold, 600 employees retrenched and various efforts to contain costs in an effort to reduce the airline's debts. Waste elimination, revenue generation and asset disposal were the main elements of that turnaround strategy, according to Thomas Omondi Achola (2019), who was Strategy Director at the time.

Achola (2019), Mugo (2019) and Mbuvi Ngunze (2019), who was KQ CEO at the time, said Operation Pride was a success. Achola (2019) said a year after KQ's biggest loss in the 2015/16 financial year, the airline recorded an operating profit the following year and again in December 2017, when KQ changed its financial year from April to March to a calendar year (January to December). However, the airline still made losses before tax "predominantly because of financing costs."

Mugo (2019) said during that period KQ cut its gross losses by 35% and grew operational profit "by over 100%." The challenge, she said, was that the carrier still had aircraft that it could not pay for and owed both local banks and the US Export-Import Bank, which were part of the consortium that had helped KQ to acquire the new aircraft.

Through a bottom-up ideation approach which involved all employees, 700 initiatives were put through a funnel and KQ ended up focusing "on around 400 of them," Ngunze (2019) said. He said that KQ saved "$280 million worth of costs" through the sale and sub-leasing of aircraft and renegotiations with aircraft lessors.

The COP, known internally as Project Safari, started towards the end of 2016. It was about renegotiation of the airline's debt to foreign aircraft financiers and restructuring of its debt of $2 billion (KSh20 billion) to Kenyan banks. Although the local banks were vehemently opposed to efforts to convert their loans into equity and took KQ to court, eventually the Kenyan Government persuaded them to support the proposal. In the end, the banks constituted the KQ Lenders Company, which came to own 38,1% of the airline, with the Government being the new majority Shareholder at 48,9% and KLM's shareholding reduced from 16% to 7,8% (Kenyan Wallstreet Team, 2017).

By November 2016, Operation Pride had begun "to bring results." Following two years of record-breaking losses, KQ had reduced its net loss to KSh5 billion in the first half of the 2017 financial year, down from KSh12 billion in the previous year, and passenger numbers had increased from 68% to 71% (Aglionby, 2016).

In mid-November 2017, KQ announced the successful conclusion of its US$2 billion debt restructuring, with the Kenyan Government having offered $750 million as guarantees for KQ's debt for 10 years. The deal diluted existing KQ shareholders by 95% and the Nairobi Securities Exchange suspended the carrier's shares for two weeks. Ngunze said the debt restructuring would enable KQ to have time "to reshape the business to pay a bit more on the tail end" (Miriri, 2017).

However, KQ CEO Sebastian Mikosz's Privately Initiated Investment Proposal, which would have seen the airline being granted permission to operate Jomo Kenyatta International Airport (JKIA), led to the Kenyan Parliament voting to nationalise the airline "to save it from mounting debts." KQ was going to be part of an aviation holding company with four subsidiaries, one of which would be JKIA. The new company would be exempted from paying excise duty on all goods, including jet fuel (Reuters, 2019).

Interestingly, the two airlines' restructuring plans appear to have run parallel to one another. SAA's *Bambanani* and the Business Restructuring Plan (BRP) in 2005 and 2006 took place just as KQ's KATAP was coming to an end. While KATAP was a great success, the SAA BRP – which led to the airline making first an operational profit and then registering profits in 2010 and 2011 – appears to have laid a solid foundation for future success.

Although the SAA BRP (which took place under the theme "simplify, right-size, re-skill and incentivise") involved comprehensive strategic re-orientation which was intended to see the airline return to profitability by 2009, both SAA's BRP and KQ's KATAP also focused heavily on cost containment and revenue generation. In the case of the latter, ideas were harvested from KQ employees, with McKinsey as a trainer and coach (Kinyanjui, 2019), while in SAA's case the BRP was driven by Ngqula's TMT, with the support of Seabury, which formed a Cash Conservation Office which scrutinised "every single invoice and every single payment" made by the airline (Ngqula, 2019).

Also in 2005, fellow African competitor Ethiopian Airlines (EAL) adopted Vision 2010, a five-year plan to increase the EAL fleet, to double its number of passengers and to triple its cargo volume. By 2010, EAL had accomplished all its goals: its fleet had grown by 60% to 41 commercial aircraft, it had doubled its passengers to 3,2 million per annum and its cargo volume had tripled (Oqubay & Tesfachew, 2019:8).

SAA's Strategy for Growth, adopted by Mzimela in 2010/11, coincided with similar strategies for KQ and EAL. EAL launched Vision 2025 in 2010, while KQ launched Project Mawingu a year later. While details of SAA's Strategy for Growth are sketchy, both EAL's Vision 2025 and KQ's Project Mawingu were bold and ambitious. Through Vision 2025, EAL planned to increase the number of aircraft in its fleet to 120 by 2025, with this number to go up to 200 aircraft by 2030 to take advantage of bulk-purchase discounts, to fly to 90 international destinations (Mills & Van der Merwe, 2020) and to double its target of US$5 billion in revenue to US$10 billion by 2025-30 (Oqubay & Tesfachew, 2019:4).

By 2015, the Ethiopian carrier had "become the largest African airline." In 2018 it transported "more than 12 million passengers (a four-fold increase since 2010) and half a million tons of cargo," and its fleet size comprised "more than 100 new-generation aircraft (a three-fold increase since 2010)" and it flew to 115 international destinations, among them Los Angeles in the USA and Tokyo, Japan. Its China-Africa routes alone were expected to carry one million passengers in 2018, making EAL "the major airline linking Africa with China" (Oqubay & Tesfachew, 2019:8).

However, in 2015 SAA and KQ were both making huge losses and were heavily indebted. SAA had been struggling to implement its LTTS for two years, while KQ launched its Operation Pride that year. By the end of 2020, SAA was still in business rescue and KQ was still in the process of being nationalised. That was despite South African Finance Minister Tito Mboweni's allocation of R16,4 billion to SAA in February 2020 to cover the airline's debt and interest payments, in addition to an emergency loan of R3,5 billion which the carrier had received from the Development Bank of Southern Arica in January 2020 (Paton, 2020).

A comparison of the three airlines follows in table 15.1 below.

Discussion of the Results

In the discussion of the results, SAA will be featured first, followed by KQ and EAL, with a comparison of the three airlines concluding the section.

While most participants held the view that SAA was not properly capitalised when it was moved out of Transnet to become a stand-alone company, there is no disputing that, over the years, the airline has had numerous Government bail-outs and bank guarantees. However, as Mzimela (2019) argued, Government guarantees increased SAA's financial liabilities.

By aviation economist Joachim Vermooten's (2020) calculation, SAA received R53,3 billion of funding from the Government between 2007 and 2020, with R32,2 billion of it being in cash and R19,1 being in guarantees, and financial assistance totalling R67,9 billion from Transnet and the Government between April 1999 and March 2020. According to the Treasury, of the R291 billion which was to have been spent on bailing out SOEs between 2008 and March 2022, R244,7 billion was to have gone to electricity utility Eskom, with SAA in second position with "a total bailout package of R38,4 billion" during that period (Paton, 2020).

Mzimela (2019) made the legitimate point that SAA's high gearing ratio meant that the airline had to pay a premium whenever they purchased goods and services, compared to airlines with lower gearing ratios which enjoyed better discounts. "When I go, as SAA, with everybody looking at the balance sheet, they say 'ah, ah, ah, there's no room for negotiation'. So, at every point, you're already starting off from a highly disadvantaged position," she said.

Table 15.1: Comparison of SAA, KQ and EAL:

	SAA	Kenya Airways	Ethiopian Airlines
Formed	1 February 1934 as a Government Department	11 January 1977 as a State-owned company	8 April 1946 as a Commercial Enterprise, but State owned
Milestones	Established as a stand-alone company in 2007	Privatised in 1996 and KLM became the majority Shareholder (26%)	Victim of Political Turmoil between 1975 and 2000 and appointment in 2004 of Girma Wake as CEO and Tewolde Gebremariam as Deputy CEO
Restructurings	• Bambanani (2004/5) • SAA Business Restructuring Plan (2006) • SAA Growth Strategy (2010) • Long-Term Turnaround Strategy (2013)	• Kenya Airways Turnaround Plan (2004/5) • Project Mawingu (2011) • Operation Pride (2015) & Project Safari (2016)	• Vision 2010 (2005) • Vision 2025 (2010)
Number of CEOs (2010-2020)	10	3	2
Decision Making	Mostly Shareholder, plus Board	TMT and Board	TMT and Board
Mandate	Commercial and Developmental	Commercial	Commercial
Constraints	PFMA, Lack of Capitalisation, Lack of Appropriate Management Skills	Terrorism, West Africa Ebola Outbreak	None
Ownership	Government	Private	Government
Financial Performance 2010-2020	Last profitable in 2011	Last Profitable in 2012	Profitable throughout the period
Number of Employees	Estimated to be around 10 000 in 2019	Estimated to be around 4000 in 2019	About 15 000 in 2019

Source: Own Composition

Writing in SAA's Integrated Annual Report, Chairman JB Magwaza (2017:38) argued that the airline had "long struggled with adequate capitalisation and a lack of capital injection from the Shareholder." He said that lack of capitalisation had weakened the airline's balance sheet and impacted negatively on the implementation of the LTTS.

SAA's poor capital base meant that in the main the airline operated much older, fuel-heavy aircraft which drained its limited resources, and that led to it charging higher prices compared to its competitors and, therefore, being uncompetitive.

To stress the importance of proper capitalisation during a turnaround, Bibeault (1999) likened it to a blood transfusion during surgery "because cash is the lifeblood of the business." Calling it "in essence a cash flow tourniquet to stop the bleeding," Bibeault (1999:242-3) said improving cash flow is paramount.

Secondly, in addition to poor capitalisation, SAA's problems are attributable to a variety of challenges. Among these are the airline's mandate, the Public Finance Management Act (PFMA), Shareholder disposition as well as Board and Management instability. By far the most formidable challenges are the airline's mandate and the PFMA with its considerable restrictions.

The origin of the problem is the South African Airways Act No. 5 of 2007, which states in its preamble that the airline is a vehicle "to promote air links with the Republic's main business, trading and tourism markets within the African continent and internationally." That founding legislation states further that South Africa – which has "a developmental orientation" – regards the airline as "a national carrier and strategic asset that would enable the State to preserve its ability to contribute to key domestic, intra-regional and international linkages" (SAA Act, 2007).

Although Ngqula (2019) and Kriel (2019) believed that their mandate, during Alec Erwin's tenure as Minister of Public Enterprise, was to run a commercial enterprise, the fact remained that SAA had a dual mandate: it was expected to serve a developmental mandate, while simultaneously being a commercially viable business. In the SAA BRP, Ngqula and team acknowledged as much when they pointed out that there were competing interests in Government, with the DPE and National Treasury having given the airline "a formal mandate to pursue profits," while pressure from other Government Ministries "serve to blunt that focus somewhat" (SAA Business Restructuring Plan, 2007).

The SAA BRP team said the national carrier often found itself facing various demands from different Government Departments, and the airline found itself "discouraged" from reducing staff numbers because of the country's high employment rate. As a result, the airline found itself in a situation where it had higher employee-per-passenger and higher employee-per-available-seat-kilometre ratios than its competitors, with some of its harshest critics being other Government Departments:

Despite – or, perhaps, because of – this ambiguous mandate, SAA often seems to please no one. Its harshest critics are the agencies whose constituencies use air transport – DEAT [the Department of Environmental Affairs and Tourism], DTI [the Department of Trade and Industry], Agriculture, and Foreign Affairs. These agencies fault SAA for offering too little capacity on too few routes.

Some of them would like SAA to focus more on volume and less on profits so as to drive economic growth directly. At the same time, other agencies fault SAA for the burden its periodic financial losses impose on Treasury. All these Government Departments have different expectations of SAA, which at times are in conflict. SAA as an SOE is expected to fulfil national objectives such as tourism, job creation, being a profitable airline and not depend on State funding, and also facilitate trade between SA and other States (SAA Business Restructuring Plan, 2007).

However, that dual mandate predated the SAA Act. According to Mohale (2019), even during Coleman Andrews's tenure, SAA had "a confused dual mandate." On the one hand, the carrier's mandate was meant to be developmental because it had to fly to areas where other commercial airlines would not find it profitable to fly, and on the other hand it was meant to be commercially successful to "fund our own expansion, our own operations and buy our own fuel and our own aircraft."

That developmental mandate saw SAA flying loss-making routes which made political sense, but for which the airline was not subsidised. In the process, the airline incurred huge losses.

To make matters worse, there was no common understanding of what the national carrier's developmental mandate entailed, apart from having to fly to countries and cities that its political masters wanted it to fly to. Former Public Enterprises Minister Barbara Hogan (2019) said she "never understood the notion of a developmental mandate for SAA," and ventured that "very few Ministers could tell you what the developmental agenda is for SAA," apart from the need to advance transformation.

The fact that there was no clarity regarding what the developmental mandate was made things "worse than just having those two mandates," argued Shaw (2019). He said the nebulous developmental mandate and everything that went with it meant that SAA was "disabled before you put it into the market."

Former DPE Deputy Director-General Matsietsi Mokholo (2019) confirmed Hogan's (2019) view that even the Department "did not have a test of saying this is the developmental mandate and for it to be achieved, this must be done." She said the developmental mandate was problematic not only for SAA, but also for the Government "because juggling those mandates was very, very problematic."

Some Ministers like Hogan – and, it would seem from accounts by Ngqula (2019), Kriel (2019) and Vermooten (2019) – Erwin adopted a hands-off approach to SAA and left the Board and the Top Management Team to run the airline as they saw fit. However, others, like Gigaba and Gordhan, adopted different approaches, as will be shown later.

Even in his instruction to the SAA Board in 2013, Gigaba (2013) had directed that the new turnaround strategy that he wanted formulated had to "highlight the conditions required for an improved and profitable operating model, with efficiencies of scale … as well as the strategic importance of the proposed route network to achieve Government's objectives."

Gigaba (2019), who complained about lack of Government clarity about SAA's role, was very firm on the need for the airline to play a developmental role, but was equally conscious of the need for the Government to ensure that the developmental mandate was not a financial burden on the airline. The Government, he said, would have had a responsibility to help SAA keep its "overheads manageable" and would have had a duty to keep its fuel levy "affordable" and to subsidise the non-profitable routes.

Thirdly, the PFMA posed yet another considerable challenge to SAA. Both the literature on the aviation sector and various interview participants during the course of this study pointed out repeatedly the competitive nature of the industry and the fact that it has wafer-thin margins.

Not only did the PFMA – which imposes, among other things, "extra-bureaucratic requirements" (Halstead, 2019) like lengthy procurement processes (Fredericks, 2019; Halstead; 2019) – slow down decision making in an industry where agility is a *sine qua non*, but it also disempowered the SAA BoD and the CEO. Neither the CEO and his TMT nor the BoD could make decisions which, at other airlines, are routinely made by their counterparts.

DPE Acting Deputy Director-General Avril Halstead (2019) explained: "Every time they want to open or close a route, they have to get approval from the Government, and so on and so on. They want to purchase a new aircraft, they have to get approval from the Government; they want to lease a new aircraft, they have to get approval from the Government."

Halstead (2019) said these approvals were in terms of "the contentious" Section 54 of the PFMA, which assigned to the Shareholder "authority for making relatively operational decisions."

According to Mokholo (2019), the PFMA obliged the SAA Board to submit to the Minister requests of transactions that fall within the Significance Materiality Framework for consideration within 30 days. She acknowledged that often the Shareholder did not respond within the 30-day period:

> *The 30-day requirement is a big problem. Legislation is a big problem for SOEs because the Shareholder, in most cases, does not respond within 30 days. When you are in a competitive space like SAA, by the time you want to enter or change a route, you come for Shareholder approval and, three months later, Emirates is already in there. Meanwhile, we are still going to consult.*
>
> *The PFMA says nothing happens without the Treasury. If the Treasury and the DPE are not aligned, they are fighting, who suffers? The airline. We have not mastered this in terms of the powers which should reside with the Shareholder and the powers that the Shareholder should delegate to the Board in terms of the Shareholder Compact, and the powers that the Board delegates to the Executives.*

Vuyani Jarana (2019), who was SAA CEO at the time he was interviewed for this research, said the PFMA was a major constraint which placed SAA at a huge disadvantage when compared to its competitors. He said by subjecting SAA to the PFMA, the Government was effectively "tying [our] hands at the back and expecting [us] to win a championship."

That was an analogy that one was to hear repeatedly during the course of this study in reference to the PFMA's effect on the airline.

Jarana (2019) explained: "BA doesn't have a PFMA; they act quickly. Emirates doesn't have that. They are State owned, but they are run like a corporate entity. Ethiopian Airlines, similar; Kenya Airways, similar. By and large all State owned, but they are enabled by being released from a very cumbersome piece of legislation where you have had to talk to so many people to be able to achieve success."

Both Jarana (2019) and interviewed SAA Board Members, including Chairman JB Magwaza (2019), were extremely frustrated – with good reason – that they were not able to appoint CEOs and Chief Financial Officers of SAA subsidiaries Air Chefs and South African Airways Technical (SAAT) without the prior approval of Gordhan as Shareholder Minister. They were livid that, on one occasion, their choice of CEO for Mango was rejected by Gordhan and that, on another occasion, the Minister took six months to get back to them on their choice of CFO for SAAT, whom they ended up losing to a rival airline.

SAA Chief Restructuring Officer Peter Davies (2019) stressed the need for agility: "In a competitive environment which is fast changing, it's quite difficult for an airline to make commercial decisions when you are being treated like a Post Office … I think it's a fact that SAA has never been allowed to operate as a normal commercial airline because of restrictions placed by the Shareholder. I'm being brutally honest."

Davies (2019) said the rules and regulations under which SAA operated had to be relaxed for two reasons: unlike a Government Department, SAA has competitors "breathing down our neck" and the airline was "in intensive care." He said there had to be appreciation of the fact that the aviation industry was "a dog-eat-dog business, a nasty business," and that SAA needed to be able to make decisions quickly, hence it had "to be treated differently in that sense."

Davies (2019) warned that if the SAA leadership was "not allowed to do what we want to do, in the time that we are given to do it, then we won't succeed; it's as simple as that."

SAA, then, found itself in a situation directly opposite to the one that turnaround scholars consider ideal for successful implementation of a turnaround strategy. A turnaround requires "the visible hand of management" (Bibeault (1999:3-7) and the CEO should enjoy "absolute authority" (Bibeault, 1999:95; Finkin, 1992). "If he or she cannot act decisively and quickly, the company is probably doomed," Finkin (1992) cautioned.

Fourthly, frequent changes of Shareholder Ministers and their different styles were also challenges for SAA. Jarana (2019) complained, for instance, that in the 18 months during which he was at the helm of the airline, he and the Board had to deal with four different Ministers. These were then-Finance Ministers Malusi Gigaba, Nhlanhla Nene and Tito Mboweni and Public Enterprises Minister Pravin Gordhan. These Ministers all had different styles.

According to Mohale (2019), frequent changes of Ministers resulted in a lack of continuity, with new Ministers feeling "compelled to re-invent the wheel and start afresh." Jarana (2019) complained about an apparent belief within the Government that a CEO appointed during a particular Minister's tenure is "that Minister's person." He attributed that to the culture of the governing ANC where, "when a Minister changes, [the new Minister] looks at you through the eyes of the previous Minister."

"The problem with the ANC," Jarana (2019) said, "is that even at its best form, when a Minister is changed, when the next Minister comes in it is as if he is from another party. Now, you can see that flowing through to SOCs. All of a sudden, you've got a position where people are not sure about whether they should trust you or not. The styles are very different."

Proactively comparing the disposition of the Ministers under whom he had served for a decent period, Jarana (2019) said Gigaba "was more liberal about saying 'listen, combat this thing and make sure that you take it out of pain; respond to the issues'," while Nene was "a little bit conservative" and Gordhan was "extremely conservative." He said even when he faced difficult challenges to which he had an answer, he was not comfortable to approach Gordhan with a proposed solution because "you would be pressed for answers, and some of those answers the Shareholder may not like or believe they are correct."

As SAA Chairman, Magwaza (2019) found Gordhan totally inaccessible, and was unable to get an audience with him. He said he had sent SAA's tweaked LTTS to Gordhan, when he was appointed Minister of Public Enterprises in 2018, and asked him to read it and sign off on it with the Board, but the Minister had not got back to him:

> *His predecessors, Malusi Gigaba, understood the strategy and said "okay, go ahead, guys, and make it work." We then had Nhlanhla Nene; he wasn't even there for six months. We were able to present to him the turnaround strategy and he understood it and said "now it makes sense; even the way you conceptualise it and talk about it, it's going to work."*
>
> *We have not even had an opportunity to present to our Minister this turnaround strategy.*
>
> *Our Minister has not had that opportunity to look at our strategy. He keeps on saying that we are missing the plot. Maybe I agree; maybe we are missing the plot, but he doesn't understand our strategy because he has not been told by the Board what the strategy is.*

Magwaza (2019) said SAA's lenders understood the strategy "better than our Shareholder, by the way."

Fifthly, not only did the Shareholder take long to make decisions, but there were occasions when SAA Board Members and the TMT felt that the Shareholder was reluctant to make decisions at all or to honour its undertakings. Jarana (2019) was immensely frustrated, for instance, that, despite having signed off on the LTTS which clearly stated that the airline would need R21,7 billion to effect the turnaround, the Shareholder had not made that money available at the time of the interview. As a result, he found himself spending a lot of his time dealing with "liquidity and balance sheet issues."

"My view," he said, "is that if you sign off on a Corporate Plan, you are not only signing off on the nice things; you are also signing off on the painful side of issues.... So, this is the issue. Commitment was made by virtue of National Treasury signing off on the Corporate Plan, but what I'm finding difficult is that it would appear to me that there's not 100% alignment within the Cabinet," he said.

While other participants were also critical of Gordhan as Shareholder Minister, Jarana (2019) and Magwaza (2019) were particularly more so. Jarana (2019) said Gordhan adopted "a father-and-child type of attitude" towards the Board, and that had the effect of killing debates. Consequently, Jarana (2019) called for "transformation in attitudes and in the minds on that side."

Magwaza (2019) said the first thing that was not right and which would not work for any strategy was having a Shareholder "who understands this thing, is anxious that it happens and it happens now" and then starts over-reaching. He said in such a situation, "then the strategy would flounder because if you are not sitting there every day and you are merely basing [your action] on what you read and your own anxiety – and you are not even managing your own anxiety – you put so much pressure on an already over-pressurised environment that people end up trying to make you happy, rather than doing the job that is required in the organisation."

According to Magwaza (2019), the role played by Gordhan as a Shareholder was not helpful to the airline:

> *You need a Shareholder who is going to understand that this is a sick organisation and, therefore, you need to allow the people whom you have brought in there, first the Board and then the Executive, to be given space to implement the strategy. Don't breathe down their throats every other week and every other minute. The first issue is about understanding what is happening and giving the Board and the Executive the opportunity to do what you would require.*
>
> *Secondly, you need a Shareholder who is prepared, when it comes to decisions, to make major, major decisions, and not run helter-skelter because of the pressure he has from other politicians. If you can't get a Shareholder who is going to say to the other politicians "please, give me time, don't come here and tell me what to do," you are going to flounder. He must be a strong Shareholder who is able to manage his own politics and not allow that politics to come and affect the organisation.*

Paton (2020) argued that being a Director of a State-owned company in South Africa "is to agree not to be a real Director at all, but to answer to a Cabinet Minister driven by political motives" which were "at odds with the commercial and fiduciary responsibilities Directors have been asked to take on." She said SAA Directors had had "the worst of it" because the airline had traded recklessly, but they did not have the authority to place it in business rescue or in liquidation without the Shareholder's consent.

Paton (2019) said when Gordhan argued that more attention should be given to governance at SAA, what he meant was that "Government should have stepped in earlier, not with money, but to run the show."

Clearly, the process of implementing SAA's LTTS – which depended heavily on the Shareholder – was not conducive to success. As Chowdhury (2002:256) argues, "it is the process through which turnaround strategies are implemented, and not their content *per se,*" which explains the difference between their success or failure.

The sixth challenge that has bedevilled SAA's implementation of its turnaround strategy was unhealthy Board dynamics. Although divisions within the Board and between the Board and Management were particularly pronounced during Dudu Myeni's tenure as Chairperson, these continued beyond her term on the Board. Magwaza (2019), for instance, was very critical of the behaviour of some of his fellow Directors who, he said, did not respect the operations-governance line and sought to involve themselves in operational matters, including the appointment of Senior Executives reporting to the CEO.

Board Member and Audit and Risk Committee Chairman Akhter Moosa (2019) was equally worried about "endless contestation" within the Board, which showed "lack of trust in the CEO" and hampered implementation of the LTTS. He felt that the Board needed to show more trust in the CEO, who felt "threatened at times," and that Jarana also needed "to engage differently to win over the Board." Moosa (2019) felt that a workshop was needed "to iron out the differences" in the BoD.

Moosa (2019) expressed great frustration with the Board-Management dynamic, which he said was far from ideal. He said while robust discussions were to be welcomed, "endless contestation and not looking at the bigger picture" – something which had come to be "the hallmark for a while now" – was holding SAA back.

"When you get into a ship like this," Moosa (2019) said, "you have got to trust the captain. You've got to trust the captain completely, and he has got to know that you trust him. He has also got to know that he has to listen to you."

He said while some Board Members had since "softened up," the situation had not improved "sufficiently to create a dynamic Board." Describing himself as being unhappy, Moosa (2019) went as far as saying "short of the entire Board being replaced, I think there has to be a culling and re-appointment of other members," preferably appointing "people who really bring aviation knowledge into the scheme of things." He said the Board needed the Shareholder's intervention.

Magwaza (2019) concurred with Moosa (2019). He said the Board undermined Jarana to the extent that he got "terribly frustrated because he sees a Board that is second-guessing him." He said in addition to agility, SAA needed "a Board with balls," which was something that Jarana did not enjoy and which had led to his resignation.

So frustrated was Magwaza (2019) with the Board that he had written to Gordhan to suggest a reconstitution of the Board, but a member of the Minister's team at the DPE had informed him that "the Minister needs a Board resolution" to that effect.

In a direct reference to the SAA Board that he still headed at the time of the interview, Magwaza (2019) said SAA needed a Board "that draws a thick line between the role of a

Board and the role of the Executive," and which did not "transgress and step over the line in terms of what it should do and what the Executives are supposed to do." He added:

> *I have a very crude expression that was given to me by my father, who said you don't buy a dog and then you do the barking yourself because the dog will be confused in that situation. So, you need to get a Board with that kind of understanding.*

In addition to its frustration with the Shareholder, the SAA BoD also had to worry about potentially being held responsible for the airline's reckless trading as a result of its precarious financial situation. Although it is required to table its Annual Report to the Parliamentary Portfolio Committee on Public Enterprises each year, the national carrier often went without doing so for months on end, until some budgetary allocation from the National Treasury in order to enable it to be able to claim that it was a going concern. The last published SAA Annual Report was for the 2016/17 financial year; at the time of writing this report, none was published for the 2018 and 2019 financial years.

However, when SAA's financial statements were finally presented before the Standing Committee on Public Accounts on 15 May 2020, they revealed that the airline had sustained losses of R5,5 billion and R5,1 billion in 2018 and 2019 respectively (Paton, 2020).

Halstead (2019) had some sympathy for the BoD which, she said, was "in a really difficult position." She said the fact that Board Members were "literally sitting on a knife's edge every day," worried if they were allowing the airline to trade recklessly, made it "difficult for them to delegate authority to Management as much as they may want to, under the circumstances."

"I don't know how frequently, but I've seen, every three months, legal opinions that they are seeking that they are still on the straight and narrow and haven't stepped off. When Board Members are feeling like they are close to the edge, they get nervous and want to make sure that they've got control of the sort of risks that may result in them stepping over," Halstead (2019) said.

Moosa (2019) said the Board had told Gigaba, Nene and Mboweni, during their respective tenures as Finance Ministers, that it was planning to place SAA in business rescue or even get it liquidated because it was insolvent. He said the Board had written "at least eight or 10" such letters to the Ministers, and "each one of those letters were responded to in a politically-correct version to say the Government is committed to SAA, that there is a sovereign guarantee."

Moosa (2019) said the Board was "not permitted to put the entity into business rescue without the consent of the Shareholder, whereas you could do it with another company."

As an eighth problem, there was unanimity among the participants in this research that SAA did not have the required management skills to implement a turnaround strategy successfully. While everybody – Board Members, Senior Executives and labour representatives – was effusive with praise for Jarana, who was very popular as CEO and was held in high regard, there was unanimity that both individuals within his Executive Committee and in the next tier of leadership within the airline were poor.

Board Member Mohammed Bassa (2019) spoke of "dead wood" and "people who come to work so that they can go home," and "people who have been appointed and promoted because of their connections with the previous Board." Kalawe (2019) said the airline needed people with "solid experience in the aviation industry" because "the guys who are there now are pen pushers," following the departure of those who understood the aviation industry.

Jarana (2019) shared Kalawe's (2019) view that employees with valuable skills had long left the airline. He said commercial skills, in particular, were "almost non-existent" at SAA. Both he and SAA Board Members said part of the problem was that the airline was not an attractive proposition as a prospective employer. SAA, he said, was "not an employer brand – it is damaged, with all the history of instability." He said efforts to recruit hard-working men and women "who are strong executives" from companies like Unilever were unsuccessful because "they can't stomach the uncertainty about the future because this thing is known to be unstable."

Davies (2019) echoed Jarana's (2019) view that, over the years, SAA had lost "a lot of good expertise," with many frustrated employees having left to join mostly Middle Eastern airlines. He said international experience had to be brought into SAA, while being mindful of the country's history.

Davies (2019) said another challenge was that those in the SAA TMT who were there when the decay set in at the airline were still around, together with those in Middle Management. He said in order to improve the chances of successfully turning an organisation around, Middle Management had to change:

> *It's Middle Management that's immune to the problem. They hold the conduit; they manage the lines of communication. They can be vicious, they can be nasty, they can be positive, they can be like damn right telling lies. It's a bit like a ball of wool that has been played with by a cat. It's normally a complete mess.*

Non-Executive Director Martin Kingston (2019) said SAA was "in dire need of skills and experience, capital and technology." He said the SAA Executive Team needed to be "not comprehensively, but pretty meaningfully re-organised."

Moosa (2019) said the SAA TMT was "partly capable," and that impacted negatively on the airline's agility because "agility demands that the Board entrusts it [the LTTS] to a capable Executive."

Interim CFO Deon Fredericks (2019) – who was seconded from Telkom – also shared the view that SAA had "limited expertise" and that people who had something to offer did not want to work for the airline. He said he had agreed to be seconded to SAA only because he was at the end of his career, hence all he could lose was his reputation, "which I try not to lose by doing the right thing at the end of the day."

Fredericks (2019) said there were people at SAA who were not adding value, but getting them out of the company would be "another difficult challenge at the end of the day."

Magwaza (2019) said the Board had come into an organisation that was "seriously depleted in terms of Executives," where some "very senior people" had been in acting positions "for something like four years." He said those individuals were not the most capable: "I mean, you get a paper written by an Executive and when you look at it you say 'ohh, gosh, what happened to this person?'"

The ninth problem that confronted SAA was the fact that, at any given stage, the majority of its Senior Executives were acting and not permanent appointees. Former Acting CEO Musa Zwane (2019) said the fact that most of the Executives at SAA were acting (including himself as CEO) did not help matters. He said that, upon his appointment as Chairman, Magwaza had told him that "when you are the actor in the position that I was acting in, you are like a castrated man; there is nothing you can do."

Former Non-Executive Director Mzimkulu Malunga (2019) said he had felt sorry for SAA's TMT, the majority of whom were in acting positions. He said these Executives were "treated badly, even by the Board:" "Nobody really saw them, if you ask me. I felt that the Board didn't think that Management mattered much."

The tenth problem faced by the airline was the absence of policy coherence on aviation. A number of interview participants pointed to the fact that South Africa allows various foreign airlines to land directly in Cape Town and Durban and to take off from those cities, in the process undermining Johannesburg as a regional hub. Zwane (2019) pointed out that many countries did not allow their main hubs to be undermined in the manner in which SAA's Johannesburg hub was undermined with the Government's blessing. Such decisions, he said, made the national carrier to "compete unfairly with other airlines from around the world."

Jarana (2019) said it was important for South Africa to insist on reciprocity of policy on aviation. He said the country had to ensure that it did not have "open skies to a point where you kill your domestic air transport mechanism" because if it was too open, international carriers would siphon traffic from Durban, Cape Town and maybe even

Port Elizabeth in future.

Jarana (2019) bemoaned the absence of "policy logic on aviation in Government." He said there was so much fragmentation, with the Government having "no strategic position on aviation." He said there was a transport policy, an aviation policy and a tourism promotion policy, "all running in parallel." He said Ethiopia, on the other hand, had aligned policy to ensure that people – including the Chinese – "go to Addis Ababa before they come here."

Mokholo (2019) said the Government had realised, in hindsight, that liberalising the skies had created problems for South Africa. She said there was realisation that the Cabotage Rules (allowing foreign airlines to pick up passengers within a country, instead of confining them to one hub) had to be changed. She acknowledged that having three domestic airports (excluding the private Lanseria International Airport) becoming international points of entry and departure placed the national carrier at a disadvantage.

"So, we said we need to stop Cabotage. We need to allow BA to fly directly into OR Tambo International Airport, and that's it. We allow Mango, Kulula, Comair, the ones that would fit domestically, to compete with SAA or to compete with Mango. On competitive neutrality, we are not saying there must not be competition with SAA, but we are saying close it (foreign airlines landing and departing from Cape Town and Durban) so that you can be able to allow this economic fairness," Mokholo (2019) said.

Bassa (2019) said most of the Bilateral Air Services Agreements that the Government had concluded with other countries were at the expense of SAA as a national carrier. He said most international passengers from South Africa now travelled on Emirates, "the single largest foreign carrier" in the country, with eight flights per day originating from South Africa. He said Emirates had 50 flights a day from India, 30 a day from the United Kingdom and 30 a day from Australia.

Mokholo (2019) said policy incoherence was responsible for the wholesale liberalisation of the skies, at the expense of SAA. She said the way the Government allowed "new entrants, especially foreign airlines, into our space was creating problems for our domestic airlines." That, she said, led to valid questions being asked about why the Government wants "to own these entities if we are not going to support them from a policy point of view."

Mokholo (2019) said the idea of developing a Whole-of-State approach was intended, among other things, to "look at how we license foreign airlines coming into the country and how we allow them to operate within the two principles of Competitive Neutrality and Cabotage Rules." She said, from the perspective of the Principle of Competitive Neutrality, the Government took the view that State-owned airlines "will pay taxes like everybody else, they will be subjected to everything else, but there should be certain things that we do or legislation to give them that added advantage." One of the ways of giving

SAA an advantage, she said, was not to allow foreign airlines to land in the country "and still even carry passengers through domestically."

Finally, and perhaps more damagingly, SAA faced a problem of discordant voices from within the Government. While Gordhan, President Cyril Ramaphosa and the governing African National Congress argued that SAA was an important national asset which needed to be supported, Finance Minister Tito Mboweni publicly questioned the airline's continued existence and even advocated for its liquidation. Speaking at an investor conference in New York in November 2018, Mboweni said: "It [SAA] is loss making; we are unlikely to sort out the situation, so my view would be to close it down. Why I say close it down is because it's unlikely that you are going to find any private-sector equity partner who will come join this asset" (BusinessTech, 2018).

Understandably, that statement caused great unhappiness within the SAA Board and the TMT. At a time when the airline desperately needed a vote of confidence as it sought to raise loans and to reposition itself among the travelling public as a reliable carrier, Mboweni's public comments undermined its efforts.

Jarana (2019) said at a time when SAA desperately needed funding to provide certainty about the future, Mboweni's statement "effectively undermined the plan." He said an airline was like a listed a company: people who booked seats on SAA six to nine months before they were due to fly were "effectively shareholders in the brand." Nobody, he said, bought shares in a company whose future they doubted.

That is why, Jarana (2019) explained, statements like Mboweni's that SAA may have to be sold, and one by Reserve Bank Governor Lesetja Kganyago "yesterday who said don't bail out SOCs," were irresponsible:

> He is quoted as having said so in the media, which I find very reckless because what is happening now is that you have a Government that is not cohesive. There is no accountability. Everyone goes and shouts. We don't need critics; we need people coming with solutions.

> You can't disown your kids; you can't disown them because you feel they are on drugs, are you with me? You can't. You need to take responsibility for your role as a parent. In the case of the Government today, and the ANC Government in particular, they have to take accountability.

> Even Tito [Mboweni], when you appoint these people who are appointed as Board Members and CEOs, they are appointed by the Cabinet, and not by one person. Now, if you appoint people who are of good will but are not making sure that they have got the requisite skills, then you can't come, when they have got it wrong, and say 'well, then kill the SOC'. If you are going to kill it, then make a decision to do so; don't shout on the streets. For some of us who have

made a sacrifice to come and make it work, effectively you are pulling the capital under our feet.

Jarana (2019) said it was strange that, until then, "the reckless statements" were made by senior politicians from the governing ANC, and not opposition parties like the Democratic Alliance, the Economic Freedom Fighters, the United Democratic Movement or the Inkatha Freedom Party. Instead, those statements were made by Cabinet Ministers, "which means there's no cohesion at the Cabinet level."

He added, tellingly: "Now the Shareholder has lost his mind, in a nutshell."

Jarana (2019) said it was strange that Mboweni and Kganyago were saying one thing about the future of SAA and Gordhan was saying another, and yet "the President is quiet about it; he is not chaperoning his Ministers in one direction." He described "the mind of the Shareholder" as "the single biggest thing" holding the airline back.

Davies (2019) said the national carrier's suppliers followed the local and global media "and all they see is that it's doom and gloom." He said Mboweni's statement about SAA had sent a wrong message to those suppliers – including travel agents – and potential customers (passengers). He said everybody had to recognise that 70% of SAA's business came from abroad, and was not generated in South Africa. He said in the case of the revenue generated by SAA on its routes to Washington DC and New York in the USA, those two routes generated "more revenue than the entire SAA domestic network."

Davies (2019) said people tended to forget that airlines were "a commodity, a fast-moving consumer good," saying there was "nothing more perishable than an empty seat on take-off; you'll never sell it again."

Fredericks (2019) was also aggrieved by Mboweni's comments on SAA, saying they worked against the airline. He said negative comments on SAA by a Cabinet Minister had a deleterious impact on the airline because it dealt with forward bookings.

"Somebody sits in London or New York and sees this newspaper article. That agent says 'Sir, let me not book you on SAA; it seems they have trouble and may not be flying in six months' time or a year', which means that suddenly you have an immediate negative impact on your cash flow as well as your bottom line. That's why I say overall there's support, but there needs to be alignment between the Minister of Finance and the Minister of Public Enterprises – they need to speak with one voice," Fredericks (2019) said.

Magwaza (2019) said SAA needed a Shareholder "who is not going to be making irresponsible statements, which then begin to scare the Board, scare the Executives and, worse of all, scare all the other stakeholders such as suppliers that maybe this thing is going to be folding up first thing tomorrow morning if there is this kind of statement." He said in addition to making suppliers jittery, Mboweni's statement led to cancellations of international ticket bookings on SAA and had the effect of undermining the LTTS.

A summary of the factors which have caused or exacerbated SAA's challenges follows in table 15.2 below.

KQ's experience, however, has been very different from that of SAA. Although the airline's challenges were not much different from SAA's in its first few years as a Government-owned carrier, with it similarly poorly capitalised and being led by a Management Team which was described as "highly inexperienced," the situation became very different after its privatisation (Debrah & Toroitich, 2005).

Like SAA, KQ also had a series of other managerial problems. Over an 18-year period, from its inception in 1977 until 1995, the airline had 10 different CEOs appointed by its then sole Shareholder, the Kenyan Government. Worsening the situation was the fact that the Board was made up of "political appointees with no specific experience either in managing a business, in general, or an airline in particular," and this left the airline without any "clear strategic direction" (Debrah & Toroitich, 2005).

However, after its privatisation and listing, KQ was run more professionally as a business, with Shareholders whose only involvement was at Annual General Meetings and through the appointment of Board Members, with a Board that did not involve itself in operational matters, but which properly delegated to the CEO. KQ's listing on the Nairobi Stock Exchange (NSE) in June 1996 was described as the largest share issue in Kenya at the time, amount to 6% of the total NSE market capitalisation (Debrah & Toroitich, 2005).

While EAL's mandate was commercial from that airline's inception, KQ's was commercial from the moment of its listing.

Not only was there no PFMA equivalent with which KQ had to comply when it came to procurement and other forms of decision making, but Management also had "not just authority, but very sufficient authority to be able to chase the dream and the vision of the Shareholders and the Management of the company," as former KQ Information Technology Director Kevin Kinyanjui (2019) put it.

Kinyanjui (2019) said the Kenyan Government did not interfere at all "because they are the ones who had committed during the privatisation that the airline had to be run commercially." Instead, the Government, he said, "literally left the running of the airline to the Board and the Management."

Table 15.2: Factors which have worked against the implementation of SAA's LTTS

Factor	Effect
Under-Capitalisation	SAA was not properly capitalised and relied on Government guarantees, thus becoming heavily indebted
Dual Mandate and Different Government Expectations	The developmental mandate, which was unfunded, posed a serious challenge to SAA, which was also expected to be profitable. Also, Government Departments like Public Enterprises, Finance, Tourism, Trade and Industry as well as International Relations and Cooperation have had different expectations of SAA
PFMA	The stringent regulations of the PFMA deprived SAA of agility and resulted in prolonged decision making
Lack of Coherent Government Aviation Policy	The granting of Bilateral Air Services Agreements to foreign airlines to land in coastal cities Cape Town and Durban and to take off from there undermined both the national carrier and Johannesburg as a regional hub
Frequent Changes of Shareholder Ministers	Frequent changes of Ministers resulted in lack of continuity, with new Ministers feeling "compelled to re-invent the wheel and start afresh"
Shareholder Reluctance to Make Decisions and Honour Undertakings	Shareholder Ministers were reluctant to make politically unpopular decisions, and failed to honour their undertaking to provide SAA with the R21,7 billion funding required to turn the airline around in terms of the LTTS
Unhealthy Board Dynamics	Divisions and "endless contestations" have characterised SAA Boards, with some of its members interfering with the CEO on operational matters
Directors' Fears about Reckless Trading	SAA's financial position, with liabilities exceeding assets, worried Board Members' about being held personally liable for the carrier's reckless trading and potentially being declared Delinquent Directors
Leadership Instability	SAA has had 11 CEOs – 7 of them acting – between 2004 and 2020
Lack of Management Skills and Expertise	Interview participants spoke of "dead wood," "people who come to work so that they can go home," and "people who have been appointed and promoted because of their connections with the previous Board"
Acting Senior Executives	Leadership instability saw many Senior Executives in acting positions over extended periods, without real authority
Discordant Government Voices	Finance Minister Tito Mboweni's statement that SAA would have to be "closed down" – at a time when the Board and Management were trying to inspire confidence – caused great PR and economic damage

Source: Own Composition

Although there was no information during this study on the number of times Ministers responsible for the airlines in Kenya and Ethiopia were changed, nevertheless there was sufficient evidence that the Governments in those countries did not have the kind of direct influence on the strategies and destinies of KQ and EAL that the South African Government had on SAA. In both countries, the Governments as Shareholders were directly represented on the Boards of Directors, with their Directors having the same level of influence as their other fellow Directors.

Subsequent to its privatisation, the biggest challenge facing KQ was a consequence of its Project Mawingu. While the basis of the growth strategy was understandable, given the airline's history of commercial success since its privatisation in 1996, perhaps an argument can be made that Project Mawingu – which involved increasing the size of the KQ fleet from 42 to 115 aircraft by 2021 and increasing the airline's destinations from 58 to 117 "in 77 countries in six continents" (Amollo, 2015; Thiong'o, 2015) – was overly ambitious. However, that argument would not be sustainable.

Firstly, EAL's Vision 2025 – which "laid out a fundamental new trajectory for the company," sought to increase the number of aircraft in its fleet to 120 by 2025, to fly to 90 international destinations (Mills & Van der Merwe, 2020) and to double its target of US$5 billion in revenue to US$10 billion by 2025-30 (Oqubay & Tesfachew, 2019:4) – was just as ambitious, if not more so. Secondly, there is no telling how successful KQ would have been in implementing Project Mawingu, were there no external circumstances which impacted negatively on the airline.

In fact, Mugo (2019), Achola (2019) and Ngunze (2019) are confident that Project Mawingu would have succeeded, were it not for a series of exogenous factors over which the airline had no control. Although she was not with KQ at the time, Mugo (2019) said the Operation Mawingu plan that she saw upon joining the airline in 2015 was "actually a good project." However, "Murphy's Law happened: anything and everything that could go wrong, went wrong."

Achola (2019) said KQ experienced "shocks along the way" following its decision to embark on its growth strategy, and the airline was unable to withstand them.

He reels these off:

> *If you look at it, there were certain events. The airport (JKIA) burnt in August during peak, the peak of peaks. When the airport burns during peak, many of the people who were booked think, actually, there is no airport. There was an Ebola attack in West Africa, where we ended up stopping to operate to Freetown and Monrovia. The airline lost $50 million. There was the Westgate attack. There was the Mpeketoni attack. So, there was a series of events.*

> *Alongside that series of events, we had various aircraft entry events, because remember we had a strategy to grow. You are getting in aircraft, you are anticipating a certain level of revenue, but because of the shocks in the market, the revenues plummet. So, if you look at the first year, for example, that's when the airport burnt and, subsequently, there was the Westgate terrorist attack. Same year. That had a huge impact on the bottom line.*

The Westgate Mall terrorist attack took place in October 2013 (Howden, 2013), the fire at JKIA took place in August 2013 and the outbreak of the Ebola Virus Disease in West Africa started in February 2014 (Centers for Disease Control and Prevention, n.d.). The Mpeketoni attack, in which at least 48 people died, took place in June 2014 (BBC, 2014).

In an implied comparison of KQ's performance on Project Mawingu against EAL's performance on Vision 2025, Achola (2019) said: "Their airport didn't burn. They didn't have the Ebola issues. They never had the terrorism issues. They have way, way lower labour costs."

If there are things for which CEO Titus Naikuni and his KQ TMT could be held responsible, those would be too much confidence and failure to factor in the actions – current or future – of competitors and to anticipate or mitigate against possible exogenous factors. While KQ could not have anticipated the terrorist attacks, the Ebola Virus Disease outbreak in West Africa and the fire at JKIA, at least it should have expected how its competitors were likely to react both at the time and during the 10-year period.

That would have been consistent with British aviation analyst and advisor Chris Tarry's advice that, as a company implements its strategy, it is important for it to "take a view not only of what [its] competitors are doing now, but also of what they are likely to do by the time [it] has implemented its strategy." That means that KQ could have anticipated that both EAL and Middle Eastern carriers would have eyed its lucrative markets, particularly in West Africa.

Following the late delivery of the Boeing 787 Dreamliner aircraft that it had ordered and the facts that its rights issue had not raised the expected capital and that its operations did not generate the anticipated revenues, KQ found itself with huge debts and had to "go to the banks to borrow money to finance both [aircraft] pre-delivery payments and operations" (Achola, 2019). Kinyanjui (2019) said Operation Mawingu led to KQ flying into "very serious headwinds," with costs overrunning revenues.

Half-way into Project Mawingu, KQ reported a loss of KSh25,7 billion for the 2015 financial year, which included unrealised losses on fuel derivatives of KSh5,8 billion.

Gross profit declined from KSh18,2 billion to KSh8,2 billion, with an operating loss of KSh16,3 billion (Amollo, 2015).

Throughout this period, KQ enjoyed the full support of its Shareholders, especially KLM and the Kenyan Government. In a statement carried on its website, Kenya's National Treasury (2015) said while "poor management and investment," "un-strategic decisions" and "the buying and leasing of planes" had left KQ "highly indebted," the national flag carrier had to be saved:

> *The slogan of Kenya Airways (KQ) is "The Pride of Africa." Therefore, KQ is an important entity for this country. In the past, KQ has been an envy of the continent. It carries our national flag and identity globally. With that in mind, the national carrier must be saved from the KSh25,7 billion loss which signals imminent collapse of the airline.*
>
> *... In order to save the "Pride of Africa," the challenges which contributed to the huge loss must be known. Currently, some challenges have been pointed out. The slump in tourism did affect many sectors of the economy and Kenya Airways was not immune. It is also true that the Ebola outbreak in West Africa affected the KQ business.*

The Kenyan National Treasury (2015) said it "might be appropriate" for the airline to make a capital call on Shareholders "partly because the capital structure, holding other factors constant, is less optimal and more significantly immediate." It said the Kenyan Government – which owned 29,8% of KQ at the time – and KLM (which owned 26,7% equity at the time) would "need to consider major capital injections to rescue the airline."

That led to the launch of Operation Pride that year and the Cost Optimisation Plan (COP), with the latter known internally as Project Safari, a year later. Intended to undo or reverse the damage caused by the earlier growth strategy that was Operation Mawingu, Operation Pride was intended to "derive at least $200 million in value from increasing revenue and cutting costs." To accomplish that goal, KQ engaged the services of both McKinsey and Co. and Seabury Group as consultants (Bekele, 2016).

As part of Operation Pride, KQ reduced its fleet by almost a third, leased its Boeing 777 and 787 jetliners, agreed to lend its under-utilised pilots to Ethiopian Airways, sold its take-off and landing slot at Heathrow International Airport in London and planned to retrench 15% of its workforce (600 employees) in order to return to profitability. Mbuvi Ngunze and his team embarked on this plan with the full support of KQ's main Shareholders, the Kenyan Government and Air France-KLM (Bekele, 2016).

The COP, which was intended to "try and save the airline, without necessarily nationalising it," was about the renegotiation of KQ's debt to foreign aircraft financiers and the restructuring of KQ's debt of KSh20 billion to Kenyan banks (Mugo, 2019).

Bekele (2019) said Ngunze "sat on a very hot seat" and "found himself paying a price for some bad decisions made some years back." He said that, as part of Operation Pride, Ngunze downsized the fleet, rationalised some routes, released some aircraft and even sold the KQ slot at Heathrow International Airport.

Financial Times Correspondent John Aglionby (2016) reported in November 2016 that Ngunze's Operation Pride had begun "to bring results." He said after two years of record-breaking losses, the airline had reduced its net loss to KSh5 billion in the first half of the 2017 financial year, down from KSh12 billion in the previous year, and passenger numbers had risen from 68% to 71%.

Apart from the aforementioned exogenous factors like the terrorist attacks, the fire at JKIA and the Ebola Virus Disease outbreak in West Africa, one of its key markets, KQ's other major challenge was the radical Kenya Airline Pilots Association (KALPA), which demanded the resignation of Chairman Dennis Awori and CEO Ngunze because they were there – as Chairman and Chief Operations Officer respectively – during the implementation of Operation Mawingu. KALPA insisted that "any turnaround strategy amounts to an exercise in futility if implemented by the same management team [that] carries responsibility for the 'poor' decision-making that dragged down the airline" (Bekele, 2016).

According to former KQ Marketing Director Chris Diaz (2019), the pilots embarked on a go-slow and threatened a strike if Awori and Ngunze were not removed. He said pilots would come to work but delay the aircraft from taking off on time, or call in sick at the last minute to cause delays.

In the end, Awori resigned in October 2016, and a month later Ngunze announced that he would also step down in May 2017. However, KALPA continued to have frosty relations with the airline after the two men's resignation, with relations even becoming worse, according to Achola (2019).

Tarry (2019) observed that unions tend to be strong and even aggressive at most airlines, especially if those airlines happened to be Government owned or to have the State as a significant Shareholder. He said airlines like BA and Air France had to find ways to manage – or, as he put it, "change" – union behaviour. It follows, then, that KQ and other airlines would have to find a way of improving relations with their unions or of getting them to change their conduct.

In a strange turn of events, an airline which had done well since its privatisation in 1996 found itself in the process of being nationalised in 2020, following a decision taken by the Kenyan Parliament in June 2019 after it had rejected new CEO Sebastian Mikosz's

Privately Initiated Investment Proposal, which would have seen the airline running the profitable JKIA. Given the challenges which were experienced by KQ when it was still fully owned by the Government, most interview participants expressed legitimate concerns that the airline's nationalisation would lead to the same kind of challenges, including the possibility of Government interference.

Kenyan Parliamentary Transport Committee Chairman David Pkosing said KQ would be part of a State-owned aviation holding company with four subsidiaries, with the holding company enjoying tax concessions "for a period to be determined" and exempted from paying excise duty on all goods, including jet fuel (Reuters, 2019). That way KQ, which charges more than its competitors for tickets to the same destinations, thus "forcing price-sensitive passengers through hubs like Addis Ababa and Kigali," would be able to reduce its prices and be more competitive (Reuters, 2019).

Kenyan researcher and writer Morris Kiruga (2019) said those who looked at EAL and marvelled at what "100% Government ownership can do for you" conveniently ignored the fact that Ethiopia had "a unique culture and a unique history." He said Ethiopia had gone "the Singapore way" and given autonomy to EAL.

"We want to copy Ethiopia, but we are not looking at the kind of culture which this thing is based on, the fact that Ethiopian Airlines comes from a primarily Ethiopian perspective. The Ethiopian perspective of the world is very unique. It was just their New Year this week. Ethiopia is unique in very many ways," Kiruga (2019) cautioned.

He said if KQ's nationalisation went ahead, it would be very important to get someone who could run the airline with "full autonomy because an airline does not need Government interference; an airline does not need small, messy things like being involved in Government corruption."

Kiruga (2019) was right about Ethiopia's uniqueness. According to Ethiopian aviation journalist Kaleyesus Bekele (2019), the salaries of EAL employees are "very minimal when compared to the salaries of SAA and KQ." Bekele (2019) said EAL CEO Tewolde Gebremariam – who once gave him a lift in "a simple Toyota car" – once told him that "we don't work for a pay cheque; we have a national obligation."

Ethiopia's unique approach to its airline is best illustrated by the resistance that the EAL Management put up against interference by the Derg government, described as "a totalitarian military regime," between 1975 and 1991 following the latter's overthrow of Emperor Haile Selassie. The EAL leadership fought back valiantly against the interference by the Derg government, calling on the experience gained during its long partnership with American carrier TWA to demonstrate "corporate independence, self-reliance, ability to operate in an unconventional setting and capacity to manage and survive setbacks." EAL Management pressured Derg officials to appoint a CEO who understood the aviation industry, and they eventually succeeded (Oqubay & Tesfachew, 2019:7).

In a second act of defiance, EAL Management threatened to resign *en masse* if the Derg persisted with its demand that EAL – which had used Boeing aircraft from inception – should purchase Russian aircraft and no longer buy from the American manufacturer. Again, the Derg authorities compromised by reversing their decision, and EAL was able to introduce Boeing 767s, which enabled it to fly non-stop long-distance flights of up to 13 hours across the Atlantic Ocean. The airline also replaced its Boeing 720 aircraft with the new Boeing 737s and expanded its technical services and training facilities.

Another important act of independence was shown by the EAL leadership in 1991. When the Ethiopian People's Revolutionary Democratic Front (EPRDF) marched on Addis Ababa, "practically placing it under siege" in an effort to oust the Derg government from office, the EAL Management took a decision "to protect and save the assets of the company from damage and destruction," in the event that the conflict spilled over into the city. The EAL Top Management Team (TMT) "unilaterally decided to move EAL's aircraft to Nairobi, negotiating with the Kenya Aviation Authority to operate and service EAL's customers from Nairobi until the political tension in Ethiopia abated (Oqubay & Tesfachew, 2019:7).

"This remarkable corporate independence, commitment and responsibility," wrote Oqubay and Tesfachew (2019:7), "was only possible because of the corporate culture developed in EAL and the training and commitment of its Management."

Finally, the appointment of Polish expatriate Sebastian Mikosz to succeed Ngunze did not have the desired outcome. There was consensus among interview participants that Mikosz – who had achieved success at LOT Polish Airlines in his native country – had not managed to win over KQ employees and to advance the airline's turnaround strategy.

In an implied criticism of Mikosz and his leadership style, Kinyanjui (2019) said he foresaw "a very difficult time for the airline again until it gets what I would call the right leadership with pragmatism, being realistic but involving and getting everybody committed to rally behind the right cause." He said it was obvious, judging by "the kind of ways and noise we hear from the airline," that Mikosz and the KQ staff were "not on the same page."

Achola (2019) said although the disconnect with employees had begun earlier – when consequences were visited upon those who were not pulling their weight – and was "sort of repaired," the chasm had since widened during the Mikosz era. Therefore, there was a bigger challenge to ensure that the next KQ CEO would have to be somebody who had a different approach to managing people:

> *The next CEO, because the current CEO is leaving, has to be like an Imam or a Rabbi or a Bishop or a Pastor, whatever religion you profess. They have to*

be actually someone who will heal the soul of the airline. They have to be a people's person. They have to realise that leadership is a conversation. They have to realise that the responsibility of the leader is to create a conversation.

They have to realise that the responsibility of the leader is to create loyal followers – and loyalty is not sycophancy, in my view. Loyalty has something to do with the things I talked about, people who share vision, people who feel valued, people who are very clear about where the company is going and people who are very clear about what their role is.

Today my sense is, when I meet KQ people, none of those things I have talked about exists. When I picture it, I think Management is on its own and the troops are on their own. I don't know where the two groups are going to end, where they are going. Your guess is as good as mine.

Mugo (2019) said she did not believe that Mikosz had succeeded at KQ. She said he had come with certain expectations "and did not expect the kind of push-back that he received both internally and externally." She said that push-back also came from Members of Parliament, who had summoned Mikosz to meetings, as well as the Kenyan Government.

"A lot of things happened. I think, for him as a person, it's not a good thing that you were looking at something you expected to succeed at and you were not making any inroads," Mugo (2019) said.

A summary of the factors which have caused or exacerbated KQ's challenges follows in table 15.3 below.

Comparisons of the SAA and KQ Case Studies

As can be seen in tables 15.2 and 15.3, there were far more factors which impacted negatively on SAA's implementation of its LTTS than there were factors which had the same impact on KQ's implementation of Operation Pride. Secondly, while by far the majority of these determinants are attributable to the Shareholder and the BoD in SAA's case, in KQ's case they are largely attributable to the TMT and the BoD.

Table 15.3: Factors which have worked against KQ's implementation of Operation Pride

Factor	Effect
Project Mawingu	Serious unforeseen – and unforeseeable – exogenous factors derailed implementation of the growth strategy, which also did not take the actions of competitors into consideration
Mounting Losses and Growing Debts	Mounting losses and growing indebtedness forced KQ to turn to the Government for support and to debt restructuring, which saw owed Kenyan banks becoming reluctant shareholders
Aggressive Pilots' Union, KALPA	Pilots' go-slow led to flight delays and cancellations, and pressure led to the resignations of Chairman Dennis Awori and CEO Mbuvi Ngunze
Sebastian Mikosz's Alienation	Polish expatriate Sebastian Mikosz did not have the desired success at KQ, largely because of cultural alienation from KQ employees and push-back from politicians
Nationalisation	Privatised in 1996, KQ stood on the verge of nationalisation early in 2020, with an uncertain future

Source: Own Composition

The Shareholder is a big factor in SAA's failure to implement the LTTS or any earlier versions of turnaround strategies. It is the Shareholder that has ensured that the airline was never properly capitalised from the beginning, although the loss suffered by the airline as a result of the fuel hedge by Andre Viljoen worsened the situation. It is the Shareholder that has lumbered the airline with an unrealistic dual commercial-developmental mandate, and it is the Shareholder that has tied the hands of the carrier's TMT and BoD with the PFMA, which leaves it severely hamstrung and unable to make swift decisions in what is a very competitive market.

It is also SAA's Shareholder, in the persons of the Presidents of the Republic (in this case Presidents Jacob Zuma and Cyril Ramaphosa), who have ensured that the airline has had four Shareholder Ministers between 2017 and 2020, each of whom has had different styles in their dealings with the national airline. While some Ministers like Gigaba and Nene are said to have been more supportive of the BoD during their tenures as Finance Ministers, Gordhan was said to have been inaccessible and reluctant to make decisions which Section 54 of the PFMA entrusted to him.

It is the Shareholder Ministers who have been reluctant to make politically unpopular decisions, such as the implementation of employee retrenchments on the eve of elections, or who have taken for ever to make decisions based on the Board's resolutions or even to approve appointments recommended by the Board in terms of the aforementioned Section 54 of the PFMA.

It is the Shareholder that has concluded Bilateral Air Services Agreements which have made it possible for foreign carriers to land in and take off from Cape Town and Durban, in the process undermining both the national carrier and Johannesburg as a regional hub. It is also the Shareholder that has created a climate where a senior Cabinet Minister like Mboweni could publicly create doubt about SAA's future and, in the process, seriously undermine the airline in the market place.

It is the Shareholder that has allowed a situation to develop where, according to the SAA BRP (2007), SAA found itself unable to please anybody in Government, with "its harshest critics [being] the agencies whose constituencies use air transport – DEAT [the Department of Environmental Affairs and Tourism], DTI [the Department of Trade and Industry], Agriculture and Foreign Affairs, [which] fault SAA for offering too little capacity on too few routes."

It is because of the Shareholder's failure to honour its commitment to provide the required R21,7 billion funding to SAA, which it approved when it signed off on the LTTS, that the airline's Non-Executive Directors found themselves worried about reckless trading and dreading the possibility of being hauled before the country's courts to be declared Delinquent Directors.

That is the context in which Jarana (2019) said the Government did not want to fix SAA, and averred that "the mind of the Shareholder is the single biggest obstacle to turning around the SOCs, especially SAA."

The BoD, on the other hand, was responsible for the internal divisions, "endless contestations" (Moosa, 2019) and encroaching in operational matters (Magwaza, 2019; Malunga, 2019; Moosa, 2019). It is also various SAA Boards which have been responsible for the leadership instability (SAA has had 11 CEOs – seven of them acting – between 2004 and 2020), something which is the exact opposite of what is required during the implementation of a turnaround strategy.

Therefore, SAA Boards have created a situation where many Senior Executives have been acting over extended periods in their positions, instead of making permanent appointments. That is the phenomenon which led to Zwane (2019) referring to SAA as "the Hollywood of Kempton Park." As Malunga (2019) explained, having Acting CEOs and other Senior Executives made it easy for various SAA Boards to become operationally involved, which suggests that they deliberately did not make permanent appointments because having Acting CEOs and other Senior Executives suited them best.

Since the CEOs were themselves acting – or, if they were permanent, they were there for a relatively short time – SAA has found itself with lack of skills and expertise. Instead, the airline has had to contend with the problem of "dead wood" and "people who come to work so that they can go home," and "people who have been appointed and promoted because of their connections with the previous Board" (Bassa, 2019).

KQ, on the other hand, had far fewer challenges which impacted negatively on its ability to implement Operation Pride and other turnaround strategies. Both KQ and EAL were in the fortunate position of not having to deal with any similar challenges directly or indirectly created by their Shareholders or their Boards. On the contrary, they had Shareholders who did not interfere at all in the running of the business, and who left the running of the airlines to their appointed BoDs.

The facts that KQ was a listed company and that it had Dutch carrier KLM as a majority Shareholder are likely to have been important contributors to the independence enjoyed by the airline's BoDs and the leadership stability which has taken place over the years. Between the same period (2004-2020) when SAA has had 11 CEOs, KQ has had only three CEOs. The last one, Allan Kilavuka, was Acting CEO only for three months, between January and March 2020, and was appointed fully into the position with effect from 1 April 2020.

More importantly, while most SAA CEOs (full-time and acting) left under some cloud (first suspended and, in most cases, eventually paid out), with only Mzimela and Jarana having left on their own accord, at KQ Naikuni, Ngunze and Mikosz all left voluntarily. Although union pressure led to the departure of Naikuni and Ngunze, there is no evidence that pressure or politics from the BoD or the Shareholders forced them out.

EAL has had a strong culture of independence since its formation in 1946 through a partnership with TWA. Except during the period of political instability between 1975 and 1991, the EAL BoDs have enjoyed independence and the airline has had enviable management stability. Between 2004 and 2020, EAL has had only two CEOs, Girma Wake and Tewolde Grebremariam, both of whom were permanent in those positions. Gebremariam was Wake's Deputy from 2004, before succeeding him in January 2011, and continues to be the airline's CEO until today.

Project Mawingu – which necessitated Operation Pride in the first place – had by far the biggest impact on KQ. In particular, it was exogenous factors – in the form of a series of acts of terrorism, a fire at JKIA and the Ebola Virus Disease outbreak in West Africa – which had a terrible effect on KQ's implementation of that growth strategy. The impact of those factors is incomparable to any other oversight or "strategic failure" (Achola, 2019) on the part of the KQ leadership team.

While an argument can be made that KQ may not have sufficiently considered current and future actions of its competitors as it embarked on the ambitious Project Mawingu, there is a good chance that the airline would have achieved many of its targets if the aforementioned exogenous factors had not materialised. Neighbouring EAL, which was not as strong as KQ in the market in 2010 (Bekele, 2019), managed to exceed its targets for Vision 2025 long before that date.

Secondly, the mounting losses and growing debts which were a consequence of Project Mawingu had a major impact on KQ's implementation of Operation Pride. In the end, they forced KQ not only to embark on the COP, but also to turn to the Kenyan Government for recapitalisation. The latter applied pressure on Kenyan banks from which KQ had taken loans to convert their loans into equity, which was something to which they eventually agreed reluctantly after the Government had undertaken to guarantee their loans.

Thirdly, the growing aggressiveness of KQ unions, in particular KALPA, made it difficult for Management to focus on turning the airline around. Not only did KALPA force Awori and Ngunze to resign as Chairman and CEO respectively, but it has also protested against the airline's plans to employ foreign pilots – at a time when the airline has a shortage of pilots. Instead, KALPA, which has complained that its members are over-worked, has insisted on only Kenyan pilots being employed.

Fourthly, while it may have made sense to employ Mikosz as Ngunze's successor on the strength of his achievements at LOT Polish Airlines, the former appears to have been guilty of a few missteps. His first error of judgment was bringing along with him five compatriots with whom he had worked at LOT Airlines. That decision, early on in his tenure, sent through a message – perhaps unintentionally – that he had no confidence in the Kenyan Executives who had run the airline with Ngunze and Naikuni. It led to the immediate resignation, four months into his tenure, of four senior KQ Executives – among them Kinyanjui – and set Mikosz against KQ employees.

Mikosz also seems to have made little or no effort to understand Kenyans and the way they did things. Instead, he complained publicly, in his fourth month in the job, about "a serious lack of trust, which makes delegation of duties very hard" and stated – somewhat insensitively – that "there is no African way of doing things; there is a good way of doing things or a bad way of doing things" (Wafula, 2017).

Perhaps unsurprisingly, Mikosz subsequently received resistance from KQ staff and a push-back from the country's politicians (Mugo, 2019).

It was also strange that a man who was employed to turn the airline around ended up becoming the agent for its nationalisation. It was Mikosz's Privately Initiated Investment Proposal, which would have seen the private airline running the public JKIA, which the Kenyan Parliament's Transport Committee seized upon to recommend the carrier's nationalisation. Mikosz's legacy, then, looks certain to be the reversal of the 1996 decision to privatise KQ.

The decision to appoint Kilavuka, a Kenyan who was CEO of KQ's low-cost carrier JamboJet, as Mikosz's successor suggests that the KQ BoD may have regretted the decision to replace Ngunze with a European expatriate.

Ultimately, the future of a nationalised KQ remains unknown. It remains to be seen if the airline will be allowed – like EAL – to operate autonomously, with a supportive Government which maintains a hands-off approach, or if the Government will again interfere in the way in which it used to do before the airline's privatisation.

So, while SAA's challenges were overwhelmingly attributable to Shareholder disposition and the BoD, KQ's were largely a consequence of unforeseen and unforeseeable exogenous factors.

Chapter Sixteen

A FRAMEWORK FOR SUCCESSFUL IMPLEMENTATION OF TURNAROUND STRATEGIES

From the preceding chapter, it is clear that South African Airways (SAA) had far more factors which impacted negatively on its ability to implement its various turnaround strategies – but particularly the Long-Term Turnaround Strategy (LTTS) – than Kenya Airways (KQ) did. The airline appears to have been expected to implement a turnaround strategy in a hostile environment which actively worked against the implementation of the self-same strategy.

KQ, however, found itself in a very different situation. It found itself in an enabling environment where the Top Management Team (TMT) and the Board of Directors (BoD) could take and implement decisions unhindered. While an argument could be made that KQ enjoyed that level of freedom because it was privately owned, the fact remains that Ethiopian Airlines (EAL) had as much operational autonomy as KQ had, even though it – like SAA – is fully Government owned.

As Oqubay and Tesfachew (2019) indicated, even during the difficult years of the Derg regime in Ethiopia, EAL was "always regarded as a flagship State enterprise with unofficial corporate independence." While Government ownership provided EAL with "stability, growth opportunities and the ability to pursue a long-term strategy rather than short-term profitability" (Oqubay & Tesfaschew, 2019), in SAA's case Government ownership has had the opposite effect.

The difference, as Fuzile Lungisa (2019), former Director-General in the Department of Finance stated, is politics. He said while some in Government wanted "to do the right things, politically doing the right may be suicidal for them" because of not only the ideological differences within the governing ANC, but also the organisation's alliance with COSATU and the SACP.

Oqubay and Tesfachew (2019:11) said the Ethiopian Government's inability to subsidise EAL made the airline more disciplined "to ensure fiscal responsibility." It would seem that the knowledge that the Government would not be able to come to the airline's financial rescue – what Tarry (2019) called "precipice management" – was always uppermost in the minds of the EAL leadership, which realised that there was no big brother waiting in the wings to save the airline if it failed to perform.

More importantly, Oqubay and Tesfachew (2019:11) concluded – correctly – that EAL's success "defies the notions that ownership determines performance and that public ownership is inferior to private [ownership]." They point out that EAL performed "considerably better than many privately-owned airlines" because of the advantages of "long-term strategic orientation rather than short-term profit orientation dominant in the Anglo-Saxon corporate world."

Tarry (2019) also argued that while State-owned carriers have "a different base, the reality is there is no reason why, from a financial performance point of view or whatever, a State-owned airline should have different objectives from a privately-owned airline."

It follows, then, that it is not Government ownership *per se* that has impacted negatively on SAA's ability to implement its turnaround strategies successfully. Instead, it has been the Government's disposition, as a Shareholder, to the airline which has had a damaging effect. It would appear that, instead of acknowledging that, unlike other State-owned companies (SOC) that provide a public good and are monopolies, SAA is in a fiercely competitive market, the Shareholder treated the airline no differently from the way it treats other SOCs, in the process suffocating it with a burdensome developmental mandate and bureaucratic legislation like the Public Finance Management Act (PFMA), which robbed it of much-needed agility.

As Oqubay and Tesfachew (2019:11) put it: "The capital intensity of the industry makes operating at full capacity critical and sustaining creditworthiness a precondition for survival and growth. Intense international competition, which leaves no room for inefficiency, further increases pressure for learning."

A poorly capitalised SAA which was not a going concern throughout the period of the implementation of the LTTS had anything but creditworthiness and had to contend with a lot of inefficiencies, including when it came to decision making. Instead, SAA found itself in a situation where decision making was laborious and took months, in an industry were agility and fleet-footedness are required.

At a time when SAA needed to "shrink, survive, grow and prosper," in that order, in the words of Tarry (2019), the airline could not proceed to reduce its staff numbers and sell non-core assets, but had to await permission from the Shareholder – which was not forthcoming. Consequently, political considerations often trumped commercial logic.

Three theoretical propositions guided this research. These placed tentative limits on the scope of the study to increase the feasibility of completing the research in the time available to the researcher (Baxter & Jack, 2008:551).

Baxter and Jack (2008), who likened propositions to hypotheses in quantitative research methodology, argued that both make an educated guess about the possible outcomes of the experiment or research in question. They said addressing the propositions during the report phase of the research ensures that the report stays focused and answers the research question.

Yin (2014) contended that while both the propositions and the unit of analysis may still be reviewed or updated in the course of a study, their presence in case study research increases the chances of that study remaining "within feasible limits."

The theoretical propositions used to guide this research were the following:

- A supportive Shareholder that leaves a capable, empowered Management Team to run a company under the direction of a similarly supportive Board of Directors increases the chances of a company's success in implementing turnaround strategies;
- Organisational stability at top leadership level increases the chances of success in implementing turnaround strategies; and
- Clarity on decision rights and accountability within an organisation increases the chances of success in implementing a company's turnaround strategies.

It was expected that this study would show that lack of stability at top leadership level within a company, dominant Shareholders and Boards of Directors that flout good corporate governance by involving themselves in operational business matters, and lack of clarity regarding decision rights impact negatively on the implementation and outcome of turnaround strategies. It was expected further that the extent to which these constructs impact on the outcome of turnaround strategies at the two airlines would differ based on their ownership structures, given the fact that SAA is a public enterprise fully owned by the South African Government, while KQ was a listed, privately-owned airline in which the Kenyan Government was a significant Shareholder.

The conceptual framework used for this study, as advocated by Miles and Huberman (1994), is shown in figure 16.1 below. It indicated that the "presumed relationship" – in the words of Miles and Huberman (1994) – among the three constructs and the outcome of turnaround strategies would be one that would reveal that:

- Companies with supportive Shareholders and Boards which adopt a hands-off relationship, which enjoy organisational stability and in which there is clarity regarding decision rights are likely to be more successful in the implementation of their chosen turnaround strategies; and that, conversely

- Companies with intrusive/meddlesome Shareholders and Boards, frequent changes in top management and unclear decision rights are likely to fail or be unsuccessful in the implementation of their chosen turnaround strategies.

From a corporate governance perspective, the theoretical framework is best illustrated in figure 16.2 below.

The findings of this research revealed that:

- SAA did not have a supportive Shareholder, a supportive BoD or an empowered Management Team, while KQ and EAL did;
- SAA – which had 11 CEOs (seven of them acting) between 2004 and 2020 – did not enjoy stability at top leadership level, while KQ did until 2017 (and EAL did since 2004 when Girma Wake was appointed CEO and Tewolde Gebremariam was appointed Deputy CEO); and
- There was no clarity on decision rights and accountability at SAA, where there was an on-going tussle between the BoD and the Shareholder, while there was clarity on both issues at KQ and at EAL.

Figure 16.1: Study's Conceptual Framework

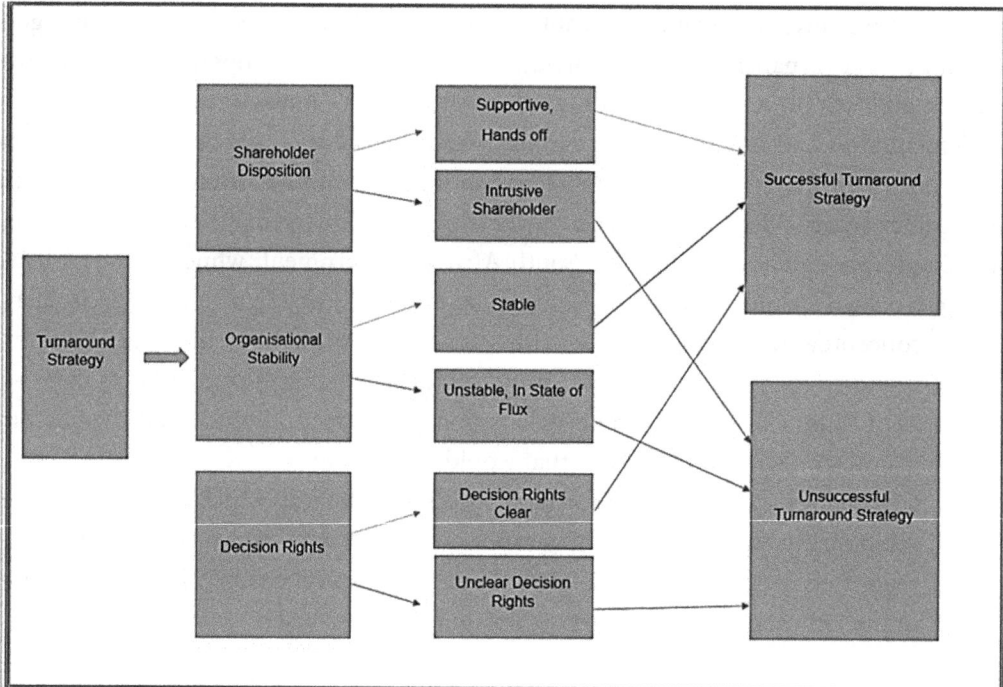

Source: Own Composition

Therefore, in accordance with the conceptual framework given above, the research findings indicated that SAA was likely to be unsuccessful in the implementation of its turnaround strategy – as, indeed, it was. In fact, no determinants of a possible successful implementation of a turnaround strategy could be found at SAA, where far too many factors worked against the airline's leadership.

These findings are shown in figure 16.3 below in the form of the chosen conceptual framework.

Figure 16.2: A Governance-Strategic Leadership Model for Turnaround Strategy Implementation

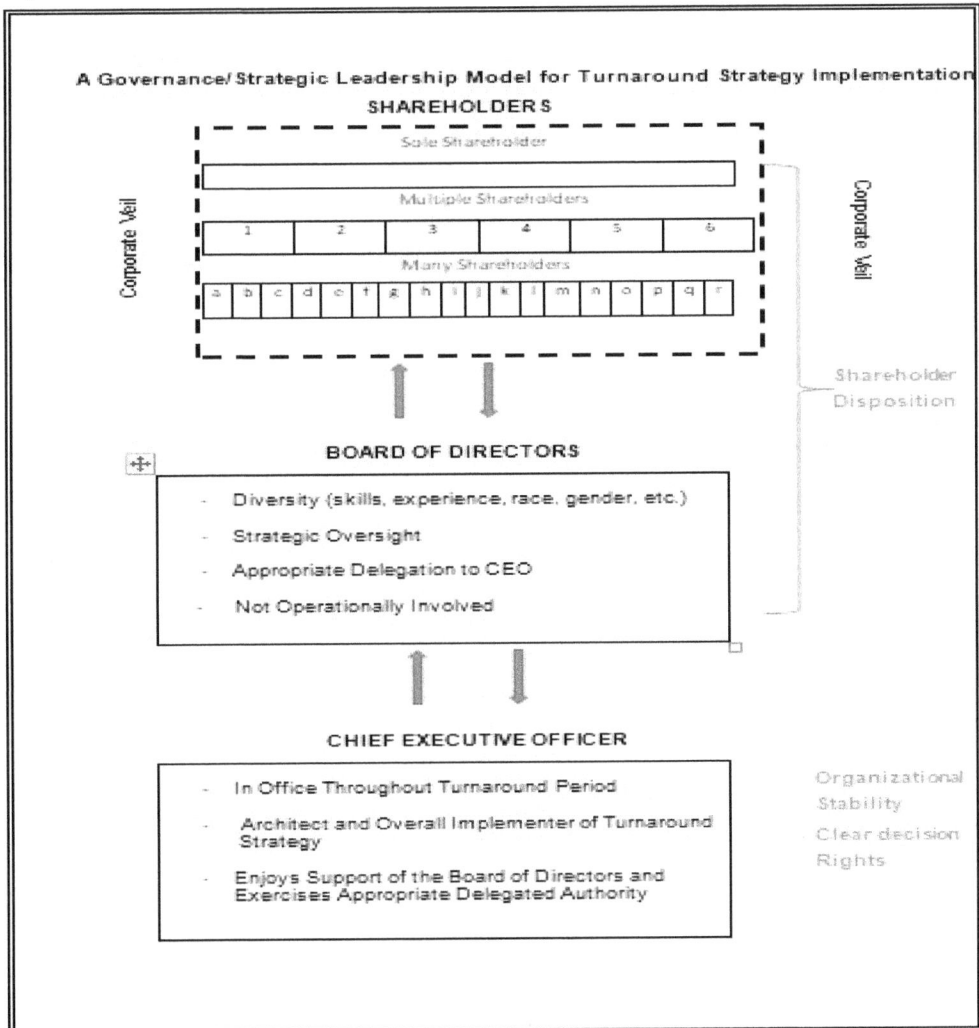

Source: Own Composition

Viewed against the background of the same conceptual framework, the findings indicate that KQ was likely to be successful in the implementation of its turnaround strategy. However, the airline was half-successful in the implementation of Operation Pride: while it managed to reduce costs considerably and to generate sufficient revenue to be operationally profitable, the enormity of the debts incurred during Project Mawingu saw the airline recording huge losses during the period covered in this research. In the end, Operation Pride alone was not enough and was soon followed by the Cost Optimisation Plan (COP)/Project Safari, which successfully restructured the airline's US$2 billion debt into equity.

However, Operation Pride was still going during the course of 2020 and the airline was in the process of being nationalised. While Operation Pride was half a success, that was attributable more to the enormity of the debt incurred during Project Mawingu, and was not a result of any of the three constructs used in this study. It is notable, however, that while Titus Naikuni successfully saw the Kenya Airways Turnaround Plan (KATAP) to its end, Mbuvi Ngunze resigned just as Operation Pride was beginning to make an operational difference, but remained on a contractual basis to see the COP to an end.

These findings are shown on the next page in figure 16.4 in the form of the chosen conceptual framework.

Based on the research on the two case studies, the emerging framework for a successful implementation of a turnaround strategy comes from the corollary to the findings on SAA's poor implementation of its LTTS.

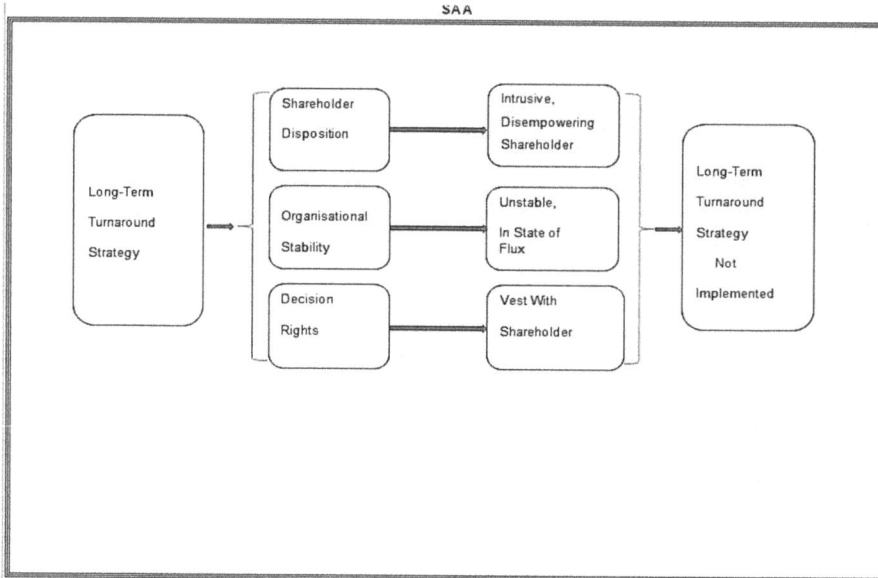

Figure 16.3: Implementation of SAA's LTTS
Source: Own Composition

Figure16.4: Implementation of KQ's Operation Pride and Project Safari

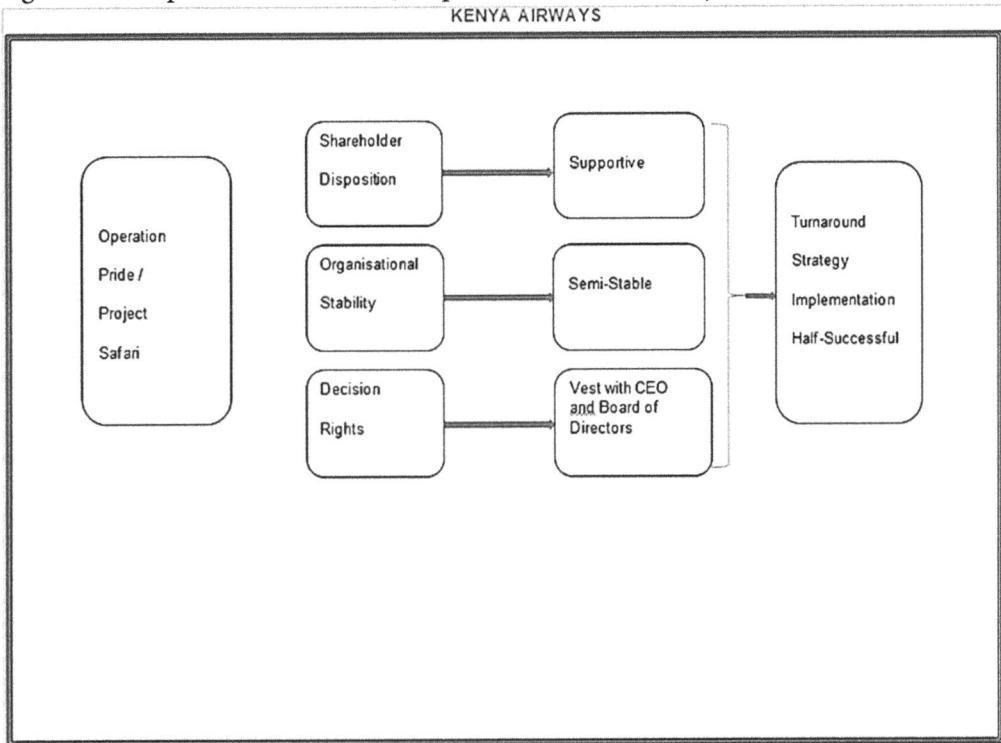

KENYA AIRWAYS

Source: Own Composition

There are eight indispensable elements of this framework, namely:

1) Firstly, a company or organisation must have leadership stability, with a CEO and a Management Team with the requisite skills and expertise. Organisational stability is a *sine qua non*. It is vital that a CEO who introduces or drives a turnaround strategy remains in office throughout its implementation. Examples are Naikuni at KQ, who had success with KATAP, and Wake and Grebremariam at EAL with Vision 2010 and Vision 2025 respectively.

2) Secondly, a CEO implementing a turnaround strategy must own that strategy. This is consistent with Bibeault's (1999:149-50) view that a turnaround leader should be "the architect of the turnaround strategy" and its implementer. If s/he was not party to that strategy's development, it is important that s/he must have an opportunity to review and/or tweak it accordingly and then own it. A CEO has a better chance of successfully implementing a turnaround strategy which s/he believes in and has ownership of.

3) The turnaround strategy must be realistic and implementable. It must speak to the direct conditions in which the company finds itself at the time, and not be "good academic papers but lack gravity," as SAA Chairman JB Magwaza (2019) put it.

4) A company implementing a turnaround strategy must be mindful of competitors' current and future actions and/or responses and be alive to possible exogenous factors and have sound mitigation plans. While it was not different from EAL's Vision 2010, the main shortfall of KQ's Project Mawingu was the series of external events over which KQ had no control, together with the actions of competitors like EAL and Middle Eastern carriers.

5) A turnaround strategy should have the buy-in and full support of all key stakeholders, especially the TMT, the Board of Directors and the Shareholders, with commitment from each to honour their respective undertakings. The main shortfall of SAA's LTTS was the Shareholder's failure to honour its commitment to provide the funding necessary to implement the turnaround strategy.

6) Adherence to good corporate governance is paramount, with the BoD responsible for strategic oversight and the CEO with the TMT responsible for operations. It is vital that the CEO should have full operational autonomy, as Wake and Gebremariam did at EAL and Naikuni and Ngunze did at KQ (although Ngunze said there were some moments when he experienced Board interference).

7) There should be a turnaround implementation fund. As Tarry (2019) argued, a turnaround "needs cash and a lot of management time and a reasonable expectation." Such a fund is vital to ensure the success of a turnaround strategy implementation.

8) Finally, there should be Government policy/regulatory coherence. In addition to its "unofficial corporate independence," management discipline and financial prudence, EAL's success is also attributable to the fact that aviation policy in Ethiopia has been supportive of the airline, unlike in South Africa and, to some extent, Kenya, where landing rights were liberally given to foreign airlines which have offered fierce competition to SAA and KQ respectively. In South Africa's case, the granting of Cabotage rights to British Airways, following its partnership with Comair, and of rights to foreign airlines to land in and take off from Cape Town and Durban has significantly undermined both SAA and Johannesburg as a regional aviation hub.

Government policy/regulatory coherence is vital not only for SOCs, but for all companies in the different sectors of the economy. Knowing the rules applicable to business or a sector of the economy and being certain that they will not change willy-nilly during the implementation of a turnaround strategy, but will be enforced consistently is vital for business in general, and not only SOCs. Policy coherence and its consistent application make long-term planning possible.

The framework is shown in figure 16.5 below.

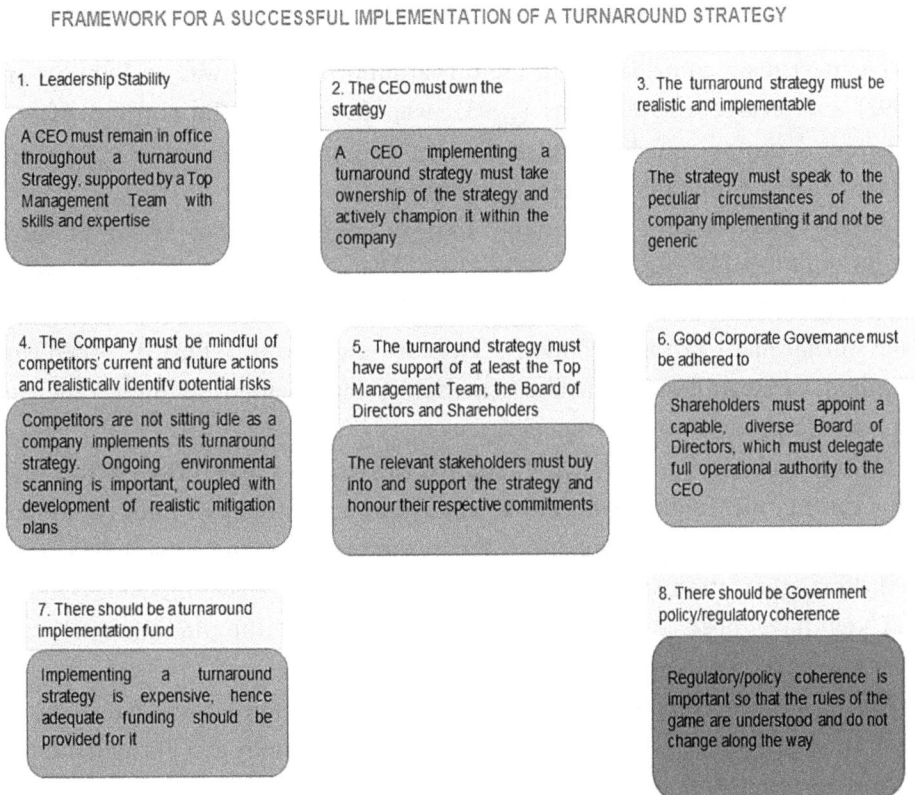

FRAMEWORK FOR A SUCCESSFUL IMPLEMENTATION OF A TURNAROUND STRATEGY

1. Leadership Stability

A CEO must remain in office throughout a turnaround Strategy, supported by a Top Management Team with skills and expertise

2. The CEO must own the strategy

A CEO implementing a turnaround strategy must take ownership of the strategy and actively champion it within the company

3. The turnaround strategy must be realistic and implementable

The strategy must speak to the peculiar circumstances of the company implementing it and not be generic

4. The Company must be mindful of competitors' current and future actions and realistically identify potential risks

Competitors are not sitting idle as a company implements its turnaround strategy. Ongoing environmental scanning is important, coupled with development of realistic mitigation plans

5. The turnaround strategy must have support of at least the Top Management Team, the Board of Directors and Shareholders

The relevant stakeholders must buy into and support the strategy and honour their respective commitments

6. Good Corporate Governance must be adhered to

Shareholders must appoint a capable, diverse Board of Directors, which must delegate full operational authority to the CEO

7. There should be a turnaround implementation fund

Implementing a turnaround strategy is expensive, hence adequate funding should be provided for it

8. There should be Government policy/regulatory coherence

Regulatory/policy coherence is important so that the rules of the game are understood and do not change along the way

Figure 16.5: Framework for a Successful Implementation of a Turnaround Strategy
Source: Own Composition

Relationship of the Current Study to Previous Research

Although a considerable amount of research has been conducted on turnaround strategies since Schendel and Parton's (1976) ground-breaking work on corporate stagnation and turnaround, much of that work has focused on elements of turnaround strategies and companies' application of those turnaround strategies. Early turnaround scholars Hofer (1980) and Bibeault (1982) distinguished between operational and strategic turnarounds, with the latter identifying three turnaround stages: an emergency stage, a stabilisation stage and a return-to-growth or redevelopment stage. Grinyer and McKiernan (1988) contributed the concept of sharp-bend performance.

The next main contribution in the turnaround literature was by Robbins and Pearce (1992) and Pearce and Robbins (1993), who introduced the concept of a two-stage turnaround process involving retrenchment and entrepreneurial re-orientation, which has remained a dominant view in the literature.

Boyne (2004) studied turnaround strategy implementation in the public sector in Britain and contributed the concept of "3Rs" – retrenchment, repositioning and recognition – to the body of knowledge. Building on Pearce and Robbins's (1993) two-stage turnaround process, Trahms, Ndofor and Sirmon (2013) added managerial cognition, strategic leadership and stakeholder management as important elements in implementing a turnaround strategy.

O'Kane and Cunningham (2014) studied the tensions which exist within a leadership team during the implementation of a turnaround strategy, while Dimopoulos and Wagner (2016) focused on the effect that corporate governance and CEO turnover have on the implementation of a turnaround strategy.

These have been the dominant contributions in the literature on turnaround strategies, as shown in figure 16.6 below.

Much of the research that has been conducted since then has focused on the application of one or another aspect of a turnaround strategy at a particular company and the kind of results that it has produced. Some research has sought to replicate one of these turnaround theories in some particular context.

According to O'Kane and Cunningham (2014:966), corporate turnaround is an area of academic study where "theory is nascent or immature." They contend that a study which includes an assessment of the management of key activities and tensions by turnaround leaders in companies with different ownership structures (family run, publicly owned or State owned) would be beneficial.

TURNAROND STRATEGY LITERATURE REVIEW

Schendel & Parton (1976)
- Corporate Stagnation and turnaround
- Corporate turnaround strategies

Hofer (1980)
- Operational and Strategic Turnarounds

Bibeault (1982)
- Operational and Strategic Turnaround
- Three Main Turnaround Stages:
- Emergency Stage
- Stabilization Stage
- Return-to-Growth/Redevelopment Stage

Grinyer & McKieman (1988)
- Sharpbend performance

Robbins & Pearce (1992-3)
Two-stage turnaround process:
- Retrenchment & Entrepreneurial Reorientation
- Successful turnarounds begin with sustained retrenchment responses

Arogyaswamy, Barker & Yasai-Ardekani (1995)
- Decline-stemming strategies
- Recovery Strategies

Boyne (2004)
"3Rs" for Public Service Turnaround
- Retrenchment
- Repositioning
- Reorganisation

Trahms, Ndofor & Sirmon (2013)
Managerial Cognition, Strategic Leadership and Stakeholder Management

O'Kane & Cunningham (2014)
Turnaround leadership core tensions

Demopoulos & Wagner (2016)
Corporate Governance and CEO Turnover

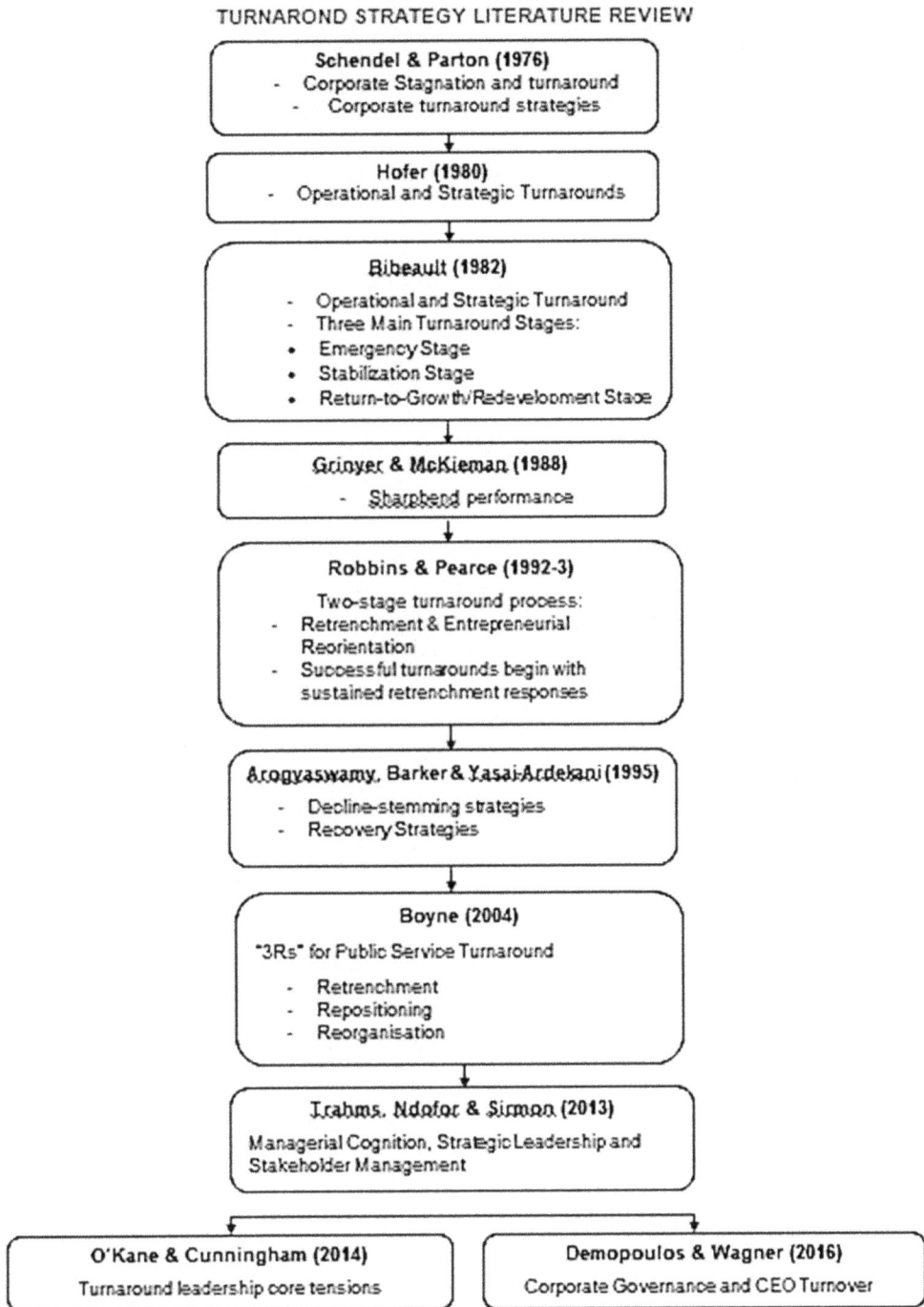

Figure 16.6: Dominant Schools in Turnaround Strategy Literature

Source: Own Composition

Schoenberg, Collier and Bowman (2013) reviewed literature that included 22 empirical studies which had investigated business turnaround strategies completed during recessionary periods from the mid-1970s to the early 1990s, and which was based on turnaround and recovery strategies used by almost 1 300 companies. They found that there was a great deal of convergence in the conclusions of those studies.

Schoenberg *et al.* (2013) found that the literature identified six predominant turnaround strategies as being effective, with four of them related to the main objectives of the strategy and the other two related to change processes necessary for the implementation of turnaround strategies.

In their conclusion, Schoenberg *et al.* (2013) remarked that they were unaware of any research on turnaround strategies that was conducted outside of Europe and the Americas. They argued that this presented an opportunity for future studies to identify turnaround strategies that are effective in different cultural contexts and to establish the reasons for the success or otherwise of individual strategies in those circumstances.

Trahms *et al.* (2013:1297) said a lot more remains unknown or understudied when it comes to organisational decline and turnaround compared to what is known, and expressed the view that a study that includes an assessment of the impact that strategic leadership, stakeholder management and resource orchestration plays in the turnaround process would be helpful.

To the extent that this research revealed considerable leadership tensions at SAA (within the TMT and the BoD respectively and between the two structures, as well as between these BoD and the TMT on the one said and the Shareholder on the other side), it has built on the work done by both O'Kane and Cunningham (2014) and Dimopoulos and Wagner (2016). However, this research covered new ground by establishing, among other things, how and why Shareholder disposition impacts on the implementation of a turnaround strategy.

This study has sought to fill the gap in the knowledge, as identified by Schoenberg *et al.* (2013), that there was no research on turnaround strategies conducted outside of Europe and the Americas.

Contribution to the Body of Knowledge

This study, which sought to develop a framework for a successful implementation of a turnaround strategy in African business, particularly in the aviation sector (with SAA and KQ as case studies), breaks new ground and, therefore, makes new contribution to the body of knowledge. By focusing on the development of a framework for a successful implementation of a turnaround strategy, based on the findings of the research into the aforementioned case studies, rather than seeking to establish which form the implementation of the turnaround strategies at the two airlines took, this research makes new contribution to the body of knowledge.

Another area in which the study makes a unique contribution to the body of knowledge on turnaround strategies is in its findings on the debilitating role played by power dynamics and political interests in the implementation of SAA's turnaround strategy. The study revealed that, where the State is the only Shareholder or a majority Shareholder, there is a direct correlation between the degree of political maturity in that country and the degree to which the Government seeks to involve itself – and even to interfere – in the running of a State-owned company.

That level of political adventurism was particularly acute in South Africa, where the governing ANC had taken over just over two decades earlier from a racial minority and regarded SOCs as strategic instruments for control, transformation, advancement of an ill-defined developmental agenda and direct involvement in the economy. The study established that there was a sense in which the post-apartheid Government regarded SAA and other SOCs as strategic spoils of conquest or war which had to be repurposed and squeezed for maximum political – and sometimes personal – benefit. This was exacerbated by internal divisions within the governing party and its tripartite alliance, which led to Boards of SOCs like SAA being yet another site for factional contestation.

With the governing ANC ideologically committed to the State's centrality in the economy, SOCs are expected not only to advance transformation, but also to play a leading role in the economy. Not even SAA, which operates in a very competitive environment, was exempted from this role.

That explains why a growing number of SOCs in South Africa have been implementing various turnaround strategies over the past few years which have not borne much – if any – success.

In the first decade of its existence (and Kenya's second decade of independence), KQ faced similar challenges to SAA. Things changed for that airline following its privatisation which was forced by the Structural Adjustment Programme (SAP) as a result of heavy indebtedness.

Ethiopia, which was never colonised, did not experience post-independence exuberance and was very measured in its approach to its airline, which was run along business lines from its inception, thanks to the partnership struck with American airline TWA. From inception, the Ethiopian Government allowed EAL "corporate independence," which served the airline well even during the difficult years of the Derg administration.

Another area in which this study makes a meaningful contribution to the body of knowledge is in the implementation of turnaround strategies at State-owned companies.

The vast majority of the research done into turnaround strategies has focused predominantly on private-sector businesses, with work which has been done on the public sector by scholars like Paton and Mordaunt (2004), Boyne (2004) and Walshe *et al.* (2010) in the United Kingdom and Ravaghi, Mannion and Sajadi (2017) in Iran having focused on public services like health, education and local government. Even then, much of that work has focused on the type of turnaround strategies used and the results that they have produced, and not on determinants of a successful implementation of a turnaround strategy or the development of a framework for a successful implementation of a turnaround strategy.

This study contributes to the body of knowledge on turnaround strategies, especially in the context of African businesses (one of which is State owned and the other privately owned) and improves the chances of a successful implementation of turnaround strategies in African airlines by practitioners. In particular, it establishes what determinants contribute towards or detract from the successful implementation of a turnaround strategy.

In addition to contributing to the body of knowledge on turnaround strategies, this study should also be helpful to African researchers and practitioners on strategy in general and turnaround strategies in particular. Apart from its theoretical contribution to the body of knowledge, it is expected that the study will prove to be of crucial practical importance to the Government of South Africa as it seeks to oversee the successful turnaround of financially ailing State-owned companies like SAA, Transnet, the South African Broadcasting Corporation, the Public Rail Agency of South Africa, Denel, PetroSA, etc. through Shareholder Ministries like the Departments of Finance, Public Enterprises, Communications, Transport, Energy and the many others which have State-owned enterprises reporting to them.

Similarly, this study is also likely to be of interest to the Kenyan Government, should it go ahead with its plans to nationalise Kenya Airlines.

From the study, it is evident that SAA – whose business rescue process had just been approved by SAA debtors and relevant stakeholders at the time of writing – is unlikely ever to be turned around successfully for as long as it is fully owned by the Government and there is no coherence in the Government's aviation policy. In order to improve the chances of the airline's survival, it would be imperative for a strategic equity partner or partners (SEP) to be brought on board, and that progress is made in the Whole-of-State approach to aviation mentioned by both former Public Enterprises and former Finance Minister Malusi Gigaba (2019) and former Department of Public Enterprises Deputy Director-General Matsietsi Mokholo (2019) during the respective interviews with them. The quantum of the SEP's shareholding will have to be such that it or they will be able to exercise considerable power through their representation on the BoD.

Finally, SAA – whether the current reincarnation or its new version – cannot possibly succeed in what is a hyper-competitive industry for as long as it is subjected to the suffocating influence of the PFMA.

Conclusion

The SAA brand is damaged almost irreparably. It will take an aggressive marketing campaign over a sustained period, accompanied by reliable performance when it comes to on-time departures and arrivals, for the airline to win decent market share and restore the great reputation that it once had. The challenge is worsened by the entry into the market of Lift Airlines and SAA's delayed return to the market after the resumption of flights following the total shutdown of South Africa's air space when the Coronavirus pandemic first hit the country in March 2020.

To accomplish that goal, a lot of money will need to be spent on marketing. This is particularly because SAA has become a laughing stock to many in the media and in politics, who routinely – and legitimately – single it out as one State-owned company which should have been sold or allowed to fail, instead of repeatedly gobbling up much-needed resources which should have been channelled to important social services like health and education, among others.

Once a very popular Cabinet Minister when he was in charge of the country's finances, Pravin Gordhan has grown increasingly unpopular in the media and among his political rivals because of his dogged backing of the national carrier. For continuing to fund SAA, he and Finance Minister Tito Mboweni get accused of "subsidising the rich instead of the poor." While that argument is motivated more by the need to score some political points, it is certain to be damaging not only to the two Ministers concerned if SAA continues to be reliant on bailouts, but also on the Government as a whole. The shocking evidence of corruption and ineptitude led before the Commission of Inquity into State Capture has also damaged the SAA brand to the general public, from which the airline draws its passengers.

With the Government heavily in debt and no longer able to bail SAA out whenever the airline comes with a begging bowl, it will be important that the strategic equity partner which is expected to come to the airline's rescure has deep pockets. For that partner to pour money into SAA, it is likely to insist on a meaningful say in the running of the airline, with some guarantee that the Government will become more of a passive Shareholder, as is the case at Telkom.

Meanwhile, while KQ – which is fortunate to have the unstinting support of the Kenyan Government – is certain to survive the tough times through which it has gone since 2015, it remains to be seen what its future as a nationalised airline holds. The extent to which it will succeed will depend heavily on the the Kenyan Government's predisposition as a Shareholder.

On the other hand, EAL, which enjoys "unofficial corporate independence" (Oqubay & Tesfachew, 2019), looks certain to continue to dominate the African skies and to be this continent's major representative in international aviation.

REFERENCES

- Abate, M. (2013). *The economic effects of progressive air transport liberalisation in Africa: The case of city-pair routes to or from Addis Ababa.* (Unpublished Master's Dissertation). Addis Ababa University, Addis Ababa, Ethiopia.

- Abebe, M.A. (2012). Executive attention patterns, environmental dynamism and corporate turnaround performance. *Leadership & Organization Development Journal*, 33(7), pp. 684-701. Available at: https://doi.10.1108/01437731211265250.

- Achola, T.O. (2019, September 17). Interview. [Transcript]

- Africa Aviation (2020, April 27). Former Kenya Airways CEO Joins IATA. Voyages Afriq. Available at: https://voyagesafriq.com/2020/04/27/former-kenya-airways-ceo-joins-iata/

- Africa Facts (c.2017). Top 10 Best Airlines in Africa, [Online]. Available at: https://africa-facts.org/top-10-best-airlines-in-africa/

- Aglionby, J. (2016). "Kenya Airways records country's worst ever loss." [Online] 21 July. Available on: https://www.ft.com/content/006aacfe-4f44-11e6-8172-e39ecd3b86fc

- Aglionby, J. (2016, October 26). Awori resigns as Kenya Airways chairman. *Financial Times.* Available at: https://www.ft.com/content/bcf6e0e6-3c7e-3da7-8acc-d65ae5fd2704

- Aglionby, John. (2016 November 24). Kenya Airways chief executive steps. *Financial Times.* Available at: https://www.ft.com/content/bed46be0-b24e-11e6-a37c-f4a01f1b0fa1

- Aglionby, John. (2017, May 4). Kenya Airways hires new CEO from Lot after huge losses. *Financial Times.* Available at: https://www.ft.com/content/7b49396b-bd05-3d7d-a6c9-98b791a07a13

- Alderighi, M., Cento, A; Nijkamp, P. and Rietveld, P. (2012). Competition in the European aviation market: the entry of low-cost airlines. J. Transp. Geogr. 24, pp. 223-233.

- Amadala, Victor (2019, December 19). *The Star*, 19 December 2019. KQ to sink further in losses despite multi-billion restructuring. Available at: https://www.the-star.co.ke/business/2019-12-19-kq-to-sink-further-in-losses-despite-multi-billion-restructuring/

- Amollo, B.A. (2015). Mawingu Project Quality and Risk Management. Available at: https://www.academia.edu/27407935/MAWINGU_PROJECT_QUALITY_AND_RISKM ANAGEMENT

- Arogyaswamy, K., Barker, V.L. & Yasai-Ardekani, M. (1995). Firm turnarounds: An integrated two-stage model. *Journal of Management Studies,* 32 (4), 493-525. Available from: https://doi.org/10.1111/j.1467-6486.1995.tb00786.x

- Associated Press. (2013, August 7). Fire forces closure of Kenya's main airport. *The Guardian*. [Online]. Available at: https://www.theguardian.com/world/2013/aug/07/kenya-airport-fire-forces-closure

- Back, G. (2019, May 15). Interview. [Transcript]

- Balgobin, R. & Pandit, N. (2001). Stages in the turnaround process: The case of IBM UK. *European Management Journal*, 19(3), 301-316. Available from: https://doi.org/10.1016/S0263-2373(01)00027-5

- Barrett, S.D. (2006). Commercialising a national airline – the Aer Lingus case study. *Journal of Air Traffic Management*, 12, pp. 159-167. Available at: doi:10.1016/j.jairtraman.2005.11.001

- Barron, C. (2019, June 2). Any SOE's success begins with the board. *Sunday Times Business Times*, p.7.

- Barron, C, (2020, September 6). Political meddling clips SAA's wings. *Sunday Times Business Times*, p.6.

- Bassa, A. (2019, April 23). Interview. [Transcript]

- Baxter, P. and Jack, S. (2008). Qualitative Case Study Methodology: Study Design and Implementation for Novice Researchers. *The Qualitative Report*, 13(4), pp. 544-559. Available at: https://nsuworks.nova.edu/tqr/vol13/iss4/2

- Bekele, K. (2016). "Turmoil At Kenya Airways Reaches Climax." [Online]. 10 May. Available at: https://www.ainonline.com/aviation-news/air-transport/2016-05-10/turmoil-kenya-airways-reaches-climax

- Bekele, K. (2016, May 10). Turmoil At Kenya Airways Reaches Climax. *Aviation International News* [Online]. Available at: https://www.ainonline.com/aviation-news/air-transport/2016-05-10/turmoil-kenya-airways-reaches-climax

- Bekele, Kaleyesus (2017, October 10). Kenya Airways Executives Exit as Expats Jump Aboard. *Aviation International News* [Online]. Available on: https://www.ainonline.com/aviation-news/air-transport/2017-10-10/kenya-airways-executives-exit-expats-jumb-aboard

- Bekele, Kaleyesus. (2019, June 5). Kenya Airways' Outgoing CEO Satisfied with Recovery Progress. AINonline. Available at: https://www.ainonline.com/kaleyesus-bekele?page=1

- Bekele, K. (2019, September 20). Interview. [Transcript]

- Bell, G. (2002, February 14). Government buys back SAA stake for R382m. Available at: https://www.iol.co.za/news/south-africa/government-buys-back-saa-stake-for-r382m-81789

- Belobaba, P.; Odoni, A. and Barnhart, C. Eds. (2009). *The Global Airline Industry.* West Sussex: John Wiley & Sons Ltd.

- Bennett, J.A. and George, R. (2004) *South African travel and tourism cases.* 3rd ed. Pretoria: Van Schaik.

- Bennett, J.A. (2005). *Managing tourism services: a Southern African perspective.* 2nd ed. Pretoria: Van Schaik.

- Bibeault, D.B. (1999). *Corporate Turnaround: How Managers Turn Losers into Winners!* Washington, DC: Beard Books

- Birns, H. (1999, December 15). Ex-SAA boss launches charter airline from Johannesburg. Flight International. Available at: https://www.flightglobal.com/ex-saa-boss-launches-charter-airline-from-johannesburg/29826.article

- Blom, N. (2018). "Comair keeps flying high, marks 72 years of profit." *Business* Day, p.1. 18 September. Johannesburg: Tiso Blackstar.

- Bloomberg (2017). Etihad Faces Tough Air Berlin Call After Alitalia Bankruptcy. 4 May 2017 [Online]. Available at: https://www.bloomberg.com/news/articles/2017-05-04/etihad-faces-tough-call-on-air-berlin-after-alitalia-bankruptcy

- Bloomberg (2018). India to sell controlling stake in troubled Air India, along with most of its debt [Online]. Available at: https://www.businesslive.co.za/bd/companies/2018-03-28-india-to-sell-controlling-stake-in-troubled-air-india-along-with-most-of-its-debt/

- Bloomberg. (2019, December 5). How many companies are turned around after going into business rescue. Available from: https://businesstech.co.za/news/business/360138/how-many-companies-are-turned-around-after-going-into-business-rescue/

- Boyne, G. A. (2004). Explaining Public Service Performance: Does Management Matter? *Public Policy and Administration*, 19(4), pp. 100-117. Available at: https://doi.org/10.1177/095207670401900406

- Boloko, A. & Barnett, S. (2020, April 21). 10 things to know about business rescue. Norton Rose Fulbright. Available from: https://www.financialinstitutionslegalsnapshot.com/2020/04/10-things-to-know-about-business-rescue/

- Boyne, G. A. (2004). A "3Rs" Strategy for Public Service Turnaround: Retrenchment, Repositioning and Reorganization. *Public Money and Management*, 24(2), pp. 97-103. Available at: https://doi.org/10.1111/j.1467-9302.2004.00401.x

- Brinson, L. (2002, March 18). Kenya Airways Expands its All-Boeing Fleet With 777s [Press Release]. Boeing. Available at: https://boeing.mediaroom.com/2002-03-18-Kenya-Airways-Expands-its-All-Boeing-Fleet-with-777s,1

- Brits, A. (2010). A liberalised South African airline industry: Measuring airline total-factor productivity. *Journal of Transport and Supply Chain Management*, 4(1), 22-38. Available from: **DOI:** https://doi.org/10.4102/jtscm.v4i1.7

- *Business Daily.* (2010, January 29). Union objects to Kenya Airways plans to lay off staff in restructuring. Available at: https://www.theeastafrican.co.ke/business/Kenya-Airways-to-lay-off-staff-in-restructuring/2560-5435716-6e9ed3/index.html

- *Business Daily.* (2014, September 22). Naikuni to Leave Kenya Airways on October 31. Available at: https://www.businessdailyafrica.com/corporate/Naikuni-to-leave-Kenya-Airways-October-31/539550-2461238-d3gufh/index.html

- *Business Daily.* (2015, September 17). KQ Chairman Mwaniki set to retire after 10-year term. Available at: https://www.businessdailyafrica.com/corporate/companies/KQ-chairman-Mwaniki-set-to-retire-after-10-year-term/4003102-2874994-qo54e0/index.html

- *Business Daily.* (2019, June 10). Michael Joseph gets three more years as Kenya Airways Board Chair. Available at: https://www.businessdailyafrica.com/corporate/companies/Michael-Joseph-gets-three-more-years/4003102-5151584-26kg9tz/index.html

- *Business Day* (2012). "1Time failure raises questions." *Business Day*, 6 November. Johannesburg: Tiso Blackstar.

- Business Insider (2018). Airlines are making more money than ever before – but they're facing mountains of problems [Online]. Available at: http://www.businessinsider.com/airlines-biggest-business-problems-2018-4?IR=T

- Businesstech (2016). "Zuma recommends SAA to all travellers after flight to New York." 17 September. [Online] Available at: https://businesstech.co.za/news/government/137083/zuma-recommends-saa-to-all-travelers-after-flight-to-new-york/

- BusinessTech. (2016, March 15). How much money SAA has lost over the past 10 years. Available from: https://businesstech.co.za/news/business/116826/how-much-money-saa-has-lost-over-the-past-10-years/

- BusinessTech. (2018, November 2). Mboweni calls for SAA Closure. Available at: https://businesstech.co.za/news/government/281399/mboweni-calls-for-saa-closure/

- Business Times. (2019). Ex-KQ CEO Titus Naikuni Lands New Job in South Africa [Online]. Available at: https://businesstimes.co.ke/ex-kq-ceo-titus-naikuni-lands-new-job-in-south-africa/

- Button, K. (2003). Does the theory of the "core" explain why airlines fail to cover their long-run costs of capital? *Journal of Air Transport Management*, 9(1), pp. 5-14. Available at: https://doi.org/10.1016/S0969-6997(02)00075-3

- Campbell, K. (2014). *African airlines face cost and political changes, need international partnerships*. Available from: http://www.engineeringnews.co.za/article/african-airlines-face-cost-and political-challenges-and-political-challenges-and-need-international-partnerships-2011-04-29.

- CAPA (2013, March 19). South African Airways hits a new low with the suspension of Acting CEO Vuyisile Kona. Available at: https://centreforaviation.com/analysis/reports/south-african-airways-hits-a-new-low-with-the-suspension-of-acting-ceo-vuyisile-kona-98087

- Centers for Disease Control and Prevention. (n.d). History of Ebola Virus Disease. Available at: https://www.cdc.gov/vhf/ebola/history/summaries.html

- Centre for Asia Pacific Aviation (CAPA) (2016). Ethiopian Airlines and Air Mauritius grow, but others face strong headwinds [Online]. Available at: http://www.centreforaviation.com/africa-outlook-ethiopian-airlines-and-air-mauritius-grow-but-others-face-strong-headwinds.

- Chalmers, R. (2001, August 2). Kulula.com takes to the skies. *Business Day*.

- Chattopadhyay, C. (2015). Aviation Industry: Challenges and Prospects. *Journal of Research in Business, Economics and Management*, 3(2), pp. 145-149. Available at: www.scitecresearch.com/journals/index.php/jrbem/index.

- Chen, R. (2017). Competitive responses of an established airline to the entry of a low-cost carrier into its hub ports. *Journal of Air Transport Management*, 64(B), pp. 113-120. Available at: http://dx.doi.org/10.1016/j.jairtraman.2016.07.015

- Child, K. (2020, December 22). Dudu Myeni loses delinquent director finding. *Business Day*. Available from: https://www.businesslive.co.za/bd/national/2020-12-22-dudu-myeni-loses-bid-to-appeal-delinquent-director-finding/

- Chingosho, E. (2005). *African airlines in the era of liberalization. Surviving the Competitive Jungle* [E-Book]. ISBN 9966-05-011

- Chowdhury, S.D. (2002). Turnarounds: A Stage Theory Perspective. *Canadian Journal of Administrative Sciences*, 19(3), pp. 249-266. Available at: https://doi.org/10.1111/j.1936-4490.2002.tb00271.x

- Cochrane, K. (2001, July 25). BA/Comair shrugs off competitor's war plans. *Travel News Weekly*, 11.

- Collins, Tom. (2019, November 6). Blame game masks Kenya Airways' struggles. *African Business Magazine*. Available at: https://africanbusinessmagazine.com/sectors/infrastructure/blame-game-masks-kenya-airways-struggles/

- Companies and Intellectual Property Commission. (2020:online). Business Rescue. Available from: http://www.cipc.co.za/index.php/manage-your-business/manage-your-company/private-company/changing-status-your-company/business-rescue/

- Courtemanche, L., Cote, L. & Schiehll, E. (2013). Board capital and strategic turnaround: A longitudinal case study. *International Journal of Disclosure and Governance*, 10(4), 378-405. Available from: doi: 10.1057/jdg.2013.9

- Centre for African Journalists (CAJ) News Agency. (2015). Skywise reacts to Mango expansion plans. Available from http//:www.metrosanews.co.za.

- *Corriere della Sera*. (2014).

- Creswell, J.W. (2014). *Research Design: Qualitative, Quantitative and Mixed Methods Approaches*. 4th ed. Thousand Oaks, CA: SAGE.

- CTAIRA. (2020:online). About CTAIRA. Available at: http://www.ctaira.com/About-us.html

- Daina, O.M.; Robert, M.S. and Gicheru, E.N. (2017). Analysis of Turnaround Strategies on Organisation Performance: Case of Uchumi Supermarket, Kenya. *European Journal of Business and Management*, 8(31). Available at: https://iiste.org/Journals/index.php/EJBM/article/view/33930/34895

- Davies, P. (2010, February 25). Interview. [Transcript]

- Debrah, Y.A. and Toroitich, O.K. (2005). The Making of an African Success Story: The Privatization of Kenya Airways. *Thunderbird International Business Review*, 47(2), pp. 205-230. March-April 2005. Glendale, Texas: Arizona State University. Available at: https://DOI:10.1002/tie.20049

- Department of Public Enterprises (2009, October 1). Appointment of new Board of Directors to South Africa Airways (SA) Board. Available: https://www.gov.za/appointment-new-board-directors-south-african-airways-saa-board

- Department of Public Enterprises (2013, September 10). "Address by the Minister of Public Enterprises, Mr Malusi Gigaba, MP, during the briefing to the Public Enterprises Portfolio Committee on the SAA Long-Term Turnaround Strategy in the National Assembly. [Online] Available at: www.dpe.gov.za

- Diaz, C. (2019, September 19). Interview. [Transcript]

- Dimopoulos, T. and Wagner, H. F. (2016). Corporate Governance and CEO Turnover Decisions. Swiss Finance Institute Research Paper No. 12-16. Available at: http://ssm-com/abstract=2040690

- Doganis, R. (2019). *Flying Off Course: Airline Economics and Marketing*, 5th ed. London: Routledge Taylor and Francis Group.

- Dresner, M.; Lin, J.C. and Windle, R. (1996). The Impact of Low-Cost Carriers on Airport and Route Competition. *Journal of Transport Economics and Policy*, 30(3), pp. 309-328.

- Du Plessis, J. (2019, March 6). Interview. [Transcript]

- Du Toit, P. (2019, June 25). Gordhan says SOEs in dire straits, threatens boards and CEOs with intervention. *Fin24*. Available at: https://www.fin24.com/Economy/gordhan-says-soes-in-dire-straits-threatens-boards-and-ceos-with-intervention-20190625

- Eisenhardt, K.M. (1989). Building Theories from Case Study Research. *Academy of Management Review*, 14(4), pp. 532-550. Available at: https://doi.org/10.5465/amr.1989.4308385

- Ensor, L. (2018, June 12). "Jarana plans job cuts to save SAA," *Business Day*, p1. Johannesburg: Tiso Blackstar.

- Ensor, L. (2018, June 12). "Vuyani maps a punishing austerity plan for SAA," *Business Day*. Johannesburg: Tiso Blackstar.

- Eze, C. (2016). Nigeria: airlines to earn U.S.$39,4 billion in 2016, Africa Carriers to Lose US$0,5 billion. Available at: http://allafrica.com/stories/201606030928.html.

- Federico, G. (2013). SAA II: abuse of dominance in the South African skies. *Journal of Competition Law and Economics*, [Online] 9(3), pp. 709–737. Available at:

- Finkin, E.F. (1992). Structuring a Successful Turnaround. *Journal of Business Strategy*, 13(4), pp.56-58. Available at: https://doi.org/10.1108/eb039508

- FlightGlobal.com. (2001). Ex-SAA chief in 29m pound pay-and-misrule claim. Available at: https://www.flightglobal.com/ex-saa-chief-in-29m-pay-and-misrule-claim-/38056.article

- Fredericks, D. (2019, March 6). Interview. [Transcript]

- Fu, X., Lei, Z., Wang, K and Yan, J. (2015). Low-cost carrier competition and route entry in an emerging but regulated aviation market – the case of China. Transp.Res. Part A Policy Pract. 79, pp. 3-16.

- Fuzile, L. (2019, April 3). Interview. [Transcript]

- Gavin, K. (2013). Operator preparedness is key to successful Africa flights. *Aviation International News*, 42(1), pp. 8-9.

- Genga, B. (2019, May 24). Kenya Airways CEO Mikosz Set to Quit Before End of Contract. Bloomberg. Available at: https://www.bloomberg.com/news/articles/2019-05-24/kenya-airways-ceo-mikosz-set-to-quit-before-end-of-his-contract

- Gigaba, M. (2013, April 19). Statement by Minister Malusi Gigaba on the occasion of the announcement of the new SAA CEO at Airways Park, Kempton Park. Available at: https://www.gov.za/statement-minister-malusi-gigaba-occasion-announcement-new-saa-ceo-airways-park-kempton-park

- Gigaba, M. (2013, September 10). SAA's Long-Term Turnaround Strategy. [Address to the Public Enterprises Portfolio Committee]. Available at: https://www.politicsweb.co.za/documents/saas-longterm-turnaround-strategy--malusi-gigaba

- Gigaba, M. (2013, September 10). Address by the Minister of Public Enterprises, Malusi Gigaba, MP, during the briefing to the Public Enterprises Portfolio Committee on the SAA Long-Term Turnaround Strategy in the National Assembly, Cape Town. [Online] Available at: www.dpe.gov.za

- Gigaba, M. (2019, February 26). Interview. [Transcript]

- Gernetzky, K. (2018). "Political uncertainty 'biggest risk to airlines'," *Business Day*, p.3. 18 September. Johannesburg: Tiso Blackstar.

- Grinyer, P. H., Mayes, D. and McKiernan, P. (1988). *Sharpbenders: The Secrets of Unleashing Corporate Potential.* Oxford: Basil Blackwell.

- Grinyer, P. H and McKiernan, P (1990). Generating major change in stagnating companies. *Strategic Management Journal,* 11 (Summer Issue: Corporate Entrepreneurship), pp. 131-146. Available at: https://www.jstor.org/stable/2486674

- Godongwana, E. (2019, July 17). Interview. [Transcript]

- Gordhan, P. (2019, December 8). Why we opted for business rescue and not for liquidation for SAA. *Sunday Times*, p.19.

- Goldman Sachs International (2004). Evaluation of Ownership Options Regarding Aer Lingus plc. Dublin: Government Publications.

- Goldstein, A. (2001). Service liberalisation and regulatory reform in sub-Saharan Africa: the case of air transport. *World Economy*, 24(3), pp. 221-248.

- Government Communication Information Service. (2001, June 27). Statement by the Government of South Africa on South African Airways Limited. Available at: https://www.gcis.gov.za/content/newsroom/media-releases/cabinet-statements/statement-cabinet-meeting-27-june-2001#statement

- Government Communication Information Service. (2016, September 2). Appointment of the Board of South African Airways (SAA). Available at:

https://www.gcis.gov.za/newsroom/media-releases/appointment-board-south-african-airways-saa

- Halstead, A. (2019, February 15). Interview. [Transcript]

- Hazledine, T. (2011). Legacy carriers fight back: Pricing and product differentiation in modern marketing. *Journal of Air Transport Management*, 17(2), pp. 130-135. Available at: doi:10.1016/j.jairtraman.2010.10.008

- Heinz, S. & O'Connell, J.F. (2013). Air transport in Africa: Toward sustainable business models for African airlines. *Journal of Transport Geography*, 31, 72-83. Available from: DOI: 10.1016/j.jtrangeo.2013.05.004

- Hill, L. and Bowker, J. (2015, November 18). SAA names Musa Zwane as new CEO. *Sunday Times Business Times*. Available at: https://www.timeslive.co.za/sunday-times/business/2015-11-18-saa-names-musa-zwane-as-new-ceo/

- History.com Staff (2009). Wright Brothers. Available at: https://www.history.com/topics/inventions/wright-brothers.

- Hofer, C.W. (1980). Turnaround Strategies. *Journal of Business Strategy*, 1(1), pp. 19-31. Available at: https://doi.org/10.1108/eb038886

- Hogg, A. (2015, April 24). Suspended SAA CEO Monwabisi Kalawe steps down. Biznews. Available at: https://www.biznews.com/undictated/2015/04/24/saa-ceo-monwabisi-kalawe-steps-down

- Hogan, B. (2019, May 6). Interview. [Transcript]

- Hopkins, H.D. (2008). Successful turnaround strategies. *Strategic Direction*, 24(8), pp 3-5. Available at: https://doi.org/10.1108/02580540810884566

- Howden, D. (2013, October 4). Terror in Nairobi: the full story behind al-Shabbab's mall attack. *The Guardian*. Available at: https://www.theguardian.com/world/2013/oct/04/westgate-mall-attacks-kenya

- IATA. (2017). Annual Review. Available at: https://www.iata.org/contentassets/c81222d96c9a4e0bb4ff6ced0126f0bb/iata-annual-review-2017.pdf

- IATA. (2020, April 14). COVID-19 Puts Over Half of 2020 Passenger Revenues at Risk [Press Release No: 29]. Available at: https://www.iata.org/en/pressroom/pr/2020-04-14-01/)

- IATA. (2020, June 17). "The Worst May Be Yet To Come" – Impacts of COVID-19 on European Aviation and Economy Increasing. Available at: https://www.iata.org/en/pressroom/pr/2020-06-18-01/

- ICAO. (n.d). Freedoms of the Air. Available at: https://www.icao.int/pages/freedomsair.aspx

- ICAO. (2020, August 5). Effects of Novel Coronavirus (COVID-19) on Civil Aviation: Economic Impact Analysis. Montreal, Canada: International Civil Aviation Organisation

- ICAO Economic Development. (2020, August 5). Economic Impact of COVID-19 on Civil Aviation. Available at: https://www.icao.int/sustainability/Pages/Economic-Impacts-of-COVID-19.aspx

- IoDSA. (2019). Guidance for Boards – Challenges Facing Public Sector Boards. Johannesburg: Institute of Directors in South Africa

- Iol.co.za. (2012, September 28). SAA Board Members Quit. Available at: https://www.iol.co.za/business-report/companies/saa-board-members-quit-1391867

- Ikade, F. (2020, January 29). Kenya Airways to Kick-start Restructuring Soon Amid Struggle to Survive. Ventures Africa. Available at: http://venturesafrica.com/google-cancels-investment-plans-in-kenyas-wind-farm/

- Ismael, Z. (2015). 'SAA to get R6.5bn bailout'. iafrica.com.

- Joffe, H. (2019, December 8). No more business as usual for SAA. *Sunday Times Business Times*, p.1.

- Joffe, H. (2020, September 27). Cuts set to fund SAA bailout. *Sunday Times Business Times*, p.1.

- Jarana, V. (2019, April 17). Interview. [Transcript]

- Jeter, J. (2001, December 30). Airline Chief Hit Turbulence in S. Africa. *Washington Post*. Available at: https://www.washingtonpost.com/archive/politics/2001/12/30/airline-chief-hit-turbulence-in-s-africa/eae8842a-743e-4b14-8527-db2dc74ec43c/

- Jonker, K. (2019, April 26). Interview. [Transcript]

- KaNkosi, S. (2018, October 10). SA's finance ministers over the past 10 years. *Business Report*. Available at: https://www.iol.co.za/business-report/economy/sas-finance-ministers-over-the-past-10-years-17416548

- Kalawe, M. (2020, March 20). Interview. [Transcript]

- Kamau, Macharia. (2019, October 29). Turnaround CEO who never got ailing KQ off the ground. *Standard Digital*. Available at: https://www.standardmedia.co.ke/business/article/2001347242/turnaround-ceo-who-never-got-ailing-kq-off-the-ground

- Kenya Airways Annual Report. (2017)

- Kenya Airways Annual Report. (2018).

- Kenya Airways. (2020, February 27). KQ Board confirms Allan Kilavuka as Group Managing Director and CEO [Press Release].

- Kenya Association of Travel Agents. (2020, January 24). KATA expresses support for the nationalisation of Kenya Airways. Available at: https://katakenya.org/22020/01/24/kata-expresses-support-for-the-nationalisation-of kenya-airways/

- Kenya Cabinets. (2018). Defied Odinga Wave for 10 Years, Isaac Edwin Omolo Okero. Available at: https://cabinets.kenyayearbook.co.ke/defied-odinga-wave-for-10-years-isaac-edwin-omolo-okero/

- Kenyan National Treasury. (2015). Comment: We Must Save Kenya Airways, The "Pride Of Africa." The National Treasury. Available at: https://www.treasury.go.ke/media-centre/news-updates/204-comment-we-must-save-kenya-airways-the-pride-of-africa.html

- Kenyan WallStreet Team. (2017, November 13). KQ Lenders Company and Gov't now own 87% of Kenya Airways. Available at https://kenyanwallstreet.com/kq-lenders-company-kenyan-govt-now-87-kenya-airways/

- Kemp, S. (2001). Airlines take on new cut-cost airline kulula.com. Africa News Service, 13 July.

- Kingston, M. (2019, January 9). Interview. [Transcript]

- Kinyanjui, K. (2019, September 16). Interview. [Transcript]

- Kiruga, M. (2019, September 18). Interview. [Transcript]

- Knoema Corporation (2019). Kenya – Contributions of travel and tourism to GDP as

- Kona, V. (2019, April 2). Interview. [Transcript]

- Kriel, V. (2008). Presentation to Portfolio Committee on Public Enterprises.

- Kriel, V. (2019, November 5). Interview. [Transcript]

- Kriel, V. (2020, January 28). SAA recapitalisation. [e-mail reply to Kaizer Nyatsumba]

- Kosgei, D. (2018). Why Kenya Airways is abbreviated as KQ and not KA. *The Standard.* [Online] Available at: https://www.standardmedia.co.ke/ureport/article/2001276950/why-kenya-airways-is-abbreviated-as-kq-and-not-ka

- Kumar, N. (2006). Strategies to Fight Low-Cost Rivals. *Harvard Business Review,* December 2006. Boston: Harvard Business Publishing. Available at: https://hbr.org/2006/12/strategies-to-fight-low-cost-rivals.

- Kuo, L. (2016). "Kenya Airways, once the 'pride of Africa', is selling off yet another piece of itself." [Online]. 27 September. Available at: https://qz.com/africa/792740/kenya-airways-once-the-pride-of-africa-is-selling-off-yet-another-piece-of-itself/

- Lacey, M. (2002, December 30). Kenya's Ruling Party is Defeated After 39 Years. *The New York Times*, p1. Available at: https://www.nytimes.com/2002/12/30/world/kenya-s-ruling-party-is-defeated-after-39-years.html

- Lawton, T., Rajwani, T. & O'Kane, C. (2011). Strategic reorientation and business turnaround: The case of global legacy airlines. *Journal of Strategy and Management*, 4(3), 215-237. Available from: DOI: 10.1108/17554251111152252

- Leigh, G. (2020, July 14). How Top Aviation Leaders See The Future of The Airline Industry. *Forbes*. Available at: https://www.forbes.com/sites/gabrielleigh/2020/07/14/how-top-aviation-leaders-see-the-future-of-the-airline-industry/#1ac60a287b85

- Levenstein, Eric. (2020, February 24). Business rescue process gives wings to SAA turnaround. *Business Day*, p.9.

- Luhabe, P. (2019, February 27). Interview. [Transcript]

- Luke, R. and Walters, J. (2013). Overview of the developments in the domestic airline industry in South Africa since market deregulation. *Journal of Transport and Supply Chain Management*, 7(1), pp. 177-128.

- Maeko, T. (2020, March 13-19). SAA losses: R26 bn. Job losses: 2 268 plus. *Mail & Guardian*, p. 16.

- Macozoma, S. (2019, June 19). Interview. [Transcript]

- Magwaza, J.B. (2019, June 24). Interview. [Transcript]

- Mahlati, Z. (2020, February 5). Guptas tried to bribe me, Kona tells Zondo Commission. Iol.co.za. Available at: https://www.iol.co.za/news/politics/guptas-tried-to-bribe-me-kona-tells-zondo-commission-42131054

- Mailovich, C. (2019). SAA's board chair JB Magwaza resigns. *Business Day*. Available at: https://www.businesslive.co.za/bd/national/2019-07-11-saas-board-chair-jb-magwaza-resigns/

- Maina, M. (2020, May 26). Kenya Airways announces FY 2019 results, bailout request denied by Treasury. AeroNewsX. Available at: https://www.aeronewsx.com/post/kenya-airways-bailout-request-denied-by-treasury

- Mananavire, B. (2016). Air Zim seeks new synergies. Available at: https://www.dailynews.co.zw/articles/2016/05/16/air-zim-seeks-new synergies

- MarketScreener. (2010, April 21). Kenya Airways PLC (KQ). Available at: https://www.marketscreener.com/KENYA-AIRWAYS-PLC-6493924/company/

- Markman, Terry [ca.1999]. Freedom in the skies: Air transport in South Africa. Johannesburg: Free Market Foundation.

- Markman, T. (2019, April 4). Interview. [Transcript]

- Mashele, T.; Moatshe, L. and Zonke, X. (2019, June 10). Interview. [Transcript]

- Masinde, A.B. (2016). Challenges of Implementing Turnaround Strategies at Kenya Railways Corporation. Available at: https://pdfs.semanticscholar.org/80b6/b357dc07bb4d271fcd46eb6eb45f07df2d86.pdf

- Mazareanu, E. (2020, May 7). Coronavirus: impact on the aviation industry worldwide - Statistics & Facts. Statista. Available at: https://www.statista.com/topics/6178/coronavirus-impact-on-the-aviation-industry-worldwide/

- Mburu, E.W. (2016). Challenges of Implementation of Turnaround Strategies and Performance of Postal Corporation of Kenya. Available at: erepository.uonbi.ac.ke>bitstream>handle>mburu

- McCann, J. (2015). *SAA's Dudu Myeni in Nene's crosshairs*. Available from: http:www.mg.co.za/article/2015/09-17-SAA's-Dudu-Myeni-in-Nene's-crosshairs.

- Meyer, John (2004). *Lighter Than Air: A Reading A-Z Level T Leveled Book*. Reading A-Z. Available at: www.readinga-z.com

- Mhlanga, O. and Steyn, J.N. (2016). The aviation industry in South Africa: A historical overview. *African Journal of Hospitality, Tourism and Leisure*, Vol. 5(4), pp. 1-14.

- Mhlanga, O. and Steyn, J.N. (2017). Impacts of the macro environment on airline operations in Southern Africa. *African Journal of Hospitality, Tourism and Leisure*, 6(1), pp. 1-15.

- Mhlanga, O. (2017). Impacts of deregulation on the airline industry in South Africa: A review of the literature. *African Journal of Hospitality, Tourism and Leisure*, [Online] 6(3). Available at: http//: www.ajhtl.com

- Miles, M.B. and Huberman, M.A. (1994). *Qualitative Data Analysis: An Expanded Sourcebook*. 2nd ed. Beverley Hills: Sage

- Mills, G. and Van der Merwe, E. (2020, February 19). SOE overhaul, the Ethiopian way. *Daily Maverick*. Available at: https://www.dailymaverick.co.za/article/2020-02-19-soe-overhaul-the-ethiopian-way/?

- Ministry of Finance. (2014, December 22). Transfer of South African Airways (SAA) to the Ministry of Finance Gazetted. Available at: www.treasury.gov.za/comm_media/press/2014/2014122201%20-%20Media%20Statement%20by%20Ministry%20of%20Finance%20on%20transfer%20of%20SAA%2022%20December%202014.pdf

- Ministry of Finance. (2016). Finance Minister Meets New SAA Board. Available at: http://www.treasury.gov.za/comm_media/press/2016/2016090901%20-

%20Minister%20Press%20Statement%20on%20Minister%20Meeting%20with%20new%2
0SAA%20Board.pdf

- Miriri, D. (2017, November 15). Kenya Airways completes $2bln debt restructuring. AfricaTech. Available at: https://www.reuters.com/article/ozabs-uk-kenya-airways-restructuring-idAFKBN1DF1TI-OZABS

- Mokholo, M. (2019, March 27). Interview. [Transcript]

- Mkokeli, S. (2020, October 29). Minister Pravin Gordhan welcomes government funding for SAA. Available from: https://www.gov.za/speeches/minister-pravin-gordhan-welcomes-government-funding-saa-29-oct-2020-0000

- Moosa, A. (2019, May 27). Interview. [Transcript]

- Mott MacDonald. (2017). Annual Analysis of the EU Air Traffic Transport Market 2016 – Final Report. Brussels: European Commission.

- Mugo, W. (2019, September 19). Interview. [Transcript]

- Munaita, P. (2015, August 1). Project Mawingu strategist had their heads in the clouds. *The East African*. Available at: https://www.theeastafrican.co.ke/news/eas/4552908-2816360-3ured9/index.html

- Mulder, C. (2019, May 17). Interview. [Transcript]

- Munene, M.N. (2012). Liberalization of Air Transport in Africa: Case of Kenya's Air Transport. Unpublished, University of Nairobi.

- Mungai, B.W. and Bula, H.O. (2018). Turnaround Strategies and Performance of Kenya Airways. *The University Journal, 1*(2), pp. 1-16.

- Mwakio, P. (2019, March 13). Tourism growth in Kenya exceeded global and regional levels in 2018. [Online] Available at: https://www.standardmedia.co.ke/article/2001316454/tourism-growth-in-kenya-exceeded-global-and-regional-levels-in-2018

- Mzimela, S. (2019, February 27). Interview. [Transcript]

- Namu, J. and Oniango, M. (2020). Kenya Airways: Fall of the Pride [Online]. Available from: www.africauncensored.net

- Ndaba, B. (2020, May 28). Dudu Myeni slams judgement declaring her a delinquent director. Iol.com. Available at: https://www.msn.com/en-za/news/national/dudu-myeni-slams-judgment-declaring-her-a-delinquent-director/ar-BB14J3jO

- Ndhlovu, R. and Ricover, A. (2009). *Assessment of potential impact of implementation of the Yamoussoukro Decision on open skies policy in the SADC region.* (GS 10F-0277P). Gaborone: USAID Southern Africa.

- Nene, N. (2019, May 27). Interview. [Transcript]

- News24. (2001, May 31). R200m for SAA's ex-CEO. Available at: https://www.news24.com/SouthAfrica/R200m-for-SAAs-ex-CEO-20010531

- Ngqula, K. (2019, November 19). Interview. [Transcript]

- Ngqula, K. (2020, January 28). SAA recapitalisation. [e-mail reply to Kaizer Nyatsumba]

- Ngqulunga, B. (2008). Presentation to Portfolio Committee on Public Enterprises.

- Ngunze, M. (2019, September 25). Interview. [Transcript]

- Njegovan, N. (2006). Elasticities of demand for leisure air travel: A system modelling approach. *Journal of Air Transport Management*, 12(1), 33-39. Available from: DOI: 10.1016/j.jairtraman.2005.09.003

- Njoka, K. (2005, August 23). Kenya: Okero Exists Buoyant Kenya Airways. *The East African*. Available at: https://allafrica.com/stories/200508230852.html

- Njoya, E.T (2013). Air transport and destination performance – a case study of three African countries (Ethiopia, Kenya and South Africa). Paper presented at the Aviation Research Workshop, 14-15 February 2013, Munster/Westfalen

- Nunes, A. (2020, July 10). How COVID-19 will change air travel as we know it. BBC. Available at: https://www.bbc.com/future/article/20200709-how-covid-19-will-change-air-travel-as-we-know-it

- Obura, Fredrick. (2019, December 16). *Standard* Digital. Kenya Airways Board appoints acting Chief Executive Officer. Available at: https://www.standardmedia.co.ke/business/article/2001353417/kq-board-appoints-acting-chief-executive-officer

- Ogbeidi, M. M. (2006). The Aviation Industry in Nigeria: A Historical Overview. *Lagos Historical Review*, 6(6), pp. 133-147.

- O'Kane, C. and Cunningham, J. (2014). Turnaround leadership core tensions during the company turnaround process. *European Management Journal,* 32(6), pp. 963-980. Available at: https://doi.org/10.1016/j.emj.2014.04.004

- Okoth, E. (2016, July 31). Turbulent times for Kenya Airways as it records Ks26bn loss. *Daily Nation*. Available at: https://www.nation.co.ke/news/Collapse-fears-as-KQ-dives-to-Sh26bn-loss/1056-2814784-xc1s7b/index.html

- Okoth, E. (2019, September 16). Interview. [Transcript]

- Omarjee, L. (2018, October 11). SA's former Finance Ministers: Where are they now? *Mail&Guardian*. Available at: https://mg.co.za/article/2018-10-11-sas-former-finance-ministers-where-they-are-now/

- Omarjee, L. (2019, June 2). 10 challenges that forced SAA CEO to throw in the towel. *Fin24*. Available at: https://www.fin24.com/Economy/10-challenges-that-forced-saa-ceo-to-throw-in-the-towel-20190602-2?

- Ombok, E. (2020, May 27). Kenya Airways sees recovery a year away as losses mount. Iol.co.za. Available at: https://www.iol.co.za/business-report/international/kenya-airways-sees-recovery-a-year-away-as-losses-mount-48575122

- Onyango, Seth. (2019, December 27). KQ faces turbulent skies in 2020 as Mikosz leaves office. PD online. Available at: https://www.pd.co.ke/business/economy-and-policy/kq-faces-turbulent-skies-in-2020-as-mikosz-leaves-office-18224/

- Oosthuizen, M. (2012). SAA and the South African Airline Industry: The Next Ten Years – 2012-2020. Cusp Consulting.

- Oqubay, A. and Tesfachew, T. (2019). The Journey of Ethiopian Airlines. *How They Did It: Getting Granular in Solving Policy Issues*, 2(1). Abidjan, Ivory Coast: African Development Bank. Available at: https://www.afdb.org/en/documents/document/policy-brief-how-they-did-it-vol-2-issue-1-the-journey-of-ethiopian-airlines-107363

- Oqubay, A. (2020, July 24). Telephone Interview.

- Organisation for Economic Cooperation and Development (2001). Regulatory reform in Ireland. Paris: OECD

- Ouma, A. (2003, January 31). Naikuni Appointed Airways MD. *The Standard*. Available at: https://allafrica.com/stories/200301310722.html

- Oxford Business Group (OBG). (2017). *Growing number of carriers joining South Africa's aviation market.* Available at: http://www.oxfordbusinessgroup.com/analysis/race-skies-more-carriers-are-joining-market-cater-growing-number-air-passengers.

- Oyugi, J.O. (2016). Challenges of the Implementation of Turnaround Strategy and Competitive Advantage of Uchumi Supermarkets Limited in Kenya. Available at: https://pdfs.semanticscholar.org/70be/4a83090844330811dfcb148f633197df7049.pdf

- Panicker, S. and Manimala, M.J. (2015). Successful turnarounds: the role of appropriate entrepreneurial strategies. *Journal of Strategy and Management*, 8(1), pp.21-40. Available at: doi.org/10.1108/JSMA-06-2014-0050

- Papatheodorou, A. & Lei, Z. (2006) Leisure Travel in Europe and Airline Business Models: A Study of Regional Airports in Great Britain. *Journal of Air Transport Management*, 12(1), 47-52. Available from: DOI: 10.1016/j.jairtraman.2005.09.005

- Pather, R. (2016). Crib Notes: Who exactly is Dudu Myeni? *Mail&*Guardian. Available at: https://mg.co.za/article/2016-09-01-crib-notes-who-exactly-is-dudu-myeni/

- Paton, C. (2018). "SAA gets another bailout," *Business Day*, p1, 24 October. Johannesburg: Tiso Blackstar.

- Paton, C. (2019, December 10). State-owned entities' fatal flaw has not been sorted out. *Business Day*, p.7.

- Paton, C. (2020, January 21). 'Thuma mina' and the woes Directors face at State entities. *Business Day,* p.7.

- Paton, C. (2020, February 20). Gordhan still calls the shots at SAA. *Business Day*, p.1-2.

- Paton, C. (2020, February 26). SAA will have debt and interest payments taken care of. *Business Day Budget 2020*, p1.

- Paton. C. (2020, May 15). SAA unveils huge losses. *Business* Day. Available at: https://www.businesslive.co.za/bd/national/2020-05-15-saa-unveils-huge-losses/

- Paton, C. (2020, August 25)). Government now looks to base SAA on Telkom model. *Business Day*, p.1.

- Paton, R. and Mordaunt, J. (2004). What's Different about Public and Non-Profit 'Turnaround'? *Public Money and Management*, 24(4), 209-216. Available at: http://dx.doi.org/10.1111/j.1467-9302.2004.00422.x

- Pearce II, J.A. and Robbins, D.K. (1993). Toward Improved Theory and Research on Business Turnaround. *Journal of Management*, 19(2), pp. 613-636. Available at: https://doi.org/10.1177/014920639301900306

- Pearce II, J.A. and Robbins, D.K. (2008). Strategic transformation as the essential last step in the process of business turnaround. *Business Horizons* Vol 51, pp. 121-130. Available at: https://doi.org/10.1002/smj.4250130404

- Petrescu, F.I. and Petrescu, R.V. (2011). *Memories About Flight!* Create Space Publisher.

- Pirie, G.H. (1990). Aviation, apartheid and sanctions: air transport to and from South Africa, 1945-1989. *GeoJournal*, 22(3), pp. 231-240. Available at: https://doi.org/10.1007/BF00192821

- Pirie, G.H. (1992). Southern African air transport after apartheid. *The Journal of Modern African Studies*, 30(2), pp. 341-348. Available at: https://doi.org/10.1017/S0022278X00010752

- Pirie, G.H (2006). Africanisation of South Africa's international air links, 1994-2003. *Journal of Transport Geography*, 14(1), pp. 3-14. Available at: doi:10.1016/j.jtrangeo.2004.10.006

- Planting, S. (2020, January 16). SAA puts assets on the block. *Business Maverick*. Available at: https://www.dailymaverick.co.za/article/2020-01-16-saa-puts-assets-on-the-block/?

- Porter, M. (1998). *Competitive Strategy: Techniques for Analyzing Industries and Competitors*. New York: Free Press.

- Pretorius, M. (2008). When Porter's generic strategies are not enough: Complementary strategies for turnaround situations. *Journal of Business Strategy*, 29(6), pp. 19-28. Available at: https://doi.org/10.1108/02756660810917200

- Raseroka, V. (2019, April 2). Interview. [Transcript].

- Ravaghi, H.; Mannion, R. and Sajadi, H.S. (2017). Organizational failure and turnaround in public sector organizations: A systematic review of the evidence. *Medical Journal of the Islam Republic of Iran*, 31(76). Available at: https://doi.org/10.14196/mjiri.31.76

- Reeves, M.; Haanaes, K. and Sinha, J. (2015). *Your Strategy Needs A Strategy: How to Choose and Execute the Right Approach*. Boston: Harvard Business Review Press.

- Rehan, A. (2019, September 23). Interview. [Transcript]

- Reuters. (2017, December 14). Standard Bank SA appoints Lungisa Fuzile as CEO. *Business Report*. Available at: https://www.iol.co.za/business-report/standard-bank-sa-appoints-lungisa-fuzile-as-ceo-12418994

- Reuters (2018, March 29). "South African Airways net loss widens to 5,6 bln rand, CEO says." [Online]. Available at: https://www.reuters.com/article/saa-results/south-african-airways-net-loss-widens-to-5-6-bln-rand-ceo-says-idUSJ8N1QO018

- Reuters (2018, August 30). Better times ahead, says Kenya Airways. *Business Day*, p.17. Johannesburg: Tiso Blackstar

- Reuters. (2019, July 24). MPs back plan to nationalize Kenya Airways. *Citizen Digital*. Available at: https://citizentv.co.ke/business/mps-back-plan-to-nationalise-kenya-airways-265549/

- Reuters. (2019, July 25). Exclusive: Kenya Airways goes full circle with two-year nationalization plan. Available at: https://www.reuters.com/article/us-kenya-airways-restructuring-exclusive/exclusive-kenya-airways-goes-full-circle-with-two-year-nationalization-plan-idUSKCN1UK22M)

- Rivers, M. (2015). *South African Airways: adapt or die*. Available at: http://africanbusinessmagazine.com/sectors/infrastructure/south-african-airways-adapt-or-die/#sthash.Am4hZxso.dpuf.

- Robbins, D. K. and Pearce II, J.A. (1992). Turnaround: Retrenchment and Recovery. *Strategic Management Journal*, 13(4), pp. 287-309. Available at: https://doi.org/10.1002/smj.4250130404

- Rupp, S. (2015). African airlines: Looking beyond statistics. Available at: http://www.consultancyafrica.com/index.php?option=com_content&view=article&id=11 83:african-airlines-looking-beyond-the-statistics-&catid=57:africa-watch-discussionpapers

- Ryabinkin, C.T. (2004). Let there be flight: It's time to reform the regulation of commercial space travel. *Journal of Air Law and Commerce*, 69(1), pp. 101-137. Available at: https://scholar.smu.edu/jalc/vol69/iss1/5

- Ryan, C. (1992). "SAA 'war' threat to be investigated," *Sunday Times*, 14 June, p.1. Johannesburg: Tiso Blackstar.

- SAA Annual Report. (2017).

- SAA Business Restructuring Plan 2007/2008 to 2009/10. (2007). Simplify, rightsize, re-skill and incentivize. [SAA plan obtained from Vera Kriel (2019, November 5]

- SAA Museum Society (n.d). South African Airways – A Brief History. Available at: http://www.saamuseum.co.za/saa-history.html

- Schendel D.; Patton, G.R. and Riggs, J. (1976). Corporate turnaround strategies: A study of profit decline and recovery. *Journal of General Management*, 3(3), pp. 3-11. Available at: https://doi.org/10.1177/030630707600300301

- Schendel, D. and Patton, G.R. (1976). Corporate stagnation and turnaround. *Journal of Economics and Business*, 28(33), pp. 236-241.

- Schoenberg, R.; Collier, N. and Bowman, C. (2013). Strategies for business turnaround and recovery: a review and synthesis. *European Business Review*, 25(3), pp. 243-262. Available at: https://doi.org/10.1108/09555341311314799

- Schlumberger, C.E. (2010). *Open Skies for Africa: Implementing the Yamoussoukro Decision.* Washington, DC: The World Bank.

- Serra, A. and Leong, C. (2020, May 6). Here's what travelling could look like after COVID-19. Available at: https://www.weforum.org/agenda/2020/05/this-is-what-travelling-will-be-like-after-covid-19/

- Shabangu, C. (2019, June 8). Interview. [Transcript]

- Shaw, A. (2019, May 23). Interview. [Transcript]

- Share, B. (1986). *The Flight of the Iolar: The Aer Lingus Experience, 1936-1986.* Dublin: Gill and Macmillan.

- Shaw, S. (2011). *Airline marketing and management*. (7th ed.). Farnham: Ashgate.

- Sithole, K. (2019, June 9). Why Exit Letters Count. *City Press Business*, p.2.

- Skapinker, Michael. (2020, June 23). What 9/11 can teach us about aviation's post-coronavirus future. *Financial Times*. Available at: https://www.ft.com/content/8c4e90f4-c61e-447d-a3ef-78d29e4cf56d

- Skiti, S. (2013, March 17). Guptas tried to "buy" SAA boss with R500k. *Sunday Times*. Available at: https://www.timeslive.co.za/news/south-africa/2013-03-17-guptas-tried-to-buy-saa-boss-with-r500k/

- Skiti, S. (2019, October 2). Yet another SAA exec suspended. *Mail&Guardian*. Available at: https://mg.co.za/article/2019-10-02-yet-another-saa-exec-suspended/

- Skiti, S. (2019, November 26). Gordhan announces an executive chairperson for crisis-hit SAA. *Mail&Guardian*. Available at: https://mg.co.za/article/2019-11-26-gordhan-announces-an-executive-chairperson-for-crisis-hit-saa/

- Smith, C. (2019, June 26). Gordhan: 5 reasons behind SAA's huge losses. *Fin24*. Available at: https://www.fin24.com/Companies/Industrial/gordhan-5-reasons-behind-saas-huge-losses-20190626

- Smith, C. (2020, May 5). Kulula.com owner goes into business rescue. Fin24. Available at: https://www.fin24.com/Companies/Industrial/kululacom-owner-comair-goes-into-business-rescue-20200505

- Smith, E. (1998). *An evaluation of the impact of air transport deregulation in South Africa.* Unpublished PhD Thesis (Transport Economics), Rand Afrikaans University. Johannesburg, South Africa

- Smith, N. (2012, October 9). SAA CEO Siza Mzimela Quits. Bizcommunity.com. Available at: https://www.bizcommunity.com/Article/196/534/83063.html

- Smith, N. (2013, February 14). Kona won't resign from SAA. Bizcommunity. Available at: https://www.bizcommunity.com/Article/196/583/89270.html

- Speckman, A. (2015). Comair battles amid tough airline market. [Online] Available at: http://www.timeslive.co.za/Comair-battles-amid-tough-airline-market.

- South African Airways Act No. 5 of 2007 (2007). Government Gazette. South Africa.

- South African Airways. (2018, April). SAA Group Presentation to Standing Committee on Appropriations.

- South African Government News Agency (2012, October 11). Cabinet concerned about SAA developments. Available at: https://www.sanews.gov.za/south-africa/cabinet-concerned-about-saa-developments-0

- South African Press Association (2012, September 28). SAA board members resigned through media. Iol.co.za. Available at: https://www.iol.co.za/business-report/economy/saa-board-members-resigned-through-media-1392021

- South African Press Association. (2012, October 8). New SAA CEO Quits. Available at: Times Live. Available at: https://www.timeslive.co.za/politics/2012-10-08-new-saa-ceo-quits/

- Ssamula, B. (2008). *Strategies to design a cost-effective hub network for sparse air travel demand in Africa.* Unpublished doctoral thesis. University of Pretoria. [Online] Available at: http//upetd.up.ac.za/thesis/available/etd-07242008-093606/unrestricted/01chapters1.2.pdf.

- Ssamula, B. (2009). Sustainable business models for the State-owned African airlines. In: Sustainable Transport: 28th Annual Southern African Transport Conference (SATC), Pretoria, 6-9 July 2009.

- Statistics South Africa (2016). How important is tourism to the South African economy? [Online]. Available at: http://www.statssa.gov.za/?p=11030

- Steyn, J.N. & Mhlanga, O. (2016). The impact of international air transport agreements on airline operations in Southern Africa. *African Journal of Hospitality, Tourism and Leisure,* [Online] 5(2), pp. 1-16. Available at: http//:www.ajhtl.com

- Stockport, G.; Cowie, A. and Dockrat, I. (2000). *The Turnaround of South African Airways.* n.p.

- Taboi, L. (2019, September 18). Interview. [Transcript]

- Tafiranyeka, M. (2014). Intra-Africa trade: Going beyond political commitments. *Africa Renewal Journal,* 28, pp.5-6. Available at: DOI: 10.18356/41e06a6d-en

- Talevi, G. (2020, August 20-26). SA's Iron Lady. *Financial Mail.* Arena Media: Johannesburg.

- Tarry, C. (2019, April 3). Interview. [Transcript]

- Taylor, S. (2020, May 4). Air Transport 2035: Four Possible Post-COVID-19 Scenarios for Aviation. Apex Media. Available at: https://apex.aero/2020/05/04/air-transport-2035-webinar-results

- Teece, D.J.; Pisano, G. and Shuen, A. (1997). Dynamic Capabilities and Strategic Management. *Strategic Management Journal,* 18(7), pp. 509-533. Available at: https://doi.org/10.1002/(SICI)1097-0266(199708)18:7<509::AID-SMJ882>3.0.CO;2-Z

- Thamm, M. (2020, May 28). Dudu Myeni was prepared to cause "untold harm to SAA and the SA economy." *Daily Maverick.* Available at:

https://www.dailymaverick.co.za/article/2020-05-28-dudu-myeni-was-prepared-to-cause-untold-harm-to-saa-and-the-sa-economy/#gsc.tab=0

- The Comair Story (n.d.). Laying down the foundation. Available at: http://www.comair.co.za/about-us/the-comair-story

- The Africa List. (n.d.). Girma Wake: Using conflict as a tool for growth, and choosing trust over fear. Available at: https://theafricalistinsights.com/latest-news/girma-wake-ethiopian-airlines-rwandair-leadership-advice

- Thiong'o, N. (2012). Kenya Airways 10-year strategy. PowerPoint Presentation. Available at: http://www.slideshare.net/thiongonick/kenya-airways-10year-strategy

- Tlhakudi, K. (2020, August 19). Restructured SAA will boost aviation sector and serve as a vital lifeline. *Business Day.* Arena Media: Johannesburg.

- Trade Law Centre (2018). African Continental Free Trade Area (AfCFTA) Legal Texts and Policy Documents. [Online] Available at: https://www.tralac.org/resources/by-region/cfta.html

- Trahms, C.A.; Ndofor, H.A. and Sirmon, D.G. (2013). Organizational Decline and Turnaround: A Review and Agenda for Future Research. *Journal of Management*, 39(5), pp. 1277 – 1307. Available at: https://doi.org/10.1177/0149206312471390

- Transnet Freight Rail. (n.d.). History Overview. Available at: http://www.transnetfreightrail-tfr.net/Heritage/Pages/Overview.aspx

- Tshabalala, B.S. (2019, May 8). Interview. Transcript.

- United Nations World Tourism Organisation. (2020). International tourism down 65% in first half of 2020. *World Tourism Barometer*, 18(5). Available from: https://www.e-unwto.org/doi/epdf/10.18111/wtobarometereng.2020.18.1.5

- United States of America. Department of State (2020: online). Office of the Historian. Oil Embargo, 1973-1974. Available from: **https://history.state.gov/milestones/1969-1976/oil-embargo**

- Vermooten, J. (2019, November 8). Interview. [Transcript]

- Vermooten, J. (2020, June 4). "News from the South." Presentation made at the 3rd Workshop on "Aviation in Africa" in Hong Kong.

- Vlok, N. (1992). "Views of South African Airways on the Deregulated Market." Speech at the International Air Transport Conference in Midrand, August 1992.

- Volkov, O. (2017, May 17). Kenya Airways appoints new CEO. Aerotime Hub. Available at: https://www.aerotime.aero/oleg.volkov/18607-kenya-airways-appoints-new-ceo

- Wafula, Paul. (2017, September 26). Strategy: Meet turnaround CEO hired to fly Kenya Airways out of turbulence. *Standard Digital.* Available at:

https://www.standardmedia.co.ke/article/2001255637/strategy-meet-turnaround-ceo-hired-to-fly-kenya-airways-out-of-turbulence

- Walshe, K.; Harvey, G.; Hyde, P. and Pandit, N. (2010). Organizational Failure and Turnaround: Lessons for Public Services from the For-Profit Sector. *Public Money & Management,* 24(4), pp. 201-208. Available at: DOI: 10.1111/j.1467-9302.2004.00421.x

- Warui, C. (2019, September 19). Interview. [Transcript]

- Wensveen, J.G (2011). *Air transportation: a management perspective.* Farnham: Ashgate Publishing Ltd.

- Whitehouse, D. (2019, November 27). Turbulence zone: South Africa can't afford to let its national airline fail. *The Africa Report.* Available at: https://www.theafricareport.com/20517/south-africa-cant-afford-to-let-its-national-airline-fail/?utm_source=newsletter_tar_daily&utm_campaign=newsletter_tar_daily_27_11_2019&utm_medium=email

- Whitney, J.O. (1987). Turnaround Management Every Day. *Harvard Business Review,* September Issue. Available from: https://hbr.org/1987/09/turnaround-management-every-day

- Windle, R.J. and Dresner, M.E. (1995). The Short and Long Run Effects of Entry on US Domestic Air Routes. *Transportation Journal,* 35(2), pp. 14-25.

- WNS (Holdings) Ltd. (2017). Top Trends Shaping the Airline Industry: A WNS Perspective. Available from: https://www.wns.com/insights/articles/articledetail/459/top-trends-shaping-the-airline-industry

- World Trade and Tourism Council (2017). *Travel and Tourism Economic Impact 2017, Kenya.* [Online] Available at: https://www.wttc.org/-/media/files/reports/economic-impact-research/countries-2017/kenya2017.pdf

- World Trade and Tourism Council (2017). *Travel and Tourism Economic Impact 2017, South Africa.* [Online] Available at: https://www.wttc.org/-/media/files/reports/economic-impact-research/countries-2017/southafrica2017.pdf

- World Travel & Tourism Council (2020). South Africa – 2020 Annual Research: Key Highlights. [Online] Available at: https://wttcweb.on.uat.co/Research/Economic-Impact/SouthAfrica2020.pdf

- World Travel & Tourism Council (2020). Kenya – 2020 Annual Research: Key Highlights. [Online] Available at: https://wttcweb.on.uat.co/Research/Economic-Impact/Kenya2020.pdf

- Yin, R.K. (2014). *Case Study Research – Design and Methods.* 5th ed. Los Angeles: SAGE

- Zalagenaite, Zvile. (2017, July 20). Freedoms of the Sky: The basics of passenger traffic agreements. Aerotime Hub. Available at: https://www.aerotime.aero/zivile.zalagenaite/19397-freedoms-of-the-sky-the-basics-of-passenger-traffic-agreements

- Zhang, A. and Chen, H. (2003). Evolution of China's air transport development and policy towards international liberalization. Transp. J. Spring, pp. 32-49.

- Zhang, B. (2017, December 11). Major airlines are finally taking on the biggest threat to their business. *Business Insider Australia*. Available at: https://www.businessinsider.com.au/how-airlines-combat-low-cost-competition-2017-12.

- Zwane, M. (2020, February 25). Interview. [Transcript]

Also by Kaizer Mabhilidi Nyatsumba:

South Africa as an International Brand: An Assessment of how it can be Marketed More Effectively

ALL SIDES OF THE STORY: A Grandstand View of South Africa's Political Transition

Nelson Mandela: The South African leader who was imprisoned for twenty-seven years for fighting against apartheid, 2nd printing (co-written with Benjamin Pogrund)

Desmond Tutu: The brave and eloquent Archbishop struggling against apartheid in South Africa, 3rd printing (co-written with David Winner)

The Shaman (poetry)

Incomplete Without My Brother, Adonis

In Love with a Stranger (short stories)

A Vision of Paradise (short stories)

Silhouettes (poetry)

When Darkness Falls (poetry)

UMLOZI (Zulu poetry)